Paul Simpson is the author and co-author of over a dozen non-fiction books including the recently released *A Brief History of the Spy*. He has edited and contributed to numerous international entertainment magazines and currently oversees the news and reviews website SciFiBulletin.com.

THE MAMMOTH BOOK OF PRISON BREAKS

Paul Simpson

ROBINSON

RUNNING PRESS
PHILADELPHIA · LONDON

Constable & Robinson Ltd.
55–56 Russell Square
London WC1B 4HP
www.constablerobinson.com

First published in the UK by Robinson,
an imprint of Constable & Robinson Ltd., 2013

A copy of the British Library Cataloguing in Publication
Data is available from the British Library

UK ISBN: 978-1-47210-023-8 (paperback)
UK ISBN: 978-1-47210-024-5 (ebook)

First published in the United States in 2013 by Running Press Book Publishers,
A Member of the Perseus Books Group

Books published by Running Press are available at special discounts for bulk
purchases in the United States by corporations, institutions, and other organizations.
For more information, please contact the Special Markets Department at the
Perseus Books Group, 2300 Chestnut Street, Suite 200, Philadelphia, PA 19103, or
call (800) 810-4145, ext. 5000, or e-mail special.markets@perseusbooks.com.

US ISBN: 978-0-7624-4940-8
US Library of Congress Control Number: 2012944636

9   8   7   6   5   4   3   2   1
Digit on the right indicates the number of this printing

Running Press Book Publishers
2300 Chestnut Street
Philadelphia, PA 19103-4371

Visit us on the web!
www.runningpress.com

Printed and bound in the UK

"The best-run prison in the world is going to have an occasional escape. We've had escapes and will have them again. I am sure, as long as there are prisoners. To ask that a prison have no escapes is like expecting a police department to prevent robberies altogether."

Fred T. Wilkinson, assistant Federal Director of Prisons, 13 June 1962, after the Great Escape from Alcatraz, quoted in the *San Francisco Chronicle*.

For Sophie, who is developing a keen interest in history, particularly the Horrible parts!

CONTENTS

INTRODUCTION

If we're honest with ourselves, no one wants to be caged up. The thought that our entire lives are at the dictate of others, and that we've lost control of our day-to-day existence, is horrifying. But most members of society agree that there are elements who need to be kept away from the general populace. This isn't the place for a discussion about whether a propensity for criminal actions is a form of mental illness, or what defines a crime: people are put behind bars, and others are charged with keeping them there. And the ones who are inside often want to get out – preferably much earlier than the due process of law will allow.

The Mammoth Book of Prison Breaks was inspired, in part, by the TV series *Prison Break*, which starred Wentworth Miller as Michael Scofield, a young man whose brother, Lincoln Burrows, was incarcerated because he had been framed for murder. In order to help free Linc, Michael committed a crime so he could be sent to the same prison, Fox River Penitentiary, but before he did so, he had a complete blueprint of the facility tattooed onto his body. Although *Prison Break* got progressively sillier as the seasons passed, the first year, which followed the attempts to break out of Fox River, showed the many possibilities and problems with such an escape.

Prison escapes have formed the core of a number of classic movies – from *Papillon* to *The Shawshank Redemption* – and there's a whole subgenre of prisoner-of-war films such as *The Great Escape* and *The Colditz Story*. Some of these are based on real incidents, magnified for the purposes of a good story; others are completely fictitious (not that that has prevented them from inspiring real-life escapes, as we will see later on.) Television has presented 'real-life' dramatizations of such exploits: two series of *I Escaped: Real Prison Breaks* have aired around the world, and many broadcasters have looked to their own country's history for source material. Some of these stories are retold in this book, although all of the assertions made in these documentaries have been re-examined and quite often found to be overly generalised.

Some of these escapes are well known, others much less so, and have often been found when a news report on one story makes a casual comment about a previous escapade. The first helicopter escape from an American jail, masterminded by conman Dale Remling, is an example of this: overlooked by compilers of such escapes, probably because it's not mentioned in the Wikipedia listing, it's a lovely story of a man revelling in temporary freedom.

As well as looking at escapes from the last hundred years, we've delved back into history: the first escapes from the Tower of London; the flight of Mary Queen of Scots from Lochleven Castle; the miraculous acrobatics of a young monk later beatified as St John of the Cross; the tunnel dug by Yankee prisoners during the American Civil War.

Each entry has been cross-checked with as many primary sources as possible: the Newspaper Archive website and Google News both have scans of newspapers from around the globe, and it's been interesting reading how five different papers have treated the same core information. Many escapees have written their own accounts of their exploits, and these have been matched with the contemporary reports where possible (and the occasional piece of 'unreliable narration' commented on). Some of the breakouts have given rise to urban myths that have eventually been presented as gospel; where possible, we have identified these. What follows aren't definitive accounts, of course, but hopefully present a wide perspective.

Inevitably there are a few stories that didn't make the cut for this volume, sometimes eliminated because it was simply impossible to find any form of corroborating evidence. An escape from a Mexican jail in which the participants managed to tunnel their way up into the courtroom in which they had been sentenced is a great tale, and worthy of inclusion in Steven Pile's *Book of Heroic Failures*, but as it isn't referenced elsewhere, it isn't expanded upon here. (Equally, trying to find those references led to a detailed account of another escape from a Mexican jail that we'd not heard of previously, which does feature.)

The book is divided into three main sections. Prisoners can go over the fences that pen them in – whether it's a fifteen-feet-high metal obstacle with barbed wire on the top, or the full might of the Berlin Wall – or they can tunnel beneath them (although there aren't that many of those outside of prisoner-of-war tales). The third alternative, which often leads to the most daring exploits, sees prisoners trying to go out through the gates that have been slammed shut behind them – hiding inside a dog basket, perhaps, or within a food lorry, or, as in the case of Frank Abagnale, persuading the jailors to open the doors themselves.

Each escape is different, and in this book we don't judge those who are doing the escaping. Details of the crimes (if crimes they were) are given, as well as a brief note of what happened to the escapees after the end of the hunt for them. But the focus is on getting from point A (inside the prison) to point B (outside).

We start with one of the most daring escapes of modern times, when, in 1983, nearly forty members of the Irish Republican Army broke out of the highest security prison in Western Europe . . .

Paul Simpson
January 2013

PART I: BETWEEN THE LINES

difficult for the hated British, they started to be almost pleasant. It wasn't until that Sunday morning in September 1983 that the cause of their change became clear: the IRA were intending to take over H7. To do that they needed access to the circle at the heart of the prison, and to achieve that, they had to be trusted.

Although many odd ideas were suggested for breakouts from the Maze – from tunnels (which weren't feasible, given that the blocks were built on concrete specifically to deal with such a threat), to hot-air balloons – the IRA realized that a proper coordinated response was the only way to combat all the various obstacles that sat in their way. Rather than have multiple people working on different strategies, one escape officer was appointed: Larry Marley, who had achieved fame for breaking out of a courtroom where he was on trial for an attempted escape. Marley and some colleagues had tried to get out from Long Kesh internment dressed as a British Army foot patrol, but had been arrested. When they were placed in a holding cell at Newry courthouse, they realized they could get through the bars of the cell toilet, and managed to not only negotiate that, but also the thirty-feet-high fence that surrounded the courthouse.

Marley was being held in H5, and became the clearing-house for all escape ideas. He realized that he needed as much information as he could get about the prison – which wasn't easy, since whenever prisoners were moved in or out of the facility, they were kept from seeing the layout. Every little snippet was passed on to an intelligence officer in each block, who arranged for it to reach Marley. Maps and photos of the buildings were smuggled in so that they could work out the relative positions of each block to the gates.

If an escape attempt was to have any chance of success, then the warders needed to be taken unawares. If the prison authorities got wind of any sort of activity, then they would have no hesitation in cracking down. The IRA men knew they needed to get inside the warders' heads, and create a softer environment where there wasn't the daily tension. This didn't go down well with some of the men inside the prison, who only a few short months before had been engaged in dirty protests against the Brits, but it achieved its aim. Larry Marley found out exactly how they could get out from the Maze. While most activities within the prison were regulated, the prison food lorry seemed to be a bit of a law unto itself. It was even allowed out of the main gate without anyone checking its contents. If the IRA men could somehow get hold of the lorry, and "persuade" its driver to take them to the main gate, then as many men as could fit in the back of it could escape. The only way that they could get hold of the lorry was to have control of one of the blocks which it visited. And the only way that could be achieved was if they had real weapons and ammunition with which to intimidate the guards into submission, so that they were aware that this was a proper IRA operation.

Firearms would need to be smuggled in from outside the prison, and it was also clear that if a large enough number of prisoners escaped (and the mantra of the escape was "think big"), then assistance would be required to spirit them across the border into Southern Ireland speedily, before the inevitable manhunt caught up with them. The plan was therefore worked out meticulously, written down, and smuggled out for approval by the IRA's GHQ. Only those who absolutely needed to know what was going on were told of the plans within the prison, and those few were kept on a very tight leash. If any hint was dropped, even inadvertently, then the person responsible would not be included on the list of potential escapees.

H7 was designated as the block to take over. The block opposite it, H8, was empty, which meant there was less chance of the escapees' activities being noticed quite as quickly. Within the group were three of the IRA's top men: Bobby Storey, Gerry Kelly and Brendan "Bik" McFarlane. All three had played their part in getting to know the prison officer by becoming orderlies with access to the nerve centre in the circle. Grilles that should have always remained shut were left open because the prison warders knew the men would be passing through some tea and toast; the inmates were occasionally left on their own while a warder popped out to make himself a drink. Although none of the prison staff would probably have admitted it, a certain level of trust had been quite deliberately gained, and a complacency that was vital to the IRA plans was beginning to be felt.

The GHQ gave the go-ahead, and arranged the various logistical elements that were needed. Even now, nearly thirty years later, the IRA will not admit how they got the guns into the Maze – apparently just in case they need to do something similar again – but five handguns were somehow brought into the prison. (Prison officers speculated that they might have been smuggled in by female visitors concealing them very uncomfortably; certainly, visitors didn't go through a metal detector – one of the elements of which the Hennessey Report on the escape was critical).

Once the list of escapees was sorted out, the escape committee worked out who could be dressed in the prison guard uniforms that they intended to take from the warders on duty. Larry Marley, still in H5, calculated exactly where everyone needed to be, so that they could maintain line of sight, and take out the prison officers on cue. He drilled the plan into the brain of another inmate on H5, Goose Russell, then persuaded the governor that the only way to keep the peace was to move Russell from H5 over onto H7. This was duly done, and Marley was also able to get the firearms across to H7 without a problem.

The date chosen was Sunday 25 September. Very little happened in the Maze on a Sunday: there weren't any workshops or football games. It might not strictly have been a day of religious observance for the prisoners, but to all intents and purposes the Maze closed down. That meant that there were less prison officers than normal. The two previous Sundays, dry runs were carried out to ensure that everyone could get into position as they needed to, and even though some of the chosen men were unexpectedly moved out of H7 into other blocks, replacements were quickly found and briefed. An unexpected setback had been the breakdown of the food lorry, and its temporary replacement with an open-backed vehicle, but the original, covered wagon was soon in service again.

The only real potential hitch that the escape committee could see arose earlier in the day, when they learned that the senior officer in the control room was going to be John Adams, probably the last prison warder that they wanted there. Whereas most of his colleagues would be subdued by the presence of the weapons, and the aggressive shouting that would accompany the IRA demands, Adams was likely to try to do something.

However, by the time they learned this it was really too late. Everything was in readiness.

At 2.15 p.m. everything was totally normal within H7. The majority of the 125 prisoners contained in the block were going about their usual routine, engaged in some form of recreational activity. The twenty-four orderlies were cleaning up and otherwise assisting as necessary. There were also twenty-four prison staff, keeping as watchful an eye on the situation as they deemed it demanded.

Fifteen minutes later, the breakout began. Bik McFarlane was the first to head towards the circle, his gun concealed. Kelly followed, along with Storey, and two other trusted lieutenants, Mead and McAllister, who were all tooled up. Mead ensured that two of the senior staff were in his sight; Storey and McAllister went into the officers' tea room; Kelly positioned himself by officer Adams; and McFarlane gained entry to the lobby of the circle in order to sweep it.

The cue was the word "bumper". When McFarlane called down for the bumper, everyone sprang into action. Storey and McAllister had to use a combination of threatened violence and harsh whispers to get the four officers in the tea room to obey them: the sight of the weapons, and the declaration, albeit softly, that this was an IRA operation, was sufficient to prevent the men from taking any action. At the same time, McFarlane overpowered the guard in the lobby, and Mead kept the two officers covered.

There was a gate between Gerry Kelly and John Adams in the ECR. Under no circumstances could Kelly allow Adams to use the panic button, the radio or the telephone, and he made it very clear to Adams that if anyone called him he was to say that everything was okay. His life relied on him being able to persuade them he was telling the truth.

As the men within the circle acted, so did the other IRA men down the wings, simultaneously attacking the guards there. All the guards were prevented from reaching the alarms, either by threats of violence, or actual assault – one officer in C-wing was hit over the head; another in D-wing was stabbed. It looked as if the IRA had taken control with minimal bloodshed and the need to fire the weapons.

However, they hadn't had a chance to carry out a head-count of the guards, and didn't realize that one of them was using the ladies' toilet. As he came out, John Adams took advantage of the momentary confusion and tried to shut the door of the control room. Knowing that if this happened the escape was over, Gerry Kelly pushed the door as it closed, then fired two shots. One of them hit Adams above the eye, rendering him unconscious.

The shots had an immediate effect: the prison guards stopped any further attempts at resistance, and allowed themselves to be moved into the classrooms, where their hands were tied behind their backs, and they were bound together. Nine of them were stripped, and their uniforms donned by waiting prisoners. Then all of them had pillowcases slipped over their heads, and an IRA statement was read to them, informing them that the IRA had taken over the block, not out of revenge or to punish the men for their action during the hunger strikes, but in order to escape. However, if anyone tried to resist, they would be dealt with. "Allow common sense to prevail," it concluded. "Do not be used as cannon fodder by the prison administration, nor the faceless bureaucrats at Stormont or Whitehall."

However, the use of the firearm was what had concerned the GHQ and the escape committee about allowing the men to have weapons. If the Army knew that the prisoners were armed – and if any prison officer died – then they wouldn't hesitate to fire at them. And had the shots been heard?

It seemed not, since there were no emergency calls from the prison central authorities. John Adams was told that he would receive medical attention once the escape was further under way. The guard at the main gate to H7 was overpowered and brought to join his colleagues. Now all the men had to do was wait.

The lorry was late. Although it wasn't on a set timetable, it normally arrived at H7 about twenty-five minutes earlier; this was a delay that would cause the escapees major problems later. It finally turned up at 3.25 p.m., thirty-five minutes after the IRA had taken control of H7. The ersatz prison officers allowed driver David McLaughlin and prison orderly Dessie Armstrong to enter the block, but as soon as they started to unload the food from the back of the lorry, they were held up at gunpoint and taken inside the building.

McLaughlin was vital to the escapees' plans: he was the person who the guard on the gate was expecting to see when they finally reached the main entrance. The presence of anyone else would have raised the alarm. It was therefore essential that he did exactly as he was told. He was shown the maps that Marley had prepared, and rather to the IRA men's surprise, the prison warder started to point out some of the small but important errors on the diagrams. When they questioned his cooperation, he pointed out that he didn't want them to think that he was deliberately misleading them with potentially fatal consequences.

Twenty-five minutes later, at 3.50 p.m., the IRA-controlled lorry was ready to leave. In the back were the escapers, some in prison uniform, while McLaughlin and Armstrong were in their usual positions in the cab. They had an extra person with them: Gerry Kelly was lying on the floor in the passenger side, aiming a gun at McLaughlin. The driver's left foot was tied to the clutch, and his door lock jammed to prevent him trying to escape. A cord led from beneath his seat to what McLaughlin was informed was a grenade – in fact, the IRA men didn't have such armament, but the driver wasn't to know that. The cord was simply tied around the frame of the seat, but he acted as if he were sitting quite literally on a bomb. Storey had told McLaughlin that Kelly was a highly dangerous man with nothing to lose; Kelly grunted appropriately, although he would later engage McLaughlin in conversation (when he asked the driver how much he earned, McLaughlin told him it wasn't f***ing enough, which Kelly later described as being quite sharp given the circumstances).

The other eighty-seven inmates of H7 remained behind, many of them armed with chisels and screwdrivers, to ensure that the prison warders didn't escape and raise the alarm. Some of those left behind vented their frustration at not being part of the flight by trashing the furniture and fittings.

Ever conscious of the gun pointing at him, McLaughlin drove the lorry to the section gate, and was waved through without any sort of search by the guard on duty. Armstrong was then moved to the floor to join Kelly, since his presence in the cab at the administration gate would have raised questions that no one wanted asked at that point. And no one did say a word: the lorry was passed through this barrier without any problems.

Only one obstacle lay in the prisoners' way: the main gate. However, to get access to this they had to go through the Tally Lodge. Although he was instructed to park out of sight, to allow the IRA men dressed as prison warders to exit the lorry, McLaughlin parked near the gate itself, telling Kelly that there wasn't any room anywhere else. The eight fake warders then went about their business, capturing the officer at the gate to the airlock, which allowed the lorry to pass through, and then went into the Tally Lodge, where they quickly overpowered the guards there.

However, this was where the delay to the lorry's arrival started to impact seriously on the carefully worked out IRA plan. They had expected to be at the lodge around 3.30, half an hour before officers started arriving for the shift change; instead, they had to deal with an ever-increasing number of captives as warders turned up for duty and were taken prisoner. Resistance from some of them was inevitable, and one of the warders managed to press a hidden alarm button.

Within seconds the phone went in the Tally Lodge. It was the Emergency Control Room querying what was going on. Storey and McFarlane ordered Senior Officer Wright to answer it, which he did with two IRA guns pointed at his temples. He told the ECR that no one there had triggered the alarm, but the ECR said that the one beneath the television had been activated. The prison officers near the TV started to move away from it surreptitiously, none of them wanting to be on the receiving end of IRA punishment. McFarlane and Storey weren't as concerned about that as getting the ECR off the line, but Wright, seeing an opportunity to alert his colleagues, asked how he should reset the alarm. The IRA men knew full well what he had done – as McFarlane later pointed out, they knew how to reset it, let alone a senior prison officer – but the warder in the ECR didn't get the message. Instead he told Wright to "push it back in, you stupid bastard" and rang off. Wright's face drained of blood as he realized what was likely to happen to him.

The IRA had far more immediate problems. They didn't have anywhere near sufficient firepower to keep the forty-plus guards under control if they decided to resist. (One of them who tried to encourage his colleagues to attack was told to shut up or be a dead hero by the IRA.) It was around now that prison officer Jim Ferris was stabbed: he had tried to run from the lodge to raise the alarm at the prison gate, but had been chased by one of the IRA men in prison warder uniform and attacked. Although the wound didn't look that serious, combined with Ferris' history of heart problems, it meant that he died later.

That attack had been seen by the British Army soldier in the watchtower who thought initially that there was some sort of scuffle going on between prison guards. He told his operations room what he had seen, and they contacted the ECR, only to be told that there had been a false alarm. But only a few minutes later – at 4.12 p.m. – one of the prison guards managed to get to a telephone and contact the ECR, who alerted the Army and the Royal Ulster Constabulary (RUC).

At this point, all hell broke loose. The IRA was losing control of the situation, and they knew that they had to get out now, or risk the whole escape collapsing. The main group of escapees were still in the back of the lorry, in which Kelly and McLaughlin were still sitting (Kelly now using a fake gun to keep the driver under control, although McLaughlin was unaware of the switch). As McFarlane ran to open the main gate, he was recognized by one of the arriving prison warders, while another one blew his whistle when he realized that the Tally Lodge was under siege.

The lorry should have been able to go through, but an alert warder called two members of staff to block the entrance with their private cars. Once this was done, the lorry was useless, and the men jumped from the back. They ran through the main gate and into the car park. Officer Gallagher was just pulling in, and six of the prisoners tried to hijack his car. Gallagher threw the keys away, and received a severe kicking as thanks. The prisoners found the keys, and piled into the car, heading for the external gate, half a mile down the road. Officer Talbot had already been alerted to the escape and was locking it as Gallagher's car came speeding towards him, closely pursued by another car, driven by warder McClure, lights flashing and horn blaring. McClure managed to ram the prisoners' car, but they skidded into the gate, forcing it open. Most of them dived out of the vehicle, across the car's bonnet, through the gate and away; one didn't get out in time, and was arrested.

Three of the IRA escapees had formed a rear guard to prevent the warders from following them, and during the melee that followed, warder Campbell Courtney was shot in the leg by Harry Murray. Murray himself was then shot by the British soldier in the sentry post; the two wounded men found themselves being treated together at Lagan Valley hospital. The majority of the other men were able to get over the fence, and away into the fields. Thirty-five men had managed to get out of the most secure facility in Western Europe.

It was a major propaganda coup for the IRA. All the government at Westminster could do was order an enquiry – which spread the blame for the escape around, although it did also commend a number of the prison officers for their actions during the hectic afternoon. But there were immediate consequences for those left behind.

The prisoners in H7 heard about the confusion at the Tally Lodge and realized that the RUC and the Army would shortly be arriving at the Maze. They returned to their cells, leaving the captured warders still tied up. The guards were eventually rescued, and that evening the H7 inmates were moved across to H8, going past a group of very annoyed prison warders armed with batons and German Shepherd dogs who took out their anger on the prisoners. Armstrong, who had been innocently caught up in the escape, was treated as an accomplice and also beaten up.

Operation Vesper was put into effect. A cordon was established around the Maze and border patrols were stepped up to find any of the IRA men who were trying to slip through to the south. It was, as one police officer told *Time* magazine, "like trying to corner a pack of wolves". Prisoners tried to hijack vehicles: fifteen of them including Gerry Kelly and Bik McFarlane stole cars from a local farm, but when one of them failed to move sufficiently quickly, three of them appropriated a sports car from a young lad, who they then had to ask how to operate it!

Around half of the original group from H7 were recaptured within twenty-four hours. Three had never made it off the prison site in the first place. A group of prison warders followed some of the escapees through a hole in the fence that they had torn, out in the fields towards the river Lagan, finding pieces of discarded prison officer uniform along the way. Fired up by the news that at least one of their colleagues had been killed, they ran on the IRA men's trail, joined by RUC officers. As the Army and RUC set up a checkpoint on the road, the warders started to investigate along the banks of the Lagan, and spotted bubbles coming up from behind some reeds. Bobby Storey and two others were caught there; Sean McGlinchey was apprehended a few minutes later. They had been free from the Maze for a mere half an hour. Storey was released in 1994, but rearrested in 1996 on other charges. Although he has been accused (under parliamentary privilege) of being head of intelligence for the IRA, he now lectures on the Maze escape.

None of the escapees was able to meet up with the assistance that had been provided for them by the IRA GHQ; upon hearing the news of the way the break out had unfolded, they had quietly disappeared. Some escapees were caught at roadblocks, others found in the fields and nearby towns by the searching Army and RUC patrols. Patrick McIntyre and Hugh Corey held a fifty-five-year-old woman hostage in her home in the foothills of the Mourne Mountains, twenty-five miles south of Belfast, and held out for two hours before surrendering.

Others made it considerably further. Bik McFarlane, with a group of seven others, took a family hostage at a farmhouse, and eventually they were all able to make a clean getaway when McFarlane persuaded the woman of the house not to reveal their presence. Rather than allow the IRA men to take her oldest child hostage to ensure her silence, the woman, and the rest of her family, swore on the Bible that they would say nothing for seventy-two hours. They kept to their word. McFarlane requisitioned materials from the house, and told the owner that she could collect recompense from Sinn Fein headquarters in Belfast. Then he and his group made their way along country roads at night to south Armagh, a republican stronghold where they were able to meet up with IRA colleagues and be smuggled across the border.

Gerry Kelly and his group made their way to Lurgan, and were able eventually to make contact with republican sympathisers there. One of them, a former prisoner at the Maze, allowed them to remain hidden in his home, in the place where he had previously secreted an arms cache. The men – joined by chance by another group of fugitives – remained hidden there, using coffee jars when they needed to urinate, and only coming out for vital bodily functions, which didn't, unfortunately for them, include showers. They were eventually freed from their new prison and smuggled across the border.

Kelly and McFarlane assumed new identities and went to live in Europe, continuing the struggle on behalf of the IRA. They were arrested in Amsterdam in January 1986, and eventually deported back to Ireland on 3 December. When they were returned to the Maze, the same senior prison officer who had been on duty on the day of the escape was waiting to escort McFarlane to his cell. He was released from the Maze on parole in 1997, but was charged the following year with offences relating to a kidnapping that took place in December 1983. That case collapsed when the prosecution evidence was ruled inadmissible, and McFarlane received compensation from the Irish government. He is now a voluntary worker for Sinn Fein.

Kelly was released in 1989 and went into politics. He was part of the team involved in negotiations with the British government between 1990 and 1993, as well as those leading to the Good Friday Agreement. He is currently the Sinn Fein party spokesperson on Policing and Criminal Justice.

Of the other prisoners, three were killed on active service with the IRA, and some battled extradition for years, until the Good Friday Agreement led to the withdrawal of the requests. According to a BBC documentary in September 2008, one of the escapees has not been heard of since May 1983.

The "great escape", as it was inevitably dubbed, wasn't the only flight from the Maze, but they were few and far between. Some of them were as doomed to failure as the IRA man who had put together a costume of cabbage leaves and was going to crawl out of the compound disguised as a row of cabbages. On 10 August 1984, Benjamin Redfearn was crushed to death while trying to escape in the back of a refuse lorry. In March 1997, a tunnel was found complete with electric lighting – it had got beneath the perimeter wall of H7 and was only eighty feet from the main wall. On 10 December 1997, Liam Averill was smuggled out of the prison dressed as a woman, as part of a group of women and children attending a Christmas party; he evaded capture until given amnesty in 2001.

The Maze prison was closed in 2000; H7 was demolished in November 2007. A monument to the hunger strikers still remains in the Free Derry area of Bogside, and some of the original Maze buildings have been given listed status.

Sources:

BBC Northern Ireland, September 2008: *Breakout* (interviews with Bobby Storey, Bik McFarlane, Gerry Kelly and Courtney Campbell)

BBC News, 8 February 2010: "Maze Prison buildings to keep listed status"

BBC News, 16 March 1998: "The Maze – home to paramilitaries"

The Guardian, 5 April 2007: "Thirty years on, the Maze reveals a secret"

The People, 14 September 2003: "Maze Escape Party Row"

BBC News, 8 December 2006: "Go ahead given for kidnap trial"

New York Times, 4 December 1986: "Dutch Extradite Two I.R.A. Fugitives"

BBC On This Day: "25 September 1983: Dozens escape in Maze breakout"

Hennessey, Sir James: *Report of Inquiry into the Security Arrangements at HM Prison, Maze* (HMSO, 1984)

McKane, William: *Unpretentious Valour* (C R Print, 2008)

Hayes, Paddy: *Break Out!* (O'Brien Press, 2004)

Breaking the Heart of Midlothian

Edinburgh's Old Tolbooth, immortalized in the works of Sir Walter Scott, stood as the town's jail for over 250 years, next door to St Giles' High Kirk. Its forbidding presence stood as a warning to the good folk of the Scottish capital, who would flock to the platform on its west side to witness the public hangings and beheadings, and regard the impaled heads above its doors, which could stay in place rotting for all to see for years. Now all that remains of the building, which was torn down in 1817, is a mosaic in the ground that marks where its doorway once stood, and even now, nearly two centuries later, it is still common to see people spit upon it in disdain.

It deserves its foul reputation. Many who entered the Tolbooth died there, either at the hands of executioners or illness and disease. As Scottish Advocate Depute Lord Cockburn wrote in *Memorials of his Time*, published in 1856: "A most atrocious jail it was, the very breath of which almost struck down any stranger who entered its dismal door; and as ill-placed as possible, without one inch of ground beyond its black and horrid walls. And these walls were very small; the entire hole being filled with little dark cells; heavy manacles the only security; airless, waterless, drainless; a living grave. One week of that dirty, fetid, cruel torture-house was a severer punishment than a year of our worst modern prisons – more dreadful in its sufferings, more certain in its corruption, overwhelming the innocent with a more tremendous sense of despair, provoking the guilt to more audacious defiance."

And defiant they were over the centuries. While some sought to escape the embrace of the Maiden (the proto-guillotine that was used as a form of execution), or being stepped off a ladder to hang before the crowds, by taking their own lives, others found ways to flee the prison altogether.

It was definitely in the interests of the prison keeper, known as the "gudeman" of the Tolbooth, to keep them within the confines of the building: if a prisoner were to escape and remain at liberty for more than twenty-four hours, then the jailer was liable for a fine of £40 sterling, a hefty sum in those days, and if the runaway had been imprisoned for debt, the jailer also had to settle that! If prisoners were caught within the twenty-four-hour period, then the responsibility for the fine was theirs. To that end, the keeper was instructed to check every single cell (known as apartments) twice daily for any signs of escape, and to ensure that they did not receive any tools to help with that.

Various abscondings from the Tolbooth are recorded, some memorable for their method, others for the people involved. One of the first comes from April 1600, a mere forty years after the Old Tolbooth became the prison, and was one of the most ingenious, if not totally successful, escape attempts in the jail's long history.

Robert Auchmutie was a barber-surgeon, who had been arrested for killing James Wauchope in a duel on St Leonard's Hill. He had some alchemical knowledge, and was aware of the destructive properties of what was then called aqua fortis, better known today as nitric acid. Feigning illness, Auchmutie claimed that he needed the window of his apartment covered to provide darkness, using his cloak to keep both the light out and prying eyes away from the aqua fortis' work on the bars. All seemed to go well, and Auchmutie arranged with his apprentice to wave his hand when the town guard was out of sight. Unfortunately for him, the waving was spotted by the guard who prevented Auchmutie from climbing down a rope to his freedom. He became a victim of the Maiden shortly thereafter.

The guards weren't always as on the ball as they might have been: there are numerous instances recorded of prisoners adopting the clothing of their visitors in order to gain their freedom. One of the earliest came in 1610 when Margaret Maxwell, Lady Amisfield, was interrogated by the Privy Council over the escape from the Tolbooth of her son-in-law Thomas Kirkpatrick. It seems as if a private interview between the pair was simply a ruse to enable Kirkpatrick to swap clothes with Lady Amisfield, which meant that he was able to depart undetected.

She, on the other hand, was caught, and although she was initially jailed in the Tolbooth, she was eventually transferred to quarters more appropriate to her social situation in Edinburgh Castle.

A couple of generations later, the idea was equally successful in enabling Alexander Smith to flee the Tolbooth. Arrested in 1681 for his part in the rebellious Covenanter movement and his involvement with the Battle of Bothwell Brig two years earlier, Smith was able to get away from the Tolbooth dressed as a woman, although he was captured near Glasgow and returned to Edinburgh. However, as he was being taken across country, fellow Covenanters attacked the transport at Inchbelly Bridge near Kirkintilloch and freed him.

The case of Robert, fifth Lord Balfour of Burleigh, is probably the most famous case of cross-dressing being used to escape from the Tolbooth. Balfour wasn't blessed with the most equable of temperaments and had fallen in love with Miss Anne Robinson, the tutor to his sisters. This match with someone of "inferior rank", as the *Dictionary of National Biography* (*DNB*) calls her, did not find favour with his parents, who sent him travelling in Europe in the hope that he would forget her. However before he departed for the continent, Balfour made his beloved promise that she wouldn't marry anyone else during his absence, and making it abundantly clear that he would kill her husband if she failed to keep to her word. (Some accounts suggest that Balfour simply wrote to her with the threat.)

However Anne found love elsewhere with Henry Stenhouse, a schoolmaster at Inverkeithing. Again, the accounts differ as to whether Stenhouse was aware of the danger he faced should Balfour return from the continent, but whether he knew of Balfour's jealousy prior to the young man's arrival on his doorstep or not, he certainly found out at that point that the lord was in deadly earnest. When Balfour learned that Anne had married, he tracked her down to Inverkeithing, and called the schoolmaster out. According to Robert Chambers' *Domestic Annals of Scotland*, Balfour told Stenhouse that he had spoken to Balfour's disadvantage and he had therefore come to fight him. Stenhouse pointed out that he had never seen Balfour before, and was certain he had said nothing against him, but the Master of

Burleigh was insistent. "I must nevertheless fight with you, and if you won't, I will at once shoot you." Despite Stenhouse making it clear that it was against his principle to fight duels, and that he had neither horses nor arms, Balfour shot him in the shoulder. Stenhouse died from infection twelve days later, on April 21, 1707. Despite a clever defence (described with commendable understatement by the *DNB* as "ingenious but inadequate") being mounted at his trial at the High Court of Justiciary in Edinburgh, Balfour was condemned to death and held at the Tolbooth before sentence was carried out.

According to legend, Balfour tried to escape twice, the second time successfully after impersonating one of his sisters, who was "very much like him in face and stature". The first time was less pleasant, and although there is some doubt as to whether it was Balfour who was the subject of this plan, it certainly seems to have taken place to assist one felon from the gates of the Tolbooth.

The prisoner was smuggled out of the jail in a trunk, after the jailors had been suitably bribed by his family to look the other way. The trunk was transported to Leith, from where it, and its human cargo, could be dispatched to the continent. Unfortunately for the man inside the case, the porter taking it to Leith was not in on the plan, so had no idea that the trunk should be kept at any particular angle. Hanging upside down, and bumped around as the porter pushed his load to the docks, the prisoner kept quiet in case he was discovered. His luck ran out, though, when the porter met with a friend who suggested they go for a drink. The porter dropped the trunk, causing the prisoner to scream in agony. The frightened porter and his friend opened it up, to find the man unconscious within. The guard was quickly summoned and the prisoner returned to the Tolbooth.

When Balfour did succeed in getting away – a mere day before his execution was due – he was avidly pursued. He was under sentence of death for "a barbarous murder" and was to be apprehended. Not simply disguised in his sister's clothing, Balfour had shaved his head, making recognition of his reddish-blond hair difficult. Prior to his escape to the continent, the *DNB* suggests that he "skulked for some time in the neighbourhood of Burleigh, and a great ash-tree, hollow in the trunk, was long shown as his place of concealment", becoming known as Burleigh's Hole. He was never recaptured, with *Chambers' Domestic Annals* and the *DNB* both suggesting that he was involved with the 1715 Jacobite rebellion, for which he was attainted by Parliament, thereby losing his title and lands. (The *Newgate Calendar* is kinder, noting that he died penitent for his crime, which seems a little less likely!)

A quarter-century after Balfour cheated the Maiden, three smugglers attempted to flee their dates with destiny, and in so doing, led to the lynching of the captain of the Edinburgh town guard, John Porteous a few weeks later. In the spring of 1736, Edinburgh baker Andrew Wilson along with George Robertson and William Hall were found guilty of raiding the Pittenweem customs house in an effort to liberate what they believed were their rightful goods. Wilson and Robertson were sentenced to hang; Hall was to be transported to the colonies. None of them desired their fate, and singing psalms to disguise the sound of their activities, Wilson and Robertson, along with two horse thieves imprisoned with them, cut through the bars of the apartment window. One of the thieves managed to squeeze himself through, but Wilson had clearly partaken too heavily of his own goods, and wasn't able to get through the gap. He and Robertson were moved to different accommodation.

On 11 April, the two men attended church at the Tolbooth kirk, which was part of St Giles' High Kirk next door to the prison. According to a contemporary report, they were accompanied by four of the town guard, and shortly before the sermon was about to begin, Wilson hauled Robertson from his seat and threw him away from the guards, exhorting him to run for his life. When the guards went to pursue the fleeing man, Wilson grabbed one with either hand, and apparently a third with his teeth. Robertson laid out the fourth guard with a punch and belted for the church exit. He was able to get out of the city gates before they were closed, and friends provided him with transport to get out of the country. Legend has it that he ran a bar near Rotterdam for many years – he certainly was never apprehended by the Scottish authorities.

Wilson wasn't so lucky. Although his selfless actions in helping his friend escape endeared him to the common crowd – and led to fears that the mob might try to free him when he was taken for execution – he was guarded more heavily as a result, and three days later went to his death at the Grassmarket. Despite the town guard's fears that there would be unrest, there were no attempts to rescue him. However, after Wilson had been executed, the mob began throwing stones at the hangman, and town guard captain Porteous over-reacted when he and his men came under attack. Whether on his own initiative, or because he was ordered to do so by the magistrates present, he told his men to fire on the crowd. Between six to nine people lay dead at the end, and Porteous found himself on the receiving end of a death sentence three months later and sent to the Tolbooth.

When the crowd learned there was a chance that Queen Caroline might pardon him, they took the law into their own hands, and Porteous escaped from the Tolbooth in a manner that he really would have preferred not to have done. After disarming the guard, and ensuring that the troops stationed nearby couldn't intervene, the mob attacked the Tolbooth, and discovered which apartment was being used by Porteous. The former guard captain desperately tried to escape up the chimney, but, unsurprisingly, this had been barred to ensure that prisoners couldn't get out that way. He was dragged out of his hiding place, and pulled through the streets to the Grassmarket where, on the third attempt, he was lynched from a makeshift gibbet.

Other escapes were more straightforward. In 1765, the authorities were worried that Leith bucklemaker William Purcell would use his transfer from the Tolbooth at Leith to its counterpart in Edinburgh as an opportunity to make his escape, but he was still brought to the capital so that he could be tried in the Edinburgh courts, accused of stealing ten of the king's weights from the port. They were right to be concerned: on the night of 10 December, he cut through the window of the West Gallery, tied a rope to the bars, and made his getaway.

A year later came one of the most famous escapes from the Tolbooth, that of the convicted incestuous murderess Katherine Nairn, who had already escaped the gallows because she was pregnant. The evidence against Nairn and her lover, Patrick Ogilvy, was based mainly on the highly suspect testimony of Anne Clark, a cousin of the Ogilvy family. She maintained that Nairn, who had married Ogilvy's brother Thomas, had begun an over-familiar relationship with Patrick when he returned from the East Indies – in those days incest wasn't defined by blood relations between the two parties but by their relationship through marriage. When Thomas learned of this, there was a row between the brothers which resulted in Patrick's departure, and, not long after, Thomas' death, apparently from poison. (There's good cause to suspect that Clark herself might have been the poisoner, particularly since the brother who stood to inherit, Alexander, had been her personal and professional partner!)

Both Patrick and Katherine denied any involvement in Thomas' death, but both capital charges were proven against them. Patrick was hanged on 13 November 1766, but because Katherine was pregnant – whether by Thomas or Patrick was never ascertained – she was allowed to see the child through to term. Her daughter was born on 27 January, and within a month the authorities began debating whether Katherine could now be put to death. When the decision was delayed for a week, a plan was put into action to spring her from the Tolbooth, which was carried out on 15 March .

Katherine had been attended by midwife Mrs Shields (or Shiells), who continued to visit her after the baby's birth. Shields pretended to be afflicted with a maddening toothache, so kept her head and face covered in a shawl when entering and exiting the Tolbooth. According to the report in James Grant's 1880s collection of anecdotes about the town, *Cassell's Old and New Edinburgh*, once the jailers were used to seeing Shields like that, "Katherine Nairn came down one evening in her stead, with her head enveloped, with the usual groans, and holding her hands upon her face, as if in agony. The warder of the inner door, as she passed out, gave her a slap on the back, calling her a 'howling old Jezebel', and adding a 'hope that she would trouble him no more'."

However, according to the Grant version of events, Katherine nearly screwed up the whole plan by going to the wrong front door – instead of heading for the home of her father's solicitor, she ended up knocking at the entrance to judge Lord Alva's abode. The servant who answered it recognized her, and raised the alarm. Katherine fled the scene, and eventually found her way to the house of her uncle, William Nairn (later Lord Dunsinane). He then kept her hidden in the cellar until he could arrange for transport to get her to Dover. She travelled across the Channel, and eventually ended up in America. An alternate, if less exciting version suggests that a coach and horses was waiting for Katherine when she left the Tolbooth, and took her straight to Dover.

The baby was not as lucky; she died or was smothered two months later. Alexander Ogilvy was put in the Tolbooth on charges of bigamy four days before Katherine made her escape; he was exiled from Edinburgh but fell to his death before he could depart. No one knows what happened to Anne Clark.

Twenty guineas was offered for the recapture of James Hay, an eighteen-year-old glazier, one of three men found guilty in October 1783 of two vicious attacks, which had left a victim close to death. Sentenced to hang, Hay was able to flee from the Tolbooth after his father helped him to file through the chains (somehow managing to avoid detection when the jailers made their twice-daily inspection). Hay's father persuaded one of the jailers to take a drink with them, and after they had got him drunk, suggested that he fetch more alcohol. The keeper left the apartment door open as he went, and Hay followed closely behind him. As soon as the drunken jailer had left the prison, Hay's father called out to the doorkeeper to "turn his hand" once more, which the man, believing that it was to allow a visitor to the prison to leave, did. Hay raced through the open gate, and hid in the nearby graveyard – where he remained for six weeks until the hue and cry had died down, assisted with food and drink by fellow former pupils of George Heriot's Hospital, which was next to the kirk. Even the princely reward didn't tempt them to betray his location, and like most of the other escapees from the Tolbooth, Hay is believed to have headed for the continent.

The Tolbooth survived until 1817, although construction on a new prison began in 1791 at Calton Hill – now the site of St Andrew's House, the home of some of the most senior civil servants in the Scottish government. The dark and foreboding building was razed to the ground.

Sources:

Skelton, Douglas: *Dark Heart: Tales from Edinburgh's Town Jail* (Mainstream, Edinburgh, 2008)

Cockburn, Lord Henry: *Memorials of his Time* (Robert Grant & Son, Edinburgh, 1946)

Grant, James: *Cassell's Old and New Edinburgh* (originally a periodical in the 1880s, now online at http://www.oldandnew edinburgh.co.uk)

The Book Smuggler

Over the years, many disguises have been used to help prisoners escape from jail, and there have also been plenty of plots which involved the potential fugitive hiding within a container. Not often have the two been combined as successfully as the flight from Loevenstein Castle by the celebrated Dutch writer and philosopher Hugo de Groot (also known as Hugo Grotius, the Latinized version of his name that was used on his writings).

De Groot's later treatises would become recognized as the foundation for international law by those who study the subject closely – he outlined the principles of the conditions necessary to qualify a conflict as a "just war" as well as defining the freedom of the seas – but as one student pointed out, "Unfortunately the escape story seems to be more important to the average Dutchman than the books Grotius wrote." He lived through one of the most turbulent periods in Dutch history, the Eighty Years War between the Netherlands and Spain, which began in 1568. He was part of the elite, and a precocious student, studying law at Leiden University aged only eleven, and gaining his doctorate five years later.

Perhaps it was inevitable that de Groot became embroiled in the political and religious conflicts of the era; he followed the moderate teachings of Professor Arminius. However when riots broke out between the Arminians and their opponents, order had to be restored, and it was decided by the Synod of Dordrecht in 1618 that the moderates' viewpoint should be banned. De Groot and two other key moderates were arrested. Tried in secret, de Groot and van Ledenberg, who had been Secretary of the States of Utrecht, were sentenced to lifelong imprisonment (some sources even claim that the sentence was imprisonment for "eternity"). Their colleague Johan van Oldenbarnevelt, the former Advocate of Holland, was executed in 1619.

Van Ledenberg and de Groot were sent to serve out their term at Loevenstein Castle, which sits on the confluence of the Maas and Waal rivers. It had originally simply been a toll building, but at the start of the Eighty Years War, the Spanish had stationed troops there. The Dutch had tried to take it from their control in 1570 but were repelled; a second attack two years later brought it into the hands of the Dutch state. William of Orange then ordered the defences to be upgraded, with ramparts built and a moat dug. The castle at the centre of this new fortress became the "Staatsgevangenis" (state prison), where political prisoners could be safely housed.

Van Ledenberg was unable to cope with the prospect of seeing out his days here and committed suicide. De Groot took a more philosophical attitude, and spent much of his time studying. His wife, Maria van Reigersbergen, chose to share his captivity, but after coming to a financial arrangement with some of the guards, was allowed to go out from the castle from time to time to buy necessities, and to make arrangements for de Groot to borrow books from his friends. De Groot spent twenty months reading ancient and modern literature, studying theology on a Sunday, and working on his thesis, *"Jus Belli et Pacis"*, which would eventually be published in 1625.

Maria began to tire of the constraints, and looked for a way to help her husband escape. The books that were sent to him on loan were dispatched in large chests, as were deliveries of linen. The guards became accustomed to seeing the containers going back and forth between the castle and the nearby village of Gorcum (modern day Gorinchem), and gradually their checks on the contents became more and more lax. By the spring of 1621, they were hardly bothering to look at all.

The chests might have been large enough to contain many heavy books, but they weren't anywhere near the size of a man. After some persuasion from his wife, de Groot tried to squeeze his frame into the four-feet length, and experimented with how long he could remain in there without it becoming too uncomfortable. Once he had developed enough stamina, Maria bored some airholes into the top of the chest, and told her maid Elyse what she was planning and the part she would need to play.

On 22 March 1621, a day when the governor was away from the castle on business, Maria begged his wife for permission to remove a load of Arminian books from her husband's apartment because, she claimed, they were distracting him too much from spending time with her. The governor's wife gave her consent, and Maria sent the repurposed chest up to the apartment. De Groot got in, and Maria then drew the curtains around his bed, leaving some of his clothes on a chair. She called some soldiers in to help her with the chest, claiming that de Groot was lying sick in bed so couldn't assist her.

Maria's heart must have leaped into her mouth when one of the soldiers jokingly asked, "How come it's so heavy? Is there an Arminian in it?" but she kept her cool, and said, "No, only Arminian books." The chest was carried down from the apartment to a boat, where Elyse accompanied it down the river to Gorcum. Maria meanwhile stayed in the apartment, and lit a lamp in the same way her husband always did to aid with his studies. When the governor arrived back later in the day, he looked up at de Groot's cell window, and came to the obvious conclusion. It was only the next day that the deception was discovered.

By this time de Groot was far away. The trip down the river had been perilous, and the fugitive had had great difficulty keeping quiet during the journey. Elyse persuaded the skipper and his son to carry the chest to their destination, rather than placing it on a sledge, and she demonstrated a similar quickness of mind to her mistress when the son commented that he believed there was something alive within the chest. "Books have life and spirit too," she said, and the boy said no more.

The chest was delivered to the house of Jacob Daatzelaar, one of de Groot's Arminian friends. Elyse immediately told him what – or rather who – was inside, but Daatzelaar refused to have anything to do with the escapee. His wife was made of sterner stuff, and sent her servants away so they wouldn't see de Groot. She then released the prisoner from his chest, and gave him a rule and trowel so he could disguise himself as a mason. De Groot then was able to accompany her brother, another mason, through the streets to a boat, which began his odyssey to Antwerp and then Paris, where he waited for his wife.

The governor was understandably angry with Maria's actions, and she was kept prisoner at Loevenstein for a fortnight until the order was sent for her release. Her ingenuity, tenderness and courage were recognized. The pair were reunited in France, after de Groot agreed not to return to the Netherlands. De Groot died in 1645 after being involved in a shipwreck from which he did not recover.

De Groot wasn't the only Dutchman of the period to be assisted in an escape from prison by his wife's actions. Six months after the flight from Loevenstein, Dominicus Sapma, another Arminian minister, was being held in jail in Amsterdam. His wife had applied to be allowed to visit him, since he wasn't committed for any "villainous action", but only because of his religious beliefs. Both she and his sister were given permission.

On 22 September, Sapma's wife and sister visited the jail around 4 p.m., following the detailed requests he had given them. His wife had a scarf wrapped around her cheek, as if she had terrible toothache. As the gate-bell rang to mark the end of visiting, Sapma put on her clothes, transferred her wedding ring to his hand, and used the scarf to cover his cheek. He then put on his wife's veil and walked out, accompanied by his sister. His wife remained behind, expecting any minute to hear the alarm being raised by the keeper's wife, an old, cunning woman whom her husband regarded as the greatest danger to the plan.

In fact, it was this woman who let Sapma out of the prison and she even said something comforting to him, when she saw that "she" was crying. Sapma's sister quickly replied on his behalf that she could not speak because of both grief and toothache. Even though they were through the gate, they weren't safe – Sapma was too tall for the woman's dress he was wearing, and had to go through the streets bent over so the height disparity wouldn't be obvious. However, they arrived at their hiding place without discovery.

When the deception was uncovered, the magistrates were extremely unhappy, and initially refused to release Sapma's wife. It probably didn't help that her first petition said that he had escaped "by the blessing of God" nor that her second claimed that she didn't think she had "transgressed their

Worships' orders". The latter was torn to pieces when it was read. A full week later, the court of Burgomasters and Schepens ordered her release.

The delay in releasing her may have been connected to another escape by one of the Arminians, Vezekius; he had taken advantage of the decision by a court in Haarlem to allow his wife and children to visit him and for them all to wander around the prison, where he found an old rusty key. To his amazement, it fit the lock of the prison gate, and he duly let himself out and took shelter in a family friend's house. His wife ended up in the workhouse in her husband's place for five days, and was only released when their maid had a serious accident and was unable to bring the youngest child into the workhouse to be suckled.

In fact, there was almost an epidemic of prison breaks by members of the Arminian movement. From 1619, ministers Johann Grevius and Prins were held at the workhouse in Amsterdam under a strict regime. Their families weren't allowed to visit, candles were withdrawn so they couldn't read in the evenings and after they made a slight complaint, the fires weren't lit. However, around the middle of June 1621, conditions improved for a short time, and Dominicus Sapma was involved with planning an abortive break out using ladders to ascend the walls. When Sapma himself was arrested, the plans were put on hold in case he was sent to the same workhouse; however the day after Sapma had used his wife's clothes to escape from the jail to which he had been consigned, some of the Arminians tried again, and only narrowly escaped without being discovered.

Nothing further happened until the summer of 1622, when word came that Grevius and Prins were going to be moved to Loevenstein Castle. Sapma knew that any rescue attempt had to be tried before that took place and on the night of 12 June, ladders dyed black were placed against the high walls of the workhouse. A group of men then ascended to the top of the wall, and let rope ladders down the far side into the inner courtyard. It didn't help that the local dogs were roused by the noise of the men bringing the ladders and the rest of their gear to the prison walls, and it was quite surprising that no one within was woken to raise the alarm.

As the first group were rappelling down the ladders as quickly as they could to get to the rooms where the prisoners were sleeping, and a second group was sitting on the roof, a local man came storming out of his house, his sword drawn, to attack the men who were waiting at the base of the ladders. He tried to raise the alarm, claiming that the men were thieves who were trying to steal the money from the almshouses, next door to the workhouse. The conspirators tried their best to shut him up, and in the end told him the truth – they were helping the Arminian ministers to escape. According to the contemporary report, "the man stood as if he had been thunder-struck, left off crying, looked a little at the work, and then wishing them good success, but in such foul language as the mob are used to utter, retired into his house." As if that weren't enough, one of the criminals inside the workhouse heard the noise of the escape attempt, and cried out, "The Arminians are getting out!" Luckily the guards at the workhouse were used to hearing him scream odd things at different times and ignored him.

By this point, the raiding party had reached the cell doors, and used copy keys that they had previously been able to make to open the two locks. Grevius and Prins were quickly assisted to ascend the rope ladders, and go down the other side. Three other prisoners joined in the escape, with all of them getting clean away. The next morning authorities were baffled when they found the empty cells. The locks were still fastened: how could the men have disappeared? It was only when two of the ladders were found outside the prison that all became clear.

Many of the Arminians went into exile until the death of their prime persecutor, Prince Maurice of Orange in 1625; they were formally allowed to reside in all parts of the Republic from 1630. Their propensity for escape has, with the exception of Hugo de Groot, been mostly forgotten over the years!

Sources:

Davies, Charles Maurice: *History of Holland from the Beginning of the Tenth to the End of the Eighteenth Century* (Parker, 1842)

Murray, John: *A hand-book for travellers on the continent* (John Murray, 5th edition, 1845)

Brandt, Gerard: *The history of the Reformation and their Ecclesiastical Transactions in and about the Low Countries* (John Nicks, 1723)

Slot Loevenstein website: www.slotloevestein.nl/ (History/Hugo Grotius pages)

Canadian Journal of Netherlandic Studies, 1985: "Grotius and the Socioeconomic Development of the United Provinces around 1600"

European Journal of International Law, 2003: "Rebels with a Cause? Terrorists and Humanitarian Law"

The Prince and the Pauper

It doesn't matter what your station in life is: you can be a king or a commoner, a dictator or a peasant. There's a chance that at some point, you may be locked up. And if you are – particularly if you feel that you have been locked up unfairly, perhaps while your country is being left to the devices of those you feel are your inferiors, and even common decency is being ignored – then you will want to escape. The nephew of Emperor Napoleon I, Louis-Napoleon, later known as Napoleon III, felt that way when he was imprisoned at the Castle of Ham in 1840; he had tried to restore the Bonaparte succession on two separate occasions, and failed each time.

After the final fall of his uncle in 1815, Louis-Napoleon's parents had been removed from their positions as rulers of Holland, and the young Louis was raised in Switzerland and Germany. In 1830, Louis-Philippe had established the July Monarchy in France, and his opponents, including the Bonapartists, saw Louis-Napoleon as a potential rallying point since he was the legitimate heir within his generation, following the death of Louis' cousin, the Duke of Reichstadt. (His other uncle, Joseph, was the next in line, but lived in America between 1817 and 1832.) In 1836, Louis-Napoleon tried to stage a Bonapartist coup in Strasbourg, but the soldiers arrested him rather than follow him. Louis returned to voluntary exile in Switzerland, but when his presence there became an embarrassment to the government, Louis chose to leave, and moved to Royal Leamington Spa in Britain. He bided his time there for two years, before trying another coup, this time in Boulogne in August 1840. This too failed to ignite popular support, and this time the French establishment decided to keep him where they could see him – in moderately luxurious quarters (certainly compared with the average prison cell) at a fortress in the town of Ham, part of the Somme region of northern France.

The Château had been originally built in the thirteenth century, but it was heavily fortified during the fifteenth, and proved to be an excellent holding place for the would-be Emperor. Its moat, high walls and heavy guard were a serious deterrent, particularly when seen from the inside. If Louis went for a walk, even if it was only on the ramparts, then he was accompanied. Warders were stationed at each door and on the stairs to make sure that he was always in sight. Ironically, some of the soldiers sent to guard him were from the two regiments that he had tried to use in his coups in 1836 and 1840, from Strasbourg and Boulogne respectively.

Resigned to his situation, at least initially, Louis-Napoleon spent much of his time writing pamphlets and essays, a few of which discussed his claim to the throne of France, as well as setting out some of the principles by which he would govern. Otherwise he would spend his time cultivating flowers, or playing games of whist with the commandant, General Montholon, and fellow prisoner Dr Conneau.

In 1844, his uncle Joseph died, leaving just Louis-Napoleon's own father, Louis, between him and the throne – if he were ever to gain it back. There were rumours around the same time of a general amnesty for political prisoners, but Louis did not want to exchange his jail cell for a life of exile. The possibility of travelling to Central America to oversee the building of a canal in Nicaragua was mooted. At the start of 1846, he asked if he could be permitted to visit his father, who was dying in Florence, Italy, but was told that it would only be feasible if he acknowledged his debt to King Louis-Philippe for allowing this. Louis-Napoleon refused to kowtow in this way, and decided that the only way that he would be released to see his father was if he escaped.

Once he'd made that decision, the first thing Louis-Napoleon needed to do was persuade the Commandant that he was waiting for an amnesty, so couldn't possibly be thinking of planning an escape. By dropping hints in their conversations, he was able to make the Commandant believe that an amnesty was likely to happen in June. At the same time, he decided that the best plan of escape was to arrange for some workmen to come to the fortress, and then disguise himself as one of them, walking out under the noses of the guards.

Even though Commandant Montholon was pretty sure that no escape plan was under way, he didn't relax his vigilance over his charges, and most of the soldiers under his command thought his precautions were ridiculous. During the night, the guard was doubled; during the day, two guards were stationed at the foot of the staircase leading to Louis' rooms. However, one of these guards disappeared each day for a quarter of an hour to fetch the newspapers. This brief space would be the only chance that Louis would have.

Luck was on the future Emperor's side. As Louis was trying to think of a way to organize this, the Commandant informed him that, at long last, permission had been given for repairs to be carried out to the part of the fortress in which Louis was housed. For eight days, Louis-Napoleon carefully monitored their movements, and the way that the guards watched them.

Montholon was taking no chances with the workmen: they normally came in and went out together. On their entrance, they walked in single file past two guards, and the same procedure was followed on their exit in the evening. If they had to work separately within the fortress, each was carefully watched, but, as Louis realized to his delight, if they had to go back out to collect items, then the scrutiny was more lax. The direct road from the fortress to the town was clearly visible from the walls of the fortress, so were they to do anything unusual, there would be plenty of time to spot it. It was this minor chink in the armour that Louis decided to exploit.

One of the other prisoners who had been incarcerated at Ham with Louis, his valet Charles Thélin, had finished his five years' imprisonment and was now permitted to go into the local town, St Quentin. The plan therefore was that Thélin would ask permission to head into St Quentin, and would then head back to prison after hiring a cab. When he left, Louis, dressed as a workman, would exit alongside him. This would mean that the guards' attention was on Thélin, not the "workman", and hopefully not draw any attention as he made his way down the road.

Everything was made ready for the morning of Saturday 23 May 1846. A disguise had been smuggled in for Louis, and he was all set to change into it when he was told that some friends whom he had met in England had arrived to see him. Their arrival was quite fortuitous in one way: Louis was able to borrow their courier's passport, on the pretext that his valet was about to make a journey. Otherwise plans were put on hold until Monday, since Louis needed to be sure that there were sufficient workmen around the place that one of them leaving wouldn't be so noticeable. To ensure that there were, Thélin asked if they could build him some shelving.

On the morning of Monday 25 May, Louis, Dr Conneau and Thélin waited impatiently for the workmen to arrive. The one guard they really didn't want to be on duty had been placed in front of Louis' door overnight: he had a bad habit of keeping a close eye on all of the workmen, interrogating them about their activities as the day progressed. Chances were he wouldn't be relieved until 7 a.m., much later than Louis wanted to leave his departure. However, by luck, the previous day, the shift pattern had been changed, and this particular guard went off duty at six.

The workmen arrived at five, as normal, and were inspected as they entered the castle. Louis' disguise was as a joiner, but, at least initially, there weren't any among the working party. He also had prepared a special pair of sabots, the wooden shoes which the workmen normally wore: these would boost his height by four inches, adding to the disguise. However, the workmen weren't wearing them that Monday.

The combination of the two setbacks was enough to persuade Dr Conneau to counsel delaying the escape attempt. The point of no return would come when they shaved off Louis' distinctive moustache: if they didn't proceed with the plan, and the Commandant spotted Louis' lack of hirsuteness, he would immediately become suspicious.

Louis wasn't going to give up his hope of freedom. He ordered his valet to remove the moustaches, and packed the few items he was taking with him: a small dagger, a package containing two letters from his mother, and one from his uncle Napoleon in which he told Louis' mother that he hoped Louis would grow and "make himself worthy of the destinies which await him". He then put on the rest of his disguise: a dirty shirt and pair of trousers, a blue linen apron, a long black-haired wig, and a bad cap. His hands and face were painted with red and black, and then, after a cup of coffee, Louis donned his sabots, put a clay pipe in his mouth and prepared to leave.

At 6.45 a.m. Thélin called the workmen over and invited them to have their morning drink, which got them out of the way. He then went down the stairs, where one of the workmen had been repairing the balustrade. Two guards were stationed there as normal; Thélin distracted one of them so that he couldn't see who else might be coming down the stairs. He chatted with the guard, who wished him a pleasant journey – Thélin was carrying a coat, and had explained he was collecting Louis' dog to take him for a walk.

Louis exited from his room, and picked up a plank, which he placed on his shoulder before going down the stairs. The other guard moved back out of the way of the plank, which Louis had positioned so that his face wouldn't be visible. He followed Thélin and the first guard towards the two wicket gates, and passed through them into the courtyard without incident. As Louis crossed the courtyard, a young locksmith's boy ran across, apparently about to start a discussion with him. Thélin intercepted him, and sent him back upstairs before he could talk to Louis.

No one else gave Louis more than a brief glance. When he accidentally dropped his pipe in front of a soldier, the guard simply continued pacing up and down. He then passed various officials, as well as over a dozen guards who were lounging around outside the guardhouse. Thélin followed close behind, now with Louis' dog eagerly bounding along beside him.

The guards at the first gate eyed Louis a little suspiciously, but they weren't sufficiently worried to cause an alarm. Louis walked through the gate, with Thélin close behind. Just one more gate to go – but as they approached it a pair of workmen were entering the fortress. As they came closer, the other workmen were surprised that they didn't know Louis, but then as their paths crossed (and Louis was beginning to worry that he was about to be discovered), one of them said, "Oh, it's Bertou!"

Louis was free. While Thélin headed into Ham to fetch a cabriolet, which he was going to drive himself, Louis started to walk towards St Quentin, still carrying his plank, as if he didn't have a care in the world. Louis had reached the cemetery of St Sulpice, around two miles from St Quentin, when he heard the sound of an approaching cabriolet. Louis was about to throw his plank to the ground when he heard a second cabriolet approaching from St Quentin; Thélin slowed down to allow this one to pass him, and Louis maintained his disguise until it was well out of sight. He then got rid of the plank and his sabots, then mounted the cabriolet, and took the reins.

When the two men reached St Quentin, Louis hopped down from the cabriolet, returning the reins to Thélin. Louis went round St Quentin, to wait for Thélin on the other side. Thélin meanwhile went to collect a fresh carriage and horses; he was also able to scrounge some breakfast for his master. By 9 a.m. Thélin had collected Louis and they, accompanied by the dog, reached Valenciennes by 2.15 where they were picking up a train to Brussels. At 4 p.m. they got on the train. From there it was an easy route, via Brussels and Ostend, back to Britain.

Louis' unorthodox departure wasn't spotted for nearly twelve hours. The governor kept sending for him, but Dr Conneau replied that Louis couldn't be disturbed, since he had taken medication which made him drowsy. Eventually the governor lost patience, and came over to Louis' rooms. When he entered the bedchamber, he discovered a dummy in the bed – but by that time, Louis was already far across the border. Conneau was given three months' imprisonment for aiding the escape; Thélin was condemned in his absence to six.

Louis never got to visit his father; the older Louis died a month after the flight from Ham. He stayed in Britain until after the revolution in February 1848 which removed Louis-Phillippe from the throne of France. He stood in the direct elections for the presidency of France in December that year and won a landslide majority. Three years later, he became dictator, and a year after that, on 2 December 1852, he became Emperor Napoleon III, ruling France until he was captured at the Battle of Sedan in the Franco-Prussian War in 1870. He was held captive in Germany for six months before being exiled to England, where he died in 1873. One of his lasting legacies to France: the establishment of a penal colony in French Guyana, which has come to be known by the title of its smallest component part – Devil's Island. Its inhabitants were not given the opportunities to escape that Louis himself had used.

Sources:

Briffaut, F.T.: *The Prisoner of Ham* (T.C. Newby, 1846)
Simpson, Frederick Arthur: *The Rise of Louis Napoleon* (Frank Cass & Co. 1909)
The Free Lance-Star, March 19, 1912 "Louis Napoleon's Escape"

The Outlaw's Last Escape

There are quite a few prison breaks that have entered mythology – from the exploits of Papillon Henri Charriere, to the prisoner-of-war escapes involving the Wooden Horse or gliders from Colditz Castle. But not that many have inspired a pageant. The escape from the Lincoln County Courthouse of Henry McCarty, otherwise known as Billy Antrim, Henry Antrim, Kid Antrim, Billy Bonney and William H. Bonney, but renowned as Billy the Kid, was first memorialized in a pageant in Lincoln County, New Mexico, in 1940, with many of the actors direct descendants of the participants in the bloody shoot out. The pageant continues to this day.

Billy the Kid has become the stuff of American legend – in addition to multiple written retellings of his story, there have been songs (notably by Billy Joel), and even a ballet dedicated to the cowboy who was only twenty-five when he died. Born around 1856, his first escape from custody supposedly occurred in 1875, a year after his mother's death when he was mostly working as a general labourer and cowboy. According to legend, at that time, the Kid was still using the name of Henry McCarty (he started calling himself Antrim, after his stepfather, shortly after this incident), and was arrested initially for stealing two pounds of butter from a ranchman living near his home in Silver City, New Mexico. He was released when he promised to behave better, but shortly afterwards he stole $70, a not inconsiderable sum, from a Chinese man, known as Charlie Sun, in Georgetown. This time he was thrown into jail by Grant County Sheriff Harvey Whitehill.

The young outlaw was held in the Silver City lock-up, and complained to Whitehill that the jailer there was mistreating him, keeping him in solitary confinement and not allowing him to take any exercise. Whitehill therefore ordered the jailer to let the Kid out of his cell to wander around a corridor. The sheriff gave two different stories of what happened next:

In the version Whitehill passed on down through his family, Billy used the freedom he had been granted to reach a chimney. An accomplice on the outside had lowered a rope down inside the building, and the Kid was able to use this to get out. However, when he was interviewed by the *Silver City Enterprise* in 1902, Whitehill claimed that he arranged for Billy to be freed from his cell, but mistakenly, the future outlaw was left unsupervised. When Whitehill realized that there was no sign of the Kid, he raced outside the jail in search of him. A Mexican loitering nearby told him that a young man had come out of the chimney. Whitehill ran back inside the jail, and looked up the big old-fashioned chimney. Clearly visible were handmarks where the fugitive had clawed into the thick layer of soot which lined the chimney. Even though the chimney was only as wide as a man's arm, the Kid had been able to squeeze his way through.

As Whitehill said to the *Silver City Enterprise* reporter, it was shortly after this that Billy the Kid "commenced his career of lawlessness in earnest". He moved to Arizona, and after an argument got out of hand, he killed Frank "Windy" Cahill in what was described as a criminal and unjustifiable shooting in 1877. He then became part of a feud between cattlemen and merchants in the New Mexico area of Lincoln County. The Kid worked for English cattle rancher John H. Tunstall, who, together with Scottish lawyer Alexander McSween, were arguing with Lincoln merchants James Dolan and Lawrence Murphy. Tunstall was murdered in January 1878 by men working for Dolan and Murphy; the Kid and others in Tunstall's employ swore revenge. Calling themselves "Regulators" they engaged in a vicious battle with Dolan and Murphy's workers. After they killed two of their enemies in March 1878, they were declared outlaws.

Sheriff William Brady and Deputy George Hindman were both killed when they tried to ambush McSween, and a bounty hunter also fell to the Regulators. In July, matters came to a head with the Regulators trapped inside McSween's house for four days. Even the army was unable to dislodge them, but when the house was set on fire, the Regulators ran for their lives. The Kid managed to survive; most of the others were shot as they fled. He and the few other remaining Regulators were outlawed for good.

Pat Garrett was elected as Sheriff of Lincoln County in November 1880 after promising to restore law and order to the area in the aftermath of the bitter feud. On 23 December, he captured Billy the Kid at Stinking Springs, four days after he and his posse ambushed the remnants of the Regulators at Fort Sumner. They were taken to Las Vegas, and then to Santa Fe, where they were held in the prison for the first couple of months of 1881. The Kid had no intention of remaining a prisoner, and started digging a tunnel, which was betrayed to the prison authorities on 28 February. As a result, he was placed in solitary confinement, and shackled to the floor of his cell by the local sheriff.

After an attempt to try him in the federal court for the murder of the bounty hunter, Buckshot Roberts, which failed when Billy's lawyer pointed out to the court that the location of Robert's death wasn't federal land, the Kid was handed back to the territorial authorities (New Mexico didn't become a state of the union until 1912). He was charged with the murder of Sheriff Brady, and after a one-day trial, was found guilty. On 13 April 1881, Billy the Kid was sentenced to be hanged exactly one month later, on Friday 13 May, in the town of Lincoln.

It took five days for Billy to be transported from Santa Fe to Lincoln, and his guards expected him either to attempt to get away, or his friends to try to rescue him. It was made abundantly clear to him that the first bullets fired would be at him, not his rescuers. In the event, the journey was uneventful, although the Kid was regularly taunted by one of the guards, Bob Olinger.

On 21 April, the Kid was escorted into his new home in the new Lincoln County courthouse, which had previously been the store run by his enemies, Murphy and Dolan. His guards were Olinger and Deputy James W. Bell, who were warned by Sheriff Garrett to watch their prisoner at all times, even though he was often chained to the floor of what had been Murphy's bedroom.

A week later, Garrett was away from Lincoln collecting taxes (or possibly collecting timber to use for the Kid's gallows). He had reinforced the instructions to Olinger and Bell, knowing that Billy would now be desperate to find a way to escape his fate. Olinger continued to taunt the Kid: the two loathed each other, because they had been responsible for the death of one of the other's friends. Some reports even suggest that Olinger had drawn a line across the room, and warned Billy that if he crossed it, he would be summarily executed. Certainly, a contemporary witness described Olinger as "a big burly fellow, and every one that I ever heard speak of him said he was mean and overbearing, and I know that he tantalized Billy while guarding him, for he invited me to the hanging just a few days before he was killed. Even after he was killed I never heard any one say a single nice thing about him."

The Kid didn't seem to have a problem with Deputy Bell, or even Sheriff Garrett; the latter wrote an account of his dealings with Billy in which he noted that the Kid acknowledged that the sheriff had acted "without malice, and had treated him with marked leniency and kindness". Those qualities were in short supply soon after 5 p.m. on the afternoon of 28 April.

There were five other criminals being held at the Lincoln County courthouse that day, and it was Olinger's duty to take them for something to eat. Billy was therefore left on his own in the jail with Deputy Bell. He asked if he could use the privy, which was in an outhouse behind the prison. Bell agreed, and unshackled him from the floor. Still bound at ankles and wrists, Billy was escorted down the stairs, and out back to the toilet, where he was left to carry out his business unsupervised. Bell then followed Billy back into the courthouse, and up the stairs.

At the top of the stairs, Billy the Kid turned round and fired a gun point-blank at Bell. The deputy crashed down the stairs, and out of the back door, where he fell into the arms of cook Godfrey Gauss, who lived behind the courthouse. Although Billy almost certainly picked up the weapon in the outhouse, it has never been satisfactorily explained who left it for him. One theory suggests that Tunstall's clerk, Sam Corbet, had visited Billy every day while he was in the courthouse, and on one occasion was able to slip him a note or otherwise let him know the one key word, "Privy". That was enough to alert Billy to the presence of something that would help him, smuggled in there by another friend, José Aguayo.

Sheriff Garrett believed that Billy had somehow got ahead of the deputy, been able to reach the armoury, and used one of the weapons from there to kill Bell. One witness claimed that Billy had told him that he had attacked Bell and used the deputy's own gun against him. Of course, had ballistics evidence been available, most of these theories would have been discounted immediately.

In the confusion that followed, Billy was able to slip his wrist-irons off – getting out of such handcuffs had been his party trick for some years, since he had very dainty wrists – and shuffled his way into the armoury, where he was able to collect Olinger's pride and joy, a brand new 10-gauge Whitney shotgun. He moved to the window.

Olinger had heard the shots, and probably initially thought that Bell had been forced to shoot their prisoner. As he entered the yard, he heard a shout from Gauss telling him that Bell was dead. A moment later, Billy yelled, "Hello Bob . . . Look up, old boy, and see what you get," from the window. Olinger did as the outlaw suggested, to see his own shotgun pointed directly at him. The Kid remorselessly let him have both barrels. Olinger collapsed to the ground, killed instantly. Billy then destroyed the gun, and threw it down at Olinger's body.

As a crowd began to gather, Billy returned to the armoury, and grabbed a Winchester rifle, two pistols and a belt of ammunition. He returned to the window, and told the crowd that he hadn't wanted to kill Bell: all he wanted was to get away. Gauss, who had been a friend of Billy's previously, threw him up a pick that he could use to get rid of his leg shackles, then went to find him a horse.

No one dared take action against Billy as he worked at the shackles, finally freeing one leg after an hour's endeavour. He then mounted the horse (on the second attempt – the first time the horse had bolted, spooked by the dangling iron remaining on Billy's leg), and rode away.

The story of Billy's escape cemented his legend. The *Daily New Mexican* said that he had shown "a coolness and steadiness of nerve in executing his plan of escape" and that it was "as bold a deed as those versed in the annals of crime can recall. It surpasses anything of which the Kid has been guilty so far that his past offenses lose much of heinousness in comparison with it, and it effectually settles the question whether the Kid is a cowardly cutthroat or a thoroughly reckless and fearless man."

The Kid stayed on the run with Garrett on his trail for nearly three months. During the night of 14 July 1881, Pat Garrett shot Billy the Kid at the home of Pete Maxwell in Fort Sumner – possibly in a deliberately set ambush. The headstone on his grave comes from the Warner Bros. film *The Outlaw*! Because Garrett had shot Billy, he never received the reward for his capture; he lost the next election for sheriff, and his reputation began to dwindle as questions were asked about the manner in which he killed the outlaw. Garrett himself was shot dead aged fifty-seven in 1908.

Sources:

El Paso Times, 24 March 1987: "Billy the Kid made 1st escape from Silver City jail"

Wild West, August 1998: "Billy the Kid: The Great Escape"

University of Nebraska: *Encyclopedia of the Great Plains*

Nolan, Frederick: *The West of Billy the Kid* (University of Oklahoma, 1998)

Nolan, Frederick: *The Lincoln County War: A Documentary History* (Sunstone Press, 2009)

Boze Bell, Bob: *The Illustrated Life and Times of Billy the Kid* (Tri-Boze Press, 2nd edition 1996)

Jacobsen, Joel: *Such Men as Billy the Kid: The Lincoln County War Reconsidered* (University of Nebraska, 1997)

Getting Even With the Bankers

Criminals often have justifications for their crimes, most of which won't resonate with the ordinary person who isn't prepared to cross the lines that crooks do to get what they want. But in the 1930s, a gang of robbers almost became heroes to the American public, and when their leader was shot and killed in an ambush by the Bureau of Investigation (the forerunner of the FBI), hundreds came to look at his dead body. The reason: John Dillinger's gang targeted a specific group of people. As Harry "Pete" Pierpoint explained, they "stole from the bankers who stole from the people". Some things never change!

Dillinger's greatest mistake was giving the Bureau an excuse to come after him. At the time, bank robbery wasn't a crime with which they became involved in the normal course of events – they might be asked to advise, and assist, but their remit only covered crimes that affected more than one state. During his escape from Crown Point Jail, Dillinger very unwisely travelled across a state line in a stolen car; from that moment on, his fate was sealed.

John Dillinger was born in 1903, and after getting in trouble with the law for theft of a car, he enlisted in the Navy. The service life wasn't for him, and he deserted his ship, heading for Indianapolis. He became friends with a pool shark, Ed Singleton, and the pair tried to rob a Mooresville grocer but the amateur robbers were quickly caught. Singleton pleaded not guilty, and received a two-year sentence. Dillinger's father convinced him to confess and, much to his horror, the young man was sent to Indiana State Prison for assault and battery with intent to rob, and conspiracy to commit a felony, for sentences of two to fourteen years and ten to twenty years respectively. When he was paroled after eight and a half years, he had become an embittered, hardened criminal. As a result of the murders, robberies and other crimes he committed between May 1933 and his death in July 1934, Dillinger was declared Public Enemy Number One.

Bank robber Harry Pierpoint had met Dillinger when both of them were in the Pendleton Reformatory, and they teamed up again when Dillinger followed Pierpoint to the state prison at Michigan City. Since it seemed likely that Dillinger would be freed soon – many people had complained about the apparent injustice of his sentence, including the grocer he had robbed – he seemed to be the ideal person to work on the outside to help free Pierpoint and his gang of fellow bank robbers, Charles Makley, Russell Clark and John "Red" Hamilton, all of whom were serving between fifteen and twenty-five years for various crimes. If he could find a way of smuggling guns into the prison, then Pierpoint would allow Dillinger to join his gang.

After Pierpoint's request for parole was turned down, Dillinger made the necessary arrangements, and ensured that various weapons were transported into the Indiana State Prison within thread boxes. The gang were working within the prison's shirt factory, and were able to gain access to the boxes. Using the shotguns and rifles, they successfully escaped on 26 September 1933. Two guards were shot during their departure.

However, Dillinger wasn't there to greet them. He had been arrested in Lima, Ohio, four days earlier, following bank raids that he had carried out in Bluffton soon after his release in May. When he was searched, the sheriff's men found papers which seemed to indicate that a prison break was being planned; Dillinger, who could be charm personified when he wanted, persuaded them that they were nothing of the sort.

Pierpoint's gang returned the favour on 12 October. Around 6.25 p.m., Pierpoint, Makley and Clark arrived at the Lima jail, claiming that they were from the Indiana State Prison (technically true) and were there to return Dillinger to Michigan City for violating his parole (definitely not true!). Sheriff Jess Sarber didn't believe them, and asked to see proper identification. Pierpoint didn't hesitate: he shot Sarber, and then screamed at him to provide the keys to the cells. Sarber refused to answer, so Charles Makley hit him with his gun butt. When Sarber still was uncooperative, his wife, who had been keeping him company in the jail, begged them to stop hurting him, and dug the keys out of a drawer. Pierpoint and his men freed Dillinger and vanished; Sarber died ninety minutes later. "Get killers. Either dead or alive! Order to Police" screamed the headlines.

At this point, the Bureau of Investigation became involved in a consultative role, identifying and locating the five men, who didn't try to stay hidden. They raided various police stations, including one in Warsaw, Indiana, as well as the arsenals at Auburn, Indiana and Peru, Indiana, stealing machine guns, rifles, revolvers, ammunition, and bulletproof vests. They then went on a bank-robbing spree, gaining notoriety. A raid on the First National Bank in East Chicago was a turning point for Dillinger. On 15 January 1934 (the FBI website mistakenly dates this to a month earlier), he shot and killed a policeman, Detective William Patrick O'Malley, while making his getaway. Dillinger denied that he was responsible for the death, but the policeman who he was holding hostage at the time, Hobart Wilgus, was adamant that Dillinger fired the sub-machine-gun burst.

Dillinger and the gang were apprehended on 23 January, after a fire broke out in the hotel where Russell Clark and Charles Makley were living. The firemen recognized them from the many Wanted posters of Dillinger's men that were circulating; the local police found three Thompson sub-machine guns, two Winchester rifles mounted as machine guns, five bulletproof vests, and more than $25,000 in cash. Arraigned in a Tucson, Arizona court on 25 January, they were dispersed around the country, with Dillinger sent by plane back to Crown Point, Indiana, on 30 January to stand trial for the murder of O'Malley. (Such air travel was a novelty, and apparently Dillinger complained the whole time.) The others were transferred to Ohio to answer charges of murder for Sheriff Sarber; within weeks, they were tried and convicted.

Once he had arrived at Lake County jail, Dillinger turned on the charm to the gathered reporters, agreeing to pose for photos with the local sheriff, Lillian Holley, and prosecuting attorney Robert Estill – both would lose their jobs as a direct result of their apparent chumminess with the alleged murderer after his escape. He claimed he was "not a bad fellow, ladies and gentlemen. I was just an unfortunate boy who started wrong," and answered Sheriff Holley's boast that she could keep him with a simple statement that she couldn't.

Dillinger appeared before the court on 5 February, and was charged four days later. Although the authorities wanted to move him away from Crown Point, his lawyer, Lou Piquett argued against it. Security measures were kept tight initially – footage can be watched online of hordes of policemen, toting shotguns, keeping guard outside Lake County – but it was gradually relaxed as Dillinger appeared resigned to his fate.

He was nothing of the sort. Using razor blades, the gangster carved himself a fake Colt .38 revolver out of washboard, with a quarter-inch copper tube inserted to simulate a barrel. (Or possibly, he arranged for a real one to be smuggled in – there is no definitive evidence either way, and three separate "Dillinger guns" can be found on display in museums, each claiming to be the fake that he created!) At 9.15 a.m. on 3 March, nine days before his trial was scheduled to start, Dillinger used the gun to take one of the guards, officer Baker, hostage. He then seized two .45 automatic pistols from a couple of National Guardsmen who had been watching over another prisoner, Herbert Youngblood, as well as a couple of machine guns. He tried to persuade other prisoners to come along, but they refused – only Youngblood was willing to accompany him. Taking deputy sheriff Ernest Blunk with them as a hostage, they exited through a kitchen and a side entrance to the jail. After Youngblood checked for any watchers, Dillinger walked Blunk through to the police garage, and then out into the street. They then went to the Main Street garage, where they took mechanic Edwin Saagar hostage, and proceeded to steal the sheriff's car! (Dillinger asked Saagar which was the fastest car in the garage, and the mechanic indicated the V8 – it wasn't a deliberate choice to cock a snook at law enforcement, contrary to the legend.) Blunk was forced to drive the car at gunpoint across country. When Dillinger let his hostages go, he handed Saagar four dollars as recompense. A postal worker who saw Dillinger's escape called the police, but was told that he must be mad. Only after he insisted did they take him seriously – and discovered the truth.

Dillinger survived on the run for four more months, but since he had crossed the state line in the stolen car, the Bureau of Investigation were hot on his trail, with Special Agent in Charge Melvin Purvis assigned to bring him in. Dillinger's girlfriend, Mary Evelyn "Billie" Frechette, was arrested in Chicago and then Purvis and his men nearly caught Dillinger, who had now teamed up with another well-known gangster, "Baby Face" Nelson, at the summer resort of Little Bohemia Lodge on 23 April. Dillinger escaped by the skin of his teeth, leaving behind an arsenal of weaponry. The Bureau were responsible for the death of civilians, and its leader, J. Edgar Hoover, brought Samuel Cowley in to assist Purvis.

In an effort to avoid recognition, Dillinger underwent painful plastic surgery on 28 May, after which he needed to recover for a month. On 22 June, Dillinger's thirty-first birthday, Hoover designated him "Public Enemy No. 1" with $10,000 offered for his arrest, and $5,000 for information that led to his capture. A few weeks later, Anna Sage (an alias adopted by Rumanian Ana Cumpanas) tipped off a police detective that Dillinger was living in her apartment as the boyfriend of her lodger – the FBI's official history claims that Sage was the madam of a brothel, and that Dillinger had visited, together with a friend of hers, Polly Hamilton. On 21 July, Sage told Purvis and Cowley that she, Hamilton and Dillinger would be going to the movies the next day.

On the evening of 22 July, the Bureau set a trap around the Biograph movie theatre in Chicago's Lincoln Park area. John Dillinger went to see the gangster film, *Manhattan Melodrama*. It finished at 10.40 p.m. and within a few minutes Dillinger was dead. Realizing that he was trapped as he left the cinema, he reached for his gun. He was hit by four of the six bullets that Bureau agents fired before he could aim – one of them went through the back of his neck, through his brain, and out beneath his right eye.

When they heard about Dillinger's death, Harry Pierpoint and Charles Mackley realized that they would need to escape from death row without any potential help from their friend. Both had been sentenced to death in the electric chair the previous March. They decided to try to emulate Dillinger's means of escape from Crown Point.

The pair created fake guns from bars of soap which they had blackened with shoe polish. On 22 September, they made their move. The weapons were convincing enough to persuade the guards to let them out of their cells, but when they reached the main door other guards opened fire on them with rifles. Makley was killed instantly, but Pierpont survived, although he was seriously injured with a bullet remaining in his spine. As a result, he had to be carried to the electric chair on the morning of 17 October 1934. Russell Clark, the third man arrested for the murder of Sheriff Sarber, was convicted of bank robbery; he was sentenced to life in prison.

Sources:

Gangster File – The Sensational Truth: Bonnie & Clyde/Al Capone/ Dillinger Online, courtesy of yakidk89's channel at YouTube. (This has a lot of useful historical footage, although the narration is inaccurate in places.)

Interview with Edwin Saagar from University of Southern California archives: http://www.youtube.com/watch?feature= player_embedded&v=e6C7kScGHLw

FBI: Famous Cases: John Dillinger (http://www.fbi.gov/about-us/ history/famous-cases/john-dillinger) (includes huge pdf files of all the correspondence between agents of the Bureau regarding Dillinger)

G. Russell Giradin, with William J. Helmer and Rick Mattix: *Dillinger: The Untold Story* (Indiana, 2009)

Burrough, Bryan: *Public Enemies: America's Greatest Crime Wave and the Birth of the FBI, 1933–34* (Penguin, 2009)

Hammond Times, 22 July 1984: "The Hobart Wilgus Story"

Chicago Herald and Examiner, 27 August 1934: "Crime does not pay!"

The Unknown Great Escape

Many of the escapes contained in this volume are well known, either because of the amount of coverage they received in the media at the time, or because they have become the source material for books, screen adaptations or plays. Others have become lost in the mists of time, including what may well be one of the largest prison escapes of the twentieth century, if not ever. The aftermath of the Great Escape from Stalag Luft III during the Second World War horrified the world when 50 of the prisoners were executed, but that number pales compared with the statistics for the escape from Fort San Cristobal on 22 May 1938. Nearly 800 prisoners fled; over 200 of these were killed, and only three made it safely across the border into France.

Construction on a military fortress had begun at the tail end of the nineteenth century in the Ezcaba enclave, not far from Pamplona in the northern Spanish Navarre region. It was designed to be a formidable defensive structure, built into the top of a mountain, within which were three buildings that could not be seen from the outside, and a moat to deter infantry attack. Unfortunately what the designers didn't anticipate was the advent of aviation, so when the fortress was completed in 1919, it was immediately redundant.

San Cristobal was used as a prison between 1934 and 1945, and throughout that time there were complaints about the dreadful conditions within its walls. Hundreds of prisoners were installed there after the October Revolution in 1934, and deaths led to a mutiny within the fort, as well as strikes in nearby Pamplona and other cities around Spain calling for a change in the way the men were treated. From November 1935, some of the 750 prisoners began to be moved out but not in particularly large numbers; three months later, an amnesty for political prisoners saw four hundred released, many of whom immediately condemned the insanitary and unhygienic conditions.

The military coup on 18 July 1936 led by General Francisco Franco saw the prison refilled to its capacity and beyond, with two thousand or so inmates housed within its walls. Conditions remained harsh, with reports of beatings, extreme hunger and outbreaks of lice. Some prisoners were apparently told that they were free to go, so set off down the mountain, only to be killed when they reached the foot. Twenty men were shot on 1 November 1936, four more sixteen days later – official records indicate that 305 prisoners died, although many of the deaths are ascribed to anorexia, heart attacks, or tuberculosis. By spring 1938, there were 2,487 prisoners held at San Cristobal, many of whom had no real idea what crimes they had committed to be incarcerated in such a hellhole. They weren't allowed to look through the windows – the guards would fire at them if they did – and their correspondence was censored, if it even reached them at all. It was against this background that a small group decided to make a break for it in May that year.

The vast majority of those who decided to flee San Cristobal that day had no idea that there was any form of escape being planned. They took the chance to flee an oppressive regime, and many of them paid the ultimate price. A small group of prisoners were looking out for any weaknesses among the prison guards' routine, and they realized that Sundays would be the best day to strike – in common with many other prisons, less went on that day since it was deemed a day of rest, so less guards were on duty. Led by Leopoldo Pico, prisoner number 319, the twenty or so men used the made-up language Esperanto to keep their plans concealed from eavesdropping guards, or fellow prisoners who might overhear something and try to gain capital with the authorities by betraying them.

On Sunday 22 May, there were only ninety-two guards at San Cristobal to monitor over twenty-five times that number of men; in Pamplona, six miles away, there were 331 soldiers. At eight o'clock in the evening, Pico and another prisoner, Baltasar Rabanillo, took hostage the guard who was bringing them dinner, seized his keys and locked him up. They then went up to the next floor of the prison, and captured the four guards there.

Pico put on one of the guard's uniforms, and then split the rest of the escapees into two groups to apprehend the other guards. One group rounded up the cooks and anyone else in the kitchen area; the other locked guards into the tool room.

However, when the freed prisoners started to cross the yard, one of the guards started to raise the alarm. According to the account given by survivor Ernesto Carratalá in his memoirs, "it was the first and only time in my life I saw a man killed. A group of my countrymen accurately, brutally and repeatedly hit the guard on the head. They did so with a hammer, and did not stop until they had overcome his resistance, and the soldier fell inert." The guard succumbed to his injuries, the only one to die – Pico had given instructions that no one was to be killed. Entering the Oficina de Ayudantía, Pico and his men disarmed the guards, and made one of them request the guard on the far side of the door to open it. When he did so, he was also disarmed, and the prisoners were then able to get access to the keys to the cells. As the other guards, who were either having their dinner or were on duty watching the perimeter, were rounded up, the prisoners were released from their cells.

All seemed to be going to plan. Within half an hour, the prisoners had taken control of the fort, and those that wanted to could make a mass getaway. However, Pico couldn't anticipate that one of the guards would return from Pamplona, see the situation unfolding and run back to the town to raise the alarm. Nor could he have expected that one of his fellow prisoners, Angel Alcazarde de Valasco, would flee from the fort to inform the authorities.

Pico had banked on the escape remaining undetected until the next batch of guards arrived to take over duties the following morning, but instead, military trucks with huge searchlights were dispatched from Pamplona, and many of the prisoners turned tail and returned to the fort. By 3.30 the next morning, there were 1692 inmates remaining in San Cristobal. Nearly one third of the total population, 795 men, had fled to the surrounding thickly wooded hills.

Carratalá, who was only eighteen years old at the time of the escape, remembers that the confusion was total. Some people thought that the war was over, and made their way to the train station in Pamplona, where they were arrested when they tried to buy a ticket. He himself spent a quarter of an hour running through the woods, but when he heard the sound of the approaching vehicles, he decided to cut his losses and head back to the prison. Like many of his comrades, he was back in his usual place by the time the military arrived.

Many of them didn't last long in the wild; 207 were shot rather than arrested; 585 were brought back to San Cristobal. Among them was Felix Alvarez, who very nearly reached the border with France. Running from the troops, who were shooting the escaping prisoners like rabbits, he and a couple of men from the same area got as far as the village of Gascue-Odieta, but a woman there reported them to the military. She did make up for it to a certain extent – before they were returned to San Cristobal, she made them what Alvarez still recalled as the best soup of his life.

The military authorities were humiliated by the sheer scale of the escape, and tried to claim that many of those who fled were common criminals "of the worst kind . . . a bunch of murderers, robbers and thieves". When they were returned to San Cristobal, they were thrown into the worst cells, on the lowest level, and were often left naked and without food for days on end, receiving regular beatings from the guards. One man, Amador Rodriguez Solla, later nicknamed Tarzan by his peers, managed to remain on the loose, hiding in a cave eating snails, frogs and plants, until 14 August.

Seventeen leaders of the escape were tried by a military court; fourteen of them were sentenced to death and shot in the centre of Pamplona on 8 September 1938; one of them was sent to the asylum in Pamplona. Pico was also illegally executed, although there are various different reports as to when. The prosecutor at the trial said he had been shot before those proceedings began; some said he was killed in the woods; others that he was captured, returned to San Cristobal and shot there. De Valasco, who had raised the alarm, had his prison sentence reduced; everyone else who was recaptured received a further seventeen years.

Three of the men did make it across the border into France; one of them emigrated to Mexico, where he never discussed his time in prison or his escape with his family.

When the French press denounced the way that Franco's regime had handled the breakout and its aftermath, the dictator issued an "official note" commenting on the French defamation of his actions, pointing out that a guard had been killed during the escape; most of the escapees had been returned to the prison; those who had been killed had fought back against their pursuers; and wondering about the activities of certain French citizens who had been visiting villages close to San Cristobal prior to the escape. It was the only comment that the regime ever made about the escape.

Conditions did improve within the prison; the director was dismissed following the mass break out, and the financial administrator was prosecuted for embezzlement. A memorial was erected on the fiftieth anniversary of the escape, but it was regularly vandalized, and was destroyed completely by members of the extreme right in 2009. The prison was closed in 1945, and the Spanish Army abandoned the fortress in 1987, with a surveillance unit remaining for a further four years. In 2001, it was declared cultural property of the state, and over the past few years excavations of the area have allowed many of the bodies of prisoners to be removed and given proper burials.

The inscription on the memorial is perhaps the best tribute to those who died in the unknown great escape: "I die without pain, since I lay down my life for freedom."

Sources:

El Pais, 21 October 2007: "La fuga de los 221 muertos"
Memoria Libertaria, May 2005: "Fuerte de San Cristobal 1938" (includes quotes from the documentary *La gran fuga de las cárceles franquistas*)

Cheating the Death Camp

Although there have been various accounts over the years of heroic escapes from the confines of the Nazi concentration and death camps, some of which do not stand up to close scrutiny, few are as well documented and accepted as the escape from Treblinka in August 1943.

The death camp had been established as part of Operation Reinhard, the Nazi's codename for their Final Solution: the total extermination of the Jewish people across occupied Europe. There was already a forced labour camp near the formerly Polish village of Treblinka; this became known as Treblinka I. Treblinka II was solely concerned with the mass murder of as many people as possible in the shortest possible time.

The death camp was begun in May 1942, and was in operation by that July: a railway branch line was built connecting to the nearby station, along which the truckloads of Jews were brought. On arrival, they would be informed that this was a transit camp, and that for hygiene purposes, they needed to take a shower before being dispatched to their new workplaces. Separated by gender, with children remaining with the women, the Jews would strip naked, reassured that their belongings would be returned to them after the showers, and the women's hair was shorn. They were then herded along a narrow passageway into a shower room. Once there, carbon monoxide gas from the exhaust pipe of a Russian tank was pumped into the room, asphyxiating them within a few minutes. The bodies were then removed from the showers, and taken to the mass burial pits before the next group were brought in to meet the same fate.

Although they were supervised by German and Ukrainian guards, Jewish prisoners had to carry out the repulsive tasks of emptying the train cattle cars of those who had died during the journey to the camp; taking the bodies from the showers to the burial pits; and searching through the clothing and belongings of their fellow Jews for anything of value. Anything that identified the items as Jewish was removed – such as the yellow stars that Jews were forced to wear – and all identity papers and passports were destroyed.

Initially, the Jews chosen for this task were replaced every three to five days by fresh arrivals, but when the former Commandant of Sobibor camp, Franz Stangl, was placed in charge, he began to create groups of Sonderkommandos, Jewish slave labourers. Roughly 700 men and a few women were, at least temporarily, saved, although they were killed for the slightest offence, and many chose suicide rather than be complicit in the murder of their own people. After new gas chambers were built, the camp operated at peak efficiency into the spring of 1943, by which time over 850,000 people had been murdered.

When Heinrich Himmler visited Treblinka that spring, he ordered that the mass graves were to be emptied, and the bodies burned. The bones were then to be crushed, and the ashes replaced in the graves. It was an attempt to hide the scale of the massacres, once the tide of the war had turned against the Nazi regime. This process took four months or so to complete; the Sonderkommandos were well aware that their own lives would be forfeit as soon as the work was completed.

There were many attempts to escape from Treblinka before the mass breakout in August 1943. Some Jews tried to flee from the trains but were shot by the guards, or worse, handed back to the Germans. This was the fate met by the Cienki brothers, who returned to their home town in October 1942 to tell their friends and neighbours the truth about the Treblinka trains. They were handed over to the Gestapo and shot. Aron Gelberd escaped the same month, but was stripped by Ukrainian farmers who found him. He managed to reach a place of safety and emigrated to Israel after the war. Others managed to get away to Jewish ghettoes, but then found themselves returned to Treblinka when these too were emptied as part of Operation Reinhard.

Attempts to hide inside the trains carrying the possessions back for resale were rarely successful. Moshe Boorstein and Simcha Laski managed it in late July 1942, and returned to

Warsaw in time for the uprising there. Two months later, Czech businessman Oskar Berger managed to conceal himself, but was caught and sent to Buchenwald concentration camp. He survived the war. Yechiel Berkowicz, Abraham Bomba, Yechezkel Cooperman, Israel Einshindler, all successfully hid in the clothing.

Tunnels were started but few reached past the perimeter fence. One man, Lazar Sharson, did use a tunnel, and fled to the Warsaw ghetto on New Year's Eve 1942. Four others with him did not manage to escape, and were hanged in front of the other prisoners in the death pit area. Some men, like Anshel Medrzycki and Abraham Krzepicki ran away naked, and were not apprehended.

The Germans were ruthless: after a spate of escape attempts, not only were the perpetrators hanged, but so were ten of the other Jewish slave workers.

At the start of 1943, a proper resistance group started to coalesce, led by Dr Julian Chorazycki, a former Polish army officer, but when he was found in April with a large sum of money which was going to be used to get hold of weapons from outside the camp, Chorazycki chose to swallow a vial of poison rather than risk giving away the names of his comrades. Jankiel Wiernik, a carpenter, became key to the arrangements, as he was one of the few people who could move between the Sonderkommandos who were based in the main part of the camp, and the others whose accommodation was near their work area in the burial pits. The prisoners lived in constant fear that their plan would be discovered: survivor Samuel Willenberg remembered one man facing death who tried to betray the conspiracy, but the Ukrainian guard to whom he was talking didn't speak German.

As the work removing the bodies neared its closure, the committee chose its date. As Willenberg later recalled, "At the Organizing Committee meeting, held late at night by the light of fires burning the bodies of hundreds of thousands of those dearest to us, we unanimously approved the decision to launch the uprising the next day, 2 August 1943.

"I will never forget white-haired Zvi Korland, the eldest amongst us, who with tears in his eyes, administered to us the oath to fight to our last drop of blood, for the honour of the Jewish people."

Kalman Teigman, a Polish airport worker who was transported to Treblinka in September 1942, gave the most public account of the revolt at the trial of Adolf Eichmann in December 1961. Eichmann had been one of the key Nazis responsible for the holocaust. He fled to South America after the war and was captured by Israeli intelligence agents in Argentina on 11 May 1960. Returned to Israel for trial, he faced fourteen weeks of testimony from over ninety concentration camp survivors, and was sentenced to death.

According to Teigman's testimony, the eventual plan for the revolt was based around access to weapons within the camp itself. Two Jewish children were employed to clean the German officers' shoes, and were working in a hut which also contained weapons. An extra key was made for the storage lock, and the children were to bring out arms in sacks: guns, bullets, revolvers and hand grenades. Smaller items would be put in buckets which were secreted around the camp – in the motor workshop, near piles of potatoes – and then at the pre-arranged time, the prisoners would grab these weapons, find a pretext to get the SS guards into the workshops, and kill them.

Like most escape attempts, it didn't go according to plan. The revolt was supposed to start at 4 p.m., with the children collecting the weapons between 2 p.m. and 2.30. One of the prisoners, Jakob Domb, shouted out to those working in the extermination area, "End of the world today, the day of judgement at four o'clock" as he went about his rubbish-collecting earlier in the day. However, a couple of the Jews broke the Nazis' strictly enforced rules and returned to their accommodation around the same time as the children were distributing the arms. They were caught by guards, and made to undress, revealing that they were carrying sums of money in readiness for the breakout. Around 3.30, one of the camp commanders began beating them to interrogate them, which scared the other prisoners, who were sure that they would break under pressure and reveal the escape plan.

Even though it wasn't quite time for the revolt to start, driver mechanic Rudek Lubrenitski took matters into his own hands, and shot at the SS guards who were administering the beating. At the same time, a grenade was thrown – the signal for the revolt to begin.

One particular prisoner's role was to disinfect the guards' huts and accommodation, for which he used a spray gun connected to a tank on his back. Instead of simply putting disinfectant in the tank, he had added petrol to the mix, and sprayed the huts with this highly flammable substance. When the huge petrol tank was set ablaze with a grenade, the fire quickly spread to the huts.

The prisoners ran for their lives, over the fence, through the minefields into the surrounding forests, with the Germans pursuing them in cars, on foot and on horseback. Many – including most of the escape committee – were killed before they could reach freedom. Rudolf Masarek manned a machine gun from the top of the camp's pigeon house to cover the escape of the others, only to be shot. Some, like camp elder Bernard Galewski who realized that he didn't have the strength to run far from the Germans, committed suicide rather than be recaptured, or asked their friends to administer a coup de grace. But, as Kalman Teigman told a BBC documentary shortly before his death in July 2012, for those who did manage to escape the feeling was "unbelievable".

Estimates of the number of prisoners who tried to escape vary from 300 to 750 but fewer than 200 remained at large by nightfall, after Franz Stangl began a massive manhunt. Of these, 70 survived the war, spreading around the world. Stangl took retaliation against those who remained: many were killed, others made to obliterate any evidence of the existence of the camp.

After escaping through Italy and Syria after the war, Stangl moved to Brazil, where he was arrested by Nazi hunter Simon Weisenthal. He was tried in West Germany, where he maintained that his conscience was clear and was sentenced to life imprisonment on 22 October 1970. He died of heart failure the following June. Eleven members of the SS personnel stationed at the camp had been brought to trial in October 1964; one was acquitted, one died before the hearing. The most sadistic of the guards, Kurt Franz, was one of four sentenced to life imprisonment.

The last word on Treblinka should rest with Kalman Teigman, who reinforced the horror of the camps at Eichmann's trial: "The way in which facts are being presented here, one might come to the conclusion that the 700,000 Treblinka deportees were not gassed by the SS men, but all simply committed suicide." Those who escaped never forgot those they were not able to save.

Fact vs Fiction

The Treblinka breakout is one of the incidents related in Canadian author Robert J. Sawyer's novel *Frameshift*, and also is fictionalized for Guillermo del Toro and Chuck Hogan's novel *The Strain*, although this includes a vampiric element.

Sources:

Holocaust Education & Archive Research Team: Treblinka Death Camp: http://www.holocaustresearchproject.org/ar/treblinka/treblinkaremembrme.html

Yad Vashem: http://www1.yadvashem.org/yv/en/exhibitions/this_month/resources/treblinka

Testimony of Kalman Teigman at the trial of Adolf Eichmann: quoted at http://www.holocaustresearchproject.org/ar/treblinka/revolt.html

Getting the Axe

Any escape from prison, particularly if it involves high-profile inmates, such as serial killers or terrorists, tends to lead to debate in the seats of government, whether it's at a local level or national. Often these discussions can become quite hyperbolic, with each plot apparently the worst scenario that can possibly be imagined, and those who were negligent, or unfortunate enough to be responsible for the breach in security, are castigated – even if subsequent discoveries show that they weren't at fault. The reign of terror of the Kray Twins and their henchmen in London was already an emotive topic when one of their friends, the so-called Mad Axeman, Frankie Mitchell, escaped from Dartmoor – and in a debate in the House of Lords two days later, Lord Derwent didn't hold back. "This particular case of Mitchell is a quite scandalous example of an error of judgement combined with a complete disregard of the safety of the public," he thundered. And when you bear in mind that Mitchell was eventually executed, apparently on the orders of the Kray Twins, because they were unable to keep him under control, you may think that, on this occasion, the noble lord had a point!

In 1958, Frank Samuel Mitchell had been sentenced to concurrent sentences of life imprisonment and ten years' imprisonment on charges of robbery, some with violence, and since September 1962 had been held at Dartmoor Prison. Although physically very strong, he had the mental age and attitudes of a child. He had a long history of violent crime, including beating a prison officer senseless, for which he was flogged. At various stages, he had been declared insane and held at both Rampton and Broadmoor. He had escaped from the latter, and held an elderly couple hostage with an axe that he found in their garden shed, earning himself the nickname of The Mad Axeman. However, since he had been at Dartmoor, he had not become involved in any incidents of violence, and in line with prison policy at the time, in May 1965 he was allowed to be employed on an outside working party. As the Home Secretary, Roy Jenkins, explained to the House of Commons on 13 December 1966, the day after Mitchell's escape, "The object of outside working parties is to test the trustworthiness and develop the responsibility of a prisoner in conditions of less than maximum supervision when his eventual return to the community is contemplated." The prison authorities believed that Mitchell had matured and they didn't anticipate that he would abuse the trust that was being shown.

Frankie Mitchell wanted to go home for Christmas. He made that clear when he was visited by friends of the Kray brothers in the spring of 1966; he repeated it after his escape when he was still effectively being held prisoner, this time by the Krays. If anything was the overriding motive for his escape, it was that. The former Governor of Dartmoor Prison had recommended that a date be set for his release, but the government refused to do so, and for someone of his restricted mental abilities, it must have seemed as if he was going to be stuck in prison for the rest of his life, exactly as the judge had apparently ordered.

Mitchell's working party often consisted of himself and another prisoner, and they would be left to their own devices on the moor. From all accounts, the prison officers were wary of Mitchell, and as long as he came back to the prison, he was often left to his own devices. During the autumn of 1966, he was able to visit local public houses in Peter Tavey, half a dozen miles from the prison, and even go into local towns to buy budgerigars, which he had taken an interest in breeding during his time in Dartmoor. That gave ample opportunity for him to be given clear instructions.

The Krays, who at that time controlled much of the villainy in the East End of London, had got to know Mitchell when they were all locked up in Wandsworth jail, and they kept in touch with him when he was moved to Dartmoor. Around Easter 1966, two of their henchmen, "Fat Wally" Garelick and Patrick Connelly visited Mitchell, giving false names, along with a girl (known as Miss A in the court proceedings). The discussion turned to the Krays, and Mitchell made it clear he didn't want to still be in Dartmoor at the end of the year. "You won't be here for

Christmas," he was told, and, according to the evidence Miss A gave at the trial of the Kray brothers and their accomplices, the two men told her that "they" were going to get Mitchell out.

In June, Garelick returned to the prison, and when Mitchell asked about the timetable for his escape, he was told to be alert, as it would have to be arranged at short notice. Garelick, Connelly, Miss A and another girl also spent some time reconnoitring the area around the prison during this trip. The plan was then presented to Ronnie and Reggie Kray in London for their approval.

The third visit at the start of December saw an increasingly anxious Mitchell insistent that he wanted to go home. Garelick reassured him that he would be, and told him that he would need to "run further" now than they had originally told him. The day before the escape, Garelick and Connelly made a final trip to Dartmoor, a couple of days after hiring a car.

The weather wasn't good on 12 December; it wasn't sufficiently bad to prevent the working party from going out to work on a fence on the firing range at Bagga Tor, but it did mean that for the majority of the day, the prisoners stayed in the base hut. In the afternoon, Mitchell asked if he could take some bread to feed the horses, something that he had done regularly near the point where the prisoners were dropped off and picked up. Usually he would be waiting there for them when the rest of the prisoners arrived. This time, there was no sign of him and it was at least forty minutes before the alarm was raised.

By this time, Frankie Mitchell was sitting in the back of a Humber car on the way back to London in the company of three of the Kray gang: Albert Donoghue, 'Mad' Tommy Smith and Billy Exley. He was taken to a flat belonging to another member of the gang, Lennie Dunn, in Canning Town, and stayed there for the next twelve days – the rest of his life.

When they realized that he had gone, the prison authorities began a massive search. More than a hundred police using tracker dogs joined thirty prison officers combing the area during one of the worst hailstorms in recent memory. The next day, a hundred Royal Marines had been divided into three search parties, backed up by two Royal Navy helicopters, but all without success. It seemed as if he had vanished off the face of the earth.

The following weekend, warders at the prison even made a

plea via the pages of the *Daily Mirror*, believing that he might want to give himself up. "If you let us know where to meet you, we will be quite willing to pick you up," they said, believing that Mitchell might be frightened of going to the police, but would be willing to surrender to people he trusted. "If he does this," a statement from the warders noted, "he will not only gain reasonable consideration for himself but will also vindicate those who trusted him and were proved wrong – and prove wrong, indeed, those who have condemned him." By this stage, though, police investigations had started to centre on the East End of London.

The Krays claimed that they assisted Mitchell to escape from Dartmoor to help publicise his case. If he could be kept on the outside without causing trouble, then hopefully the authorities would reconsider his lack of release date. He therefore – with a great deal of assistance – wrote letters to four separate newspapers, which were authenticated by his thumbprint on the bottom. They weren't quite identical, but it was clear that they had been written from a template, with all of them highlighting the indeterminate nature of his sentence, and asking for a release date. The letters were printed in *The Times* and the *Daily Mirror*. However, the government response was clear: he had to return to prison before any consideration would be given to his case.

All the time, Mitchell was kept under lock and key, with at least one member of the Kray Firm guarding him. When he became insistent on some female company, Lisa Prescott, a hostess from the Winston club, was provided on 19 December. Mitchell very quickly became attached to her, telling his guards that they were going to get married, and refusing to contemplate moving out of the flat without her. Prescott herself was kept cowed by the Kray henchmen and only allowed to leave the flat in the company of one of them.

Mitchell was getting annoyed with his situation. He didn't feel that he was being treated seriously by the Krays and was threatening to leave the flat to visit them. He probably didn't understand that this was designed as a temporary escape, and that the intention was that he return to Dartmoor but with a clear end to his sentence in sight. When the henchmen suggested that he should go back on 23 December, he refused, saying he wanted to stay out at least over Christmas.

That refusal probably sealed his fate. According to the court case, and the evidence of Freddie Foreman, Mitchell was persuaded to leave the flat, perhaps on the pretext that he was being taken to spend Christmas in Kent with Ronnie Kray. He was assured that Lisa Prescott would be following within the hour. When he got into the back of a waiting van, two of the Krays' gunmen were waiting for him. At close range, a fusillade of bullets was pumped into the Mad Axeman. Certainly sounds of muffled bangs were heard from within the vehicle, and then the two men who had walked out with Mitchell returned to the flat, and made a phone call. "The dog is dead," one of them said, before ordering the others to completely clean the flat. Prescott was then taken to another flat and threatened by Reggie Kray to keep her mouth shut. She was told that "they gave [Mitchell] four injections in the nut". Mitchell's body was disposed of at sea.

Ronnie Kray didn't deny that Mitchell was dead, but blamed it on one of his men, Billy Exley, and three Greeks, who had offered to get Mitchell out of the country. However, when they couldn't cope with him, they shot him. (Equally, another member of the Kray firm said that Ronnie told him: "He's f***ing dead. We had to get rid of him; he would have got us all nicked. We made a mistake getting the bastard out in the first place.")

Either way, Frankie Mitchell achieved his aim of not being in Dartmoor at Christmas. Wally Garelick received an eighteen-month sentence for his part in the escape.

Sources:

Daily Mirror, 19 December 1966: "Dartmoor warders in plea to Mitchell"

Evening Argus, 29 October 2003: "Ex-Kray henchman spared jail"

Hansard, 13 December 1966: "House of Commons: Dartmoor (Prisoner's Escape)"

Hansard, 14 December 1966: "House of Lords: Dartmoor Escape of Frank Mitchell"

TheKrays.co.uk

Foreman, Frankie with John Lisners: *Respect* (Arrow, 1997)

Glasgow Herald, 26 June 1968: "Crown story of Frank Mitchell's murder after escape from Dartmoor"

Caught Because They Could

Cinema audiences in 2002 were treated to a fun romp starring Leonardo DiCaprio as a young criminal being pursued by a dogged FBI agent played by Tom Hanks. Directed by Steven Spielberg, *Catch Me If You Can* was a highly fictionalized version of the life of Frank Abagnale junior, a conman who had achieved great success before his twenty-first birthday. But while the film didn't hesitate to conflate events and characters, Abagnale's story was astounding enough without any additions. According to one report, there was even a plaque on the wall of Atlanta Federal Penitentiary commemorating Abagnale's escape from the prison since apparently he was the first person to do so. (He wasn't, but he was one of the very few who did.)

It is very difficult to verify many of the claims that are made in Abagnale's book, also called *Catch Me If You Can*. According to the former conman himself – who has subsequently gone straight, and acts as a security consultant – not everything should be taken at face value. "I was interviewed by the co-writer [Stan Redding] only about four times," Abagnale writes on his company's website. "I believe he did a great job of telling the story, but he also over dramatized and exaggerated some of the story. That was his style and what the editor wanted. He always reminded me that he was just telling a story and not writing my biography. This is one of the reasons that from the very beginning I insisted the publisher put a disclaimer in the book and tapes." As with some of the other stories in this volume where the primary evidence comes from the escapee's own account – such as Henri Charriere or Casanova (a comparison that the younger Abagnale would probably have enjoyed) – this should perhaps be taken with a pinch of salt.

Abagnale's account of his life as a conman from the ages of sixteen to twenty-one – posing as a Pan Am co-pilot, a paediatrician who worked for nine months as an administrator in a large hospital, a lawyer, a college professor and a Los Angeles stockbroker – makes for highly enjoyable reading, but by the end of his short-lived career, he was on the run in twenty-six different countries around the globe. He spent six months in the infamous Perpignan prison in France, where he was thrown naked into a cell, about five feet cubed, and told he would be there for his entire year-long sentence, with no bedding or anything beyond a bucket. From there he was transferred to Swedish custody for trial on fraud charges, and found their prisons were comparatively luxurious. After being found guilty of a lesser crime, he served six months in Sweden (much of it in hospital recovering from his treatment by the French), and then, thanks to the intervention of a Swedish judge who didn't want to send Abagnale on to Italy for prosecution there (thence to Spain), he was deported to the United States. Knowing that he was facing a prison sentence there, Abagnale resolved to escape from the custody of the guards deporting him.

Using the knowledge he had gained while working as a pilot, Abagnale removed the toilet unit, and lowered himself to the ground through the hatch cover used for the vacuum hose once the plane had landed in New York (at that time, there weren't the restrictions on moving around the cabin or using the restrooms during take-off or landing that there are today). He made his way to Montreal, and was on the verge of catching a flight to Brazil – which didn't have an extradition treaty with the United States – when he was arrested by a member of the Royal Canadian Mounted Police. The Mounties transferred him to the Border Patrol, and from there Abagnale was in FBI custody.

He eventually ended up in Atlanta where he was taken to the Federal Penitentiary to await trial. Built in 1902, the medium-security facility had a capacity of around 3,000 inmates, and a reputation for being nigh-on impossible to escape from. In April 1971, when Abagnale arrived there, the prison, like much of the rest of the American penal system, was under higher scrutiny than usual. Geed up by civil rights groups, congressional committees and the Justice Department were investigating the treatment of convicts, and undercover agents were regularly being placed into the system to report on conditions. For a man used to living on his wits like Abagnale, this was a heaven-sent opportunity.

It helped that he wasn't properly checked into the prison by the US Marshal who delivered him there. The Marshal didn't have the correct paperwork, and more or less insisted that the prison admissions officer take Abagnale without it. To the jaded eyes of the guards, this more or less confirmed that there was something suspicious about Abagnale, and right from the outset they were convinced that he was an undercover prison inspector, out to get more of their colleagues fired.

Although he initially protested that he really was a prisoner, Abagnale quickly saw the benefits to the deception. There clearly was an increased interest in prison conditions – and they would be forcibly brought to the public's attention by the riots at Attica prison in New York in September 1971, caused by the atrocious state of the penal system – and the Atlanta authorities didn't want to be found wanting. Abagnale received special treatment, and decided to use it to make his escape.

According to his own account, Abagnale contacted Jean Sebring, an old girlfriend of his in Atlanta, and when she visited him, posing as his fiancée, he outlined his plan. Sebring had been contacted by Sean O'Riley, the FBI agent who had doggedly tracked Abagnale for some time (and the basis of the character Hanratty, played by Tom Hanks in the movie), and possessed one of his business cards. At Abagnale's instigation, she then claimed to be a freelance writer and gained an interview with US Bureau of Prisons Inspector C.W. Dunlap – and got hold of one of his cards too. This she was able to pass to Abagnale during her next visit.

While Abagnale continued to allow the guards to believe that he was spying on them, Sebring took O'Riley's card to a local printer, and spun a story that she wanted to surprise her father with a set of business cards with his new telephone number on them after he moved apartments. Everything else needed to be identical to the original. Far from any connection to O'Riley, the new numbers in fact belonged to a couple of payphones in a shopping mall.

Once Sebring had given Abagnale one of the new cards, he moved into action. Shortly before 9 p.m. he told one of the guards that he really was a prison inspector, and passed over Dunlap's card, saying that an emergency had arisen and he needed to see the lieutenant on duty. The guard dutifully took him along to the lieutenant, who was as pleased as his subordinate to learn that Abagnale had come clean about his true identity. Abagnale explained that he would have been released the following Tuesday, but he had been forced to reveal himself, since he needed to speak to an FBI agent regarding a case. With that, he handed over the card, complete with the FBI seal, address – and fake phone numbers. The lieutenant didn't consider for a moment that there was anything amiss (and one has to assume that no one had told him, or others in the prison, exactly what Abagnale was on remand for!) and called O'Riley's "office" number.

Sebring answered, and the lieutenant passed the phone to Abagnale, who carried out a fake conversation during which it transpired that "O'Riley" was undercover, and couldn't come into the prison to speak with Abagnale. The only way that the two men could meet was if Abagnale could pop outside the prison and have a chat for a few minutes. The lieutenant couldn't see any problem with that; after all, as far as he could see, Abagnale was going to be out of their hair in a few days' time anyway. He assented to Abagnale meeting O'Riley. After fifteen minutes or so, a car pulled up outside the prison and the lieutenant himself escorted Abagnale to the door. The conman jumped into the car, driven by Sebring, and disappeared into the night.

(For the sake of historical accuracy, it should be noted that both Sean O'Riley and Jean Sebring were probably names created by Abagnale and Redding for the book: O'Riley's real name was Joe Shea, and he and Abagnale remained friends for the rest of the FBI agent's life.)

While the prison guards initially tried to bluff that Abagnale had managed to forcibly escape from custody – something considerably more hardened criminals had failed to do over past decades – the truth of his con was soon revealed. A manhunt followed and Abagnale managed to evade capture by FBI agents by posing as a member of the Bureau himself. However two months later, he was arrested in Washington DC, and served four years in Virginia before being paroled to Houston, Texas.

After a period of dead-end jobs, he suggested to his parole officer that he could advise banks on how to avoid being conned – and ended up becoming one of the greatest poachers-turned-gamekeepers in American history.

Fact vs. Fiction

As mentioned, Abagnale's own account was heavily fictionalized during the writing process – many of the institutions he claimed to have conned denied that he did so, perhaps, as he suggested, to avoid embarrassment – but his escape from prison, even if it wasn't quite as flamboyant as he suggests, certainly occurred. The incident is not included in the movie version: in that, he escapes from the plane and is then arrested a little later.

Sources:

Abagnale, Frank W. with Stan Redding: *Catch Me If You Can: The Amazing True Story of the Youngest and Most Daring Con Man in the History of Fun and Profit!* (Grosset & Dunlap, 1980)
Abagnale & Associates website: www.abagnale.com
Weekly World News, 7 April 1981: "The Great Imposter"
BBC News Online, 27 January 2003: "Conman who came in from the cold"

The World's Most Impregnable Prison?

The struggle to end the apartheid regime in South Africa produced many heroes: men and women who refused to give in to the oppressive demands of the white minority who ruled the country. Many of the government's opponents were thrown into jail with no idea when, or indeed if, they would be released. But some people were determined to get out and, at the end of 1979, three men – deemed terrorists by those in charge – were able to escape from the notorious Pretoria Prison.

Tim Jenkin was brought up in South Africa, and didn't question the way of life until he went to visit Britain after leaving school. He returned to South Africa to study sociology at university, and found himself increasingly questioning what was going on around him. At the end of the three-year course in April 1974, he and his friend Stephen Lee headed to London and contacted the African National Congress (ANC). They were trained with practical and survival skills to act as a propaganda cell in the South African underground, and sent back in July 1975.

One of their main jobs was to produce "leaflet bombs", simple timed explosives that threw bundles of leaflets high in the air near a targeted group of people. They could be hidden inside cardboard boxes or ordinary shopping bags. Their first was released in March 1976 to mark the anniversary of the Sharpeville massacre in 1960, and seemed to be successful, although the arrest of other ANC operatives and the harsh sentences that they were given made it clear that they were involved in a very risky business. The work escalated through 1977 and early 1978, with banners supporting the ANC and pamphlets exhorting the South African people to "Awake!" and throw off the Vorster regime.

In February 1978, Jenkin and Lee started to realize that they and their team were under police surveillance, but didn't take sensible precautions. On Thursday 2 March, they were arrested and charged under the 1967 Terrorism Act. While waiting trial, both read Henri Charriere's book *Papillon*, and although Jenkin recognized how incredible the story was, it started him seriously thinking about the mechanics of escaping: the need to devote every moment of every day to the escape, to have contingency plans for the contingency plans, and to make sure you can survive on the outside.

The first part of the plan was to ensure that they had some money, and the two men created "chargers" similar to those supposedly used by Papillon: tubes that could be inserted in the anus containing rolled-up money. On 15 June 1978, Jenkin was sentenced to twelve years' imprisonment, Lee to eight. Straight after the hearing, Jenkin obtained some aspirin from his mother to make sure he stayed constipated, so that his charger would remain in place while they were transferred to their new home: Pretoria Prison.

Built in the late 1960s for white male political prisoners, Pretoria Prison was part of the prison complex known as Pretoria Central. This comprised a central prison for criminals of all kinds from across the country; Pretoria Prison for local felons, as well as the political prisoners; and a maximum security prison for the condemned, habitual escapees and recidivists. It was regarded as one of the most secure prisons in the world. Any escape would need to start from the prison yard, so that was heavily guarded by day, and searchlights to keep it floodlit at night, as well as a vicious guard dog.

Jenkin and Lee monitored the routine: the dog sometimes didn't arrive until after lock-up at 4.30 p.m.; there wasn't a guard on duty in the watchtower between lock-up and 10 p.m. But they would still need to get as far as the yard before they could contemplate getting over the wall from there. To do that, they needed to learn how to pick locks.

Close examination of the lock on his cell door enabled Jenkin to create pieces that would form a wooden key in the prison workshop, and to his amazement, it worked first time. He then needed to create a key for the outer door lock, but that took longer, as he didn't have as easy access to check the dimensions. After a near disaster when a test key broke in the lock, he realized he would need to check the next version when the door was locked, so had to create a device to be able to reach the lock from within the cell. Using a broomstick handle connected to a piece of wood, which had the key fixed to it, he was able to unlock the second obstacle, after three months of trial and error.

Another political prisoner, Alex Moumbaris, became part of the escape group; most of the other prisoners were interested in escaping, but not as concerned with the technical aspects as Jenkin and Lee were. Other plans were discussed, such as sneaking out through the yard gate when the watchtowers guard's attentions were elsewhere, or when he sheltered from a thunderstorm, but these were dismissed as impractical. By the end of 1978, Jenkin, Lee and Moumbaris were subject to oversight of their plans by a "Washing Committee", consisting of Moumbaris and one of the most respected prisoners, Dave Kitson.

It was around then that they started to consider escape routes that began somewhere other than the prison yard. Their success with creating keys meant that a more direct exit through the front door might be feasible. Maybe they could capture the night warder, and use his keys to get out of the prison? There seemed to be too many risks inherent in that approach, but it did make them think about simply opening any locks as they progressed through the prison. To that end, they worked on their lock-picking skills, and created a key for the prison workshop so they could get at a supply of tools that they might need. They also made keys for every other door that they could get at which didn't use duplicates of the ones they had already made, sometimes using soap impressions of the keys if the warders left them in the locks, or on other times actually taking the locks out of the doors and then taking them apart.

There were ten different sorts of locks on the doors between them and freedom, and they were able to create copies of all bar three of them. They therefore built a set of lockpicks from pieces of bent wire, which they were confident they would be able to use to get through those three doors.

At the start of 1979, it seemed as if they were ready to go; at that stage, the plan still involved taking keys from the night warder for his car, but otherwise letting themselves out of the prison using the keys that they had. However, shortly before they were going to try, the prospective escapers heard that outside contacts had offered some assistance, if they could have a bit more time to set things up. Although Moumbaris was still keen to try, the others agreed to wait until mid-April. This allowed them time to develop their lock-picking abilities further, and build better devices.

Jenkin's decision to prepare for all contingencies included making sure that they knew what they would do if the promised outside help failed to materialize. They would steal the warder's car, and head towards Jan Smuts Airport (or take the airport bus if for some reason the car wasn't available to them), where the group, that now comprised eight people, would split into two parties. Jenkin, Lee, Moumbaris and two others would hire a car at the airport – one of the group had been left with his identity documentation by the security police, which included a driving licence – and drive towards northern Lesotho, around five to six hours away. Although Jenkin would have preferred to make for Swaziland, a couple of hours nearer, he was outvoted.

There was also a discussion over the use of firearms, and taking the warder's rifle or pistol. The majority of the group were against it – not least because they were worried that they would be pursued as armed terrorists and risked being shot on sight – so as a back-up, Jenkin, Lee and Moumbaris prepared a wooden replica of a Beretta 7.62mm pistol. When they saw how good it looked, the others agreed to incorporate it into the plan.

Unfortunately, no reply came from the outside contacts before the next proposed date, 21 April, so the attempt was postponed once more. They made contact at the start of May, pointing out that they hadn't had time to get everything ready, so the escape committee suggested that those on the outside should set the date. Jenkin, Lee and Moumbaris were becoming impatient – they were particularly concerned as the money they had secreted was being phased out as legal tender, and if they weren't careful, all of their painful efforts would have been for nothing.

During the wait for a reply – it took a month each way for communications – two of the eight escapers dropped out, including the man with the driving licence. That necessitated a rethink of the plan, but in the end, that worked out for the best, as the remainder had to devise a way to check the locks of the three doors that they had previously been unable to access. If they then had keys for every door, they weren't going to need to accost the night warder for his keys, and they could make their escape stealthily.

Various prisoners had to be taken out of the jail during late June and early July for medical appointments, and they noticed that a new guard post was being built by the front of the prison, with the gate moved closer to the front door. Worried that this would mean a twenty-four hour watch on the gate, Jenkin, Lee and Moumbaris considered making an attempt but in the end they realized that it was too risky.

Jenkin and Moumbaris made several tries to check the heavy sixth door, which they had not been able to get at previously, and by mid-October they had found a key that worked. Once through that door, they could check the others which lay between that and the exit, and also find out how the sentries operated at the front gate – in effect, they were carrying out a dry run for the actual escape. Another one of the escape group dropped out during the planning of this stage, as he felt the necessary diversionary tactics weren't worth the risk. In early November, Jenkin and Moumbaris carried out the reconnaissance, and managed to check all the locks except the very outer door.

With only five left in the group, the decision was taken not to bother with outside assistance – the men felt happier relying on their own devices – and then when it became clear that there would not be time to carry out another recce, two more dropped out. A date of 11 December was agreed; if for any reason Jenkin, Lee and Moumbaris could not try then, plans would be put back by twenty-four hours.

Civilian clothes had been obtained from various sources, including a whole mound of them that had been left accidentally within the prison. Their own clothes, which might be given to dogs to track their scent, were washed. The three men got rid of any personal items and destroyed documents and notes. A bag with their escape equipment – the sets of keys and lockpicks, as well as any workshop tools that they might need along the way – was hidden in the shower room, and as they took a final shower before lock-up, they collected the keys they needed for the first stage.

As soon as the section door was secured behind their jailers after lock-up, the trio set to work. They created dummies in their beds from overalls stuffed with clothing, books and towels, with shoes propped up vertically. Their prison uniforms were left in hot soapy water to eliminate the scent, and they dressed in their escape kit: sports shorts, socks and white T-shirts. They then let themselves out of their cells, replacing the heads on the brooms to confuse the guards, and picked up the rest of their escape equipment from the shower room. They also put on gloves and balaclavas, despite the summer heat: they didn't want to be recognized by the guards.

The other prisoners created a small diversion to get the guard out of the way, and the three escapers quickly passed through the doors until they only had three between them and freedom. By five o'clock, they had reached the final door, and when Moumbaris looked outside, the main gate was open.

But none of the keys that they had created would fit the final door. They tried picking the lock, but nothing would make the bolt turn. In the end, they decided the only way forward was to chisel the door open, even if that meant that they lost the major element of surprise which they had been counting on. None of the other doors in the prison that they had opened would show any signs of force so their means of escape should mystify the authorities. Moumbaris chiselled away at the wood behind the locking plate for half an hour until the bolt came clear when he pulled the door handle.

With that, they walked out into the street, and went round to the adjacent main road. There they caught a cab to the airport, and then the airport bus into Johannesburg, getting to the train terminus around 8 p.m. – the time when the guard would be carrying out his inspection back at Pretoria Prison. Lee parted company with them there, as he had friends in Johannesburg. Jenkin and Moumbaris caught a train east, and disposed of all their escape equipment and the keys out of the window as they passed through the countryside. The only things they retained were the fake gun and the chisel. From the town of Springs, they started to walk towards the border with Swaziland, about one hundred and twenty miles away, and were able to get lifts for part of the way.

Their escape wasn't noticed until the following morning. Various guards had come and gone through the door which they had chiselled through without noticing anything out of place. The cells had been cursorily checked, but it seemed as if everyone was asleep. A major hunt was begun for three dangerous terrorists – even though no one could work out how they had got out, until a bunch of keys was discovered. The guard on duty was arrested, and police mobilized throughout the country to prevent them crossing the border.

It was too late. The two men were already in Swaziland, but their problems weren't over. Luckily they approached the United Nations High Commission for Refugees, who told them not to go near the Swazi authorities: they would simply return them to South Africa. They were then passed to representatives of the ANC who got them across into Mozambique and then to Angola, where they were reunited with Lee, who had followed a similar pattern with the ANC.

The South Africans tried a propaganda campaign to blacken the names of some of their opponents by claiming they had masterminded the escape: white ANC member Joe Slovo, and the Soviet ambassador in Lusaka, Vladimir Solodovnikov were both accused. It took the guard five months to clear his name of involvement, and he horrified the court by explaining that he had been forced by the secret police to make a statement admitting assisting the escapees. The discrepancies between this confession and the facts of the case made it impossible for him to be found guilty.

The political prisoners were moved across to the maximum-security wing of Pretoria Central while the security arrangements in Pretoria were upgraded. When they returned, closed-circuit TVs, electrically operated doors, and much more visible cells had been introduced. Escape, it would seem now, would be impossible.

Sources:

Jenkin, Tim: *Escape from Pretoria* (Kliptown Books, 1987)

A Monument to Failure

There may have been more contrived ways to get out of prison, but claiming that a black and white TV set, covered with a blanket, is a bomb that has to be got rid of has to be near the top of the list. But that was the ruse that six desperate prisoners successfully employed to get out of Mecklenburg prison in 1984 in an attempt to evade the death sentences that had been passed against each of them. Speaking nearly a quarter of a century later, the guards who were attacked and placed in fear of their lives were still plainly traumatized by the events of that evening; one had previously told the press on the tenth anniversary, "You don't ever get over it. You can't take nothing for granted. The only reason you walk out of here every day is because the inmates let you walk out . . . I'm very aware of that."

Mecklenburg Correctional Center had only been opened in March 1977, seven years before the escape, and was called "a monument to failure" by the Virginia State Governor, Mills E. Godwin Jnr, since it was designed to house the worst of the worst who would never be allowed to return to ordinary society. It was supposed to be the wave of the future, with keyless cells that were operated from central control booths, but, as novelist Sibella Giorello memorably put it, "While the keyless design made theoretical sense, in practical terms the place turned into a detached day-care center – for grown men begging for attention." As the intensive investigation that was carried out following the escape showed, the prison might have been touted as virtually escape-proof, but if security procedures weren't established properly, or followed correctly, then it was more, rather than less, vulnerable to prisoners taking advantage.

Between 1977 and 1998, Mecklenburg housed Virginia's death row, and there were plenty of physical security measures in place to keep them from threatening the population ever again. Double fencing topped with rolls of barbed wire, and entrance gates both on the buildings and on the outer perimeter fence, were designed to ensure that only authorized movements were permitted, with sally ports that acted like airlocks – the doors were opened separately on each side.

Death-row prisoners, of course, have nothing to lose. Even the tiniest breath of freedom is worth any risk for them (one of the escapees would later comment at his execution that no one could take away the days he had on the outside from him). On 31 May 1984, six of them were able to show that Mecklenburg was a monument to failure in a very different way.

Linwood Earl Briley had been sentenced to death for the robbery and murder of a disc jockey, just one of the eleven to twenty victims that he and his younger brother James had slaughtered during a ten-month robbery spree. James himself was being executed for robbery and capital murder during rape – he had killed a man, after raping his pregnant wife and killing his five-year-old son. Willie Leroy Jones had shot and killed a pair of married retired shopkeepers, then set fire to their home. Earl Clanton had murdered a librarian. Derick Peterson had killed an office manager during a robbery. Lem Tuggle, the only Caucasian of the escaping group, had shot a fifty-two-year-old woman while on parole following another murder charge. As one of the FBI officers chasing them later said, they weren't people fit to breathe the same air as ordinary folk.

Others had been part of the escape planning initially, but in the end decided not to join them. One, Dennis Stockton, was also on death row, and kept a detailed diary of his life there – the source of much of the information about the escape.

Discussions about a break out began in late October 1983, when Linwood Briley was rapidly approaching the end of the appeals process, and would soon be given his execution date. His brother James, had been involved in an abortive attempt by three female visitors to smuggle guns and drugs into the prison in October 1981, and as a result, everyone coming in and out was searched thoroughly. The best way to escape seemed to be by taking over the building that housed death row, and then walking out in guards' uniforms; they would call the gate, warning them there was an explosive in the building, and have them send a van across.

As most prisoners do, they were watching the guards' routines closely, and picking up as much information as they could. They were particularly making a note of the extension numbers for each part of the prison, and the codes that the guards used for ease of communication. Sometimes if they heard something on the radio when they were chatting with the guards, the prisoners would innocently ask what it meant – or on other occasions, they would intimidate the information out of them. The notoriously bad-tempered Earl Clanton was able to learn a great deal this way. They also discovered what size uniforms the guards wore, so they knew who would be ideal targets when the escape began.

At the start of March 1984, James Briley, who had become the mastermind of the plot, called a meeting of the prospective escapers, and went through the plan. It didn't change a great deal between then and 31 May, although a number of the "escape committee" ended up not being involved – some because they didn't think the subtlety involved in the subterfuge was necessary. They'd rather try to get hold of some guns and blast their way out.

The escapers began gathering and preparing weapons from scrap metal, which they hid in their cells. There were numerous searches of the block over the next few weeks, some prompted by information passed by other death-row inmates to the authorities, but nothing was ever found.

A date of 15 April was agreed – the day on which US citizens have to file their tax returns with the federal authorities. The Brileys thought it would be a good way to reward the taxpayers who had subsidized their time in prison. At that point, some inmates started talking about dropping out of the escape. Jones and Tuggle only arrived on death row at this stage, and were immediately brought on board. However, when they took stock, they realized they didn't yet have enough weapons, so everything was pushed back a month. Although Stockton had received his execution date by this point, he became increasingly concerned about the plan and dropped out.

Despite the ringleaders agreeing to wait, another tip was received by the prison authorities on 19 April, which suggested that the escape was set for the following day; a very thorough search revealed no weapons, and the prison was kept under extra security for a few days. On 3 May, Linwood Briley's execution date was formally given to him by the court, and again, there were rumours that someone would try to help him abscond when he was out of the prison, but nothing happened. On 13 May, Stockton wrote a detailed letter to the prison security chief, explaining that the prisoners had secreted weapons in hollowed-out parts of the walls, that they planned on taking hostages and killing other prisoners if they didn't cooperate, and that the escape was imminent. Although the others suspected he was the snitch who had betrayed them earlier, this was the first time that he had done so, and despite all this information the search which followed on 17 May still failed to turn anything up.

No one picked up on the obvious sign that betrayed how close to fruition the Brileys' plan was: on the morning of 31 May, the six prisoners who were going to escape all had a shave. Linwood Briley removed his beard and combed his hair; Lem Tuggle also smartened up – neither of them now resembled the photos in their police records. The word was spread around the escapers to get ready.

Around 6 p.m. as usual, the prisoners were let out into the recreation yard. Tuggle asked Stockton for advice about the best routes to take from the prison, and Willie Turner, another robber and murderer who had been one of the key plotters, borrowed some masking tape from one of the guards. As the men were called in from the yard, they clustered around the guard at the sally port, and in the confusion he didn't notice Clanton slip away and enter the guards' bathroom, opposite the entrance to the control room – as the prisoners had noticed, this wasn't locked, a fatal error on the prison authorities' part. This was compounded by the guards' failure to take a headcount as the men went in and out. No one realized that Clanton hadn't gone to his cell with the others.

The inmates had made a mistake of their own: they had forgotten that a nurse regularly did her rounds passing out medication. Nurse Barksdale was the focus of attention from the men, but she had been reassured that because of the way the cells operated in Mecklenburg, she was safe. She wasn't aware that at least two of the escapers hoped that their paths would cross with her before they left the prison.

The nurse tried the bathroom door, but couldn't open it – Clanton had locked himself in. Thinking quickly, James Briley claimed that the previous guard shift had spotted the problem so the nurse went to the adjacent pod – separated by a locked door – to get some water.

At 9 p.m. everything was set. One of the guards, Corporal Harry Crutchfield, was checking an apparent clogged toilet in one of the cells; Derick Peterson took his knife and held it to the guard's throat, warning him not to make a sound. At the same time, James Briley called out to Ricardo Holmes, the guard in the control room, asking him if he could pass a book across from his cell to one of the other prisoners on the far side. This wasn't unusual, but it meant that for the few seconds the guard was out passing the book across, the door to the control room was open.

As soon as Holmes started down the corridor towards Briley's cell, the killer shouted, "Now, Goldie!", and Clanton dived out of the bathroom and into the control room, hitting the button that opened the sally port to the outside. Holmes turned, tried to grab Clanton, but was prevented from doing anything further by the two Briley brothers holding their homemade knives. The other prisoners were released from their cells, and quickly overpowered the guards. Most of them were then forced to strip, since the prisoners needed their uniforms. Once they had done so, their hands were tied behind their backs, and Crutchfield's mouth was also covered with tape. The prisoners who weren't coming on the escape were also locked up.

Nurse Barksdale wasn't so lucky. She had finished her rounds before the escape attempt began, but her guard escort mislaid his elevator key, and came back into the death-row pod with her. They were both taken hostage, with Barksdale fearing she was going to be raped by Linwood Briley and Clanton. To her eternal relief, although she was molested by the men, they were stopped from going any further by one of the other prisoners, Wilbert Evans. Around the same time, another inmate, Willie Turner, prevented James Briley from killing a few of the guards, although it was made very clear to the warders that if the escape attempt failed and the men came back to death row, the murderers wouldn't hesitate to kill them.

Other guards were captured as soon as they approached the pod, enticed in by calls from the control room asking for help with an injured inmate. The most critical one was the shift commander, Lt Larry Hawkins, who was forced to ring the gate and order a van to be brought around to the sally-port gate in the perimeter wall since they had "a situation". To gain power of the main control booth for the building, and thus the sally port to the general prison yard, the prisoners rang through to the guard there, and told Officer Corlene Thomas that there had been a call for her on an outside line, and that someone was coming over to relieve her temporarily so she could return it. Although Thomas was a little surprised by this, she was reassured by the sight of a guard coming over, and opened the door for him – allowing Derick Peterson to enter, knock her over, cuff her, and take control of the booth. He could then open the doors to allow the men to exit the building and head towards the sally port leading to the outside.

That was the signal for the prisoners dressed as guards, now also sporting riot gear to further disguise themselves, to head towards the loading bay outside the prison. They brought with them the "explosive" that needed removing from the pod – a small black and white television, covered in a blanket, which the "guards" would periodically spray with foam from a fire extinguisher to ensure it stayed "safe". The van arrived a few minutes later – it had been delayed because the driver, Officer Barry Batillo, had decided to bring an older van when Hawkins told him that they were going to be moving a bomb. (As the state police report later commented, Batillo didn't seem to see anything wrong with six officers' lives being at risk, but he wasn't going to take any chances with a new van!)

The men came out of the sally port carrying the bomb on a stretcher. Batillo was ordered to turn the van around and back it halfway through the gate, so it wouldn't close on them when the inner door was opened; he believed he was being ordered to do so by Hawkins, so obeyed, and then when James Briley shouted that they were carrying a live explosive, he ran for his life. The guard in the tower briefly argued about opening both gates at once, but seeing the apparent urgency of the situation, she relented.

Linwood Briley took the driver's seat, with the others putting the "bomb" in and then jumping in behind, and drove off. At 10.48 p.m. they were out of Mecklenburg, and started heading south-east from the jail, wanting to get over the state line from Virginia into North Carolina as quickly as possible. They abandoned the van in Warrenton, around thirty miles from Mecklenburg, where the Brileys, Tuggle and Jones parted company with Peterson and Clanton.

By this time, the hostage situation on death row had ended. Thirty minutes after the Mecklenburg Six had departed, the hostages were freed, and control of the pod returned to the authorities. Around midnight, other officers began arriving to take charge; two hours later, the Department of Corrections director Robert Landon was informed of the escape, as was the state governor, Chuck Robb. Around two hundred North Carolina law officers, along with tracking dogs, began combing the countryside around the area where the van was abandoned – it had been found very soon after the inmates fled from it. Aircraft and Virginia state troopers were also checking the land around Mecklenburg, in case only some of the fugitives had been in the van. "This is our top priority right now," Allen H. McCreight, special agent in charge of the Richmond office of the FBI, told the press. "It's a big one."

The manhunt would go on for nineteen days, during which many in Richmond lived in fear, particularly those who had been involved in the prosecution of the Brileys. "I think what concerned me the most was that I had seen first-hand what they were capable of doing. I knew their determination to seek revenge. You never forget the smell of death and the smell of blood from what they did," one former Richmond detective, Woody, now city sheriff, later recalled. They were not aware that the Brileys had no intention of coming back to Richmond; they wanted to get far away.

Clanton and Peterson only lasted nineteen hours. They tried to hitch a ride around midnight with hospital orderly Andrew Davis, asking him where they might be able to get some drugs or find some nightlife. When he said he didn't know, and tried to throw them out of his truck, he was attacked but managed to get away. Rather than use the truck, the fugitives ran off in the opposite direction (leaving their knife in the car) and hid in the local woods overnight, before getting rid of their guards' uniforms in the morning. Getting hungry, they headed into Warrenton and bought some cigarettes, wine, bread and cheese with money that they had stolen from the prison guards the previous night. They then stupidly made phone calls – Peterson tried to call his mother. At 6 p.m., while they were still eating their wine and cheese in a local Laundromat, the two fugitives were arrested without putting up a struggle. Earl Clanton was executed on 14 April 1988; Derick Peterson on 23 August 1991.

The other four also stole a vehicle, a blue pickup truck, which was spotted that night at a twenty-four-hour gas station in Thornburg, around fifty miles north of Richmond. Lem Tuggle was being kept in the back of the truck, facing backwards, and was becoming disorientated: "All I could see was the back of the highway signs," he complained later. The men had decided not to stay in Richmond: the Brileys knew that that would be the first place the cops would look for them. Instead, they parted company with the other two in Philadelphia, where they bought some second-hand clothes from a thrift shop and dumped their prison uniforms. Linwood Briley gave Tuggle and Jones $25 each, keeping the remainder of the $800 they had taken from the guards, and sent them on their way. Jones desperately wanted to stay with the Brileys but Linwood firmly refused.

Jones and Tuggle took the van and continued to head north, reaching Vermont, and camping just across the Massachusetts border in the Green Mountain National Forest for three days. Ten days after they had escaped from Mecklenburg, they stopped about ten miles short of the Canadian border, and to raise some funds, Tuggle went back to a gift shop he had noticed in the small town of Woodford. He stole $100 from the elderly owner, who had the presence of mind, despite a knife to her throat, to take the licence plate number of the van. The state police put out an APB for it and within a few minutes Tuggle had been apprehended. He surrendered without an argument, and was returned to Mecklenburg. Lem Tuggle was the last of the Mecklenburg Six to be executed.

He recorded a cassette tape giving his account of the escape which was smuggled out of death row, and subsequently uploaded onto YouTube. He received a lethal injection on 12 December 1996.

Jones thought he had been abandoned by Tuggle. He broke into a house and called his mother, who told him to turn himself in. He thought about it for a few minutes, then went to another house and asked to use the phone. He then called the state police, explained who he was, and agreed a meeting point. At 5.30 p.m. he was picked up and taken back to Mecklenburg. Derick Jones needed two separate supposedly lethal jolts of electricity to kill him on 22 August 1991.

The Brileys took longer to catch. They had gone to ground in Philadelphia, working at Dan's Custom Car Factory. Known as Slim and Lucky, James and Linwood had been introduced to the eponymous Dan by their uncle, Johnnie Lee Council, and fitted straight into the small business, to all intents and purposes out-of-towners just working to keep a roof over their heads. However, after Lem Tuggle admitted he had dropped the brothers in Philadelphia, the FBI began surveillance on Council, who quickly led them to the Brileys.

The Bureau staked out the garage, sending in an undercover informant to befriend the Brileys, then on the evening of Tuesday 19 June, as the feared mass murderers were barbequing chicken and drinking beer, the FBI swooped. Although the brothers tried to deny who they were, scars on James' chest were a giveaway. They were arrested and held on $10 million bail before returning to Mecklenburg.

Linwood Briley went to the electric chair on 12 October 1984. Not long before he did so, he told an interviewer, "I had my nineteen days. They couldn't take that away." James followed him six months later, on 18 April 1985.

Major changes followed at Mecklenburg. Many inmates had felt that the prison had been like a powder key, ready to explode, and in July it did, with full-scale riots breaking out on two separate occasions. (Although some sources suggest that the fear of these led to the Mecklenburg Six breaking out earlier than they had originally planned, this does not appear to be supported by the evidence.) The warden and the chief of security were both suspended without pay for ten days, and then moved to other jobs. Five of the guards taken hostage were fired, including the two control-booth guards. When Dennis Stockton's diary was smuggled out and published in *The Virginian-Pilot* newspaper in September, many of the deficiencies of the system were brought to light. Two months later, the Department of Corrections boss Robert Landon resigned.

"We have done all we could to ensure nothing like that ever happened again," the assistant warden maintained in 1994. New guards were hired and the system changed so that individual guards didn't control all the locks. All the cell windows – which had been taken apart and used to form some of the knives the prisoners created – were now checked daily, and the evening recreation period was abolished. That didn't stop men trying: Willie Turner, who had prevented James Briley from killing the guards during the break out, was able to create huge numbers of weapons which were found in his cell, including a three-foot-long Samurai sword made from pieces of his bedframe, as well as keys for nearly every door in the building that took them. However, as his execution date grew near, Turner's mental stability crumbled, and eventually his stash was found. He was transferred to Greensville prison and sent for a lethal injection on 25 May 1995. A gun was found inside a typewriter in his cell after his death.

Mecklenburg Correctional Centre ceased to be the home of the death-row prisoners in 1997; it was closed down in 2012.

Sources:

Jackson, Joe and William Burke Jnr: *Dead Run* (Times Books, 1999)
Los Angeles Times, 3 July 1994: "Wounds Deep 10 Years After Nation's Largest Death Row Escape"
Lem Tuggle Death Row recording (YouTube: http://www.youtube.com/v=UA-DdHiTnsA)
Times-Despatch, 13 December 2011: "McDonnell orders Mecklenburg Correctional Center Closed"
Times-Despatch, 31 May 2009: "Death-row escape [graphic]"
Free Lance-Star, 31 May 1994: "Virginia's greatest jailbreak"
Times-Despatch, 2 June 1984: "2 Mecklenburg escapees captured;

prison officials were warned twice"

Times-Despatch, 1 June 1984: "Death row inmates are hunted in N.C."

Times-Despatch, 1984: article by Bill McKelway reprinted at http://www.leelofland.com/wordpress/escape-from-death-row-the-briley-brothers/

Checking Out of Hotel K

No matter what you may read in some of the more conservative papers in the United Kingdom, prison is not a safe or pleasant place to be. True, there are some old lags who have become institutionalized, and find the environment inside prison much better than anything they can find in the outside world. But they are the exceptions, not the rule – and many of the prisons around the world are anything but safe or pleasant.

Take, for example, Bali's infamous Kerobokan prison, known to its inmates as Hotel K. In its time, it has housed the Muslim bombers responsible for the Bali nightclub massacre, a Balinese King convicted of killing his brother, Australian yachtsman Chris Packer after he was found with illegal weapons on his boat, and international chef Gordon Ramsay's brother, Ronnie. First impressions might suggest that it's moderately pleasant but the moment a new inmate steps through the doors, he or she is entering a world of violence, filth and deprivation. Unsurprisingly, many of those who have been arrested on drugs charges want to escape from its confines, despite the sometimes lax approach demonstrated by the guards. Sex, drugs and alcohol are easily available, if you've got the cash, and some prisoners have even been able to get "days at the beach" with guards. But if you try to escape and fail, then chances are you'll be beaten up as much by your fellow inmates as by the guards.

There have been some successful escapes from Hotel K, which was built hastily in 1976 to replace the original jail in Denpasar that had been demolished to allow a shopping mall to be built. It holds both men and women, and usually has about three times the 320 prisoners that it was designed to contain. At various times, parts of the perimeter walks have crumbled, affording prisoners a chance to escape.

The greatest escape – which led to major improvements in security at the jail in the short term – saw 289 prisoners abscond on the afternoon of Sunday 5 December 1999. It was masterminded by "Tony", who was incarcerated for his part in the murder of a Javanese debt collector. Tony had watched as his brother, Saidin, a former soldier, had cut off the man's head after he had threatened to kill the family of one of his friends. Although Tony hadn't actively participated in the killing, which his brother had been hired to carry out by the threatened friend, he had helped his brother to roll the man's headless corpse into a ditch not that far, ironically, from Hotel K, and was sentenced to imprisonment in the notorious jail.

Saidin was released from Hotel K within a few months: the Balinese court had failed to hear his appeal case within the mandated length of time, so there was little option but to release him. His brother wasn't so lucky, but he had no intention of remaining within Kerobokan any longer than he needed to.

Once in Hotel K, Tony became involved with Filipino prisoner Nita Ramos, one of the many drug dealers incarcerated, as he prepared for his escape. Tony (and Saidin while he was still there) had a powerful reputation within the jail as a result of the brutality of their crime, and few prisoners would take the chance of crossing them. All the male inmates were ordered to save their daily ration of kerosene, used for cooking, and everyone was instructed, under pain of death, to run when the escape started. Those who had the most to lose, whose sentences were coming to a close, were included, even though everyone was aware that if they were recaptured, their sentences would be increased.

In Hotel K, the fifty-three prisoners held in the women's portion, Block W, were locked up for the night at 4.30 p.m. Within a few minutes, smoke could be seen rising from the men's part of the prison, and by 4.45, it had become thick enough that the women began to fear for their lives. Its cause: kerosene-soaked mattresses, which had been placed in every cell block of the men's section. Tony had set the first pile alight within his own block, and as soon as the guards raced towards that, others were ignited in a coordinated pattern, so that the fourteen guards were quickly stretched beyond their capacity to cope, particularly when the prisoners began to take them captive too and keep them together in an office.

Tony's reputation ensured that nobody betrayed the plan, and it all seemed to proceed smoothly, although the prisoner who was deputed to collect Nita Ramos on Tony's behalf failed to persuade her to come along with him. None of the women, including Ramos, had any idea that the prison break was planned, and in the confusion, Ramos believed that she was being targeted under cover of the fire, rather than effectively being rescued. Her cell door was the only one that was opened, which led the Indonesian police to suspect that she was complicit in the escape.

Mobile phones were rife within Hotel K, and many of the prisoners had actually booked taxis to come to collect them from the jail. Once Tony had used a stolen bunch of keys to open the front door, and the other prisoners had used iron bars to smash open the other locks, the inmates piled out of the prison. Others set fire to the registration office, and burned as much paperwork as they could find, in the hope of eliminating their records and wiping their histories (which was more likely to be successful in the period before computerization became commonplace).

Two hundred and eighty-nine prisoners escaped under cover of the fire; by sunset 104 of them had been recovered. Some hadn't made it out of the prison at all, caught in the refuse area. Five prisoners stopped automatically when a police officer shouted at them to freeze or he would shoot – even though he was unarmed. Others were found in local cafés, taking the opportunity to eat some fresh plates of the rice dish nasi goreng, or simply wandering around the streets aimlessly. Four were found in toilets, another on the Kuta beach. One simply took advantage of the prison break to visit his family, but asked his brother to tell the police he would return the next morning of his own volition – which he did.

Tony was one of the 130 prisoners who were never recaptured, disappearing to Malaysia. Those who were returned to Kerobokan faced harsh treatment at the hands of the embarrassed guards: they would be beaten, and then chilli-laced water would be used to "cleanse" the wounds. Fresh fences were placed around the cell blocks to prevent a similarly coordinated attack from taking place again. Even when fires were started during riots in 2012, the new security measures ensured that no prisoners were able to escape, even though they had control of the prison for over seven hours during one incident in February that year.

Other escape attempts from Hotel K weren't as successful as Tony's. Sentenced to eleven years for drug possession, Brazilian civil engineer Rogerio Pecanz Paez was desperate to get out and although he would eventually become resigned to his fate, adopting the Buddhist faith, he did try an ingenuous scheme to abscond, with the help of his Italian cellmate, a mechanic named Ferrari.

After ensuring that no locals would want to be in the cell with them – the Brazilian could put on a convincing impression of a lunatic when he wanted to – Paez made a load of noise to cover the sound of Ferrari cutting through the bars of their cell window using a blade that had been smuggled into the jail inside a papaya. Ferrari was only in Hotel K for four months, but used the time to assist Paez in return for a daily supply of drugs. Each night the two men would work on the bars before gluing them back into place so they appeared normal to the guards during the day.

Unlike many of those who tried to escape from Hotel K, Paez made his plans sensibly, arranging for a motorbike to be waiting outside the prison, on which he could travel to a waiting boat. That would take him to Java, where he had already arranged with a corrupt immigration official to stamp his fake French passport with a tourist visa and entry stamp, so he could depart from Jakarta airport. He even had snakebite anti-venom ready in case he encountered a cobra during his escape, and a hammer to smash the jagged glass stuck in the top of the prison's outer wall.

It seemed foolproof but then, as Paez describes in his blog, a "small detail went wrong". The only thing missing was a clip to use as a form of grappling iron that he could throw over the wall, attached to the rope which he had previously prepared. However, while sawing a metal bar off the roof of the medical clinic, he snapped the piece off – and the loud noise it made alerted the other prisoners. Although he tried to get rid of the bar, Paez was put in solitary for possessing it. On his release he was put in a different cell. Amazingly, the bars in his old cell continued to fool the guards for some weeks, but when they discovered the deception the Hotel K authorities gave Paez a severe beating, and sent him to the maximum-security tower where his fellow inmates included the Balinese terrorists.

American Gabriele Natale was foolhardy when he tried to escape from Hotel K. The forty-two-year-old building contractor only had five months of his sentence left to serve when, drunk and high on drugs, he decided to abseil from an empty watchtower, over the walls and into the street. There was a hole in the inner wall of the prison where the old concrete wall had collapsed into a tunnel that had been used for smuggling alcohol into the jail. Ignoring the snakes that infested the grass between the inner and outer wall, Natale went through the hole, climbed into the tower, and used two bedsheets that he had brought with him to get over the wall. Looking like the surfer dude that he had been before his imprisonment, he hoped to catch a taxi and escape before a pursuit began.

Unfortunately, Natale's escape was spotted, and a gang of guards and local prisoners chased after him, with one of them using a motorbike to knock Natale into a nearby rice field. The American was given a severe beating outside the prison, which continued when he was brought inside, and only the intervention of the US consul, hastily summoned by one of the other prisoners, prevented him from being kicked to death. Although Natale survived, his escape attempts were over (he was released from Hotel K later in 2005). Others took advantage of the hole that was there, which the authorities covered with metal sheets – Rudi Setyawan, a convicted murderer, escaped on 18 March 2005.

The riots in spring 2012 focused attention on the conditions at Kerobokan, and it seems new prisons will be built in Indonesia to alleviate the stress, with the authorities hoping that these will prove to be successful in keeping the inmates on the correct side of the fence.

Sources:

Bonella, Kathryn: *Hotel K: The Shocking Inside Story of Bali's Most Notorious Jail* (Quercus, London 2012)

Rogerio Pecanz Paez's blogspot (not updated since 2005): http://rogeriopaez.blogspot.co.uk/2005/07/hell-on-bali-island-of-gods-real-drama.html

Prisoner details from: http://www.phaseloop.com/foreignprisoners/prison-indonesia02.html

and http://beatmag.com/daily/tag/prison/page/3/

Sealed with a Kiss

The creators of the police detective series *CSI: Miami* emulated the popular use of a theme song by The Who in the original *CSI: Crime Scene Investigation* show, and chose the British rock band's 1971 track "Won't Get Fooled Again". It's a song that might well have been adopted by the Quincy County sheriff's department in 2008, when they realized that one of the convicts in their charge was about to try to escape using a trick that had worked very successfully for Christopher Glover, aka the Phantom, and his girlfriend, Shannon Rideout, in 1995. Passing over a handcuff key during a loving kiss was not going to happen twice!

Twenty-year-old Christopher Glover was being held at the Norfolk County Correctional Center in Dedham, Massachusetts in November 1995. The centre was comparatively new: it had only been opened three years previously, with its 501-bed capacity costing $33 million, replacing the large stone Dedham Jail in which murderers George Hershey, Nicola Sacco and Bartolomeo Vanzetti had been incarcerated. While not as imposing as its predecessor, the Correctional Center still posed a considerable deterrent to those wishing to escape from its confines – not least the fact that it was built between the north and south carriageways of Interstate 95, the only prison in North America constructed between the lanes.

The old jail had seen its own escape attempts, the most notable taking place on 26 January 1975. Four inmates – alleged armed robbers James Mamey, Robert Perotta, and Thomas Carden and alleged murderer Louis Goforth Jnr – managed to get hold of a gun, which had been thrown over the jail wall by an accomplice outside, and tried to order Norfolk County Correction Officer Joseph Stroy to open the jail's main door. Carden had used the gun to hold up Joseph Colligan, one of Stroy's colleagues, telling him not to move or he would blow the guard's head off, then used his keys to open up the cells containing Mamey, Perotta and Goforth before locking Colligan up. However, the main door was controlled from the "cage", which Stroy was manning. Despite looking down the barrel of a gun a mere six feet away, Stroy refused to open the door; when he reached for the alarm, he was shot for his pains with a bullet that damaged his spinal cord but lodged too close to his aorta to be removable safely. The prisoners used a broom handle to trigger the mechanism and escaped, carjacking a vehicle to flee the jurisdiction. Based on tip-offs, three of the quartet were recaptured within a day in Boston; the fourth surrendered to authorities two days later in New York's Bronx. Stroy eventually lost his leg as a result of the bullet wound and died prematurely aged sixty-four.

Christopher Glover had finally been captured after some months of criminal activity in the Quincy area, carjacking vehicles and taking them for dangerous drives around the local roads. On many occasions, the police were simply unable to keep up with him, and he earned the nickname "the Phantom" as a result. He was arrested in April 1995 after a week-long crime spree, and one stunt which pushed the police too far: he allegedly stole a police car, and tried to run the officer down. Arrested in Florida, he was sent back to Massachusetts for trial.

Since he didn't particularly fancy serving the sentence for car theft and assault that was coming his way, Glover decided that he would make a break for it. Rather than try to find a way around the various security measures that surrounded the Correctional Center, he decided that the ideal time to flee was during one of his court appearances. If he could evade his guards and get to a vehicle then he could make good his escape: he was expert enough to be able to hotwire any vehicle and once behind the wheel, he knew there was a fair chance that he could outrun any pursuit.

However, of course, there was one major problem: for all transport between the jail and the court, he would be hand-cuffed. Somehow he would have to remove the handcuffs before he got out of the prison van so that his hands were free to manipulate the wires. To do that, he would need a key.

You might think that getting hold of a key to police handcuffs would be difficult, that perhaps those wishing to purchase them need some form of official identification. Nowadays you can simply Google names of suppliers. In 1995, there were plenty of places where they could be obtained – perhaps not totally legitimately, but certainly very easily. Glover's nineteen-year-old girlfriend, Shannon Rideout, didn't have a problem in finding one that would fit the cuffs, but she still needed to get it to him without setting off the metal detectors which swept visitors to the jail.

On 9 November 1995, Rideout came to visit Glover at Dedham. Before she entered the jail, she wrapped the key in a piece of duct tape which masked the metal from the detectors; once inside the prison, she slipped the key into her mouth. Nobody was at all surprised when the attractive young couple exchanged a long, lingering kiss when she was due to leave.

A week later, Glover made his move, surreptitiously removing the handcuffs while in the back of the van. The moment that the prison officers opened the rear doors to escort him into the courthouse in Quincy, Glover legged it and as quickly as was practicable, he stole a car. By chance he was spotted, and the police were on his tail far more rapidly than he would have liked.

Glover abandoned the car, and tried to flee on foot, but again, luck wasn't with him. He was identified by one of the Quincy police officers, who followed him to a gas station. Glover attempted to carjack another vehicle but this belonged to a handicapped senior citizen who found it difficult to follow Glover's orders. Glover claimed that he had a gun, which turned out to be a can of Mace, and after a stand-off, Glover was arrested. He was sentenced to six and a half years for the escape and carjacking charges. Shannon Rideout was given two suspended two-year terms, and two years' probation.

A decade later, Sean Ciulla, who was being charged with third-offence shoplifting and giving police a false name, also managed to escape from guards at the Quincy Courthouse on 5 November 2007, although he made his move after his hearing rather than before. Ciulla was shackled with wrist irons and leg irons when he slipped away from the prisoners who were being loaded into a transport van back to the correctional centre. According to one account, Ciulla's absence wasn't noticed until the van arrived back in Dedham. All that the manhunt could find was his discarded shoes.

He was recaptured two weeks later, after investigators used cell-phone records to track him down to a North Quincy apartment where his girlfriend and another woman tried to prevent police from entering the property while Ciulla made an escape through a back window. They spotted him, barged in and arrested him. Ciulla faced charges of escaping from custody, and his case turned on whether he had jumped out of the van – as described by one of the other prisoners, and which was regarded as more serious by the law – or simply not boarded in the first place.

On 10 December 2007, around the same time as Ciulla was being arraigned, James N. Miller was arrested by Quincy police officers on drugs charges after being involved in a car chase which finished with him slamming his SUV into a house on an intersection. He was sent to the Norfolk Correction Center, and started plotting his escape, assisted by his girlfriend on the outside, Theresa Fougere. The mistake the pair made was discussing their plans on the phone from the prison: although, as Sheriff Michael Belotti pointed out, it wasn't possible for the authorities to monitor every call that went in and out of the prison, their policy was to "aggressively monitor all inmate communications that we are entitled to monitor under the law to ensure that the public remains safe".

From what the sheriff described as "intelligence" gathered by jail officials, the sheriff's department listened in on the conversation and learned that Fougere was intending to pass Miller a key under cover of a kiss and a hug when he made his next appearance at the Norfolk Courthouse on 11 January. "This goes beyond just the stage of planning. This was close to execution," the sheriff told the *Boston Herald*. "Anytime you have these types of escape events, it undermines public safety." Fougere was questioned and a set of handcuff keys was found in her possession. She was therefore charged with attempting to aid a felon to escape, conspiracy, and attempting to commit a crime. Miller ended up facing charges of attempted escape as well as drugs possession. The Quincy Department certainly weren't going to get fooled again.

Sources:

History of Dedham Jail: http://www.waymarking.com/waymarks/ WM61F6_Dedham_Jail_Dedham_MA

http://norfolksheriff.com/history/

The Boston Globe, 27 July 1989: "Joseph Stroy, 64; Correction Officer Shot In '75 Dedham Prison Escape"

The Day, 27 January 1975: "Four flee Mass jail"

Bangor Daily News, 27 January 1975: "Prison guard shot"

The Day, 12 November 1976: "'Phantom' gets four years"

Associated Press, 26 January 1996: "Girlfriend's kiss helps man escape"

Real Prison Breaks, Cineflix Productions, 2011

The Patriot Ledger, 6 November 2007: "Prisoner escapes sheriff's deputies at Quincy court, remains at large"

GateHouse News Service, 14 May 2010: "Hingham Police: Hull man faces larceny, drug charges"

The Patriot Ledger, 23 November 2007: "Escaped prisoner captured in North Quincy"

Boston Herald, 1 January 2008: "Jailers make sure magic kiss doesn't free con"

Hide and Seek

The best escape and evasion plans can fall victim to any number of unforeseen circumstances. As Prussian Field Marshall Helmuth von Moltke the Elder pointed out, no battle plan ever survives contact with the enemy. And as prison escaper Daniel Mitchem discovered to his cost in the spring of 1995, that enemy might even be someone within your own family.

Mitchem and fellow escaper Sebastian Eccleston were inmates at Bernalillo Detention Center, in Albuquerque, New Mexico. Known as the Downtown jail and situated in the heart of Albuquerque, the facility was replaced by the modern Bernalillo Metropolitan Detention Center in 2004; it now houses the Regional Correction Center. Both men were being held for murder – Eccleston was accused of murdering a former Manzano High School football star Ricky Comingo on 13 December 1994, in what was either a drive-by shooting or a confrontation following a near collision in traffic (Eccleston and his co-defendants gave different versions of events). Mitchem had been convicted of killing a forty-four-year-old man in 1993 who refused to get out of his vehicle when Mitchem tried to carjack it; he had begun a thirty-six-year sentence earlier in March 1995.

At the time of his offence, Eccleston was officially already on the run. In October 1994, he escaped from a juvenile jail by going over the top of a ten-feet-high fence that was topped with double-edged barbed wire. Eight days after the shooting of Comingo, Eccleston was recaptured after he led police on a 115 mph chase, during which he wrecked a van he had stolen which was filled with guns. He then made a dash for the mountains, but a helicopter stopped him from getting away from the SWAT team that took him down.

Although some sources suggest that Eccleston and Mitchem used their membership of a "God pod" religious studies group at the prison as a cover for exploring escape routes, it seems as if that program wasn't officially set up until 2003. More likely, during their work time, they noticed that there was an air shaft to which they could gain access in the utility room on the same floor as their cells. The two men braided their sheets together to form a rope, and, on the evening of 27 March 1995, the cellmates filled their beds with makeshift dummies, made from clothes and socks stuffed with paper, before heading for the utility room. There they abseiled down the sixty-five feet to the first floor, and then headed for a maintenance area. Breaking into one of the employee lockers, they found a propane torch, wire-cutters, a hacksaw and a wrench. These they used to break out of the prison.

Guards went round the cells as usual during the night but didn't notice that anything was wrong. The next morning, one of the maintenance workers discovered the home-made rope and raised the alarm. A headcount revealed that the two had disappeared – and they were long gone.

Mitchem didn't survive on the outside for long. He headed for the home of his former girlfriend, twenty-two-year-old Ernestina Rodriguez, the mother of his two-year-old daughter, some thirty-five miles from the prison. Suspecting that she might be involved, the police came round to question her for a third time on the morning of 29 March. Rodriguez was still not willing to cooperate, but the same couldn't be said of her little girl. The child, who had obviously been primed by her parents not to say anything, couldn't control herself and had to tell the policemen her great secret. Pointing at the refrigerator, she said, "Daddy's in there!" And he was: somehow Mitchem had been able to curl his six-foot frame inside the fridge. Wearing only his gym shorts, Mitchem surrendered to police. He returned to prison to serve out his sentence; Rodriguez was charged with harbouring and aiding a felon. The story even made the supermarket tabloid favourite, *The Weekly World News*, for their Halloween edition later that year.

Eccleston was rather harder to find. He dropped off the map

until July 1995 (the *Real Prison Breaks* episode suggests he went to South America, although no evidence of this is provided), when his story was featured on the TV programme *America's Most Wanted.* The team searching for him received a call from the mother of Amy Custer, a girl who had got to know Eccleston some five years earlier. In mid-July, Eccleston had turned up at Custer's home in Sherburne, New York, demanding her help, and when she realized who he was, threatened to kill her if she turned him in. Custer's mother recognized Eccleston from the broadcast, and alerted the authorities.

When they reached the apartment on 27 July, the team from the Chenango County Sheriff's Department realized they had a struggle on their hands: Eccleston wasn't going to go easily, and once they were able to confine him in the bathroom, put up a tremendous struggle. As Sheriff Thomas Loughren noted to the *Norwich Evening Sun* reporter, it took three of them to subdue the eighteen year old.

Eccleston was found guilty of the shooting and, after a revised hearing, is serving a combined sentence of forty-six years, and will become eligible for parole somewhere around 2037.

Fact vs. Fiction

As noted above, the "God Pod" regime at Bernalillo began in 2003, according to its own records; the physical descriptions given of Mitchem by *Real Prison Breaks'* "expert", local lawyer Patrick V. Apocada, aren't accurate either. They also make suppositions about Eccleston's movements after the escape that aren't backed up by any shown documentary evidence.

Sources:

Associated Press report, 29 March 1995: "Escape Artist: Inmate had broken out before"

Albuquerque Journal, 4 February 2011: "Counties May Change Jail Agreement"

New Mexico Supreme Court, 13 November 1997: "STATE OF NEW MEXICO, PLAINTIFF-APPELLEE, v. MARIO ARTHUR BACA, DEFENDANT-APPELLANT"

KRQE, 25 January 2011: "Plea cuts sentence for athlete's killer"

Weekly World News, 31 October 1995: "Man breaks out of jail – and his daughter, 2, turns him in!"

Gadsen Times, 27 July 1995: "New Mexico fugitive caught in New York"

Buffalo News, 28 July 1995: "Fugitive Teen captured in Upstate N.Y."

Real Prison Breaks, Cineflix Productions, 2011

A Trucking Great Escape

Actions have consequences, often ones that simply cannot be foreseen at the time. Jay Junior Sigler's escape from a prison in Florida's Everglades in April 1998, masterminded by his friend Christopher Michelson, may be best known for the use of a truck to break through the fences to allow them to get free, but during their time on the run they were pursued by police and were responsible for the death of an innocent civilian who was in the wrong place at the wrong time. They may not have thought for one moment that such an outcome was likely – or even possible – when they made their plans, but as the judge at their trial made abundantly clear, no matter what reasons they felt they had for escaping, it was irrelevant to the death that they caused – one which they apparently callously indicated they didn't care about when they were arrested.

Their escape took place from the Everglades Correctional Institution, twenty miles west of Miami, which had not long been in use as a prison; it was built in 1995 and was originally designed to be used as a mental health facility. However, it became part of Florida's drive to build more prisons, and was described shortly before completion as a "south-west Dade County version of Devil's Island". At the outset, there was no air-conditioning, nor electrical sockets for prisoners to plug televisions or radios into. Weight-lifting equipment was banned in case it was used for prisoners to build up their strength to commit later crimes. There was even a charge of $3 levied for any non-emergency trip to the prison's health centre. In response to a major break out at Glades Correctional Institution in Palm Beach County in January 1995 security was tightened: the butterfly-shaped cell blocks were mounted on concrete slabs to prevent prisoners from tunnelling out. Motion sensors were buried around the perimeter, and there were two chain-link fences, between which were seven rows of razor wire.

Childhood friends Jay Junior Sigler and Christopher Michelson had both served sentences at Everglades for the same offence of robbing a pair of Austrian tourists in 1990. Michelson was released after eight years, but Sigler was a habitual violent offender prior to this particular robbery, and was given a twenty-year sentence, something both men felt was unjust, leaving him still trapped within the Everglades after Michelson's release. It was another Austrian who gave Michelson the inspiration for the escape plan: bodybuilder and future California governor Arnold Schwarzenegger. In the movie *The Terminator*, released in 1984, Schwarzenegger's character, an indestructible cyborg Terminator, uses a vehicle as a battering ram to break into a police station. Similar scenes occurred in the movie's sequel, and it was while watching these films on television that Michelson thought of using a truck as an offensive weapon. If he could get up enough speed, he could ram through the outer fence, crush through the razor wire, and demolish the inner fence, allowing Sigler to run through.

Michelson knew he couldn't carry out this sort of plan on his own, so once he was on the outside he recruited help from Sigler's mother Sandra, his sister Kelly Mitchell, and her new partner John Beaston. Michelson had in fact gone to live with Sandra Sigler after his release from prison, staying in her single-storey house in North Miami and making his plans. At fifty-eight, a lifelong smoker with a hacking cough, Sandra Sigler was a far cry from the "Ma Barker" figure that the papers at the time tried to present: she worked at a nearby mail-processing centre, working the night shift handling parcels. One of the police officers investigating summed her involvement up neatly: "Sandra Sigler acted out of mother's love," Florida Department of Law Enforcement Special Agent Lew Wilson told reporters a few days later. "Mom was a willing and active participant, but I don't believe she was the brains behind this." As far as Sandra Sigler was concerned, her son didn't belong in the Everglades, and she would do whatever was necessary to bring him home.

A tractor-trailer rig was stolen and driven by John Beaston, who had served time for drugs offences and trafficking in stolen property. On the morning of Saturday 11 April 1998, a mere eleven days after Michelson had been released from Everglades, the escape began. With Michelson in the cabin beside him, Beaston piloted the rig down an access road to the Everglades, and floored the accelerator. The heavy vehicle made short work of the prison's outer fence, and ploughed its way through the razor wire and two other fences to the inner fence, behind which Sigler was waiting. Beaston jumped out and fired a shotgun several times. Other prisoners, who thought this might be the cue for a mass breakout, were quickly discouraged from approaching the rig, and a couple of prison officers were slightly injured as they took cover. Sigler dashed across the yard to join his friends.

There was no way that the rig was moving again, but Michelson had thought of that. Sandra Sigler had followed the truck down the access road in a yellow Cutlass Supreme, and was waiting for the three men. (Michelson's brother was meant to be driving the getaway car, but, according to Sandra, he was too stoned to drive!) The fugitives piled into the car, and Sigler sped away, heading for the next rendezvous, where Kelly Mitchell was waiting with other cars.

The police response was immediate and rapid: within twenty minutes of the escape they had captured Sandra Sigler, Kelly Mitchell and John Beaston at a gas station nearby as they tried to swap cars. However, Jay Sigler and Christopher Michelson were able to elude the police, and escaped in Sigler's mother's car.

An alert was immediately put out for the black Chrysler, but it seemed as if the two men had vanished – they spent the night in Lake Worth. The first sighting of the vehicle came the next morning, Easter Sunday, in Pompano Beach, Florida, around forty miles from the prison. While they waited for backup, the patrol officers tried to tail the fugitives discreetly. They hoped to set up a perimeter around the fugitives and box them in, but Michelson, who was driving, realized that the law was on their tail. He turned into an alleyway, accelerated up it (to a speed of 90 mph, according to witnesses) and pulled out into the road, ignoring the stop sign and not looking where he was going. In the way was a stationary car, in which fifty-five-year-old father of three Dennis Howard Palmer was seated. Michelson and Sigler hit it at great speed. The two fugitives survived the crash, with some injuries. Both were too shocked to run from the police, who found a sawn-off 12-gauge shotgun and shells inside the car. When they were asked about the death of Palmer, they seemed not to care one way or another.

Dennis Palmer was killed instantly at the scene, and as a result, Michelson was charged with first-degree murder. The next day, all four co-conspirators, as well as Sigler, were brought up in court. Michelson couldn't believe he was being charged with murder, but because the death occurred during the commission of a felony, the charge was accurate. Prosecutors eventually also charged Jay Sigler with murder, and his mother testified against him at the trial to spare herself any more time behind bars. They were convicted of second-degree murder and vehicular homicide. Each received life sentences; Sigler was deemed eligible for parole in 2025, Michelson not at all. Both men later appealed and the charges and sentences were reduced. Both men apologised to the Palmer family after the sentencing.

At the Everglades, prison superintendent Joe Butler oversaw the rebuilding of the fences, noting wryly to reporters that "Anytime anyone crashes through your fence and starts shooting, it gets your attention. This was like the stuff you see on television. It's out of a movie." He didn't think there were major security implications, or that the attempt would spark a series of copycat raids. "I think anyone would think this was a very unusual situation," he pointed out. "How often do you hear about a semi-truck . . . crashing through your security system?"

Fact vs. Fiction

The *I Escaped: Real Prison Breaks* reconstruction of this breakout is wrong in a number of details (the nature of the fences; who was driving the truck; the colours of the cars). It should be treated with caution.

Sources:

Florida Sun Sentinel, 9 March 1995: "Latest Prison No Slice of Heaven"

Lakeland Ledger, 17 November 1999: "Mom Testifies Against Son in Fatal Jail Break"

Pittsburgh Post-Gazette, 13 April 1998: "Fugitive is arrested after fatal car crash"

John Beaston criminal record: www.angelfire.com/fl4/fci/john beaston.html

CBS News, 13 April 1998: "Arrests Foil Mom's Jailbreak Plan"

Florida Sun Sentinel, 14 April 1998: "Love, Loyalty Spawn During Escape"

New York Times, 13 April 1998: "Florida Fugitive caught After Fatal Crash"

BBC News, 13 April 1998: "Robber sprung from jail by mom"

Seattle Times, 13 April 1988: "Florida Escapee's Freedom Doesn't Last Long – After Brazen Prison Breakout And Fatal Wreck, He Is Caught"

Chicago Tribune, 13 April 1988: "Florida Escapee, Friend Caught After Car Chase"

Sarasota Herald-Tribune, 13 April 1988: "Convict, Partner Caught After Deadly Crash"

Orlando Sentinel, 14 December 1999: "Former Cellmates Get Life For Killing Man In Escape"

Florida Sun Sentinel, 14 December 1999: "2 Prison Escapees Get Life Sentences"

Florida Sun Sentinel, 6 December 2001: "Murder Charges Against Pair Reduced"

Love on the Run

One of the pieces of advice that is passed on from older to younger prison guards is never to believe a word that a prisoner says to you unless you are absolutely certain of its veracity. Prisoners have a great deal of time on their hands and they constantly probe for weaknesses. But guards are only human and susceptible to flattery – and as a result, guard Lynnette Barnett aided convicted murderer Terry Banks to simply stroll out of the Crossroads Correctional Center in Cameron, Missouri, believing that they were desperately in love.

Crossroads was opened in March 1997, two years after Terry Banks was convicted of murder. Fifteen hundred inmates can officially be housed on the premises, divided into six housing units. According to the Missouri Department of Corrections, the perimeter consists of "a three-fence system, an electric motion-detection system on the interior chain-link fence, a lethal electric fence, and a razor-wire-covered, outer chain-link fence. In addition to the perimeter fencing, an armed vehicular patrol provides additional perimeter security on a twenty-four-hour basis." It's a maximum-security prison; once you're in there, the only way you're coming out is at the end of your term. The term "lethal" in the description isn't hyperbole: the voltage that is shot through the wires is twenty times the lethal dose required to execute a man. The 4,100-feet fence is known as "The Intimidator".

Terry Banks wasn't going to be intimidated – at least not by that. He had been arrested aged nineteen for killing the former husband of his seventeen-year-old girlfriend, Sheena Eastburn. Tim Eastburn was a drug dealer, and Banks, along with his friend Matt Myers, went to his house to rob and kill him. Sheena Eastburn lured her husband into the kitchen, and Banks fired the first shot from outside the house using one of Eastburn's own rifles; Myers finished Eastburn off inside. Banks' father, Charlie, was convinced that his son had fallen in with "the wrong girl"; the FBI noted that Banks "killed for drugs, for money, and for her". Myers turned state's evidence and received a sixty-seven-year sentence for second-degree murder. Banks and Eastburn received life sentences for first-degree murder. (In summer 2012, Sheena Eastburn attempted to appeal that sentence partly on the grounds that she wasn't guilty of first-degree murder: she claimed that she was trying to get her ex, with whom she was still having a sexual relationship despite their divorce, out of the house so that Myers and Banks could return the stolen gun. Banks had fired at Tim Eastburn out of jealousy when he saw the couple kissing.)

Banks wasn't a model prisoner by any definition. Between his conviction and his escape, he had fourteen conduct violations, although none of them was for anything more serious than possession of contraband or intoxicating substances. By the summer of 1999, he was chafing at the restrictions of prison life, and wanted to get to the outside.

He targeted Lynnette Barnett, a guard at Crossroads a year older than him, who was going through some severe personal problems. Her marriage had fallen apart, and she was living in her mother's boyfriend's basement. Her ex-husband, Dave, was also in the correctional service, working at the Western Missouri Correctional Center, and following an irretrievable breakdown of communication between them, had taken out an injunction preventing her from returning to the matrimonial home. Barnett was assigned to the food warehouse building at Crossroads, where Banks was working.

Much as Lynette Barnett's family didn't want to believe that she was a willing accomplice in Banks' escape on Friday 29 October 1999 – her mother was convinced that she'd been told, "You don't help me get out of here, my outside contacts will kill your entire family" – it became apparent when videotapes of prison activities were scrutinized that the pair were definitely acting almost like lovesick teenagers. One tape, from nine days before the escape, shows them crossing a storage area holding hands, only releasing their grip as they approach the door when someone might see them.

"He caught her in a weak moment in her life," Cameron police lieutenant Don Fritz explained. "She was down and susceptible to a male figure coming in and trying to be strong for her. That's all [the prisoners have] got time to do in there, is try to con somebody. To them that's what life is all about. It's just a game to them." FBI agent Kurt Lipanovich agreed: "She was infatuated. If you want to say she's in love, fine. He's in love with his freedom."

Whether Banks really was that calculating and cynical is perhaps open to question, given that it certainly seems as if the two continued acting in their lovey-dovey way during their time on the run. Maybe he genuinely did fall for the guard. Either way, she was in a position to help him get out.

The plan was incredibly simple: Banks would pretend to be a guard and leave the prison alongside Barnett. They would then drive away into the sunset and a new life. To achieve this, they needed two things: a guard's uniform and identification. The former was easy: Barnett had lost a lot of weight during the time of her divorce, and she was able to put her current uniform on underneath her old one in order to bring it into the prison. The latter needed a bit more planning, but even that didn't present too many obstacles.

On 27 October, Lynnette Barnett went shopping in the local town and asked a local printing centre if they could duplicate her identity card, since her boyfriend had lost his and would be in serious trouble if it was discovered. The first shop refused to make a blank copy; the second one she approached agreed. With a little bit of ingenuity, she was able to make a card for Banks in the name of Chad Matthews, one of the other guards. Barnett also bought men's clothing, and filled her truck up with fuel, topping it up shortly before she got home, so she had a complete tank ready for Friday.

Although Banks was stopped for a moment at the desk by one of the guards since his identity card didn't have the proper computerized magnetic strip. Such snafus with the technology weren't uncommon; his name matched the badge, and it was within the prison records. It was enough: prisoner number 514829 walked out of Crossroads, seven minutes before the next scheduled headcount.

After cashing Barnett's pay cheque at a Kansas City liquor store, the fugitives headed straight to meet with Banks' father Charlie, who was alerted to the escape when investigators called to let him know that Terry was out. A warrant was issued for Terry's arrest on 3 November, but the pair seemed to have disappeared without trace. The first anyone knew of their whereabouts was on 3 December when police located Lynette's truck. Charlie had sold it to a friend of his brother's on 18 November; Lynette's prison-issued gear, including pepper spray and handcuffs, were hidden within the vehicle.

Around that time, Charlie took his son and girlfriend down to Victoria, Texas, a quiet locale where they could disappear easily. Both changed their appearances, dying their hair, and hung out with Jeanne Jones, a friend of Charlie's. They watched television, smoke and drank, and went to parties. And that was their undoing.

With the trail gone cold, investigators turned to the TV programme *America's Most Wanted* for assistance. The broadcast on 11 December featured Banks and Barnett, and although some people laughed off the resemblance between Charlie's friends John and Heather, at least one person thought that the coincidence was too large. He contacted the free 1-800 number given at the end of the programme and told investigators that he believed he had met Banks and Barnett in the company of a scruffy older man named Charlie. This last detail persuaded law enforcement that it was a good tip – no mention had been made of Charlie's existence in the broadcast.

On 16 December, FBI agents in Victoria visited the site of the party, but had no luck finding the pair; although they tracked down the apartment where they had been living, Barnett and Banks had left because it was too cold. Based on a tip from an informant, they learned that the fugitives had gone to stay with Jeanne Jones and her boyfriend Paul in a camper van in the Southwinds Mobile Home Village. Officers began surveillance on the camper, and spotted them, along with Charlie, Jeanne and Paul.

At dawn the next day, twenty-five officers surrounded the trailer, ready for trouble – there was a rumour that Banks was carrying a gun. Jeanne, Paul and Charlie all exited the camper peacefully, but Banks and Barnett refused to even acknowledge they were there initially. Eventually, first Barnett and then Banks gave themselves up.

Despite her family still believing that she was the innocent victim in the affair, Barnett received a five-year sentence for her part in the escape; fifteen years were added to Banks' life term. Bart Spear, the prosecuting attorney, defended his decision to prosecute Banks, despite the fact that his sentence couldn't in reality be added to, saying, "If I never prosecuted somebody who escaped from prison, I might be sending the wrong message. You can't have people escaping from prison. That's not a good thing."

Sources:

The Houston Press, 16 March 2000: "Love on the Run"

Review Of The Department Of Corrections Crossroads Correctional Center, 23 August 2000

The Joplin Globe, 29 July 2012: "McDonald County woman seeks new trial following 1995 murder conviction"

Laredo Morning Times, 19 December 1999: "Escaped murderer, Missouri guard captured"

Lawrence Journal-World, 12 December 1999: "Officer crosses to wrong side of law"

Caught in The Net

Hostage situations can play out in many ways, with demands ranging from the mundane to the extraordinary. Plane hijackers may insist on the release of fellow terrorists from prisons; bank robbers might ask for a getaway vehicle to be provided. Negotiators are trained to keep a dialogue open, and not to be fazed by anything that may come their way. But in March 2001, even experienced police officers were surprised by the demands made by William Davis and Douglas Gray, two murderers on the run from Stringtown, Oklahoma. They wanted pizza – and the chance to finish watching the movie in which they were engrossed: *The Net*, a thriller starring Sandra Bullock.

A Correctional Center has stood in Stringtown since the early 1930s; at various times it has been a venereal disease hospital, a prisoner-of-war camp and a vocational training school, but in 1968 it became a secure sub-unit of the Oklahoma State Penitentiary, with new fences and towers erected. As a medium-level secure facility, it became known as the Mack H. Alford Correctional Center in honour of one of its longest-serving wardens. Stringtown itself has a tiny population – only 396 in the 2000 census.

William D. Davis and Douglas E. Gray were two of the more dangerous prisoners held at Alford in 2001. Davis had committed a brutal murder, stabbing a homeowner eighty times during a robbery in 1974; in 1988, Douglas Gray had bound a school teacher to a chair after taking her hostage and then killed her. Both were serving life sentences; they had nothing to lose.

Both men were assigned to work in the prison manufacturing facility, making road and street signs. These were packaged up, and taken through the front gates – past the barbed-wire-topped fences – to the local post office, from where they were despatched around the country. Because the carts of signs went through on a regular basis, the guards tended not to check them too rigorously, and the two lifers thought that they might be able to conceal themselves inside a cart and effectively mail themselves to freedom.

They realized that they could not simply hide underneath the post: the extra weight of two grown men would easily be spotted. So they changed the labelling on the packages to state that they were much heavier than they were, giving a total weight for the cart that would equate to the parcels plus themselves.

On the morning of their break out, 16 March 2001, Davis and Gray prepared the packages as normal between 9.30 and 10.30 a.m., and then fellow convicts helped them to hide inside the specially rigged cart. This was wheeled out as normal at 1.30 p.m. and placed in the mail truck. And despite the correctional facility supposedly having an absolute rule that no vehicle left the premises until it had been thoroughly searched and unless the guards were sure that all the inmates were accounted for, the mail truck was waved through. The guards on the gates believed that it had been checked by their colleagues inside. At 1.55 p.m., the prison received a call from the mail supervisor at the Stringtown post office. Two inmates had jumped out of the cart, pulled a knife on him, and taken the vehicle.

They didn't keep it for long; they abandoned two other vehicles they stole shortly afterwards and soon headed into the wooded hills that surrounded the prison. There they stole guns, ammunition and some of her husband's clothes from seventy-six-year-old Ida Dunn, who lived in a trailer in an isolated spot in the forest.

While a major manhunt was under way for them, with tracking dogs and helicopters coping with the wintry conditions, the two men kept out of sight, sleeping in the snow-covered woods, and stealing food where they could. Eight days after their escape, they came across a ranch belonging to Jack Sheffield. When the rancher came to check on his cattle, he was jumped by the two men. Although he believed initially that they were going to shoot him, he was bound by Gray and taken hostage as they drove his pickup truck the 150 miles toward Oklahoma City.

However, about twenty miles before they reached their destination, Davis and Gray pulled into the side of the road and tied

Sheffield to a post before driving off. He freed himself quickly and ran for ten minutes to Arcadia, a small town near Edmond, where he raised the alarm. Soon after, realizing they had been spotted by the police, Davis and Gray abandoned the truck and ran into the woods.

They soon came upon the home of Mildred and Gilbert Tuepker. Seventy-two-year-old Mildred was chatting on the phone with her daughter Jan, who lived in Delaware, when she spotted the two men approaching the house. She told her daughter to call the police, and before the connection was cut off, her daughter heard one of the men say, "We're running from the police. Get inside."

Alerted by Jan Tuepker, Oklahoma police and SWAT units raced to the scene, where Davis and Grey were holding the two seniors hostage. They evacuated the neighbours from their properties, and settled in for the siege. What they didn't realize was that the two fugitives had vowed to commit suicide rather than be captured and returned to prison.

The police sent a "throwphone" into the property, rather than use the landline that Mildred Tuepker had been using previously. Throwphones were part of the arsenal of law enforcement agencies at that time: whereas with an ordinary phone, the hostage taker had the option of simply not using it, the throwphone consisted of a microphone and a loudspeaker. If Davis and Grey said anything, the police could hear it, even if the phone was switched off.

Edmond police officer Kris Fite was appointed negotiator, and found Gray a difficult person to talk to initially. Gray warned the police that the two hostages would be harmed if they tried to enter the house, and for over five hours Fite tried to calm the men down and coax them out of the house. Eventually, he was able to persuade Gray to release Mildred Tuepker in return for being allowed to speak to his mother, who tried to persuade her son to release the hostages unharmed.

After Mildred was sent out of the house, negotiations continued. Davis asked for a pizza and the men asked if they could finish watching *The Net*, a thriller that was being broadcast on TV. It seemed as if the situation was slowly winding down.

But then everything took a turn for the worse. Police became highly concerned when Gray revealed the existence of the suicide pact between the two men. After Gray put the phone down, he took Gilbert Tuepker into a bedroom, and asked him where the best place in the house would be for them to shoot themselves. Gilbert told them that the kitchen was probably the spot to choose. He waited in the bedroom as first one, then a second shot rang out.

Not knowing whether this meant the two fugitives had followed through with their pact, or if Gilbert had been shot, Oklahoma County Sheriff John Whetsel came close to ordering a strike on the house. But then Gray came back on the phone, and told Fite that Davis had tried to kill himself but failed. Gray had therefore put his friend out of his misery, shooting him in the head. Gray sounded increasingly depressed but Fite continued to argue with him, and eventually, eight hours after he first took the Tuepkers hostage, Gray surrendered to the police. "Everybody is going to think I'm a coward," he said, as he was led away. He received an extra forty-year sentence for the escape. Gilbert Tuepker walked out of the house unharmed.

Sources:

Deseret News, 26 March 2001: "Couple's captivity ends with one suicidal fugitive dead, one in custody"
Amarillo Globe-News, 26 March 2001: "Oklahoma escapees had made agreement to commit suicide"
Mack Alford Correctional Center prospectus
Real Prison Breaks, Cineflix Productions, 2011: John Sheffield, Kris Fite interviews

A Final Smell of the Grass

The use of capital punishment by society has always been a matter of considerable debate. Do we subscribe to the principle of "an eye for an eye", and those who take a life deserve to forfeit their own? Or should there be compassion? Or, indeed, is keeping someone locked up for the whole of their natural life a harsher, and more appropriate, punishment than being put to death? Those on death row have their own unique perspective on the question, and understandably, many of them are constantly seeking ways in which to escape from prison and experience freedom once more.

One such person was Charles Victor Thompson, who was convicted of the murders of his former girlfriend Dennise Hayslip and her new partner Darren Keith Cain on 30 April 1998 (Hayslip actually died a week after being shot, giving her enough time to name her killer to the police). He was sentenced to death the following year, and after the Texas Court of Appeals allowed a new punishment hearing, a second Harris County jury upheld the original decision on 28 October 2005. Before the new verdict, Thompson had written, "From the day you hear the decision that the death penalty will be sought, a little part of you dies silently."

Less than a week after it was confirmed that he would receive the mandated death sentence, Thompson simply walked out of the Harris County Jail, much to the consternation of those jurors who had been assured by the presiding judge that Thompson would be isolated and would have no means of escape. During the period Thompson was free, the relatives of his victims, as well as the jurors, went into hiding; Thompson himself claimed – in an interview he gave a month after his capture, and via the book written about his trial and escape, *The Grass Beneath His*

Feet – that he vowed to himself that he would not do anything violent when he was on the outside. Given the vicious nature of the double murder, and the threats that he had purportedly made during his trials, perhaps it is not surprising that those possibly affected chose to err on the side of caution.

According to an editorial in the *Houston Chronicle* a few days after Thompson's recapture, he was one of at least nineteen prisoners who had absconded from the Harris County Jail in the preceding ten years, but because he was officially on death row, security around him should have been correspondingly tighter. County Commissioner Steve Radack even admitted, while Thompson was still on the run, "It's amazing to me that we don't have more incidents like this. You have to bear in mind there's constantly people coming into our jail at the same time there's constantly people leaving as people are arrested and make bond. It's a continuous dynamic and a lot of work."

Thompson took maximum advantage of that dynamic, and the overcrowding in the prison, which had led to the prison being decertified by the state previously, meaning that staff simply couldn't keep track of all the new faces that were around. "The day you're sentenced to death, [escaping] is on your mind, regularly. You know you're going to die," he told reporters afterwards. He knew that getting out of death row in Building 12 at the Allan B. Polunsky Unit would be nigh-on impossible: the harsh conditions within the unit and the regular changes in routine would prevent any sensible planning. However, the 1200 Jail in Harris County was a completely different affair. A new building, only opened in 2003, on Baker Street in the heart of Houston, it isn't that far from the Amtrak yard, and security certainly seemed to be lax. He needed to get away from there before he was handed back to the warders at the Polunsky Unit.

The convicted murderer was still having meetings with various attorneys, which were held at the 1200, while he was waiting to be transferred. To get out of the jail, Thompson knew he had to pass various checkpoints, and obviously he could not wear handcuffs or his prison uniform. However, he also knew that he would have a chance to change, since guards didn't stay in the room with prisoners during legal consultations – as long as he could get out of his handcuffs – and legal papers weren't searched. He therefore kept hold of the civilian clothes – dark-blue shirt, khaki pants and white tennis shoes – that he had been permitted to wear during his resentencing hearing: he had managed to secrete them inside his file of legal papers following his court appearance at the end of October.

This wasn't the first time that he had tried to keep hold of civilian clothes. A set had been found in his cell four days after he was transferred into the Harris County jail prior to the resentencing hearing. According to Thompson, he was assured by Sergeant James Watson that the district attorney's office wouldn't be told about the discovery before his resentencing and that it would be simply dealt with as a contraband violation. The sheriff's office denied this, saying that the DA's office told them that the mere discovery of civilian clothes wasn't enough to sustain a charge of attempted escape.

Thompson also claimed that he brought a handcuff key from the prison within the accordion file of papers. He has never admitted how he got hold of the key in the first place ("I'll take that to my grave," he swore after his capture), although many people were highly suspicious that Petra E. Herrmann, the chairwoman of Alive e. V., an anti-death-penalty organization, visited Thompson the day before his escape. It should be made clear that the police cleared her and other visitors of any involvement, but the fact that the authorities at the Polunsky Unit were adamant that the metal detectors used on Thompson before he was sent to Harris County would have revealed the presence of the key does lend credence to the theory that Thompson was aided by someone whom he saw in Houston.

One item that he definitely brought from the prison was his death-row identification badge, which had his photo on it. It was the basis for his most audacious bluff.

On Thursday 3 November 2005, Thompson had a meeting with James Rytting, a new attorney, after being granted permission to seek fresh counsel following his trial. He had watched the routines at the jail carefully, and, as he pointed out after his arrest, many of the staff simply weren't doing their jobs properly. Certainly, he should not have been left in the room with the lawyer with the door unbolted. But Deputy John Thurman didn't lock the door, so when the lawyer left, Thompson remained in the open room, unsupervised. Rytting claimed that he told guards after the meeting that he was "done with Thompson", which should have led directly to him returning to his cell. Instead no one went to check on the prisoner.

After checking to ensure that he was right in his belief that the guard outside the door had gone to supervise the inmates at recreation – and that therefore there was no one around to catch him in the act – he used the key to unlock the handcuffs, and removed them. He stripped off his prison uniform, changed into his civilian outfit and hung his prison identification on his collar.

And then, quite brazenly, he walked to the elevator, and took a ride to the first (ground) floor. When he was asked for his identification, he showed the death-row badge, on which he had made one minor, but significant alteration: the word "offender" was covered in tape, which he hid with his fingers. Deputy Tonya Ward escorted him to colleagues, as she had done on previous occasions when she saw a non-standard form of identification. When those deputies queried what Thompson was holding, saying that they'd never seen one of those badges before, the escaper claimed that he was from the Texas Attorney General's office carrying out an undercover internal investigation at the jail – something that had happened with some frequency since it opened – and needed to go outside to meet his partner. Not wanting to get in the way of such a person, the deputies opened the door. As simply as that, Charles Victor Thompson was a free man.

Consciously telling himself to walk, not run, Thompson strolled out into the Houston heat, and wandered down the road, all the time expecting the hue and cry to begin. After a short while, he ducked out of sight, stripped off his shirt and trousers, and looking like one of the many joggers out on the streets, started to make his way towards the train tracks. As a grain train passed him, Thompson ran alongside it to match its speed, then hauled himself onto a ladder. He stayed on that train for about twenty minutes, jumping off when it stopped in the suburbs. After a brief attempt to carjack a vehicle – and being discovered by its female owner before he could work out how to operate the security device on the car – he decided to head back onto the trains, and after keeping out of sight underneath a free-way until it was dark, he jumped on board another train. He was heading through East Texas on his way out of the state. "I was pretty dirty and happy," he said of that train ride. "The scenery was nice, and it was nice to be free."

Once Thompson's absence was discovered, a major manhunt began. The primary concern was that he would go after those he had threatened. Dennise Hayslip's mother was blunt: "They say all he wants to do is run. I don't believe that. I really think he wants to get revenge," she told reporters before heading for hiding.

Finding no trace of him in Houston, apart from the clothes he had abandoned behind one of the other jails, the search was widened. On 4 November the US Marshals office offered a $10,000 reward for his capture, and charged him with unlawful flight to avoid prosecution, designating him a federal fugitive and allowing them to bypass normal extradition proceedings between states. They believed that the discovery of the clothes he used during the escape meant that he had an accomplice who had provided him with a fresh set, not realizing he had simply lost a layer of clothing.

There were various sightings that the marshals investigated: deputies were sent to Tidwell, north-east of Houston, after a county employee thought she had seen Thompson. It turned out to be another convict, but one released properly. Thompson was in fact miles away. He was well on his way through the southern states: on Friday morning the train on which he was travelling entered Louisiana, and Thompson saw up close the effects of Hurricane Katrina, which had devastated the area at the end of August that year. When the train reached the end of the line in Shreveport, Louisiana, on Sunday morning, Thompson masqueraded as a worker trying to get home after the storm. People took pity on him, allowing him use of a shower, and feeding him – they even gave him $25 to help him out and gave him a lift to a truckstop. The money was to prove his downfall.

Thompson knew he needed larger sums of money in order to escape out of the country, probably to Canada. He therefore located a pay phone and made contact with what he would only describe later as "an international assistance agency" that promised they would arrange funds via Western Union. Thompson would need to call them later that day to receive the code word that he'd have to give in order to collect the money.

While he was waiting, he bought a six-pack of Natural Light, a beer with about 4.2 per cent strength. It was the first alcohol he had drunk in a long time. Borrowing a bicycle from in front of a store, he cycled to a nearby park and had a drink. That went straight to his head, and when he returned to the payphone to make the call, he was drunk.

And that's where the US Marshals found him just after 8 p.m. on 6 November, speaking on the phone. The Gulf Coast Violent Offenders Task Force tracking Thompson had received a tip that he was in Shreveport, and contacted the local US Marshals office. According to Deputy US Marshal Mickey Rellin, who carried out the arrest, Thompson didn't try to get away. "I asked him, 'Who are you?' No answer," Rellin recalled to CNN. "'Who are you?' No answer. 'Who are you?' I then made sure that he could see my badge and my credentials, and he said, 'Are you the US Marshals Fugitive Task Force?' And I looked at him and said, 'What do you think?' He says, 'Then you know who I am.' And I said, 'Well, who are you?' And then he said, 'Yes, I'm Charles. I know you're looking for me.'"

Thompson's own account mentions the beer, but plays down the effect it had on him – he blames the woman to whom he was speaking on the phone for his arrest. She had just mentioned the $10,000 reward she had seen on *America's Most Wanted* when the marshals arrived. She's not named, but "was not only a friend, but a woman Charles had come to love and respect. She was a woman he entrusted with his life and his future." Certainly, he was in contact with a woman named Kyla based in Australia, who vigorously defended Thompson in an online forum after the resentencing hearing but stopped posting about him once the escape was under way. All he had left to his name when he was captured were the contents of his pockets: a black shoelace and a bottle of shampoo.

His lack of resistance surprised the officers involved. "You got to keep in mind he's been twice sentenced to death," Harris County spokesman Lt John Martin told CNN the night he was arrested. "He has absolutely no incentive to cooperate with law

enforcement officers, and frankly, nothing to lose by strenuously resisting being taken into custody. So you know, of course,
we imagine the worst. We imagine him putting up a fight, maybe
gaining access to some type of weapon. And you know, my big
concern was for the safety of the officers while they were trying
to take him into custody, as well as the general public who's
obviously in danger just by him being out there on the streets.
So again, we were greatly relieved that he was taken into custody
without incident."

The fugitive was taken to Caddo Parish Jail, and from there
he went back to Harris County Jail. On 8 November, a judge
ordered that he was barred from contact with the outside world,
except to meet with his lawyer until he was returned to death
row, and while he was in Harris County, he was to have a two-
deputy escort when he left his cell and to be strip-searched
when he returned to it. Lt John Martin drily commented, "I
think he should immediately recognize the futility of future
escape attempts. He will be much more scrutinized. This will
not happen again."

There were multiple repercussions following his escape,
which the Harris County law enforcement authorities put down
to human error. According to Lt Martin, "We have a number of
procedures that simply weren't followed." Sheriff Tommy
Thomas fired a twelve-year veteran of the sheriff's office for not
restraining Thompson properly and failing to lock the visitor
booth. One sergeant chose to resign rather than face discipli-
nary action. The others – who had unwittingly aided Thompson
by not scrutinizing his documentation carefully and buying into
his story – received punishments ranging from a letter of repri-
mand to a ten-day suspension without pay.

It was a little embarrassing for the Houston authorities when
it was revealed two weeks after Thompson's return that they had
lost track of another convicted felon, who was based at a halfway house in the city. Christopher Wilkins, who was imprisoned
for firearms offences, walked out of the Leidel Comprehensive
Sanctions Center on 2 October 2005, and didn't come back. US
Marshals were alerted but in the six weeks that he was on the
run, he became a suspect in three murders, an aggravated
assault and two auto thefts. At least Lawrence Darnell Thomas,

a carjacker who managed to get away from members of the Houston Police Department as he was being transferred to jail on 15 November, was recaptured within hours.

In October 2008 Thompson lost one of the statutory appeals against his sentence. As of this writing he remains on death row. "I think my second bite at the apple was my retrial," he told the *Houston Chronicle* a month after his escape. "I think my fate is determined . . . But, I'm a prisoner of hope."

Sources:

Rodriguez, Robert: *The Grass Beneath His Feet* (AuthorHouse, Bloomington, Indiana: 2009)

Houston Chronicle, 7 November 2005: "German group not involved in escape, authorities say"

Houston Chronicle, 14 December 2005: "An interview with escapee Charles Victor Thompson"

USA Today, 5 November 2005: "Search on for Texas death row inmate"

Houston Chronicle, 4 November 2005: "Victim's mom says the 'Chuckster killer' wants revenge"

Houston Chronicle, 5 November 2005: "Somebody is helping him"

Houston Chronicle, 7 November 2005: "Escaped killer is captured"

Houston Chronicle, 9 November 2005: "Thompson had no money when arrested"

Current status: http://www.tdcj.state.tx.us/stat/dr_info/thompson-charles.html

CNN, Nancy Grace show (broadcast 7 November 2005)

Details on the murders: http://www.murdervictims.com/Voices/CainHayslip.htm

Houston Chronicle, 15 December 2005: "Thompson says jailbreak was easy"

Prisontalk Online Community Forum: "Charles Thompson Resentenced to death (my side of the story as well)" archived September 2012

Houston Chronicle, 29 October 2005: "Jury sends Tomball man back to death row"

Houston Chronicle, 23 November 2005: "Fired deputy faults jail policies"

Houston Chronicle, 22 November 2005: "Deputy fired, 7 others disciplined over jailbreak"

Houston Chronicle, 9 November 2005: "Judge limits visits, tightens security around killer"

Houston Chronicle, 9 November 2005: "Jailhouse ramble heads should roll after killer's escape revealed intolerable negligence"

Houston Chronicle, 8 November 2005: "Captured killer back home"

Houston Chronicle, 24 November 2005: "Escape of suspect in 3 killings sparks outrage"

Houston Chronicle, 15 November 2005: "Escaped suspect captured"

Escaping a Dog's Life

The Lansing Correctional Facility, originally known as the Kansas State Penitentiary (KSP), has housed many well known and infamous prisoners since it opened its doors in July 1868. The Barker-Karpis Gang that terrorized Americans in the early 1930s was formed when Al Karpis (aka Alvin Francis Karpowicz) met Fred Barker when they were both serving time within its walls. Truman Capote's novel *In Cold Blood* gave publicity to the case of Perry Smith and Richard Hickock, who were held at the prison following their murder of the Clutter family in Holcomb, Kansas, in November 1959. Serial killers Francis Donald Nemechek and Richard Grissom, Jnr have both been incarcerated at the KSP.

It is also the home for a different sort of prison industry – the Safe Harbor Dog Program, which helps bring new life to dogs who would otherwise be destroyed. Safe Harbor began in 2004, when a small group of unwanted dogs was taken into Lansing. Since that time, around a hundred inmates have been trained as dog handlers. They start by socializing the animals, and then, once they are better equipped to deal with others, they house-train the animals and work on obedience training. Safe Harbor has operated for nearly a decade – but nowhere on their website now will you find reference to the woman who set it up and was the primary force behind its growth.

That's because on 12 February 2006, Safe Harbor's founder, Toby Young, assisted murderer John Manard to escape from Lansing. She went on the run with him, and, after a high-speed car chase, was captured alongside him. Toby Young is not the sort of role model Safe Harbor wants to adopt.

The problem was that John Manard said what Toby Young wanted to hear. As "Jennifer", a former Lansing correctional

officer, posted at the time of the escape (before Young's complicity was confirmed):

> "IF" (sic) she is guilty (innocent until proven guilty), yes, it
> wouldn't surprise me. In the time I worked at LCF, I saw
> many staff 'walked out' for getting caught up in an inmate.
>
> All it takes is one mistake, and a clever inmate will use it
> against you. If you give an inmate something they shouldn't
> have, no matter how innocent, they have something to use
> against you, and it is all downhill. They have blackmail
> material, and life as you know it is over. That is just how
> things are."

Prison volunteers, like correctional officers, receive training that
is supposed to help them to deal with this sort of situation. It
doesn't necessarily mean that the training is going to stick,
particularly if an inmate does their best to make them feel
special. Toby Young fell for Manard, hook, line and sinker.

John Manard was found guilty of what Judge Peter Ruddick
described as a "vicious, unprovoked and totally random" felony
murder and aggravated robbery. Aged just seventeen, Manard
and his friend Michael Yardley shot Donald England on 13 June
1996, when they tried to carjack his vehicle as he was waiting for
his ex-wife to have a haircut. Since the state couldn't prove deci-
sively which one of them was responsible, they were both held
accountable under the "felony murder" system (any participant
in a felony is held criminally liable for any deaths that occur
during or in furtherance of that felony). On 23 April the following year, Manard was sentenced to life imprisonment, to be
followed by a ten-year term, and told that he would not be eligible for parole until 2019 at the earliest. (Manard later claimed
that he didn't think he would get a chance at parole until 2028.)

At his trial Manard claimed through his attorney that he had
simply signed up for a robbery and hadn't intended anyone to
get hurt, describing himself as "a seventeen-year-old kid who
was simply scared to death". After sentencing, he apologised to
England's widow and sons for what he had done. Perhaps
understandably, he also felt aggrieved that even though he
hadn't fired the fatal shot (and the prosecutor in the case

believed this was probably the case), he was still given the same punishment as the man who had.

Sent to Lansing initially as a maximum-security prisoner, Manard kept his head down, and earned his way into the medium-security section. That was where he first came in contact with "the dog lady" as Toby Young was described by the prisoners. The former business professional who worked for the Sprint Corporation until 2001, and was married to her high-school sweetheart had recently survived a brush with thyroid cancer.

Working at a veterinary clinic, Young realized how many stray dogs there were around Kansas City, and, on the suggestion of a colleague, looked into the possibility of setting up a program at the local prison for prisoners to help retrain the dogs so they could be given to new owners. A TV series had featured these so-called "cell dogs" around the country earlier in 2004, and after discussions with the warden at Lansing, the first canines were brought into the prison on 13 August that year.

Over the next couple of years, Young became a regular visitor to the prison, bringing supplies for the dogs, exchanging the animals, and working with the prisoners. She received all the training that the state deemed necessary for being among the inmates of the prison, so was granted pretty much clear access to whatever she wanted when she needed it. The Lansing authorities were delighted with the positive publicity that the program was bringing the prison, and Young became a trusted part of the prison's extended workforce.

Young was also pleased with the way that the program was working, not just for the dogs who were no longer bound to be euthanized and would find better lives, but also for the prisoners with whom they were spending their time. Cell-dog programs across the world report that such activities give prisoners a release from the humdrum, often brutal world of the jailhouse, and can contribute to their eventual return to society. Manard was one of the first to become a trainer, joining the program in October 2004.

Quite when Manard decided to cultivate Young's friendship and turn it into something that he could manipulate to escape from Lansing is not clear. For a long time after their recapture,

Manard maintained that he was desperately in love with her, sending twenty-seven-page letters to the *Wall Street Journal*. From his cell soon after their recapture, he wrote to the local TV station: "We have a fairy tale love the size of infinity that's been lived by 2 real people. She means more to me than my own life."

Two years later he wrote to the *Wall Street Journal*: "I miss her so much, I'd have to wipe out an entire rainforest to put it on paper." He sent messages to her via a reporter who was compiling a story on their love affair and escape claiming, "I still love her with all that I am . . . I miss her more than my own freedom, and I've never doubted her loyalty and love." But how much of that was genuine is impossible to tell, particularly as much of what Manard would claim about the events of February 2006 were demonstrably false. No matter what Manard might try to state, Toby Young knew exactly what she was doing.

Manard also knew exactly what she was doing: Young was able to drive in and out of the prison, and was trusted so much that there was a very high degree of probability that her van, with its cargo of slavering mutts, wouldn't be searched properly, if at all. Over the months, the twenty-seven-year-old Manard flattered the forty-eight-year-old prison volunteer's ego, complimenting her choice of clothing, and being a shoulder to cry on for her when she described the problems that she had with her fire captain husband.

Not all the handlers were as impressed with Young as Manard. When one of them confronted her in the prison yard in October 2005, Manard came to her rescue, and from then onwards became her "escort" and unofficial bodyguard around Lansing. This brought the two of them into constant contact. In December that year his feelings for her were apparently so strong that he asked her if she would run away with him if he was able to escape from prison. When she replied that she would, Manard told her his plan.

Young claimed that Manard originally intended to mail himself from the prison, but she dissuaded him from that. He then explained how she could help: he would squeeze himself into one of the pens used to transport the dogs to and from the prison. Other inmates would then place him in her van, and she would drive through the gates. Heartbeat detectors wouldn't work, since they would register the dogs who would all be scrabbling and barking furiously. They could drop the dogs at Young's house, switch vehicles, and head off to a new life at a resort in the mountains, far away from Kansas.

Manard starved himself, losing around thirty pounds in weight so he could get his 6 foot 2 inch body into the dog carrier. Young smuggled in a cell phone for Manard to use (a key point used by those who maintained from the onset that Young was not the innocent victim she initially appeared to be), and they kept in constant contact – on one occasion, Young's husband read a text on her phone, which she quickly claimed must be a wrong number. (Her husband has never granted an interview regarding his side of the story.) She also drew out around $42,000 from her retirement plan, and bought a 1997 Chevrolet vehicle for their getaway – rather unfortunately, providing a real address to the dealer from whom she bought it: the address of their hideaway in the Tennessee mountains to which they were heading!

On Sunday 12 February, Manard was helped into the dog carrier by other inmates after the Safe Harbor dog session came to its end, and was taken to Young's van. At 10.40 a.m. Young approached the gate, where guard Earl Green was on duty. Green knew Young and although he later claimed that surveillance footage proved that he did search the van, he admitted that he didn't give it the thorough inspection that he should have done. Every box large enough to carry an occupant should have been shaken down. They weren't. (Green was initially fired, then, after he made a fuss claiming he was being made a scapegoat, was allowed to resign: prison officials showed that there were at least five occasions on which he failed to search Young's van properly.) Ten minutes later, Manard was out of Lansing. The dogs were dropped off and they picked up the new van, along with two handguns, hair dye and an electric razor. The lovers were on their way to Tennessee.

Four hours after their departure from Lansing, a headcount showed that Manard was missing. The manhunt initially worked off the principle that Young wasn't involved, and that, for some as yet unknown reason, Manard had decided to take her along, since she hadn't been found with an abandoned vehicle. Local people were convinced that she could not possibly be involved: on the Crime Scene KC blog, which by chance had spoken with Manard at the end of 2005 when interviewing a random inmate about Christmas as a prisoner, one woman, "Christine" wrote:

> Do you seriously think she would ever do that? Ridiculous. The media can put any spin on any story they want and make it into entertainment for the masses who chose to believe and not ever really look for the truth. She did not aide him, she did not hide him. They DID NOT search her van when she left. And now the warden needs someone to blame that a prisoner is missing and someones (sic) life is at risk. End of story. She would never turn her back on her husband and children, on the dogs, nor on the other inmates so incredibly impacted by what she did and will do when she returns.

But the evidence was clearly showing otherwise. "Toby Young was involved in planning this escape," Department of Corrections press officer Bill Miskell said bluntly at a press conference on 13 February. "She withdrew a substantial amount of cash. She took two handguns from her home." Young was "well known and well liked by everyone," Miskell added. "It appears that her familiarity with the staff may have played a part."

By this point, according to the account she gave in 2011, Toby Young was beginning to suspect that she might have been used by Manard. (This doesn't tally with what she said at the time.) Rather than indulging in the loving conversation of their time inside Lansing, he was far more interested in eating junk food – after all, he had been in prison for the last decade! Once their fifteen-hour journey was complete, Manard was talking about his desire for freedom to do whatever he wanted to do: this was his first time in the outside world as a legal adult.

Over the next few days, Manard and Young lived in their cabin, occasionally popping out to see a movie – ironically including *Walk the Line*, the biopic of singer Johnny Cash, which is partly set inside Folsom State Prison – or going shopping. Their purchases included two fine guitars and a parakeet! On 24 February, they went to the local shops in Chattanooga, but when they returned to their Chevy to head back to the cabin, they discovered the law was on their tail. Young maintained that she didn't expect police to be looking for them, although she admitted that they had not looked at a paper or the TV, nor listened to the radio, probably because Manard wanted to stop her from worrying. (Manard also kept the only key to the cabin; Young couldn't have left if she wanted to.)

The manhunt had taken some time to get going. Young's family and friends were questioned, all of whom were horrified and mystified by her actions. Her father read a statement saying that family members "simply don't have any ideas why or how this happened". To them she was the archetypal do-gooder, who would no sooner run off with a convicted first-degree murderer as fly to the moon. "Our training emphasizes to volunteers what they should and should not do for the inmates," spokesman Bill Miskell had pointed out. "There is no doubt that she knew the boundaries."

However, when the dealer who had sold Young the truck recognized her photograph, he dug out the file – which gave the cabin in Alpine, Tennessee as the address to which to send the title paperwork. The US Marshals headed for the cabin while Tennessee police issued a BOLO (be on the look-out for) on the truck. Young and Manard were out when the Marshals arrived, but by coincidence, the parking lot in Chattanooga in which they were grouping was the one that serviced the mall where the fugitives were shopping.

When Young and Manard came out of a Barnes and Noble bookstore and got in the truck, an alert marshal spotted it. Tennessee Highway Patrol and US Marshals chased the truck, with Manard determined not to be stopped. A 100 mph car chase ensued, with Manard escaping from blocking manoeuvres tried by the law officers, pulling a U-turn and trying to flee down the other carriageway. The police became increasingly concerned that an innocent was going to be hurt in the chase, and shortly after 9 p.m. they blocked the Interstate. Manard moved onto the hard shoulder and drove around them. But as he swerved back onto the highway, he lost control of the truck, shooting straight across the tarmac, missing a police car by inches. Seconds later there was a violent crash as the truck impacted with a thicket of trees.

Although Manard put up a brief struggle, he seemed more concerned that Young wasn't injured and tried to claim that she wasn't involved. They were taken straight into custody.

"The Warden and the Secretary of the Lansing Correctional Facility is obviously quite pleased that John Manard and Toby Young have been apprehended," the Department of Corrections spokesman said. "The apprehension that occurred last night is the best possible outcome. There were no serious injuries and John Manard and Toby Young are back in custody."

Young's concerns were more for her dogs. "I want to figure out how the prison dog program can go on. You know, there are some people I can figure that can run it, because it's a good program."

Manard had an extra ten years added to his sentence for Aggravated Escape from Custody; Toby Young received twenty-seven months for Aiding and Abetting an Escape, and Aiding a Felon. Young obviously genuinely believed that Manard loved her: originally in interviews, she quoted the French philosopher Pascal: "The heart has its reasons that reason knows nothing of."

Fact vs. Fiction

An account of the escape is available: *Mark West & Molly Rose* (named after the pseudonyms Manard and Young adopted) is an interesting take on events. The *Real Prison Breaks* episode, while fascinating for its use of the footage from the recapture of the fugitives, paints a picture of Manard as a ruthless killer that is at odds with the contemporary testimony, and even from its own interviews.

Sources:

http://www.safeharborprisondogs.com: the Young-free history of the dog training programme

http://www.doc.ks.gov/facilities/lcf/history: History of KSP

Associated Press, 10 March 2006: "Inmate says love of woman prompted Lansing escape"

Wall Street Journal, 9 February 2008: "The Heart Has Its Reasons"

Crime Scene KC, 13 February 2006: "John Manard: The pre-escape interview" (which links to a transcript of the full phone conversation)

Kansas City Star, 24 April 1997: "Teens get the maximum"

USA Today, 16 February 2006: "Dog trainer helped inmate escape in crate, authorities say"

Associated Press, 22 April 2006: "Fired Lansing guard says he was a scapegoat"

Associated Press, 2 May 2006: "Lansing prison guard allowed to resign"

Real Prison Breaks, Cineflix Productions, 2011

Nursing a Grudge

Some fugitives are on the run for days or weeks and concentrate on keeping themselves away from the forces of the Law; others only manage to stay on the run for part of a day, yet still can cause a great deal of distress and harm in that short time. Billy Jack Fitzmorris' one-day crime spree in April 2007 was a classic example of the latter: between 8 a.m. and 4 p.m. he took multiple hostages, robbed two banks, was involved in a high-speed chase, ended up besieged by a SWAT team – and ordered a ham and pepperoni pizza.

Fitzmorris was being held at the Northeast Ohio Correctional Center (NOCC), in Youngstown, Ohio by the US Marshals service, awaiting sentence in a drug case. NOCC is a private prison housing around two thousand inmates; at the time Fitzmorris was a resident, roughly two-thirds were housed there via a contract with the federal Bureau of Prisons, the other third were being held for the US Marshals. Run by the Corrections Corporation of America (CCA) ("America's Leader in Partnership Corrections" according to its website), NOCC is now described as a low-security prison, although originally it housed more dangerous prisoners.

In April 2005, Fitzmorris was already on parole from a state sentence for burglary when he was caught in possession of marijuana, cocaine and a stolen gun, and more drugs and another weapon were found at his home. On January 29 2007, he made a plea bargain, agreeing to plead guilty to one count of drug trafficking, and another of firearm possession. Three weeks later, he signed the following statement: "I accept full responsibility for the conduct underlying my pleas of guilty before Judge Frost. I regret becoming involved in narcotics trafficking and blame only myself. I am truly remorseful and accept complete responsibility for my actions."

Aware that he was facing anything up to forty-five years in prison – effectively a life sentence for a man of thirty-four – Fitzmorris was determined to escape, feeling that he had nothing to lose. He didn't try to get away from the NOCC though: he was rather smarter than that. Learning that prisoners who required medical treatment weren't dealt with on the premises but were taken to St Elizabeth's Hospital, he decided to create an injury, self-harming to produce a head wound that would need to be handled at the nearby medical facility.

At 8 a.m. on 2 April 2007, Fitzmorris was transported to St Elizabeth's by two private guards from NOCC. It was his second visit, after he had manufactured an excuse for treatment earlier in the week. When one of them left the treatment room on the eighth floor to heat up some food, Fitzmorris asked permission to use the lavatory. His hands were tied in front of him with plasti-cuffs, and the remaining guard couldn't see that there was a problem – at Fitzmorris' trial for the escape, the guards claimed that their supervisor hadn't warned them how dangerous their prisoner was. In the restroom, Fitzmorris was able to cut through the plasti-cuffs with a pair of nail clippers that he had smuggled inside his shoes from the prison.

His hands now free, and with a makeshift weapon, Fitzmorris overpowered the remaining guard and took his gun. The two medical technicians in the room, as well as two trainees from the CCA, were at his mercy. "Hey, I'm already looking at life, I don't have anything to lose," he told one of the technicians, Christine Jones. When the other guard returned, Fitzmorris was able to disable him. He then forced one of the guards to strip off his trousers, shirt, jacket and cap. Fitzmorris put that clothing on, placing the gun down for a few seconds, but relying on the power of fear and the constant threats he was making towards them to prevent any of his hostages from acting against him. "I don't want to hurt anybody, but I'll blow your brains out if you don't do what I say," he kept repeating. With a final warning to them not to follow him, Fitzmorris left the room, claiming that he was waiting for his brother to come and pick him up. (The US Marshals noted that there was no evidence that any of Fitzmorris' family were aware of his plans to escape that day.)

Fifty-four-year-old car mechanic Richard Orto's day then proceeded to take a turn for the worse. He was waiting in the parking lot for a space to free up so he could collect his mother from the hospital, before going for a game of golf with his son who was home on leave from the Marines. To his horror, he found a .38 calibre revolver pointed at his face. Fitzmorris told him to put the car in "park" and move over. The scared car mechanic did so, and Fitzmorris slid behind the wheel, instructing Orto to buckle up both of their seatbelts and remove the battery from his phone so it couldn't be traced. Orto was then held hostage for the next two and a half hours, as Fitzmorris drove away from Youngstown towards his mother's home in Columbus, Ohio. Unaware at the time that Fitzmorris was nowhere near the premises, officers and federal agents from local counties, as well as a search dog, all descended upon the hospital and subjected it to a room by room search.

During the drive, Richard Orto later claimed that he never looked beyond the gun that was holding him hostage. It never left Fitzmorris' hand – a hand that Orto could describe in some detail to the court, even if he didn't have a clue as to his captor's features. However, talking to the *Columbus Dispatch* shortly after the incident, Orto recalled that Fitzmorris was desperate and nervous, sweating profusely and mumbling to himself. Knowing that his life was in Fitzmorris' hands, Orto tried to engage him in conversation and offered him a cigarette. Fitzmorris accepted, and started to tell Orto how he had got into trouble with the law when he tried to make some easy money on a drug deal. The two even stopped to buy some more cigarettes, but Orto couldn't raise the alarm, as Fitzmorris carefully parked where his hostage would constantly be in his line of sight.

When they reached the suburb of Powell, Fitzmorris drove past a bank on Sawmill Parkway, then turned round and went past it again. After he did that a few times, he pulled into a parking lot and switched off the engine, taking the keys from the ignition. Ignoring Orto, who took the opportunity to undo his seatbelt and unlock his door, Fitzmorris went to the car trunk, and started putting some plastic bags that he found in there into the pockets of his jacket. He then pushed the gun down into the sleeve of his jacket and zipped it up.

Realizing that Fitzmorris was highly unlikely to be able to unzip the jacket and get the gun in the time it would take him to get away, Orto opened the passenger door and raced in a zigzag across the parking lot towards the nearest shop, a UPS despatching point. As Fitzmorris drove away, Orto ran into the store and demanded that the workers call the police. He reported what had happened as the news started to come in of a robbery at the First Citizens National Bank opposite.

Fitzmorris didn't stop at one bank robbery. A few minutes after hitting the bank in Powell, he raided the Ohio Savings Bank in Upper Arlington. Police, now aware of what he was driving from Orto's call, spotted him on a freeway west of Columbus and tried to get him to stop. He didn't, and a high-speed chase followed, heading onto the suburban streets of Hilliard.

After losing control for a moment, Fitzmorris rear-ended a stationary vehicle and wrecked his stolen car. He jumped out and headed into Norwich Street, a small side street of houses. Passing a couple of properties, he ran up the steps of a two-storey house and kicked the door in – all of this with the police following, and news-channel helicopters capturing every moment of it (the footage of the smash and his subsequent entry to the house can still be seen on YouTube).

The house belonged to John and Karen Zappitelli, who ran their accountancy business from their home. Karen and employee Geneva Herb were in the property when Fitzmorris smashed his way in. Herb raced upstairs and was able to escape from a window, rolling down the roof of the porch area and falling into the shrubbery, from where she was rescued by police officers who were quickly surrounding the building.

Karen Zappitelli was left inside with Fitzmorris. As her husband waited behind a police barricade, a three-hour siege ensued. As she recalled during evidence in a civil action she brought against the NOCC and the guards who had been overpowered by Fitzmorris, the fugitive "was totally irrational," she said. "He was a mad, irrational, panicked, desperate man . . . All I could do was stay calm. I didn't want to provoke him."

Fitzmorris dragged Zappitelli upstairs, where they spent the majority of the time during the stand-off. According to

Zappitelli, he sat behind her, with one leg wrapped around her, and one arm on her jacket. If she moved in a way that he didn't like, she would know about it instantly. He took her phone and began to make calls, talking to his family and to police negotiators, who were anxious to bring the situation to a speedy and blood-free resolution.

Although Fitzmorris worried negotiators led by Sergeant Mark Cartwright at one point when it seemed as if he was determined to go out in a blaze of glory, they were relieved when he asked for a pepperoni and ham pizza to be delivered. This was brought to the door by SWAT team officers two hours into the siege. Within half an hour, Fitzmorris had surrendered peacefully.

It was the last time he'd do anything in that way: his subsequent trials were marked by his disrespect and contempt for the judge, and the warning that he would kill the next correctional officer that he laid his hands on. Three jails refused to house him during the period before his trial for the original offences (for which he received a thirty-five-year sentence) after he damaged cell sprinklers on multiple occasions, and was caught with contraband in his shoes and shoved up his back passage – including on one occasion a brass outlet cover from a courtroom floor.

The US Marshals even made an application for him to wear a stun belt during his trial for the escape after his behaviour; if he tried anything, a hefty electrical jolt would make him unable to move. Although that motion wasn't granted, the Marshals had to restrain him during the trial after he turned over his attorney's desk, swore at the presiding judge and spit at the prosecuting attorneys. He was sentenced to a total of 960 months' imprisonment (eighty years) for the crimes during the one-day spree; prosecutors recommended that the Bureau of Prisons send him to the Supermax facility in Colorado.

The trials didn't end there. Both Richard Orto and Karen Zappitelli brought actions against the private prison company and the two guards who had let Fitzmorris escape. Both cases ended in a negotiated settlement.

Sources:

YouTube footage showing Fitzmorris entering the house in Hillard: http://www.youtube.com/watch?v=KuBJsbKT4cw

The Vindicator (local Youngstown newspaper), 5 April 2007: "Inmate's escape puts private prison under microscope"

NOCC description: http://www.cca.com/facility/northeast-ohio-correctional-center/

United States of America v. Billy Jack Fitzmorris, filed 5 May 2011: "On Appeal from the United States District Court for the Southern District of Ohio: Opinion"

The Columbus Dispatch, 8 October 2008: "Carjacker's gun remains man's most vivid memory"

The Vindicator, 3 April 2007: "Spree that began at St. E's ends with surrender"

The Columbus Dispatch, 7 April 2007: "He spent 3 hours next to a loaded .38"

The Columbus Dispatch, 16 November 2010: "Hostage ordeal left woman feeling like a 'freak,' jury told"

The Columbus Dispatch, 17 November 2010: "Woman seized by escapee ends suit"

US Attorney's Office, 23 February 2009: "Billy Jack Fitzmorris Sentenced to 80 Years Imprisonment for Escape, Bank Robberies, Gun Crimes and Hostage Taking"

10TV.com, 25 February 2009: "Bank Robber, Hostage-Taker Throws Fit In Court"

The Columbus Dispatch, 17 September 2008: "Escaped Inmate Releases Hostage In Exchange For Pizza"

The Vindicator, 24 May 2007: "Abducted man sues private prison, St. E's"

The Columbus Dispatch, 15 August 2008: "Prosecutor wants stun belt on career criminal"

Real Prison Breaks, Cineflix Productions, 2011: Christine Jones interview

PART II: UP, UP AND AWAY

A Towering Achievement

In medieval times, being sent to the Tower of London was the equivalent of hearing you were being imprisoned in Alcatraz, the Maze or a Supermax facility. People went in and only came out when the authorities dictated. Over the centuries of the Tower's use as a prison, of course, a few people did manage to escape, but far less than you might imagine. According to the official Book of Prisoners held at the Tower, between 1100 and 1916, only thirty-six people managed it, the majority of them in the sixteenth to eighteenth centuries (the period when it was most in use). The last man was an unnamed subaltern during the First World War; the first, to the shame, no doubt, of the Tower warders, was the very first prisoner held in the fortress.

Her Majesty's Royal Palace and Fortress, better known as the Tower of London, was founded straight after the Norman conquest of Britain in 1066; the White Tower was built twelve years later, and had become a prison by 1100. Its first prisoner was Ranulf Flambard, Bishop of Durham, who had been responsible, under King William II, for the construction of the wall around the Tower as well as tax collection throughout the kingdom. Flambard wasn't popular with William's brother, who succeeded him as King Henry I, and he was imprisoned in the Tower in August 1100 for extortion.

According to legend, the bishop was allowed to escape by his custodian, William de Mandeville. On the Feast of Candlemas (2 February), a flagon of wine was sent in to Flambard by friends on the outside. Inside it was a length of rope. The bishop removed the rope then generously shared the wine with his guards, and once they were drunk and asleep, he let the rope out over the wall of the Tower. He climbed down, but when he realized it wasn't quite long enough, he had to jump the remaining few feet. Once on the ground, he scurried to a boat waiting on the river Thames, which took him to a ship that transported him across the English Channel to safety with King Henry's brother Robert Curthose. Ranulf returned to England shortly afterwards, but did not end up back in the Tower.

Nearly five hundred years later, Jesuit priest Father John Gerard carried out an equally hazardous escape from the Tower, and unusually, we have a full account of the incident which Gerard himself penned a few years later. Gerard's father had been imprisoned in the Tower himself after becoming involved in one of the plots to free Mary Queen of Scots from her imprisonment at Tutbury in Staffordshire; he was able to buy his way out of prison, but would return behind bars in 1586 for his part in the Babington Plot, an attempt to remove Queen Elizabeth from the throne of England.

Gerard was brought up as a Catholic at a time when those who professed the faith in that Church were subject to persecution. He was educated on the continent, since there were limited opportunities for Catholics in England, and returned home in 1584, aged twenty, although that journey soon ended with a sojourn in Marshalsea Prison. After three years back in Europe, Gerard came back to England, charged with keeping the Catholic faith alive. Between 1588 and 1594 he acted as an undercover agent for the Society of Jesuits in England, frequently evading arrest through good fortune. He was betrayed in April 1594 but when he refused to recant his faith, or to reveal who had been assisting him, he was put in close confinement, and eventually sent to the Clink prison, south of the Thames. After he became a focal point for Catholics even while imprisoned there, the authorities moved him on 12 April 1597 to the Tower of London, where he was given a room in the Salt Tower, part of the Inner Ward of the Tower, built in the thirteenth century.

Gerard was tortured in the Tower on at least three occasions – his autobiography gives a graphic account of the manner and effects of the various schemes that they devised to try to get him to talk – but whenever he was asked to confess, he simply said, "I cannot and I will not." Once the torture stopped, Gerard was allowed to recover, and during that time he asked to be allowed to have some oranges. Although he used the peel to create rosaries, he was keeping the juice for a more clandestine purpose. He wasn't allowed a pen or paper, but was given a quill to pick his teeth. Part of this he adapted into a pen, and used the orange juice as ink. In this way, he was able to send messages to his friends outside the prison on the wrappers he was permitted for the rosaries – invisible to the naked eye, such messages could be read if the paper on which they were written was warmed up. After a few months, his warder permitted him to use a pencil and paper, and Gerard wrote innocuous lines to his friends in pencil while using the orange juice to pass on instructions. When he realized that the warder was illiterate, he stopped worrying about what he read.

The priest also began conspiring with other prisoners within the Tower of London. He knew that fellow Catholic John Arden was imprisoned in the Cradle Tower, which was opposite his cell. Arden was under sentence of death but had been kept in the Tower for over ten years. His warder, Bonner, eventually agreed to allow the two men to dine together – and, unknown to the jailer, celebrate the Mass. In his autobiography, Gerard claims that at that stage he had no thoughts of escape; he simply wanted to share communion with a fellow Catholic. But when he realized how close the Cradle Tower was to the moat that goes round the outer fortifications, he thought it might be possible to use a rope to get down to the wall beyond the moat.

Gerard wrote to two friends, John Lillie and Richard Fulwood, asking them to come to the far side of the moat on a specific night, bringing a rope with them. They would tie that to a stake, then Gerard and Arden would throw an iron ball attached to a stout thread across. Lillie and Fulwood were then to tie the cord to the free end of the rope, which the two imprisoned men could then draw up to them.

Before they went ahead with what was bound to be a risky venture, Gerard checked to see whether his warder would be willing to be bribed to allow him simply to walk out. When the warder refused point-blank, saying it would make him an outlaw and he would be hanged, Gerard reverted to the original plan.

On the chosen night, 3 October, Gerard was taken across to Arden's cell and locked in by the warder. Once the jailer had gone, the two men cut through a bolt on the inner door leading to the roof and made their way up the stairs. Fulwood, Lillie and a third man were rowing down the Thames as planned – but the plan was thwarted when a local man started chatting with the accomplices, believing they were fishermen. By the time they had got rid of him, and allowed time for him to fall asleep, it was too late for them to land and try the escape. Reluctantly deciding not to proceed, the three men started to row away but discovered to their horror that the tide had turned, forcing their boat against piles driven into the riverbed. Their boat capsized but luckily they were rescued. Once they knew their friends had been saved, Arden and Gerard returned to the cell, hoping the warder wouldn't have noticed the broken bolt.

Nearly being drowned didn't deter Lillie, who wrote to Gerard the next day saying that "with God's help we will be back tonight". Gerard was able to persuade the warder to allow him back to Arden's cell for a second consecutive night, and before he left his own room he wrote three letters, assuring the authorities that the warder wasn't complicit in the escape.

This time, things went more smoothly, at least initially. The three rescuers were able to land safely and fix the rope to a stake. The iron ball was thrown without a problem, and the cord attached to the rope. However, well-meaning interference from one of Gerard's priestly colleagues meant that the rope was much thicker than Gerard had anticipated – Father Garnet had wanted to be certain it could support Gerard's weight, but it made it much harder to pull it up.

Eventually the double rope was ready, but then they realized that it was stretching almost horizontally between the top of the not particularly tall tower and the stake on the far side. The plan had been to slide down the rope using a combination of gravity and the men's weight. That wasn't feasible – they would have to go down hand over hand, and Gerard's hands had been seriously injured during his torture.

Arden went first, and his weight made the rope even more slack. Gerard therefore had to twist his legs around the rope to make sure he didn't fall. After three or four yards going face downwards, Gerard's body swung round under its own weight and he nearly fell. It took him ages to get as far as the middle of the rope, but once he reached it, his strength deserted him. With a great deal of effort he managed to travel nearly as far as the wall, where John Lillie was waiting. Lillie grabbed his legs and pulled him over the wall, then put him safely on the ground.

The original plan had been to pull the rope away from the top of the tower, but in the end they cut it, and allowed half to dangle against the wall of the tower. That was probably wise, as otherwise it would have made a big splash as it fell in the moat, alerting the authorities. After a brief restorative drink, they headed for the boat. After rowing a good distance, they landed, and went into hiding on the outskirts of the city.

Gerard had made sure that Bonner, his warder, was given a chance to flee. Each day, the man had met with Lillie to exchange letters on Gerard's behalf, and on the morning of the escape, the warder went to the rendezvous as normal. There he was handed a letter that Gerard had written for him, which offered him safety. The warder gratefully accepted the offer, particularly after he learned from a colleague that Sir John Peyton, the Lieu-tenant of the Tower of London, was searching for him after the escape had been discovered.

The three letters Gerard had left behind were taken to the Privy Council, and although Peyton asked for permission to search the whole of London "and the liberties" for the fugitives, he was told not to bother. "You can't hope to find him," Gerard said the Lieutenant was told. "If he has friends who are prepared to do all this for him, you can count on it, they will have no diffi-culty in finding him horses and a hiding place and keeping him well out of your reach."

John Gerard stayed in England for some time, continuing his work, but a number of friends of his were implicated in the Gunpowder Plot in November 1605, what Gerard described as an attempt "to remove at a single stroke all their enemies and the principal enemies of the Catholic cause". He escaped with the help of the Spanish and Netherlands ambassadors in April 1606, and remained in Europe until his death in 1637.

The Restoration of the Monarchy in 1660, which followed the English Civil War and the rule of the Protectorate under Oliver Cromwell and then his son Richard, saw Colonel John Lambert imprisoned in the Tower. Lambert was a key figure around which the Parliamentarians hoped to rally to prevent the return of Charles Stuart, and his escape was a huge coup. He was helped by some of those who worked there, according to the account of his escape, which comes to us via the famous diarist Samuel Pepys. His diary for April 1660 relates the story, as it had been told to him.

The Royalists had taken control of the Tower in March 1660, and Sir Arthur Hazelrigge and Lambert were sent there. On 12 April, around 8 p.m., Lambert made his escape by sliding down a rope from his window, using a handkerchief on each hand to prevent friction burns. Six of his men were waiting for him and hurried him onto a barge. Meanwhile, in order to give Lambert plenty of time to make a clean getaway, his bed maker got into his bed and put on his nightcap. When the warder came round to lock the door for the night, the curtains were already drawn, and the woman gave a brief reply when the warder wished Lambert a good night's sleep. The following morning, the warder was horrified to see the woman there: "In the name of God, Joan, what makes you here?" he demanded. "Where is my Lord Lambert?" She told him that Lambert was gone, but she could not tell where. Hardly surprisingly, Joan was incarcerated.

Lambert was free for less than a fortnight: his attempt to foment an uprising collapsed, and he was returned to the Tower on 22 April. He didn't give up easily: according to one report, after he tried to escape for a second time, he was caught by the sentries on guard and confined in irons. That still didn't quench his fire: in March 1661, it was reported that he had consulted an astrologer over whether to try to escape or not. As a result, he was transferred to Castle Cornet in Guernsey in November 1661, and then to St Nicholas Island off Plymouth, where he died in 1684.

The other escape from the Tower of London that is regularly cited as one of the most audacious tried from any prison was that of William Maxwell, Fifth Earl of Nithsdale, who was spirited out of the grounds by his wife Winifred, Lady Nithsdale after all her petitions to King and Parliament had come to nothing in the aftermath of the Jacobite rebellion of 1715. As with

Father John Gerard's exploits, a full contemporary account of the escape exists, courtesy of a letter written by Lady Nithsdale to her sister, who was Abbess of the English Augustine nuns at Bruges. This was faithfully reproduced by John Burke in his 1836 history of "the Commoners of Great Britain and Ireland", and is as detailed as any modern exposé would be.

Following the accession to the throne in 1714 of a Hanoverian Protestant king, George I, there was considerable uprest, and a full-scale uprising in Scotland (known subsequently as The Fifteen). This led to the Battle of Preston in November 1715, at the end of which 1468 Jacobites were taken prisoner, including 463 Englishmen, among them George Seton, Fifth Earl of Winton, and the Earl of Nithsdale. Both noblemen were sentenced to death and sent to the Tower of London.

Three months after the battle, Nithsdale escaped from the Tower. His wife had travelled down from Scotland to be with him, and demonstrated her determination from the start: the roads were blocked with snow, so the stagecoach couldn't go beyond York. Accompanied by her maid, she therefore rode down on horseback, even though the snow was often deeper than the horses' waists.

Arriving in London, she wasted no time. She asked to be allowed to visit her husband, but was told that this would only be possible if she agreed to be confined with him. Knowing that that would completely hinder her from organizing either his pardoning or his escape, she refused, but managed to bribe her way into the Tower most days to see him.

Lord Nithsdale was keen that his wife petition the king for him to be pardoned, and even though she thought it would serve no purpose, she agreed. George I wanted nothing to do with her: he ignored her as she entreated him to accept her petition, but she grabbed hold of the skirts of his coat, and was pulled along with him from one state room to the next before one of his servants grabbed her around the waist, and the other removed her hand from the king's person. As she suspected, even once it had been received, the petition didn't do any good, and when news of the way George had treated her began to spread, the king's reputation suffered – and thus made him even less well disposed towards the Nithsdale family.

It quickly became clear to Lady Nithsdale that the king and the lords intended to make an example of her husband, and she tried to make him understand that the only way to avoid the executioner's axe was to escape from the Tower. Even as she went through the motions of trying to persuade the lords to intercede with the king to pardon the prisoners, she was putting her plan into action.

By the third week of February, she was a regular visitor at the Tower, and on Thursday 22, she came across in the evening, full of bonhomie and cheer, telling the guards that she was there to pass on good news to the prisoners: the lords had agreed to intercede with the king. This was true, to an extent: they had indeed passed such a motion, but with strings attached that Lady Nithsdale knew her husband couldn't (and shouldn't) accept.

Lord Nithsdale was scheduled to die on the morning of 24 February. The morning before, Lady Nithsdale made sure that everything was set up to spirit her husband out of the country if she could successfully get him out of the Tower. That evening, she pressed two women into service: the lady with whom she lodged, Mrs Mills, and Hilton, a friend of her servant Evans. The tall and slim Miss Hilton wore two riding hoods on their way into the Tower: the second was to be worn later by Mrs Mills, who, thanks to her advanced pregnancy, was very similar to Lord Nithsdale in stature. The plan was simple: Lord Niths-dale would exit the Tower wearing Mrs Mills' riding hood, and with any luck, the guards wouldn't look too closely at the "pregnant woman" leaving.

Lady Nithsdale did her best to ensure the guards were confused. The various women with her came in and out as required to bring the garments in, and Lady Nithsdale addressed them loudly by name. She then adjusted her husband's appearance, using items which she had brought into the Tower on previous occasions. She painted his eyebrows to match those of Mrs Mills, and gave him a wig of similar-coloured hair. Since he hadn't shaved, she rouged his cheeks to disguise his facial hair.

Timing was critical. Lady Nithsdale knew full well that her disguise wouldn't stand up to much examination, so she needed to get her husband past the guards as dusk was falling, but before the candles were lit. As soon as he was ready, she led him out of his room, as he dabbed a handkerchief at his eyes, pretending to be the upset Mrs Mills going off on an errand. She carefully walked in front of him, in case his masculine gait gave away the deception to the guards, and was relieved when she could pass him over to her maid Evans, who was waiting at the foot of the stairs. Evans was supposed to hand him over to Mr Mills, but he panicked when he saw Lord Nithsdale, so Evans used her own judgement and hid the fugitive with some friends.

Meanwhile, Lady Nithsdale had returned to her husband's cell, apparently waiting for her friend to return after running the errand. She kept up a dialogue with herself, imitating her husband's voice, then once it became clear that Evans and Lord Nithsdale had got away, she stood in the doorway of the cell and said loudly that she would have to go and sort out the situation that had arisen, but hopefully would return to see him later that evening. She did her best to ensure that the escape wouldn't be noticed by pulling the string of the latch through so the door could only be opened from the inside, and told her husband's servant not to disturb him until he called.

Lady Nithsdale then went by a roundabout route to the house of her friend, the Duchess of Montrose (her description of using coaches and hired sedan chairs to throw people off her scent could come from a spy thriller) to find out what the reaction to the escape was. King George was understandably furious but Lady Nithsdale couldn't care – she was reunited with her husband in a small attic room where they stayed until he could be smuggled out by the Venetian Ambassador. She then stayed in England until she had an opportunity to sort out her affairs, so her son wouldn't suffer, making a perilous trek up to Scotland to retrieve various papers from her home.

This added insult to injury as far as the king was concerned. He issued orders to have her arrested, claiming that she "had given him more trouble and anxiety than any other woman in Europe". Realizing that she had pushed things as far as she dared, Lady Nithsdale departed for Europe. She and her husband lived in poverty in Rome at the court of the Stuart Pretender for the rest of their lives.

* * *

George Seton, Fifth Earl of Winton, apparently also escaped from the Tower, although he is not included in the list of escapees in the Tower's official records. According to Sir Walter Scott, he "made good use of his mechanical skill, sawing through with great ingenuity the bars of the windows of his prison, through which he made his escape". He too ended up in Rome.

The most recent "escape" was perhaps the most casual. According to the report in the *Evening Post* in 1919, a subaltern imprisoned there told a court martial that he simply walked out one evening and went to the West End of London for a good dinner. However, when he returned to the Tower, the gates were shut, so he came back the next morning. "It was not done in the Jack Sheppard kind of way," the officer's solicitor told the court, "but was a boyish prank. Moreover it was of benefit to the authorities by calling attention to the slackness there."

Maybe it was a good thing that the Tower ceased to be used as a prison shortly afterwards!

Sources:

Gower, Ronald Charles Sutherland: *The Tower of London volume 2* (George Bell, 1901, scanned by Forgotten Books)

Farr, David: *John Lambert, Parliamentary Soldier and Cromwellian Major-General, 1619-1684* (Boydell Press, 2003)

Morris, John: *The Life of Father John Gerard, of the Society of Jesus* (Burns and Dates, reprinted by BiblioBazaar, 2010)

Gerard, John translated by Philip Caraman, S.J. *The Autobiography of a Hunted Priest* (Ignatius Press, 2012)

Burke, John: *A Genealogical and Heraldic History of the Commoners of Great Britain and Northern Ireland* (Colburn, 1836)

Evening Post, 5 July 1919: "Escape from the Tower"

A Heavenly Breakout

Most of the prison breaks featured in this book required assistance from the outside in order to be successful. Whether it's someone throwing a hacksaw over the prison walls to a predetermined spot, or being ready with a getaway car, a change of clothing and fake papers, the majority of escapees need help to complete their tasks. Sometimes of course that help is given unwittingly, or under coercion. On other occasions, it can take a more supernatural form.

The escape of Juan de Yepes Alvarez, better known to worshippers of the Roman Catholic Church as St John of the Cross, from the Carmelite monastery in Toledo, Spain has been ascribed to the assistance of the Virgin Mary, who appeared to the future saint in a dream. Whether you believe he had divine assistance, or was just extremely lucky, his flight was certainly extraordinary – as witnesses at the time would point out, no ordinary person should have been able to use the route that he took.

Brought up as a devout Catholic, young Juan entered the Carmelite Order in 1563 aged just twenty-one, and was ordained priest after four years. He was asked by Theresa of Avila to assist her attempts to reform the Order, and they worked together establishing a much more strict rule in their new houses across Spain. They became known as the "Discalced" (the "unshoed") and became extremely unpopular with the Calced Carmelites, who still held sway. At a chapter meeting in May 1575, it was noted that "[b]ecause there are still some, disobedient, rebellious and contumacious, commonly called discalced friars, who against the patent letters and statutes of the prior general have lived and do live outside of the province of Old Castile . . . and who, excusing themselves with fallacies, cavilling, and misrepresentations, have been unwilling humbly to accept the mandates and letters of the prior general, it shall be intimated to the said discalced Carmelites, under apostolic penalties and censures, including, if necessary, the aid of the secular arm, that they shall submit with the space of three days, and if they resist they shall be severely punished."

At the same time, there was great suspicion in Spain generally of the changes within the Church. The Inquisition had been established to encourage Jews and Moslems to convert to Christianity, or leave Spain, and those in the "new" movements within the Church were open to betrayal and denunciation to the Inquisition, leading in many cases to death sentences.

Although he tried to steer clear of the politics within the Church, Fray Juan de Santo Matia, as he was now known, was unable to keep out completely, and on 2 December 1577, he was arrested and taken to Toledo. He refused to renounce the way of life established by Theresa of Avila, and a result, was declared contumacious and a rebel. This meant that he was excommunicated from the Church, not allowed to say or receive the Mass, and locked up for much of the time in a tiny room, about six feet wide and ten feet long, with only a tiny slit to allow air and light in. From time to time he would be allowed out, only to receive a haranguing from the ministers, described as "a little friar, scarcely good enough to be a convent porter!" and told that "he seeks to reform others when he needs to reform himself". This would be accompanied by scourging with a cane by other friars while the Miserere was said – regarded as the most degrading and severest punishment that could be doled out to a friar. Juan refused to retract his views, and his silence only served to rile his captors further.

Kept in filthy conditions, Juan's health began to deteriorate, and he suffered from dysentery. Throughout this, though, he composed poetry in his mind (and to many, he is still regarded as the Poet Laureate of Spain), which examined his faith and the way of the Cross. After about six months, a change of jailer gave him a few benefits, including a clean tunic – the old one had become encrusted with blood from the beatings that he endured – and a pen and paper, on which he began to write his poems.

In the heat of summer, Juan began to wonder if he would survive, and hoped that he might have the opportunity to say

Mass for the Feast of the Virgin Mary (15 August). He was told in no uncertain terms by the prior of the monastery the night before that that was not going to happen on his watch. By this stage, Juan was apparently so frail that he couldn't rouse himself from the floor, despite an encouraging kick from the prior.

Yet a couple of days later, he escaped. According to his first biographer, writing early in the seventeenth century, he had been visited earlier in the month during the night, by a vision of the Virgin Mary, who told him that his trials would soon be over, and he would be leaving the prison. Depending on which version you read, this either simply gave him the moral strength to look around for an escape route, or the Virgin actually put a vision in his mind's eye of the way to go. It seems likely though that Juan took advantage of the change of jailer, who allowed him some latitude to leave his cell, and was able to calculate that he would be able to let himself down from a window over the city wall to within ten feet of the top of the wall's battlements using the rugs the jailer had provided, cut into strips. He would need to be able to get out of his cell, and he used the time when his door was left open to work at the metal staples that secured it to the wall.

It is worth noting that Juan himself never claimed that he received a vision: he told the nuns who assisted him later that he had received "help, consolation and inner impulses" from Christ and the Virgin after he prayed for aid for his escape.

Around 2 o'clock on the morning of 16 August 1578, Juan guessed that the visiting friars who had been billeted in the guest room next to his cell were now asleep. However, when he pushed at the door, and the screws holding it padlocked shut came away from the wall, the clatter of the padlock woke them. Juan waited until they fell asleep again, and then headed out to the gallery that contained the vital window.

He attached his makeshift rope to a joist, and began to lower himself down into the darkness, and let himself fall, trusting that he would be safe. He landed on a grass embankment, a mere couple of feet away from a sheer drop down to the rocks. Giving chase to a dog led him down into a lower courtyard, and he managed to get over the wall, into an alleyway in the city. (He later couldn't recall how he had been able to climb over the wall – he felt as if he was suddenly taken up and over the obstacle.)

Juan rested quietly for a few minutes, regaining his strength, hiding in a darkened doorway to avoid any passers-by. As the angelus rang, at 5 a.m., he made his way to the convent of St Joseph, which housed an order of Discalced nuns. Although a friar was not usually permitted to enter the convent, a quick-thinking member of the order said that she was too ill to go to the confessional, which meant that Fray Juan could be allowed in to hear her confession. The nuns then hid Juan from the search parties from the monastery, accompanied by constables, who tried to turn the place upside down looking for the missing friar. That night, he was taken to a hospital in Santa Cruz.

Luck, or divine intervention, certainly played its part in Juan's escape. As the warders discovered the next morning, the "rope" down which he had lowered himself was formed of tiny strips, which shouldn't have been able to bear his weight. And rather more pertinently, the joist to which he had attached the rope was not secured at either end, and certainly should have come loose when he began his escape. His jailor, Juan de Santa-Maria, said: "As I am certain he could not escape by any other way, I regard his flight as miraculous, and ordained by Our Lord, in order that he might help the reform of the Discalced. And, although I was deprived of my rights and privileges for some days, still, in spite of all, I was glad that he had escaped, and so were some other religious, because we had compassion on him, seeing him suffer with so much courage."

Fray Juan continued to serve as a Discalced Carmelite; he died in 1591 aged forty-nine. He was declared a saint in 1726, with his two key pieces of writing, *The Spiritual Canticle* and *The Dark Night of the Soul*, regarded as some of the best pieces of Spanish poetry and mystical theology.

Sources:

Kavanaugh, Kieran: *John of the Cross: Selected Writings* (Paulist Press International, 1987)

Moore, Thomas: "Our Lady and Saint John of the Cross" www.ourgardenofcarmel.org

Brenan, Gerald: *St John of the Cross; His Life and Poetry* (Cambridge University Press, 1975)

Tunnelling Out of the Attic

There are few people who won't recognize the name of Casanova – the great lover who cut a swathe through the willing women of Venice and its environs in the eighteenth century. Thanks to highly romanticized screen versions of Casanova's already embellished memoirs, he has gained a reputation as a swashbuckling, hard-living, hero. The reality was probably rather more mundane, but there is plenty of evidence from other sources to back up at least one of his more outlandish stories: his escape from the dreaded Leads prison cells at the Doge's Palace in Venice. He is an inspiration to any prisoners who get so tantalizingly close to escape but are thwarted at the last moment; that didn't just happen to Casanova once – he faced such problems twice, and in the end only surmounted them with what he made out to be divine intervention.

Giacomo Girolamo Casanova de Seingalt was born in Venice in 1725, and before his twenty-first birthday had enjoyed a brief career in both the Church and the military, neither of which particularly suited him. A more hedonistic lifestyle, gambling, womanizing and otherwise enjoying himself, was far more to his liking, but inevitably along the way, he made enemies among those in authority, and in July 1755, it became clear that he was about to be arrested. Certain that he had done nothing wrong, Casanova refused to flee Venice, but the next morning, agents of the presiding Tribunal came for him, using books of incantations of magic as their evidence against him.

Casanova was imprisoned in the Leads, the lofts of the ducal palace, which took their name from the huge sheets of lead with which the roof was covered. The only way in or out was by the gates of the palace, the prison buildings, and the bridge connecting the palace to the cells, known as the Bridge of Sighs since it was the last sight of the outside world that prisoners would have before their sentences began. He was kept in one of the cells directly above the Inquisitors' Hall, and only very occasionally allowed out to walk around the rest of the attic area. Without trial, Casanova was sentenced to serve five years in this apparently unescapable prison, without even a bed initially, just an armchair.

During one of his brief trips out into the attic, he examined the contents of a chest, and found a piece of polished black marble, about an inch thick, 6 inches long and 3 inches broad, which he hid, anticipating being able to find a use for it. A little later, he found an 18-inch-long iron bar. With saliva acting instead of oil to lubricate the work, he sharpened the bar into an 8-pointed dagger which he hid within his armchair. However, he knew that if he tried to break through the door of his cell, he would have to deal with at least three guards, and he was unlikely to succeed. So Casanova decided to tunnel his way out of an attic room!

His plan was admirably simple: he would dig down to the ceiling of the room beneath him, then on the night he broke through, he would use his sheets as a rope to lower himself down, then hide under a table until the doors were opened the next morning. At that point, he would make a dash for freedom, using his dagger as a weapon to fend off any sentries.

Keeping the work from discovery was the first problem. Casanova had previously made a fuss about the state of the cell, and his jailer, Lawrence, now swept out the room to rid it of fleas each day. Once sufficient progress had been made with the hole, it would be obvious to anyone looking at their feet when the floor was swept, so Casanova carried out an elaborate charade to stop the sweeping, claiming that the disturbance of the dust made him ill. However, before he could start work properly, another prisoner was brought in to share his cell, who insisted on the cell being swept, so there was a further two-month delay before he got under way.

Once he was alone, Casanova was able to work quite speedily, digging away at the deal beam, removing the debris in a napkin and hiding it in the garret, and then placing his bed over the ever-increasing hole. He got through three layers of wood without encountering too many more difficulties, but then hit a layer of marble pebbling. He used a bottle of strong vinegar to weaken the cement that bound the marble together, and was able to chip through it before reaching the final board.

Casanova was on the point of breaking through that last obstacle when a new cellmate was brought in to share his small room, although luckily he was only there for a week. By 23 August, Casanova had completed his task, and decided that he would make his move four days later when he knew that the room adjoining the Inquisitors' Hall would also be empty.

On 25 August, two days before he intended to escape, Casanova was moved to a new cell which his jailer thought he would prefer, since it had access to more light, something Casanova had complained about previously. The young lord couldn't believe his bad luck – but at least his armchair, with his dagger still hidden inside, was brought along to his new lodgings. He then had a tense two-hour wait while his jailer went to fetch his other belongings, and, of course, found the hole in the floor when he moved the bed. Although his jailer threatened him, Casanova said that he would tell the authorities that he had received the implements to make the hole from the jailer unless he kept quiet. After a few days, the jailer accepted the situation.

It was clear to Casanova that he wouldn't be allowed to try the same trick twice, and an examination of his surroundings made him realize that the only way out of this cell would be through the ceiling. Luck smiled on the young man once more: the jailer offered to exchange books for him with another prisoner. Using ink made from mulberries, Casanova started a correspondence with Marin Balbi, a portly monk, incarcerated in the cell next door; while Casanova didn't trust Balbi's discretion, he reasoned that he had little choice but to involve him in the escape.

The new plan was for Balbi to break through the ceiling of his own cell, go up into the eaves, and then break through the ceiling of Casanova's cell from above. He could hide the hole in his cell behind pictures of saints that he would ask the jailer to obtain (shades of *The Shawshank Redemption!*) The only snag: the dagger was still in Casanova's cell. A plate of pasta became an essential part of Casanova's plan to pass it across.

Casanova had originally thought of hiding the implement inside a large Bible and asking the jailer to give the book to the monk. However, the dagger was a couple of inches too long, and stuck out either side of the binding. Casanova therefore asked permission to make a dish of pasta for his fellow prisoner as thanks for the books he was lending him, and borrowed a huge dish from the jailer to put it in. That evening, the jailer duly carried the pasta dish through, balanced on top of the bible, not noticing the bar sticking out from either end of the book.

Balbi broke through the ceiling in eight days, covering the hole with a picture of a saint pasted up with breadcrumbs. It took him eight more days to get through a wall that separated the two cells and within a couple of days, was nearly through the ceiling of Casanova's cell. All that remained was to remove the final piece of board, hoist Casanova up, and then the pair, along with Balbi's cellmate if he wanted to join them, could make a hole in the roof of the ducal palace. From there, Casanova was happy to rely on chance to find a way to get to the ground safely.

But once again Casanova's planning was derailed. The afternoon before they were due to escape, a new cellmate, Soradici, was brought into Casanova's cell. After a few days, during which Soradici had quickly proved himself untrustworthy, Casanova decided to play on the other man's fears, and persuaded him that he had received a vision of the Virgin Mary. An angel was going to rescue Casanova from the cell in the next few days and he would take Soradici with him if he promised to give up spying. Soradici was gullible enough to fall for this story, particularly once he heard the sound of Balbi breaking through the ceiling as he prepared for the escape. Casanova was able to cow him into submission, threatening him with strangulation if he breathed any word of the escape attempt to their jailer.

Casanova had decided to make his breakout on All Hallows Eve, when he knew that the Inquisitors wouldn't be sitting, and therefore there was no chance of any new prisoners being brought either into his or Balbi's cell. He instructed Balbi to make the final breakthrough at midday, and warned Soradici that he would be required to cut the beards of both Casanova and the angel. At noon exactly, Balbi entered the cell as if by divine intervention, through the ceiling. The awe-struck Soradici made the necessary adjustment to the two men's beards, then Casanova went to see if Balbi's cellmate was going to join them. It was obvious that the old man wouldn't be able to deal with the rigours of the climb, so he agreed to remain in his cell, praying for the escapees.

After reconnoitring the roof space, and confirming that it would be easy to get out onto the roof itself, Casanova then spent four hours cutting up sheets and blankets, and threading them together to form ropes – he claimed that he was able to create 100 fathoms (600 feet) from everything in the cell, although 100 feet seems more likely. He and Balbi then made the hole in the roof, and levered the sheet of lead out of the way, only to discover that the moon was bright enough to cast shadows. If they went straightaway, they would easily be seen from St Mark's Square.

It was at this point that Balbi realized that for all of Casanova's posturing, the young nobleman really didn't have much of a clue how to proceed once they were on the roof, and both he and his cellmate tried to persuade Casanova to give up the escape. Soradici lost what little courage he had during this time, and elected not to join the other two as they crossed the rooftops, particularly as a fog was descending. Casanova and Balbi divided the rope and parcels containing their personal belongings, between them, and then, at 11 p.m., they went out onto the roof.

Once they were on the exterior of the ducal palace, Soradici pulled the lead sheet back into place. The two escapees inched their way on hands and knees across more than a dozen lead sheets, which were treacherous in the night air, up onto the apex of the roof. Casanova left Balbi sitting there while he went to find somewhere to tie the rope, so they could let themselves down to ground level.

The problem was that nothing presented itself, and Casanova was on the verge of giving up when he spotted a light in a garret room. Sliding down the roof to the level of the room, he saw a window with a grate protecting it. As midnight struck, his resolve was hardened, and he used his handy dagger to remove the grate. He then lowered Balbi into the room, but with nowhere to tie the rope to, was unable to let himself down – and the room was far too high for him to risk jumping to the floor. Another examination of his surroundings produced a 12-foot ladder, which, after some manhandling, he was able to manoeuvre into the room and use to reach the floor.

After Casanova grabbed a quick power nap to regain his strength, the two men examined their new surroundings, and discovered that they were in the state archives. At 5 a.m., no one else was stirring, and they were quickly able to descend to the ducal chancery, which looked out over the little courtyards around St Mark's Square. They broke through the door of the chancery, but were defeated by the main door leading to the grand staircase.

Casanova got changed back into his best clothes, in which he had been arrested the year before, but was spotted when he looked out of the window. The gatekeeper opened up the room, thinking he'd locked someone in, and Casanova and Balbi barged past him, and ran for the canal, where they hailed a gondola, and loudly stated their destination was Fusina. As soon as they were under way, Casanova apparently changed his mind, and asked to go to Mestre, in the opposite direction.

When they reached Mestre, Casanova hired a coach to take him to Trevisa, only to discover that Balbi had disappeared into a café for a cup of hot chocolate! The delay retrieving him meant that Casanova was accosted by an old acquaintance who he was convinced would give him up to the authorities. He tried to bluff that he had been released but when the man refused to listen, Casanova took him out of sight, and prepared to kill him. Luckily for both of them, the man wriggled out of Casanova's grasp and ran for the hills.

Balbi was determined to stay with Casanova, regarding their fates as linked. Casanova knew full well that any search would be for the pair of them together, since they made an unusual, and very distinctive, combination. He therefore told Balbi to make his own way to an agreed rendezvous, and when the monk initially refused, started to dig a hole in the ground. After working for fifteen minutes, he casually pointed out to Balbi that he should make his peace with God, as he was about to bury him there, dead or alive. Balbi took the hint and the two men made their separate ways across country. Casanova was eventually able to rid himself of Balbi after arranging a new billet for him in Bologna. Balbi disgraced himself there, was recaptured, spent two further years in the Leads, and was then returned to his monastic order. Eventually the Pope released him from his monastic vow, and he lived it up in Venice for the rest of his life.

Casanova reached Paris in January 1757, and had to regale audiences with the tale of his escape. He was finally able to return to Venice in September 1774 after he carried out a few pieces of commercial espionage for the Inquisitors, but life wasn't the same for him. He died in Bohemia in 1798.

Sources:

Casanova, Giacomo (translated by Arthur Machen): *The Memoirs of Jacques Casanova de Seingalt 1725–1798* (The University of Adelaide Library, 2012)

Kelly, Ian: *Casanova: Actor, Lover, Priest, Spy* (Tarcher, 2011)

The Prison Breaker

While many convicts might wish to become known by this nick-name, it was first awarded to one of the most daring characters featured in this volume: Jack Sheppard. Although he was only twenty-two when he was hanged at Tyburn in London on 16 November 1724, he left behind a legacy of prison breaks, immortalized in print by no less an author than Robinson Crusoe and Moll Flanders creator Daniel Defoe, and the subject of a sermon which has been passed down the centuries in which the details of his escape were used as an analogy for living a godly life. His exploits inspired John Gay's *The Beggar's Opera*, which itself became the basis of *The Threepenny Opera*, and a novel by William Harrison Ainsworth that on its first publication outsold Dickens' *Oliver Twist*. During his lifetime, he captured the imagination of early eighteenth-century London, and ironi-cally may even have lost a chance at cheating the hangman one more time because of the mob's affection for him.

Most of the information we have on Sheppard derives from the *Newgate Calendar*, a collection of biographical accounts that started off as a monthly bulletin of executions produced by the Keeper of Newgate Prison in London, but which developed into a highly readable anthology of tales from the cells. It may not necessarily have always been accurate – various pieces of editorializing in its pages suggest that it often followed the maxim attributed to Mark Twain: "Never let the truth get in the way of a good story" – but it provided vicarious thrills for eight-eenth and early nineteenth century audiences. In the case of Sheppard it certainly borrowed material from the prison break-er's own ghost-written account, to the extent that modern editions often directly quote Sheppard's text in place of those parts of the *Calendar*.

Of course, Jack Sheppard wasn't the only person to try to escape from Newgate, although he was definitely the most famous. In 1450, one keeper, Alexander Manning, was jailed himself after being found guilty of negligent custody of his prisoners over the previous years, and allowing a mutiny to take place.

In the aftermath of the 1715 rebellion, one of the Jacobites by the name of Barlow had tried to get out from the Red Room that Sheppard would break into during his own escape, "close-shaved and neatly dressed in female clothes", according to the *Calendar*, with a crowd of women surrounding him. He got as far as the keepers' lodge before one of the warders grew suspicious and threw him to the ground. Barlow tried to keep up the pretence, as the women told the prison officer off for such behaviour, and might have got away with it if the Special Commissioner who was dealing with the rebels hadn't arrived at that moment. Carleton Smith wouldn't take the bribe that Barlow offered, and ensured that he was returned to the cells. Barlow was hanged around the same time that Sheppard was gaining a reputation for himself.

Born in 1702, Jack Sheppard's path to a criminal career began about six years after his father died, when he and his brother were very young. Sheppard began drinking in the Black Lion alehouse in Drury Lane, and became very close to some of the prostitutes who frequented the pub, including Elizabeth Lyon, also known as Edgworth Bess, who would eventually become commonly regarded as his wife, and Polly Maggot. Sheppard had been apprenticed as a carpenter, and although he initially behaved honestly, after a time he began stealing from his workplaces, and then branched out into housebreaking. He eventually quarrelled with his master, and became a freelance carpenter, casing places by day and robbing them by night. Not long after he carried out a raid in Mayfair, Lyon was arrested, and placed in the roundhouse at St Giles; when he was refused entry to visit her, Sheppard knocked down the beadle in charge, smashed the door and carried her away.

It wasn't that long before Sheppard was a guest of the roundhouse himself. His brother Tom was also a thief, and the pair had teamed up to carry out various robberies. When

Tom was arrested, he tried to implicate his brother and Lyon, but they couldn't be found. Sheppard was betrayed by another of his companions, James Sykes, who got Jack drunk and then handed him over to the police. Sheppard didn't remain a prisoner for long; after a brief interrogation, he was sent to the roundhouse, but broke through the roof and escaped that night.

His second escape was a little trickier. Within a few days of absconding from the St Giles Roundhouse, Sheppard found himself in the one at St Ann's, in Soho, after a pickpocketing in Leicester Fields (modern Leicester Square) went wrong. Lyon came to visit him, was recognized as his accomplice and arrested. The pair of them were sent to New Prison in Clerkenwell by the magistrates, and because they were believed to be married, they were allowed to share a room, known as the Newgate Ward (which has led to some confusion over the years; this wasn't part of Newgate Prison.)

Sheppard and Lyon were visited by various friends over the next few days, who were able to provide them with some necessary tools. Early one morning, Sheppard filed off his chains, then made a hole in the prison wall. The Newgate Ward was on an upper storey, and was some 25 feet above the ground. Sheppard removed an iron bar and a wooden one from the window, then tied a blanket and sheet together and fixed them to one of the remaining bars. Sheppard lowered Lyon down to the ground, then climbed down the makeshift rope himself, only to find themselves still trapped in the yard, with a 22-foot-high wall in front of them. However, Sheppard was undeterred and the two of them clambered over the gate, using the locks and bolts as hand and foot holds.

Jack Sheppard continued working as a thief but he was making enemies, notably Jonathan Wild, who became annoyed when Sheppard refused to fence his stolen goods through him. Determined to curb the younger man, but unable to lay his hands on him, Wild plied Elizabeth Lyon with brandy to make her give up Sheppard's address. This she did, and he was arrested and indicted at the Old Bailey on several charges of robbery. On 30 August 1724, he was sentenced to death and imprisoned in the old jail of Newgate to await sentence.

Newgate Jail had been rebuilt in 1672 following its destruction in the Great Fire of London six years earlier. One of the unusual features was the area around the cells holding the condemned prisoners: the inmates came down a dark passage to a hatch, which had large iron spikes preventing anyone from passing through. Once again, outside friends were able to smuggle tools in to Sheppard, and he cut through one of the spikes so that it barely remained in position. On the day that the warrant was sent for Sheppard's execution, Lyon and Polly Maggot went to visit him. They distracted the guards as he broke through the final piece of the spike, leaving a hole wide enough that he could wiggle through. The two women quickly dressed him in a nightshirt they had brought to disguise the irons he was wearing, and hurried him out of the prison. Some of the other convicts tried to follow him, but the prison officers saw the gap in the hatch and prevented any other escapes. Sheppard headed for the waterfront at Black-Fryers-Stairs (Blackfriars), and headed upriver to the Horse Ferry at Westminster.

Sheppard realized that London was perhaps becoming too dangerous: Wild and his men would be looking for him, as would the officers of the law. He and a friend, William Page, headed up to Warnden in Northamptonshire for a few days to stay with Page's family. However they weren't made welcome, and within the week they had returned to London. On Friday 4 September, the day he was due to hang, Sheppard cheekily wrote a letter that was printed in *The Daily Journal*, addressed to "Jack Ketch", the popular nickname for the hangman, saying that he was drinking a toast to his health, and wishing his friends who had hanged, a "bon repo" – a good sleep.

Jack was quite right: he should have stayed away from London, and he would have been well advised to keep out of trouble when he did return. However, old habits died hard: the day after his return from Northamptonshire, he and Page stole three watches from a shop in Fleet Street. When he tried to fence them, he was advised to lay low, and the two men headed up to Finchley, north of London. However someone informed on them to the Newgate prison turnkeys, and on 10 September they were arrested. Page surrendered immediately; Sheppard tried to make a run for it, but faced with armed prison officers, gave up, begging them not to shoot him on the spot. He was taken back to Newgate, and this time the warders were taking no chances. He was put back into a portion of the condemned hold known as the Castle, where a heavy pair of irons was wrapped around him, and he was then chained to a staple fixed in the floor.

Such trifling inconveniences weren't going to stop Jack Sheppard from escaping from Newgate. If he could get hold of the right tools, he was convinced that he could get out of his chains and away from the prison. Unfortunately, the guards were keeping a close eye on him: every visitor was carefully watched to make sure that they didn't try to pass him anything he could use. On one occasion when he was left on his own, he spotted a small nail within reach, and used that to pick the horse padlock that was used to fix the chain to the staple in the floor. He used the freedom initially simply to stretch his legs, and to have a chance to sleep properly, rather than fixed to the chair, but one day his keepers came back in to check on him before he had a chance to get back into position. After he showed the jailers the ease with which he had picked the lock, they added a pair of handcuffs to his restraints. Sheppard desperately begged them not to do so, and even his former master, from whom he had stolen some of the items for which he was going to be hanged, tried to persuade them not to handcuff him.

It was all an act: Sheppard knew full well that he could slip the handcuffs without any difficulty, but he wanted to lull the keepers into a false sense of security. Within minutes of them leaving him, he had removed the cuffs but made sure that they were always on when he was being monitored. He even chafed the skin around his wrist to make it look as if he had been trying to remove them, in an effort to gain sympathy from his jailers, but to no avail (although some of his visitors took pity and gave him money).

On Wednesday 14 October, the sessions began once more, and that morning there was an uproar when Jonathan Wild's throat was cut in the courtroom by one of Sheppard's fellow thieves, Blueskin Blake. Much to the annoyance of many, including Sheppard, Wild wasn't killed, but was seriously injured, and in the aftermath of the attack, the attention of the keepers at Newgate was diverted. This made it an ideal time for Jack Sheppard to carry out his escape.

On the afternoon of 15 October, around 3 p.m., Sheppard slipped his handcuffs and then broke a link in the chain holding him to the floor. He pulled the shackles further up his legs so they wouldn't impede his progress, then made a hole in the chimney of the room. From there he was able to pull out an iron bar, about two and a half feet long, and an inch square. With that he broke through the ceiling of the Castle, and pulled himself up into the Red Room, which had been used years before to hold prisoners captured after the Battle of Preston during the 1715 Rebellion. The room and its doors hadn't been used in seven years, so Sheppard had to remove a nut from the lock before he could go further.

In the Red Room, he also found a large nail on the floor, which became very useful as he progressed through the upper floors of Newgate prison. He had to break through the wall to get at the bolt that held the door to the chapel fastened, but was lucky that no one imprisoned nearby heard him. In the chapel, he broke off one of the iron spikes, and proceeded to attack the door between the chapel and the leads (the area of the roof covered by lead sheets). The next door was very securely fastened with a heavy lock, and although he was disheartened for a few minutes, he finally regained his composure and set to work. Between the nail and the spike, he made short shrift of the padlock, and got through it.

It had taken him five hours to get this far, and he heard the clock at St Sepulchre's chime eight as he broke through yet another door, which had more bolts, bars and locks than any of its predecessors. Initially he tried to break through the lock, but when that proved impossible, he attacked the door itself – and the lock came away from the wall.

Sheppard was now one door away from the outside; the Newgate authorities didn't think anyone could get this far without permission, so it was only bolted on the inside. It was the work of a second for Sheppard to climb through it, out onto the roof. He clambered up the roof and looked over the wall, working out where his best exit point would be. The shops outside the prison were still open, so he had to be especially careful that he didn't screw up the escape at this late stage.

He headed back down to the Castle and collected the blanket that had been placed over him at night. His luck continued to hold: one of his visitors from the afternoon had promised to return that evening but hadn't done so, so the alarm still hadn't been raised – the guards were still dealing with the disturbances that had followed the attack on Jonathan Wild the previous day. He retraced his steps to the leads, fixed the blanket with the spike from the chapel to the wall of Newgate, and used it to drop down onto the roof of one of the houses next to the prison, owned by a turner named William Bird.

Sheppard tried to creep softly down the stairs from the garret of the house – luckily, the door to the roof had been left open – but the woman of the house heard his irons clinking together. Rather than risk capture, Sheppard hid in the garret for a couple of hours, and around 11 p.m., made his way downstairs. When a visitor to the house left three-quarters of an hour later, Sheppard followed him out, omitting to shut the outer door behind him. To his own surprise, he was a free man once more.

The next two hours were spent heading away from Newgate, and around 2 a.m., he found himself in Tottenham Court, where he hid in an old house in the fields for a few hours. He was still wearing the fetters around his legs, which were beginning to swell and bruise as a result of the physical punishment they had endured. He stayed hidden throughout the Friday – it poured with rain all day, so no one came looking for him. That evening he used some of the money that he had been given by visitors to his cell to buy some cheese, bread and beer, but the chandler's shop at which he purchased his necessities didn't have a hammer available. He spent Saturday the same way, and on Sunday morning ran out of patience, and tried to break through his fetters with a large stone.

On Sunday, the owner of the house found him, and was immediately suspicious when he saw Sheppard's chains. The fugitive spun him a story about being sent to Bridewell prison for not providing support for a bastard child, which the man accepted although he asked Sheppard to leave. Later that day, Jack tried the same story on a shoemaker, who got hold of a hammer and a punch from a blacksmith, in return for the quite considerable sum of twenty shillings, and broke through the fetters. The manacles and leg irons eventually ended up in the possession of Kate Cook, another of Sheppard's mistresses.

Sunday night saw Sheppard disguised as a beggar staying in Charing Cross, and taking great pleasure in talking about his own exploits. His escape was the only topic of conversation; he was already the subject of various ballads, which he delighted in listening to during his wanderings through Piccadilly and the Haymarket the following day.

Sheppard stayed free until the night of 31 October. He had promised his mother that he would do his best to leave England – although he had no intentions of doing so – and she had even gone to St James' Palace to try to gain a pardon for her son. Jack wrote a letter to his friend Blake who was still confined in Newgate, urging him "if thou art still a man, [to] show thyself such, step forth, bilk the prigs, and return to thy confederate and dear friend". (Blake did try to escape but without success.) He broke into a pawnbrokers in Drury Lane, and used the items he stole to dress as a dandy and parade around town. He went out on the town with two of his mistresses, and invited his mother to join them. Despite everyone warning him that he was being foolhardy, Sheppard got progressively more drunk, and by the time the inevitable happened, and the officers of the law caught him, he was incapable of resisting.

He was returned to Newgate, where this time they were taking no chances. In addition to the handcuffs, fetters and chains, two guards were constantly with him, day and night. He received a procession of visitors, including many of the nobility, whom he begged to plead with the king for a pardon, or at the very least a commutation of his death sentence to transportation (his brother Tom had been transported shortly before Jack escaped from Newgate).

Sheppard was given an opportunity to cheat the hangman, when he appeared before the Court of King's Bench on 11 November. He begged for a pardon, and was told that the only way that he would receive clemency was if he would name his associates in his last escape. For once, Sheppard told the truth: no one except God Almighty had aided him. He was reprimanded for profanity, and his date of execution set for Monday 16 November.

Even at this late stage, Sheppard didn't give up all hope of escape. On the morning of 16 November, he took communion, and was then taken down to the Newgate yard to be handed over to the executioners who would transport him to the gallows at Tyburn. To his horror, they insisted on handcuffing him, and he desperately tried to resist this, hitting out at the officers. After they had restrained him, the guards searched Sheppard's pockets and found a small pocket knife: Sheppard had intended to cut through the ropes that were binding him for his final journey, and leap from the cart into the huge crowds that were lining the route from Holborn to Tyburn.

On the way to the gallows, the procession stopped to allow Sheppard to drink a pint of sack (a sweet wine fortified with brandy), and when they arrived at the place of execution, the thief passed over a piece of paper to someone in the crowd, which was believed to be the account of his life. He behaved with great decency on the scaffold, according to contemporary reports, but his slight build, which had been so useful to him during his escapes, told against him now, and he was slowly throttled to death by the rope as he hung there.

Even at this stage, Sheppard still had one plan up his sleeve – one last desperate throw of the dice. After fifteen minutes, his body was cut down, and the idea was that his friends would take it away and transport it rapidly to a doctor's surgery, where blood would be let from the "corpse" allowing it to revive. Unfortunately, there was such interest in the hanging, and such a large crowd, that by the time his friends reached the body, it was too late. His remains were taken to a pub in Long Acre, and then buried in the churchyard of St Martins in the Fields that evening.

Sheppard's escape from Newgate became the benchmark for such daring feats over the next couple of centuries; in Bram Stoker's *Dracula*, the character of Renfield is imprisoned, and apparently "Jack Sheppard himself couldn't get free from the strait waistcoat that keeps him restrained". As the *Newgate Calendar* noted, "A great warrior could not have received greater attention than this famous criminal."

Sources:

Rictor Norton, *Early Eighteenth-Century Newspaper Reports: A Sourcebook*, "Jack Sheppard, Jail-Breaker", 9 October 2003 <http://grubstreet.rictornorton.co.uk/sheppard.htm>

Moore, Lucy: *The Thieves' Opera* (Viking, 1997)

Ainsworth, William Harrison: *Jack Sheppard A Romance* (Project Gutenberg reprint, 2005 from the 1922 edition)

Grovier, Kelly: *The Gaol* (John Murray, 2008)

Heppenstall, Raymond: *Tales from the Newgate Calendar* (Futura, paperback edition, 1983)

Anchoring the Giant

Ronnie Biggs and his fellow participants in the Great Train Robbery in 1963 weren't the first train robbers to make a habit of escaping from prison. Nearly seventy-five years earlier, the perpetrator of one of the most daring locomotive raids was also a veteran escape artist. Oliver Curtis Perry brought "Wild Western Ways" to the Empire State of New York in the 1890s, and spent many years in and out of jails as a result.

Described by the *Utica Saturday Globe* after one of his escapes as "the King of Desperadoes" and "the most sensational and daring train robber and all around criminal of the nineteenth century, outdoing Jesse James in cunning and boldness", the twenty-six-year-old Perry was responsible for a raid on the "American Express Special" on the night of 29 September 1891, a train running from the New York state capital, Albany, out towards Buffalo. The carriage which he targeted was carrying cash, bonds, jewellery and valuables – sometimes a million dollars' worth – guarded by one messenger (who, to be fair, was armed). Rather than the brute-force methods used by robbers in the Wild West, though, Perry had been cunning: he had sawn a hole in the door of the carriage, squeezed through, and then held up Burt Moore, the messenger. Once he had filled bags with his loot, Perry had retreated through the hole, swung beneath the carriage to cut through the air-brake, and thus stopped the train. He had then vanished into the dark canyons near Utica.

The Pinkerton's National Detective Agency was put on the case, with Robert Pinkerton himself taking a hand in the investigation. Although they announced that they had "a pretty good clue" to the robber, their enquiries stalled until one of the train crew believed that he had recognized Perry, who used to work on the New York Central Railway before an accident had left him penniless and unemployed. Many of Perry's friends from the city of Troy, where he had lived in the two years before the case, spoke out in his defence: they admitted that he had been a wayward youth, but was now on the straight and narrow. City Missionary and Sunday School teacher Miss Amelia Haswell, who had tried to reform Perry, was particularly noticeable in her spirited comments on his behalf. Perry himself wrote to the detectives in December to clear Burt Moore of any involvement in the robbery; although the letter was postmarked Guelph in the neighbouring province of Ontario, Canada, no one could trace any other sign of Perry there.

Perry hadn't taken anywhere near as much as he might have done from the robbery – American Express originally tried to claim it was as little as $150, but a figure nearer $5,000 seemed more likely – and when this ran out, he decided to visit what he had come to regard as his own private bank for withdrawals: the American Express Special. On 20 February 1892, he struck again. This time, however, it did not go so smoothly.

The problems began when Perry jumped onto the wrong carriage initially and had to make his way along the roof to the money car. Rather than reuse the stealth tactics he had employed the previous September, the robber simply broke the glass window of the carriage, and pointed his gun at the American Express messenger, Daniel McInerney. Unlike Moore, McInerney was ready to defend the goods in his charge: he pulled his gun, but as he fired, Perry did the same, his bullet hitting the messenger's gun, sending it flying and breaking his fingers. McInerney reached for the air-whistle cord, but it failed to work both times he tried. He then kicked out the lamp as Perry fired again. This shot grazed McInerney's temple; a third hit him in the thigh.

Although he was concerned at McInerney's injury, Perry was far more worried by the fact that he couldn't find any cash in the car. A desperate search didn't reveal any, and as the train slowed down, Perry abandoned the hunt, and swung himself back up onto the roof. McInerney and the conductor, who had been alerted by a faint sound from the air-whistle, believed that he must have jumped off when the train slowed down. Getting rid of the disguise he had worn for the robbery, Perry coolly climbed back into the Express and waited until it reached its next proper stop, in Lyons. There he jumped off, wandered around the station, and onto the platform, as if he was simply waiting for a passenger to arrive. Unfortunately for Perry, the conductor recognized him and realized that he must be the robber. Perry hijacked a coal train and tried to flee, but the Express engine was uncoupled, and it set off in pursuit. After running out of steam, quite literally, Perry abandoned the coal train and headed across country, stealing a horse. That put not just detectives but local angry farmers on his trail, and after a chase he was eventually arrested and taken to Wayne County Jail in Lyons. His career as a train robber was over; his time as an attempted escapee was just beginning.

While Perry waited for his trial, he became an object of curiosity to the locals, particularly members of the press. He elected to defend himself, and was remanded for an appearance before a Grand Jury. However, much as he may have appeared to be enjoying the cut and thrust of the debate in court, Perry was determined to escape. His father came to visit him in jail, and was searched on his departure: to the surprise of the authorities, this respectable builder had a drawing in his pocket, with a note in Perry's handwriting explaining the exact dimensions and shape of key that were required to unlock the corridor door within the jail. Instead of receiving a key back, Perry found his ankles shackled with heavy iron cuffs connected to an eight-inch-long log chain, and his father banned from visiting him, despite his protestations that he knew nothing of the paper.

Perry didn't seem too fazed by his new restraints: "I think you ought to get a jail strong enough to hold me without this. I ain't very hard to hold," he told his warders, who noticed that their prisoner's thin legs almost seemed to slip out of the shackles. A new closer-fitting pair was created, leading to Perry claiming that the Lyons jailers must be afraid of him "for they anchor me down as if I was a giant".

He continued to play up to the public image that was being created of him as a charming gentleman crook, all the while planning his next escape. He worked with other prisoners to create a lead key for the corridor door, but he was caught while trying it out. During the thorough search of the prison that followed, the sacking was removed that had been wrapped around his shackles to stop them from rattling – and the shackles fell in two. Perry had been able to cut them apart using a saw that he kept hidden inside a Bible. Inside his clothes, the Sheriff found five $50 bills sewn into the lining, a reserve kept in case of emergencies – or for bribing guards.

Perry was moved into a smaller cell, and watched even more carefully. He was kept apart from the other prisoners and his meals were passed through a hatch in the cell door. In his desperation to get out, he tried to break his new shackles by dropping one of the legs of his iron bed onto them; instead, he ended up with his wrists shackled as well.

When he was finally put on trial, Perry pleaded guilty, on the advice of Amelia Haswell, who was convinced that he would receive a lighter sentence as a result. He didn't: Perry was given forty-nine years and three months in total, of hard labour, the various component parts of his sentence to be served consecutively. Even with remission for good behaviour, it would be 1921 before he would see freedom.

Perry was sent to Auburn Prison to serve his time. It had been built in 1816, and saw the first execution by electric chair in 1890. It lent its name to the Auburn System of prison governance, under which inmates kept silent at all times, and moved around in the "lockstep" – each man shuffled forward, holding the shoulder of the man in front. Although Perry quickly fell foul of the system, the authorities believed that they had broken him after he served time in solitary confinement.

They were wrong. Placing him in the centre of a row of cells, and ordering no one to speak to him might have kept Perry isolated, but it didn't stop him planning. He was kept in the cell twenty-four hours a day with no contact with guards or prisoners, but on Sunday 23 October 1892, Oliver Perry escaped, after digging a hole in the twenty-two-inch thick dividing wall between cells. His neighbour was assigned to the prison tailor workshop, so his cell door was left open when he was at work. Perry had been concealing the hole with a towel, and after having supper, he had nonchalantly gone through the hole, through the open doorway, and out into the corridor. Since all the other prisoners were at work, there was no need for a lot of guards on the prison wing; Perry was easily able to avoid being seen by the single warder on duty. Getting out into the yard, he hid in an outhouse, waiting for dark, so he could scale the wall and escape.

When his flight was discovered, the prison was turned upside down, but no one could find any trace of Perry. However, later that evening, he was spotted as he crept across the yard, and one of the warders hit him so hard that his nightstick broke. As a result of the failed escape attempt, just under ten years of remission was removed from his sentence, meaning he would be in jail for at least forty years. He continuously found himself in trouble with the authorities, culminating in a forty-four-day stretch in the dungeons. After that, he became increasingly violent, and although there were some who believed that he was putting on an act to get out of Auburn, on 27 December 1893, he was declared insane. It's interesting to note that the doctor certifying him pointed out to the authorities at the asylum, "He is a desperate man, and you cannot be too careful, or he may well escape from your place."

He was sent to the Matteawan Asylum for Insane Criminals, which had only opened a year earlier, and found himself immediately in a cell on an isolation ward. The outer walls of the block had a lining of sheet iron between its brick layers, there were wire shutters and iron bars on the windows, and the ceilings had been held in place with stone flagging. The cell doors were made of two-inch-thick oak, and the locks didn't go all the way through. Prisoners could be watched day or night for any signs of faking. While Perry's release date from Auburn might have been four decades in the future, at least there he had an end in sight. Those sent to Matteawan were there for an "indeterminate sentence" according to the asylum's superintendent, Dr Henry Allison.

For eighteen months, Perry put up with the regime. He was allowed visitors, including Amelia Haswell, and complained about the conditions at the asylum. In April 1895, he decided enough was enough. On the night of the ninth, as night watchman Carmody came in to do his rounds, he was set upon and relieved of his keys by three of the inmates.

Perry had been alerted to a possible escape route when one of his fellow prisoners, Patrick Maguire, told him that a long ladder had been left in the prison chapel by workmen who were repairing the ceiling. Perry had been overseeing the creation of keys for the doors from the iron spoons that some men in the isolation ward were issued with in place of knives and forks for their meals. Maguire had been a jeweller as well as a burglar, and was able to make a small saw from a thin strip of steel that was inside the sole of the prison-issue slippers, and used this to adjust the keys into the necessary shape. Although the two locks on each door were different, one pair of keys opened all the doors in the corridor.

Maguire was able to pass a bottom lock key to another prisoner, Frank Davis; on his way to supper, Davis unlocked the bottom lock of Maguire's cell. Once the warder had carried out the post-meal inspection, Maguire had cut through the strands of wire mesh on the cell-door peephole, stuck his arm through and used his key to open his top lock. Letting himself out, he went across the corridor to Davis's cell, opened the top lock, and took the bottom lock key back from Davis, thus letting him out. They then unlocked Oliver Perry's cell. Thus when the warder came down the corridor to answer one of Perry's perennial complaints, he was startled to find that three of his charges were free to attack him. They covered his mouth to stop him raising the alarm, and pushed him into Perry's cell, where his mouth was stuffed with rags and he was tied to the bed frame.

Using the warder's keys, Davis, Maguire and Perry released two other prisoners, John Quigley and Michael O'Donnell, and let themselves through the ward door, locking it behind them. They moved softly past the attendants' rooms, and up to the chapel, unlocking the door with the warder's keys again. Once inside, they used the ladder, which was still in position, to reach a small hatch in the ceiling which led to an attic. The dormer window wasn't securely fastened, and was quickly opened, allowing them to head out onto the roof. From there it was the work of seconds to reach iron drainpipes and shin down them.

Even though they were spotted as they reached ground level, the five men were able to get away, still wearing their asylum uniforms, with no proper shoes. Quigley only managed to stay on the run for two days, before he was picked up on Good Friday, begging for food. Maguire and O'Donnell were found forty miles from Matteawan very shortly afterwards. Frank Davis survived for five days, but he too was returned to Matteawan.

Perry only lasted one day longer. He had made his way to Weehawken on the New Jersey shoreline, but when he was challenged by a police officer, he tried to run. Falling from a narrow ledge on a cliff, he was arrested, and, after an extradition battle between the states of New Jersey and New York, he was sent back to Matteawan, although he took advantage of the publicity surrounding his case to complain about the inhumane regime at the asylum. Within two months, he was declared "free from any active mental disturbance" and sent to Auburn – not before he had tried one more escape plan, trying to bribe a keeper to help him. The keeper had reported this to Dr Allison, and Perry was returned to solitary confinement for the final few days of his stay at the asylum.

The authorities were not convinced that Perry hadn't received outside help for his escape from Matteawan. According to the keeper Perry had tried to bribe, Perry had informed him that one of the other warders, William Hopkins, had supplied the keys. When Hopkins was questioned, he claimed that Amelia Haswell had sent him a parcel of jewellery in the autumn of 1894 in return for his help in the escape: Hopkins provided keys, a file and blank keys to Maguire, and had unlocked the cell door. He was also meant to leave a set of clothes and a gun for Perry to pick up once he had left the asylum, but had got drunk and forgotten. Hopkins had disposed of the jewels already, but Pinkertons were able to track them down and return them to American Express – they were part of the loot from Perry's first train robbery. Haswell admitted that she had sent the jewels, but said that they were Perry's property and he had asked her to arrange for a friend to sell them. After a lengthy court case, Haswell was vindicated.

By the time that Amelia Haswell's name was cleared, Oliver Perry had committed the act that would send him back to Matteawan. Putting two large needles onto a piece of wood, he had quite deliberately blinded himself. Two months after being recommitted to the asylum, he used broken glass to complete the job. But was even this drastic act part of an escape plan? In 1897 some of his poetry was published which suggested that he was hoping for sympathy – after all, what could a blind man do? His hopes for a pardon were dashed, and in 1901, Perry was sent to Dannemora State Hospital, within the grounds of Clinton prison. He died there on 5 September 1930.

Sources:

Spargo, Tamsin: *Wanted Man* (Bloomsbury, 2004)
New York Times, 20 August 1895: "Miss Haswell Makes Denial"
New York Times, 30 August 1895: "Examination of Miss Haswell"
New York Times, 17 April 1895: "Perry Happy in Jersey"
Montreal Daily Herald, 22 October 1892: "Escape of a Long Term Prisoner"
New York Times, 10 April 1895: "Perry Still at Liberty"
Weekly Auburnian, 24 February 1892: "Capture of Perry"
The Utica Journal, 14 April 1895: "Wasn't Oliver Perry"
Hartford Weekly Times, 11 April 1895: "Train Robber Perry"

Bringing Out the Big Guns

When the gangsters who had ruled Chicago were sent behind bars, many thought that would be the last the world heard of them. But there were a few who were determined to ensure that they were not forgotten, and when Roger "The Terrible" Touhy and members of his gang broke out from the supposedly escape-proof Stateville Prison, near Joliet in Illinois, their reputations were sufficient to merit the attentions of one of the top law enforcers in America. It was FBI chief J. Edgar Hoover himself who successfully led the hunt and got his men. And perhaps not surprisingly, the pursuit became the basis for a movie, praised for not glorifying but authentically recreating the gangster lifestyle.

While the FBI still maintains in its history of Touhy on its official website that he was responsible for the kidnapping of John "Jake the Barber" Factor for which he was sentenced to imprisonment in Joliet, authorities from 1954 onwards seemed to accept Touhy's version of events. Touhy maintained that he was framed for the kidnapping by Al Capone and Factor in order to get him out of the way (one of the chapter titles in his autobiography is the rather mild "Al Capone Didn't Like Me", which underestimates the depth of feeling quite dramatically). What Touhy never tried to deny was that he was a gangster.

One of six sons of a Chicago policeman, five of whom would turn to crime, Roger Touhy started his criminal career after the introduction of Prohibition with the passing of the Eighteenth Amendment to the US Constitution, and the Volstead Act, both in 1919. He formed a trucking company with two of his brothers, and they expanded into illegal beer and spirits distribution in the north-west suburbs of Chicago. Touhy then began working with Matt Kolb, who was supplying Capone's

Chicago Outfit with a third of its beer, and they set up their own brewery. Around the same time, he added illegal gambling to his portfolio.

Touhy's success irked Al Capone who tried on two separate occasions to persuade him to hand over control of his operations. Both times Touhy refused, and although Capone kept negotiations going, he also tried a takeover by force; Touhy was backed by Mayor Walter Cermak, which led to an escalation of the hostilities. When Capone arranged for Kolb to be killed in October 1931, all-out war began.

Capone tried to frame Touhy for the kidnapping of brewery heir William A. Hamm in 1933, but the charges failed to stick – the FBI were well aware that Ma Barker's gang, along with Alvin Karpis, were responsible. However, Capone's second try was more successful, and thanks to perjuring witnesses and corrupt lawyers, Touhy and two of his henchmen were sentenced to ninety-nine years. The rest of Touhy's mob were also eradicated: three weeks after Touhy was imprisoned, his machine-gunner Basil "The Owl" Banghart, was also sentenced to ninety-nine years for involvement in the Factor kidnapping (Banghart was set up by Capone to collect the ransom money, although perjured evidence stating that he was a key player in arranging the kidnapping swayed the court against him).

In 1935, the two men were reunited at the Stateville Correctional Centre, where 3,000 or so prisoners were surrounded by a nine-feet wide, thirty-three-feet high prison wall, made from solid concrete and steel. After war was declared by Congress on 8 December 1941, following the attack on Pearl Harbor, many of the younger guards were called up for duty or took better-paid jobs in munitions factories. They were replaced by old-timers, some of whom took a distinctly lax approach to their duties, or very raw new recruits. This left around seventy-five guards to watch over 3,256 inmates on the day that Touhy and his friends escaped. The Warden Joseph Ragen had resigned over political meddling in the prison running; his replacement, Edward H. Stubblefield, was nowhere near as strict.

If you believe Touhy's own account, he was brought in on the escape attempt quite late in the day; it seems more likely that he

was involved in the planning and implementation early on, as
the FBI suggests. Certainly, the balance of power had shifted
once the members of the Touhy Gang were behind bars: Basil
Banghart was the driving force now, as would be demonstrated
once the men were on the outside. Labelled "a regular sharpie"
and "tougher than Tough Touhy" by Chicago detectives, Banghart began his criminal career as a car thief. He had escaped
from the penitentiary in Atlanta, Georgia, on 25 January 1927
after sawing through the bars of his cell window, and running
through the local swamps to evade the tracker dogs; he later
managed to escape from custody by persuading passers-by that
the pursuing police officer was the one who needed stopping.
After serving another two-year sentence, he was arrested for
armed robbery and sent to South Bend jail in Indiana. There he
blinded a warder with pepper, used the man's keys to get hold
of a machine gun, and shot his way out of jail. He started his
term for the Factor kidnapping at Menard state prison, but was
sent to Statesville after he and other inmates attacked a warder
and commandeered a truck, breaking through the prison gates
before being recaptured.

With a minimum of thirty-three years to serve before either
man could be considered for parole, Banghart and Touhy didn't
need to rush any attempt to escape, and in any case the latter
was trying every legal avenue that he could to gain an appeal
and prove that he was framed. Banghart was probing the Statesville system for weak points: he claimed that he spotted that the
guns the guards used had a hundred yard effective range, but
the towers were 300 yards apart.

The first thing that the prisoners would need were guns
even if, as Touhy noted, "guns in a prison are like a firebug in
a high-octane gasoline refinery". These were obtained by Big
Ed Darlak (sometimes spelled Darlack), a murderer serving a
199-year term. His brother Casimir got hold of two .45 calibre
revolvers, and stashed them in the bushes near the prison.
They were then brought in by one of the trusties, Percy Campbell, when he was allowed out to collect the American flag
from outside the prison. Darlak therefore was brought in as
one of the escapers, alongside robbers Martilick Nelson,
William Stewart and St Clair McInerney, as well as serial

escaper James "Gene" O'Connor. O'Connor, whose real name was Eugene Lathorn, (which is how the FBI refer to him in their accounts, leading to some confusion between different sources) had gone over the wall previously, after switching off all the lights in the prison and getting hold of a ladder from the carpenters' shop. On another occasion, he had had himself nailed inside a furniture crate that was being sent to the nearby town, and had been driven through the gates in a truck. Each time, though, he had been apprehended, returned to Statesville, and his date of release set further away.

As well as guns, the escapers would also need a getaway vehicle. O'Connor was responsible for sorting that out. He had built up a relationship with Hugh Kross, the guard in one of the towers, stealing food from the prison storehouse and selling it to him. When O'Connor joked that one day he'd come up to see him in the guard tower, the old warder had told him that if he did so, he wouldn't shoot him. O'Connor arranged to bring some goods for him on the date the break was set, 6 October, so he would need to have his car near the tower.

Although all the preparations were ready, the escape didn't happen on the sixth: O'Connor decided to wait to see if any of the prisoners had betrayed them in return for a lighter sentence. Instead they went on 9 October 1942. At lunchtime, Touhy was waiting for the prison garbage truck to arrive. The driver, Jack Cito, was attacked (he claimed that Touhy threatened him with a large pair of scissors; Touhy says Cito had to say that to avoid being accused of collusion), and Touhy took the truck.

The only way in or out of the guard tower was via a door on the outside of the fence. The plan therefore was to get into the guard tower from the prison side, and then exit down the stairs. Touhy drove the truck to the mechanical store, where the other escapees were waiting. They overpowered the guards on duty there, ripped out the telephone wires, and grabbed some of the ladders, making two of the guards sit on them to keep them steady as they made their way to the tower in the north-west corner of the prison yard. At first, the truck wouldn't start, but a number of other convicts who were watching the escape with great interest helped them bump-start it.

With the two revolvers, and a homemade Molotov cocktail which O'Connor had assembled just in case it was needed, they put the ladders together and leant it up against the tower, and, taking the two guard hostages with them, went up to the small cubicle at the top after blowing out the glass with a single shot, causing Kross a slight glass cut.

Once at the top, O'Connor kicked the ladder away, much to the surprise of his colleagues. He then threw the rope, which Kross had previously used to haul the stolen goods out of the yard up into the tower, over the other side of the wall. Nelson shinned down it, O'Connor threw him a key for the tower door (the lock was only on the outside), and he opened the door, allowing the others to come down, pile into Kross's car and escape. Before they left the guard tower, they appropriated the weaponry up there: two high-powered rifles and a load of ammunition. The whole escape had taken seventeen minutes, from the initial hijack of the truck to driving away in Kross' Ford.

Prison governor Stubblefield wasn't on duty at the time of the escape, but even before he had arrived back from Springfield, the manhunt was under way. Within forty-five minutes, all highways within twenty-five miles of Joliet and Statesville were blocked by Illinois state police. Expecting the fugitives to head in their direction, the Chicago police began checks. Ten cars filled with officers from the State Attorney's office in Chicago joined the patrol of local highways. Local airfields were warned to set guards, since Banghart was an amateur flier and might well try to steal a plane. According to news reports, mob leaders, fearing that Touhy and Banghart were set on vengeance, went into hiding.

In fact the escapers were nowhere near as organized as the authorities or their previous enemies believed. No proper plans had been made for a hideout, or what to do to evade the law. The FBI claimed that the fugitives ran through a roadblock and abandoned the car that night in the suburb of Villa Park; Touhy says that they drove round in circles without being spotted before eventually getting rid of the car. He knew of one person who might help them, someone whom he had not communicated with while he was in Stateville, and thus wouldn't be on any of the lists of contacts that the police would be poring over to find them. Disguised in an old raincoat that they found in a garage, Banghart went by bus into Chicago to make contact.

The morale among the escapees was low. "If Banghart doesn't score," McInerny noted, "We might as well go back to the main gate at Stateville and apply for readmittance." But Touhy's friend came through, with a new car, some money, and the address of an apartment where they could hole up. This all sounded like good news, until they saw the state of the basement flat. "Warden Ragen wouldn't allow a pig from the Stateville farm to set one cloven hoof in the place," was Touhy's acid description years later. He was quick to get himself out of there and into a different apartment, particularly when Nelson and McInerny started drinking and causing fights.

Banghart knew that they needed to make some serious money in order to afford a proper lifestyle, possibly even including plastic surgery, which would set them back around $100,000. He tried to keep the others under control, and when they went out to get supplies, he would follow at a distance, carrying his shotgun wrapped inside a newspaper.

By this time the search was being conducted by the FBI. The prison escape was the responsibility of the state police – it wasn't a felony at the time – and the fugitives had not crossed state lines, so the Bureau couldn't get involved initially. However by the autumn of 1942, the military draft was in operation, and when the men failed to present themselves for registration under the Selective Service Law, they became draft delinquents, and thus the Bureau's responsibility. This was a little bit disingenuous, as Touhy was over draft age and had served in the US Navy during the First World War, but it provided the excuse that FBI leader J. Edgar Hoover needed for clearing up the mess. The full resources of the Bureau were directed towards the hunt.

Although checks were kept at every border crossing, and every law enforcement organization in America was put on alert, the focus was firmly on Chicago. The Bureau agents calculated that Banghart would be keeping the group close to his former base of operation, and that the men would probably have assumed identities from people whose wallets they had pickpocketed, in case they were stopped in the street for any petty misdemeanour. The first of the fugitives who was caught because of these checks was Nelson.

He and Stewart had been abandoned by Banghart and the others after they had gone out and got roaring drunk. Banghart had pistol-whipped them severely, leaving them unconscious, and when they had recovered, they had gone their separate ways: Nelson had headed to Minneapolis, Stewart to a former girlfriend's house. Nelson contacted his mother in northern Minneapolis on 15 December; she immediately told the police. The FBI deduced that he would probably be living in a cheap hotel, and started to cross-check residents of these with the names of Chicago citizens who had lost their wallets recently. A mere twenty-four hours later, "Harold Seeger" was located in just such a motel, the door to his room barricaded, and a gun under his pillow. He was arrested, but refused to talk.

As it transpired, his silence didn't make a difference. On the same day that Nelson was arrested, the FBI tracked down Stewart. The same principle had been applied: when Stewart had made contact with a friend in Milwaukee, the call was traced to a payphone on North Broadway in Chicago. The FBI saturated the area with agents, asking people if they had seen Stewart, and received multiple confirmations that he had been there.

Stake-outs in the vicinity produced results on 16 December. A known associate of Stewart's was spotted standing awkwardly on a street corner, clearly waiting for someone. The Bureau agents were disappointed when the rendezvous wasn't with Stewart but with another man, whom they followed anyway to a hotel on West Harrison Street. A check of the register revealed that "James Shea", who had lost his wallet and ID three weeks earlier, was living there. Rather than arrest Stewart immediately, and get the same lack of cooperation that their colleagues were receiving from Nelson, the agents decided to be patient and follow him.

Four days later, their patience paid off. Stewart met up with two other men, who the agents guessed were couriers acting as go-betweens for Stewart and the other gang members. They therefore arrested Stewart, and started to follow the new pair of suspects. The next day, 21 December, they saw one of them meet Banghart and Darlak in a crowded downtown area. Banghart was carrying his shotgun beneath his newspaper, as he always did when he went out, and rather than risk a shoot-out in a crowded area, the agents switched their surveillance on to him.

This proved harder than they expected; Banghart was used to throwing off tails, and the agents were lucky that they weren't spotted. However, over the next five days, they were able to ascertain the location of the other gang members. McInerney and O'Connor were in one apartment; Darlak and Banghart were in another, with Touhy a regular visitor.

Touhy had had a couple of close shaves during the preceding few weeks. When he visited one friend, he realized that there were FBI agents waiting for him, and he was able to give them the slip. On another occasion, a Chicago patrolman addressed him by name – but the cop simply wanted to thank him for a kindness he had done during the Prohibition era, and didn't report him. In fact, he paid for Touhy's fuel at the filling station where they met.

On 27 December, FBI agents confirmed McInerney and O'Connor's identities by obtaining some discarded bottles from their apartment while they were out, and checking the finger-prints. J. Edgar Hoover then travelled to Chicago to oversee the final plans for the raids on the apartments personally. Where at all possible, civilians were removed from the neighbourhoods of the two apartments, so that there was less chance of collateral damage. Lines of fire were calculated to ensure the safety of all the agents involved. The local police's assistance was needed to close off the streets once the operations got under way.

The following evening, McInerney and O'Connor left their apartment, returning by 11.20 p.m. Two Bureau agents were waiting for them inside; others took up position in and around the building. Alerted by something, the two fugitives went to their apartment door with guns drawn. As soon as they opened the door, one of the Bureau men called out that they were federal agents and told them to put their hands out. McInerney and O'Connor fired into the darkness but missed. The FBI agents were shooting at two targets silhouetted in the door frame; they didn't miss. The two men were blown back by the force of the bullets, and fell over the banister to lie dead on the second-floor landing. In McInerney's pockets were the address of an undertaker, and an excerpt from a poem.

Even as the FBI agents turned their attention to the other apartment, Touhy was starting to get an uneasy feeling, suggesting to Banghart that they should look for a new hiding place after he spotted men talking to each other out on the sidewalk late at night. Banghart told him not to worry.

The next morning at 5 a.m., they were woken by powerful searchlights directed into their apartment. Through a loudhailer they heard an FBI agent tell them they were surrounded, and advising them to surrender immediately. They were given ten minutes to think about it; if they hadn't come out by then, the FBI would go in, shooting. Realizing that their escape was over, the three men – Banghart, Touhy and Darlak – surrendered. They were amazed to find J. Edgar Hoover himself presiding over the arrest. "You're a lot fatter than you are on the radio," Banghart told him.

Banghart was shipped to Alcatraz. Touhy was informed that, under an obscure Illinois law, he was liable now to serve Darlak's term as well as his own; his sentence was therefore now 199 years. Banghart and Touhy continued to maintain that they had been framed for the kidnapping, and in 1954, a federal judge agreed with them. Touhy was released in 1959, but was shot twenty-five days later. He died within an hour, after commenting to a newsman, "I've been expecting it. The bastards never forget!" Banghart was freed in 1960, and spent his final twenty-two years living on a small island in the Puget Sound.

Sources:

Touhy, John: "Jake the Barber, Roger Touhy, and an Escape From the Big House" (Search International, 2001)

FBI website: "Famous Cases and Criminals: Roger 'The Terrible' Touhy's Gang"

Touhy, Roger with Ray Brennan: *The Stolen Years* (Pennington Press, 1959)

United States of America Ex Rel. Roger Touhy, Relator-Appellee, v. Joseph E. Ragen, Warden, Illinois State Penitentiary, Joliet,

Illinois, Respondent-Appellant., 224 F.2d 611 (7th Cir. 1955) Federal Circuits

New York Times, 10 October 1942: "Touhy Mob Heads Break From Prison"

Time magazine, 19 October 1942: "Back to the Roaring '20s"

Escape from Scotland's Gulag

Although it would become best known for its implementation of the Stop programme to deal with sex offenders, Peterhead Prison in the Scottish county of Aberdeenshire spent many years as a home for some of the worst offenders within the Scottish legal system. Described by an Open University Study in 1991 as "a prison of no hope", it was nicknamed Colditz by its inmates in 2010, not because of its impregnability, but because it was too cold. The temperature didn't affect one of the most famous escapers from Peterhead, "Gentleman" Johnny Ramensky, though. He managed to leave its confines on five separate occasions over a twenty-five-year period, once by swimming away on a cold November morning.

Built in 1888, Peterhead Convict Prison always had a bad reputation. It was the first such prison built north of the border – until then, convicts were sent to serve their sentences in England – and was always behind the times in receiving upgrades. Electricity wasn't fully available until 2005 – a year before serious discussion began about closing the prison down. In 1987, it became well known after Prime Minister Margaret Thatcher ordered the elite Special Air Service regiment into operation on the mainland UK for only the second time (officially) to end a siege and rescue a hostage being held by prisoners.

Safe-blower Johnny Ramensky was born to Lithuanian parents in North Lanarkshire in 1905, and moved to the Gorbals in Glasgow aged eight, following the death of his father. He drifted into a life of petty crime, and was sent to a borstal in 1921 where he spent three years learning the tricks of his trade – as has been noted on many occasions, these young offenders' institutions often were the most effective school that any of its inmates attended. He embarked on a career of housebreaking, receiving an eighteen-month sentence in 1925 after pleading guilty to sixteen charges and a further three-year sentence in 1927.

Ramensky was sent to Peterhead prison for five years in 1934 after blowing a safe at a bakers in Aberdeen, and made his first escape from there in November. Two years earlier, a man had managed to get away from a work party in the Peterhead quarry, but had been shot by the warders. Gentleman Johnny was the first to do so from within the walls of the prison. He was able to get over the walls between six and seven in the morning – either using a ladder or standing with his back against the wall, and heaving himself up it just using his shoulders, since he was incredibly strong. He was in ordinary prison uniform, with ordinary black shoes, but this wasn't designed for the depredations of a Scottish winter.

As soon as his absence was noted, a major manhunt began, with farms searched and road junctions monitored. Ramensky travelled as far as Ellon, fifteen miles south-west of the prison, and evaded the police, who had blocked the only route over the river Ythen on both sides, by swinging on the girders and stonework of the bridge. After waiting until darkness fell, he then headed south towards Foveran, but was spotted running across a field. He was apprehended, and despite carrying an iron bar in his hand, he surrendered without a fight. He had been on the run for twenty-eight hours. He was returned to Peterhead, where the governor ordered that he was shackled. The newspaper reports of this treatment led to questions in the House of Commons, and the decision to abolish this form of punishment in Scotland.

Ramensky's decision to abscond is often, wrongly, ascribed to the fact that he was denied permission to go to his wife's funeral. In fact she didn't die until three years later; Ramensky wasn't allowed to attend the ceremony – the authorities at Peterhead didn't make any allowances for him after he had embarrassed them by escaping.

A further spell of imprisonment followed his release in 1938, when he blew open a safe at the Empress Laundry in Aberdeen. He gained a certain notoriety when he informed the police after he was convicted that there was still an undetonated charge within a second safe on the premises.

When war was declared in 1939, Ramensky wanted to join up, but his various petitions to do so were turned down. On his release in 1942, he adopted the name Johnny Ramsay, and ended up in the Commandos. There are many stories about his safe-blowing exploits during the war, many probably apocryphal, but his less-legitimate talents were certainly put to good use.

Ramensky was given the opportunity to "go straight" after the war, but turned it down, and was back in prison again, this time at York, by 1947 (he was only demobbed in September 1946!). Thanks to lobbying by his girlfriend and the local MP, he was moved to Scotland, but on his release, he blew open a post office safe in Glasgow, and was sent to Peterhead on 20 February 1951.

By this time, Peterhead wasn't as escape-proof as its staff liked to think. On 12 December 1950, its inability to hold onto the prisoners was brought up in the House of Commons, and the Under Secretary of State for Scotland, Peggy Herbison, noted that "Twelve prisoners have escaped from Peterhead Prison during the last three years. Nine were recaptured within twenty-four hours, one within two days and two within three days. They committed no offences while at liberty except, in two cases, the theft of motor cars to assist their escape." However, inquiries held after each escape noted that "there is neither laxity of administration nor, indeed, of discipline in this prison".

Eighteen months after Ramensky returned to Peterhead, he escaped once again. Annoyed at not being allowed to travel to visit his very sick mother, he got out of his cell and climbed on to the roof of the prison, then jumped down into the yard below. Newspaper stories at the time suggested that he had lathered himself with soap and slipped through the bars of his cell, but this seems rather less likely than he had found a way to deal with the locks. He had left a dummy in his bunk to avoid detection.

From the prison yard, Ramensky was able to scale the prison walls, and once outside at 4 a.m., he stole a children's bicycle, which he replaced with an adult one from the Glenugie distillery a few minutes later. At 5 a.m. he was seen five miles from

Peterhead, heading down what is now the A90, on the same route that he had followed eighteen years earlier. Unfortunately for him, although he succeeded in remaining free for forty-six hours, he was picked up at Balmedie, ten miles south of Ellon, where he was found the previous time.

Ramensky was released in 1955, but once again found it difficult to remain out of prison, sent for a ten-year stretch this time by Lord Carmont, who told him, "You have shown that you are a menace to society. Any sentence of less than ten years would be useless." At the start of 1958, he made the first of his three escapes from Peterhead that year.

On a cold January morning, Ramensky made a spur of the moment decision to go, taking advantage of laxity on the part of the guards supervising the queues for breakfast. He got through a skylight, then up a gas pipe onto the roof. From there, he headed down to the yard, broke into a shed, and borrowed a ladder! This he placed on top of a bin, and was just able to reach the stonework at the top of the wall. Hoisting himself over, he made a run for it – but he was spotted by men working at the distillery. It meant that Ramensky only had a twenty minute head start, and this time the police spared no expense. Tracker dogs were used, and the Aberdeen market was disrupted by checkpoints that were set up around the city.

Ramensky was much closer to home. Rather than set out south as he had done previously, he remained in Peterhead, hiding on the roof of a local school, and then wandered around the town in a warder's uniform that he had found in a shed near the prison. However, with all the publicity surrounding the escape, he wasn't destined to remain free for long, and twenty-eight hours after he had left the prison, he was back behind bars.

He inspired another prisoner to try to make a run for it. John Spence Gilmour escaped from a working party in the turnip fields near the prison on 18 June 1958, but was spotted and quickly recaptured.

Nine months later, Ramensky was back on the loose. He got out onto the roof and over the wall on a Friday night, but the now fifty-three-year-old safe-cracker was finding it harder to evade pursuit, although he did stay free for forty hours this time. He was found by a seven-year-old boy in the hayloft at his father's farm. As the boy's father went to the prison to get help, Ramensky tried to make a getaway, but he was barefoot and bleeding. Near the distillery, he surrendered to police.

Christmas 1958 saw Ramensky's final escape attempt, although he kept his own counsel as to how he was able to stay on the loose for nearly nine days. According to James Crosbie, he had actually stayed hidden under the floorboards of the doctor's office in the sick bay while everyone was looking for him outside the prison, with food provided for him by another convict. However, he came out of his hiding place too quickly, and was caught when he asked a lorry driver for a lift, not realizing that the man was a former warder at Peterhead! After Ramensky jumped out of the back of the lorry, the driver reported his passenger to the authorities. He was also spotted by a number of other people in the area, and was picked up by the police. Ramensky never admitted who, if anyone, had helped him.

After that, Johnny Ramensky was watched around the clock, with six officers specifically tasked with monitoring him. He didn't get out of Peterhead again until he was officially released. After further spells in prison, he died in Perth prison in 1972. His funeral was attended by hundreds of mourners.

Although Ramensky was by far the most famous escaper from Peterhead, he wasn't the only one. As James Crosbie recounts in his anecdotal history of the prison, there were many different attempts. Crosbie himself was caught red-handed with a hacksaw blade working his way through the bars of his cell.

Some were doomed instantly to failure, such as the time when a prison warder was stabbed in the back with cutting shears but still managed to hit the alarm bell to summon the riot squad. That didn't deter the perpetrator, robber William Varey, who tried again later in 1985, using an imitation gun to lock seven warders in a cell. Four years after that, he was able to cut through the prison's double perimeter fence and stay on the run for two days, eventually getting caught around twenty-five miles from the prison.

Other prisoners were able to elude capture for a decent length of time. Edward Joseph Martin set a record for his time away from the prison in 1955, staying free for thirty-one days. Murderer Donald Forbes, who had killed a man while on parole for murder, stayed loose for six days before being captured in Edinburgh after going over the wall on 31 August 1971. He tried to run again two years later, but was caught in the act. Manuel Cohen escaped from the Aberdeen Royal Infirmary on 2 October 1976 when he was transferred there from Peterhead while suffering from jaundice. Since he realized he was very easy to spot because of the distinctive yellow skin colouration caused by the disease, he holed up in a house that was rented by three nurses. He held them hostage overnight but they were able to persuade him to let one of them go to buy some food and cigarettes. She, of course, went straight to the police, and he was returned to custody.

In 1997, murderer Thomas Gordon was helped by local youths to escape from the Peterhead Cottage Hospital when he went for a physiotherapy appointment. One guard was sacked over the incident; Gordon was caught at Euston station in London when he was recognized by a resident of Peterhead town who had seen the publicity.

Despite Scottish leader Alex Salmond describing Peterhead as "the jewel in the crown of the prison service" and claiming that "Peterhead prison has an international reputation and to close it would be a disaster" in 2002, the demolition of parts of the prison began in February 2012, with a new facility set to open in 2014.

Sources:

Daily Record, 16 September 2010: "Inmates dub Peterhead prison 'Colditz'"

HM Inspectorate Of Prisons HMP Peterhead Inspection: 30–31 March 2005, published June 2005

Jeffrey, Robert: *Gentle Johnny Ramensky* (Black & White, 2011)

"Peterman": "Four Examples": http://www.peterman.org.uk/four-petermen.htm

Glasgow Herald, 19 June 1958: "Peterhead Prison Escape"

Glasgow Herald, 4 October 1976: "Police capture escaped prisoner in students' flat"

Glasgow Herald, 5 October 1976: "Escaped prisoner in court"

Glasgow Herald, 21 October 1989: "Police recapture Peterhead prisoner"

Hansard, 12 December 1950: "Peterhead Gaol (Escapes): Oral Answers to Questions – Scotland"

Glasgow Herald, 5 March 1997: "Guard sacked after Peterhead escape inquiry"

Crosbie, James: *Peterhead Porridge* (Black & White, 2007)

Making Dummies in Internment

Many of those involved in the struggles in Ireland regard themselves as participants in a war, striking a blow for freedom against the oppressors. If they are captured (or interned), they see it as their duty to escape so they can continue the fight, much the same way that prisoners of war did during the Second World War. When the IRA began its border campaign in the mid-1950s, many of those arrested in the Republic of Ireland were sent to an internment camp at the Curragh, in County Kildare.

Amongst them was J.B. (Joe) O'Hagan, who, fifteen or so years later, would go on to feature in one of the most daring escapes on Irish soil (see chapter 29). He had joined the IRA aged eighteen, and was interned in Belfast's Crumlin Road Jail for the majority of the Second World War. Although the decade following the end of the war was comparatively peaceful, he was happily recalled to active duty in December 1956. As Sinn Féin President Gerry Adams said at his funeral, O'Hagan "was an example of a physical force republican who was prepared to support and exhaust other means of struggle. He saw armed struggle as a means rather than as an end, but he never ceased to be an unrepentant republican and to work always for the establishment of an Irish Republic based on national rights for the people of this island." There were nearly two hundred internees in the Curragh, many of whom were itching to get out.

Unfortunately for O'Hagan, he wasn't as important in the pecking order as he would later become. When O'Hagan and another member, Charlie Murphy, was chosen by the IRA's camp staff to work on an escape, the army's General Headquarters (GHQ) Chief of Staff instructed that a different pair of internees should use the route being planned. With so many

IRA members interned, the leadership knew that they needed some of their most experienced men back in the struggle. Dáithí Ó Conaill and Ruairí Ó Brádaigh were to be freed first. Although Ó Conaill was only twenty at the time, he was a rising star within the IRA. As second-in-command of the Pearse Column, he was involved in the raid on the Royal Ulster Constabulary's (RUC) barracks at Brookeborough in January 1957, and had served six months in Mountjoy Prison. On his release from the Dublin jail, he had been rearrested and sent to the Curragh.

Ó Brádaigh was even more senior. He had joined Sinn Féin in 1950, aged eighteen, and was appointed to the Military Council of the IRA four years later. He led a raid on a British Army barracks in Berkshire in August 1955 which obtained huge quantities of firearms and ammunitions for the IRA, and when the border campaign began, he was in charge of training one of the four "columns" (the armed units carrying out the IRA strikes), and, like Ó Conaill, had raided RUC barracks. While serving a six-month sentence in Mountjoy, he was elected as a Teachta Dála (member of the Irish Parliament) for Sinn Féin, although like his fellow TDs, he refused to sit in anything other than an all-Ireland parliament. Once his sentence was over, he too was rearrested and dispatched to the Curragh.

The plan was moderately simple: during a football match, a blanket was smuggled out and placed on the ground near the perimeter fencing. The spectators then kicked pieces of grass over it to disguise it, and the two escapees crawled underneath it. They had previously prepared dummies which were put in their beds, so the guards' headcount would be correct. As an extra precaution, to make sure that the guards who were check-ing the perimeter fencing for any signs of disturbance were distracted, a very nice cap was left on the ground. Ó Conaill and Ó Brádaigh waited until nightfall, then cut their way out of the camp. When the prison guards started enquiring about the ownership of the cap, rather than setting off all the alarms, the other IRA men knew that their comrades had succeeded. Ó Brádaigh became the first TD to go on the run since the 1920s. The following month, he was elected as Chief of Staff, a posi-tion he would hold twice in his career; he later became leader of Republican Sinn Féin, from which he retired in 2009. Ó Conaill became IRA Director of Operations but was shot and captured in 1959; he shared Ó Brádaigh's view of the struggles against the British, and joined Republican Sinn Féin when it was founded in 1986, five years before his death.

Although there were some in the camp who believed that internment wouldn't continue for much longer, Joe O'Hagan and the younger IRA members were determined to get out to become part of the fight once more. It was clear that the movement was suffering because increasingly inexperienced, if still enthusiastic, youngsters were having to carry the burden. He and others decided that they would take the risk that the Army soldiers guarding them would open fire if they tried a mass breakout.

Despite not receiving official sanction from the camp escape committee, O'Hagan and over thirty of his fellow internees made a break for it on the afternoon of 3 December 1958. They dealt with the guards in the yard and cut through the wire fence. As they had hoped, the ordinary soldiers didn't open fire on them, but the sergeant in charge did, using his hand gun to try to disable the escapees by shooting them in the legs. The soldiers also had no compunction about using less lethal force: ammonia grenades were chucked at the escaping prisoners, and Joe O'Hagan, who had gone back to help one of his friends who had got caught up in the barbed wire, fell victim to the gas. In the end, though, sixteen men were able to get away from the Curragh.

Those counselling patience were right; internment was lifted in March 1959, and O'Hagan and his compatriots were free to continue the campaign.

Sources:

Robert W. White, *Ruairí Ó Brádaigh: The Life and Politics of an Irish Revolutionary*, (Indiana University Press, 2006)

Paddy Hayes, *Break Out! Famous Prison Escapes* (O'Brien Press, 2004)

An Phoblacht, 3 May 2001: "Unassuming and mighty man laid to rest"

An Phoblacht, 29 April 2001: "JB O'Hagan dies"

The Real-Life *Fugitive*?

Over two decades, audiences watched the adventures of Dr Richard Kimble – firstly, on television in the 1960s, with David Janssen playing the man who had been framed for his wife's murder, and then thirty years later when Harrison Ford took on the role, pursued by the implacable Tommy Lee Jones. *The Fugitive* was popular because viewers identified with the wrongfully imprisoned doctor who took desperate measures to prove his innocence. As the TV series ran, a real-life fugitive kept breaking out of prison for pretty much the same reason: Alfred George Hinds was keen to prove that he wasn't guilty of the jewellery robbery for which he received a twelve-year sentence in 1953. And although Alfie Hinds' escapes weren't as spectacular as the train wreck featured in the movie version of *The Fugitive*, they baffled prison officers for some considerable time.

Alfie Hinds was a crook; that, he never denied. His father was a thief who had died while receiving ten lashes of the cat o'nine tails for his part in an armed robbery, and young Alfie was brought up in a children's home, from which he ran away aged seven after receiving harsh treatment at the hands of those in charge of him. He drifted into a life of petty theft, and was sent to Borstal in the 1930s; he was drafted into the Army during the Second World War, but he deserted.

The crime for which Hinds was arrested and convicted in December 1953 was to make him a household name over the next dozen years. According to the police, Hinds committed the robbery alongside William Frederick Nicholls. At the trial, the Lord Chief Justice described Nicholls as the principal offender in the robbery at the Maples department store in London, and the jury refused to believe Hinds' protestations of innocence. That left Hinds facing a twelve-year stretch in Nottingham prison.

(Nicholls eventually admitted that Hinds wasn't involved, leading to questions regarding his evidence in the House of Commons in June 1961.)

Hinds tried all the normal routes: he appealed, but it was turned down; he made a petition to the Home Office, but it was dismissed. As far as he could see, the only way in which he could make his story known, and thus achieve justice, was to be on the outside. But how to get out without compounding his problems?

Hinds wrote an account of his various escapes, which was published as *Contempt of Court* in 1966, and became the accepted version of his escapades, at least until his co-escaper in the Nottingham incident spoke with writer Paul Buck in 2008. The prison in which he found himself had been built in 1912, replacing the original city jail, and presented the usual obstacles: high interior walls, barbed wire and an outer barrier. According to Hinds, he reasoned that if all he did was escape from lawful custody, then he wasn't committing a criminal offence, just breaking prison rules. He didn't want to face separate criminal charges which would be much harder to deny while trying to prove his innocence of the offence for which he had been sent down. He therefore believed that if he didn't discuss the plan with anyone, he wouldn't be liable for a conspiracy charge; if he didn't do any technical action, such as creating a key, or opening a lock, then he couldn't be responsible for the breakout – all he was doing was taking advantage of an opportunity that presented itself. Of course, there was no question of any violence during the flight: that would be the fastest way to ensure that no one was thinking about his part in the jewellery robbery, but only his escape. And if someone else did all of the technical parts of an escape, and Hinds happened to come along at exactly the right moment and decided to go along, then who could blame him – at least, technically?

Hinds therefore latched on to an escape attempt already being prepared by Patsy Fleming, another robber. Fleming had already made a key for a grille that, once opened, would allow him access to the coal cellar. From inside the cellar, he could open the flap on the coal chute, and crawl up into a small well that was covered by a grating. When he undid the padlock on that, he would be in the prison yard.

The first time that Fleming tried out the route, on the night of 25 November 1955, it was a failure; although he was unable to get as far as the grating, the key, which someone else had made for him, didn't fit. Fleming had to give up and return to the cells, covered in coal dust, which he hastily showered off. The man responsible for the ill-fitting key denied there was a problem, but when Fleming tried again on 28 November, he sensibly took a hacksaw blade with him, just in case! It added ten minutes on to the escape, but was worth it.

Fleming went over to the prison workshop, where he tried to use a clamp to widen the bars on a window so he could get in, but when he realized that it was insufficiently strong, he broke in through a wire-meshed fanlight. Inside were two door frames that Alfie Hinds had made, which fitted together to form a makeshift ladder. Fleming took them out through the workshop door, leaned them against the interior prison wall, and used them to get over. He then ripped his way through a barbed-wire fence, and then climbed over the eight-foot-high outer wall, arriving in a private garden nearby.

He wasn't overly happy to find he had a companion. When he reached the garden, he heard Alfie Hinds calling out to him. Hinds had followed him through the coal cellar, and over the walls, simply taking advantage of the available route. Fleming didn't argue and allowed Hinds to tag along. They were collected by one of Fleming's friends, and managed to get through a roadblock that had been put up after the escape had been discovered by hiding in orange boxes. They were then driven down to London, where they parted company. Fleming was caught three months later in the East End.

Fleming's version of events is rather different. Hinds' account paints Fleming as the instigator of the escape, and Hinds as simply someone who came along for the ride. However in 2008, the elderly robber insisted that Hinds had been in charge, and that he had been alongside Fleming the whole way through the escape, creating the key for the padlock as they were in the coal cellar. Fleming was insistent that Hinds could make any key, and that he had also created one to get them into the prison workshop. He also claimed that it was one of Hinds' contacts who had collected them and driven them to London.

Whichever way the escape happened, Hinds was able to get out of the country and head to Dublin, where he believed that he was safe. He made numerous pleas for publicity for his case – his recorded comments which were broadcast on the new commercial television station (ITV only began broadcasting in September 1955) led to questions in the House of Commons, and the wonderful question from Sheffield MP John Burns Hynd: "Will the Minister not consider extending similar facilities through the Press, radio and television to other criminals who have loyally remained in prison, so that they make an appeal for public sympathy?" Nicknamed "Houdini Hinds" by the press, he supported himself by working as a painter/decorator for 248 days before being arrested at gun point. He had even spent part of that eight months attending law lectures at Trinity College, Dublin.

As far as Hinds was concerned, his arrest was illegal: he hadn't actually escaped from prison, and therefore, without any hesitation, he brought legal proceedings against the police for false imprisonment. However, it became clear to him that he wasn't going to succeed with this action, so he decided to escape, with a view to starting proceedings in the Irish Court. He wasn't going to cease his current action, though: it was providing him with the method of escape, from the very heart of the seat of justice, the Law Courts in the Strand in London.

Hinds' second period of freedom lasted considerably less time than his first, and just over a month after his escape on 24 June 1957, he found himself in court giving evidence in the case that was being brought against his brother Albert and a friend of his, John Maffia, for unlawfully aiding his escape. Flanked by three prison officers, rather than the usual single guard, Hinds explained that on a previous visit to the Law Courts, he had spotted that a lavatory door was locked; if he could somehow lock his escort inside the toilet, then he would be able to make his getaway unimpeded. He therefore had a chat with a prisoner at Pentonville who was shortly to be released; this man, who Hinds refused to name, but told the court was "quite a notorious locksmith", duly arranged to leave a key for the lavatory underneath a table in the staff canteen at the Courts.

On 24 June, Hinds was escorted to the Law Courts by Prison Officers Martin and Hadley, who hadn't been there before. He therefore led the way to the canteen, and went to the designated table. However, when he reached underneath to find the key, he had a bit of a shock, since there was no key waiting for him. Instead there was a small parcel, which seemed to be wrapped up in paper and secured to the table with adhesive plaster. Hinds pulled off the plaster, screwed it up and put the package in his pocket. When the two prison officers became engrossed in a conversation with one of Martin's former colleagues, Hinds was able to open the parcel. Inside there was a small padlock, but no key. He realized that something must have changed, and he had been given an alternate way of dealing with the situation – although he clearly was going to have to think on his feet.

When the three men left the canteen, they went upstairs and came to the lavatory, and when he saw two new "eyes" fitted to the door and the frame, Hinds understood exactly what was going on. They were so new – glaring like searchlights, he later said – that he realized that he had to act immediately, or someone would get suspicious and wonder why they were there. He only had one shilling in his pocket, but he would worry about that once he got away from the guards.

Hinds went to the lavatory door, with a packet of legal papers held in his left hand, and his mackintosh in his right, covering the padlock. He pushed the door open, and Martin went straight in, and down to the end. Hadley seemed to be suspicious of Hinds, and stayed a couple of yards from him, expecting to follow Hinds in and close the door behind them. Swiftly, Hinds turned, and pushed Hadley through the door, slamming it shut, and fastening the padlock between the two eyes to keep it shut. It was clear to the veteran thief that the lock wouldn't hold two angry prison officers for very long, so he ran as fast as he could down the corridor, and skidded into the first opening on the right, hearing pounding on the door and shouting from behind him.

Slowing down, Hinds passed through groups of solicitors' clerks who were milling around the law courts, and out of the building. Although the shouting must surely have attracted attention by then, no alarm had been raised in the vicinity of the courts, so he made for Temple underground station.

As he went through the barrier, he heard someone call out "Alf". Hinds turned to see his younger brother there, shocked at finding him suddenly free. Hinds had asked Albert to come to the courtroom that day when his brother had visited him the previous Saturday, but, so Hinds told the court, his brother had not been expecting his escape, and, likewise, he didn't expect to run into his brother in the middle of a Tube station. He had intended to head to a hide-out in London until he could get out of the country. Albert told the court that he had heard a shout that "Hinds had escaped", and he himself had been chased by one of the prison officers. After he had shaken off the man, Albert spotted his brother in the Strand and followed him down to the Tube station.

According to Hinds' testimony, Albert had previously arranged with John Maffia to go to Bristol, and he then suggested that it would be a good idea if Alfie went with them. With hindsight, Hinds regretted taking up the offer, as it led directly to his re-arrest. He claimed that they didn't tell Maffia that he had escaped, but spun a tale that he had been acquitted on the appeal. Instead of going straight to Bristol, though, they went to Heathrow Airport, where Hinds just missed a flight to Dublin. They therefore carried on down the Great West Road, arriving at Bristol Airport in time for a flight. Albert went to buy the ticket, but he was so nervous that he made the girl behind the ticket counter very suspicious. Thinking that he might be connected to a local murder enquiry, she contacted the police – who were delighted to apprehend Alfie Hinds once more. He had been free for less than five hours.

Hinds was sent to Chelmsford Prison, and became one of the few ever to abscond from the place – his escape makes him one of its most famous inmates, according to a local website. To get an idea of what Chelmsford looked like at that stage, watch the feature-film version of the prison sitcom *Porridge*, which was filmed on location within its walls.

Again, if you believe Hinds' own account, he wasn't necessarily the instigator of the plan, but was happy to go along with it. Fellow prisoner Georgie Walkington had worked out a way to get out, and Hinds was simply a helpful assistant on Sunday 1 June 1958 when the two men went over the wall with keys that Walkington had been able to obtain.

Walkington was meant to be cleaning his cell while many of the other prisoners attended the church service. When he went down to the ground-floor landing to collect a bucket of water, he made his way into the linen store. From there, he went through a hatch and along a passageway. At the end of this was a set of double doors, for which Walkington had a key, which led to the prison yard. Separating the yard from the compound was a wall with a pair of big gates; Walkington had keys for these too.

Hinds caught up with Walkington as the latter reached the double doors; he had persuaded Walkington's friend, who was bolting up the hatch behind him, that he was part of the escape. Unfortunately, when they reached the gates, the key didn't fit, so Hinds suggested balancing two of the wheelbarrows used for carrying coal around the prison one on top of the other, and they could then climb over the gate. Rather than see the barbed wire on top of the gate as an obstacle, Hinds fastened his jacket to it, and the pair of them were able to haul themselves up, even though Hinds fell at one point and broke his glasses.

The two men went along the top of the wall, until they found a suitable point to jump the twenty-five feet to the ground. Hinds injured his leg in the jump, so Walkington pressed ahead through the graveyard that adjoined the prison until he reached a car that was waiting for them. Despite his injuries, Hinds drove them through Essex back roads, through the Blackwall Tunnel into Kent, to a friend of Walkington's, who was appeased by a suitably large payment to put up with the risk of harbouring Hinds.

Alfie Hinds managed to stay on the loose for twenty months this time, making his way back to Dublin via Liverpool and Belfast. While continuing to lobby the Houses of Parliament and the media about his false conviction (he sold his story to the *News of the World* for a reported £40,000), he used the alias William Herbert Bishop to become part of a ring smuggling cars from the Republic of Ireland into Belfast. However, he was caught during a police operation against that. He was returned to Britain and was sent to serve the remainder of his term at Parkhurst Prison. That didn't stop him from taking legal action: he sued a police officer who mocked his claims of innocence, and continued to make applications to the Home Office for his immediate release from prison, and applying for a free pardon. After one was turned down, he told Lord Justice Sellers, "I am not going to remain in prison. It would be very hard for me to leave again. But I assure you I am going to." Officers at Parkhurst discovered in February 1962 that he had fixed the lock on his cell so he could get out at will. But eventually, after thirteen appeals had failed, he gained his pardon, and, as a free man, regularly spoke about escapes (an ITN documentary showed him explaining the pros and cons of various methods).

There was an interesting footnote to his case: in 1967 some Westminster students rather foolishly thought they could get the better of him, and "kidnapped" him as part of a Rag Week stunt. They frogmarched him along the road to a basement room in the college – but they weren't able to hold Houdini Hinds for long. Within a very short time, Hinds had got hold of a bunch of keys and locked them in!

In later life, Hinds moved to Jersey and became secretary of the Channel Islands branch of the Mensa Society, a reflection of the keen amount of work that he had engaged in learning the ins and outs of the British legal system. He died on 5 January 1991.

Sources:

Time magazine, 16 March 1962: "Alfie, the Elusive"
Hansard, 23 February 1956: "Alfred George Hinds"
Hansard, 22 June 1961: "Alfred George Hinds"
Hansard, 30 July 1964: "The Case of Alfred Hinds"
Hansard, 2 December 1964: "Prison Escapes"
Glasgow Herald, 30 July 1957: "Alfred Hinds Tells How He Planned His Escape"
Hinds, Alfred: *Contempt of Court* (Bodley Head, 1966)
Buck, Paul: *Prison Break* (John Blake, 2012)

The Escape that Changed the Law

Ronald Joseph Ryan was hanged at Pentridge Prison on 3 February 1967 for the murder of prison officer George Hodson during an escape from the jail on Sunday 19 December 1965. He was the last Australian to suffer this sentence – in large part because, even at the time of his execution, there was considerable doubt as to whether he committed the crime for which he was condemned. (The reaction of the Premier of Victoria, Henry Bolte, who had pushed for the execution, when he was asked what he was doing as Ryan was hanged – "Oh I don't remember, I suppose I was having one of the three S's – either a shave, a shit or a shower" – didn't endear the process to many either.)

Ryan was serving an eight-year sentence for breaking and entering. He didn't really start a life of crime till he was about thirty-one years of age but his time in jail saw his wife divorce him, wanting to separate herself completely from him. Ryan objected strongly to this, and planned to escape from Pentridge so he could win her back, and then take her and their children to Brazil, which didn't have an extradition treaty with Australia. He used his time inside profitably to gain the education that he hadn't received as a child and was regarded as pretty much a model prisoner.

His accomplice in the escape was Peter John Walker, who was in the middle of a twelve-year stretch for bank robbery. The date for their escape was chosen because it was the day of the prison staff Christmas party, and therefore there weren't as many guards on duty as normal. Abandoning his reading of *Exodus*, Leon Uris' book about the founding of Israel, Walker joined Ryan and they scaled a sixteen-feet-high inner wall with the help of two wooden benches. Pausing to collect a homemade grappling hook which Ryan had made from a broom handle and some wire and thrown into the long grass within the no-man's-land area, they headed for the outer wall. They were able to climb this using blankets linked to the hook, and successfully reached the top of the wall.

It was at this point that Ronald Ryan's life changed irrevocably. He and Walker were faced with guard Helmut Lange, who, seeing two convicts where they simply should not be by any sensible definition, froze on the spot. Rather than grabbing his M1 carbine rifle, which would be a match for the piece of galvanized iron pipe that the two men were brandishing, he did nothing. That allowed Ryan the opportunity to grab the gun. As far as anyone knows, Ryan understood the basics of using a weapon – point it, pull the trigger and fire – but evidence given by Lange at his trial would suggest that he didn't know much more than that. Certainly, he didn't disengage the safety catch. If he had pulled the trigger, all that would have happened is an undischarged bullet would have been ejected.

Although initially he pulled the wrong lever, Lange eventually opened the gate, allowing the two men to gain their freedom. Ryan and Walker ran out from Pentridge, and Ryan then threatened a Salvation Army prison chaplain to gain his car keys. Brigadier James Hewitt hadn't come to the prison by car that day, and in his anger at being foiled, Ryan hit him with the butt of the rifle. He then tried to use the gun to flag down a passing car.

By this point, Lange had raised the alarm, and his fellow guard, George Hodson, came out from the prison. He took the iron bar from Walker and pursued him. At the same time, other armed warders were involved in the hunt, with one of them, Robert Patterson, claiming that he fired a shot into the air when a woman unexpectedly got in-between him and Ryan.

At pretty much that same moment, Hodson fell dead. Fourteen witnesses gave evidence at the trial that followed and all confirmed that only one shot was fired – but many of those witnesses were convinced that the shot came from Ryan's gun. Some said that they saw it recoil, others that there was smoke. Yet M1 carbines at the prison were loaded with smokeless ammunition, and the weapon doesn't have any recoil. Former prisoner Harold Sheehan eventually claimed that Ryan had been kneeling down at the time the shot rang out, but his statement in 1993 was twenty-six years too late to save Ryan.

Perhaps not realizing that Hodson had been killed – or by that stage, knowing that they were in far too deep to stop now – Walker and Ryan commandeered a car and sped away. They changed cars twice more before heading for a safe house which had been arranged for them in the north-western Melbourne suburb of Kensington. The next day they moved into a flat in Elwood, to the south of the city, belonging to Christine Aitken.

The hunt for the two men was fuelled by anger at the death of the prison warder. Newspapers claimed that Ryan had shot Hodson three times after seizing him, and the Chief Secretary and Attorney General, Arthur Rylah, issued a warning to the two fugitives that the Hanging Act was still in force. On 23 December, they robbed a bank in Ormond, and on Christmas Eve, Walker murdered Aitken's boyfriend, Arthur Henderson. After that, they returned to the safe house in Kensington, hiding until their accomplice obtained a car for them. On New Year's Day 1966, they drove the 550 miles to Sydney.

They didn't last long there. Ryan wanted to reconnect with an old friend in Sydney, but she wasn't home when he called. Her daughter agreed that she would meet with Ryan and her mother at Concord Repatriation Hospital on the evening of 6 January. However, the woman had recognized Ryan and contacted the police. (Some sources suggest that they were betrayed by ex-con Lennie McPherson to whom they had gone for faked passports.) When he and Walker went to the rendezvous, the police were waiting for them. Even though Ryan was carrying a loaded revolver, he was captured without incident; Walker also gave up without a struggle. Multiple weapons were found in the boot of the car, alongside an axe, a hacksaw, a jemmy and coils of rope.

On the journey back to Melbourne, Ronald Ryan admitted that he had shot George Hodson. Or at least, that was the police version of events. According to Detective Sergeant K.P. Walters, Ryan told him: "In the heat of the moment you sometimes do an act without thinking. I think this is what happened with Hodson. He had no need to interfere. He was stupid. He was told to keep away. He grabbed Pete (i.e. Peter Walker) and hit him with an iron bar. He caused his own death. I didn't want to shoot him. I could have shot a lot more." Detective Senior Constable Harry Morrison had his own conversation with Ryan to relate: "The warder spoilt the whole show. If he had not poked his great head into it he would not have got shot. It was either him or Pete." To his dying day, Ryan denied making these statements. In fact, the only document signed by Ryan during this period stated that he would give no verbal testimony.

It wasn't enough to save him. Even conflicting testimony from various witnesses didn't sway the jury. Ryan explained to the jury what had happened in the guard tower: "At no time did I fire a shot," he said. "My freedom was the only objective. The rifle was taken in the first instance so that it could not be used against me." He maintained that he had kept the rifle so that ballistics evidence would prove that he hadn't fired the shot – but the bullet that killed Hodson passed through the prison warder, and was never found. Nor was the cartridge from which it came. And with only one bullet missing, and no sign of an undischarged bullet in the watchtower, it was easy to deduce that the only bullet fired was the one that hit Hodson.

Although the jury believed that the mandatory sentence of death would be commuted, they still found him guilty; one jury-man, Tom Gildea, was convinced that if they had known they were sending Ryan to the gallows, they would have convicted him of the lesser charge of manslaughter.

None of his appeals was successful, and, after a tot of whisky, Ronald Ryan walked to the gallows calmly at 8 a.m. on Friday 3 February 1967. "Please make it quick," he asked the hangman, who duly obliged.

The controversy didn't die out. One of the eyewitnesses who gave evidence at the trial wrote to the *Australian* newspaper in 1992 stating bluntly, "Let me assure you and your readers that Ryan did kill Hodson . . . It was a sickening sight. I also witnessed a slight puff of smoke come from the carbine Ryan used. This was probably as a result of a bullet passing through a well-oiled barrel bore."

Helmut Lange, whose rifle was used to kill Hodson, if Ryan really was the killer, refused to accept a bravery commendation,

222   *Mammoth Book of Prison Breaks*

and committed suicide in April 1969. Some of Ryan's supporters claim that Lange didn't hand over the bullet cartridge that
he had found in the tower, which would have proved Ryan's
story that he never fired the gun. According to a Melbourne
newspaper report, Hodson's daughter literally danced on Ryan's
unmarked grave at the prison in 2007 before the remains were
exhumed, cremated, and buried alongside his mother's ashes.

Had it not been for the death of George Hodson, Ryan's
escape would have been almost a run-of-the-mill affair. Instead,
it led to major protests, and the eventual abolition of the death
penalty in Australia.

Sources:

Herald-Sun, 19 January 1997: "Ryan: the case"

Supreme Court Trial Transcript – *Queen v. Ryan & Walker, 15–30 March 1966*

Sun, 31 March 1966: "Ryan Guilty"

The Australian, 7 February 1992: "Witness breaks silence to damn Ryan"

Opas, Philip, *Throw away my wig: an autobiography of a long journey with a few sign posts* (Turton-Turner, 1997)

Stoljar, Jeremy: *The Australian Book of Great Trials* (Murdoch, 2011)

Their Mission, Should They Choose to Accept It . . .

One of the most audacious heists of the twentieth century, that has entered popular mythology, was the Great Train Robbery that took place near Mentmore in Buckinghamshire, England, in the early hours of Thursday 8 August 1963. Over £2.5 million was stolen from the Royal Mail train, much of which was never recovered. Many of the robbers were found, tried and imprisoned: of them, two made daring escapes and managed to stay on the run for some time.

The two who evaded justice were Charlie Wilson and Ronnie Biggs, names that have become synonymous with the Great Train Robbery. In the case of Wilson, this was justified: he was one of the prime movers in the plotting. Ronnie Biggs, on the other hand, had a less important role: his job was to hire the replacement driver who would be needed to move the train the half-mile down the track, from where it was stopped to the rendezvous with the truck that would transport the loot. In the end, the new driver couldn't handle the type of locomotive, so Jack Mills, the original driver, was forced to take his place.

Eleven of the robbers were found guilty of conspiracy to rob and armed robbery, and on 15 April 1964, sentences of thirty years each were passed on them. Appeals three months later upheld the judge's decision on the majority of them, including Wilson and Biggs. Within a year, both men were on the run.

As soon as he heard the thirty-year sentence, Charlie Wilson knew there was only one logical course of action: he had to escape, or face the prospect of life in prison until he was at least seventy. He was initially sent to the Victorian-built Winson Green prison, on the outskirts of Birmingham, where warders were ordered not to allow him any contact with other prisoners. However, it didn't take long before the restrictions were not enforced as firmly, and after a couple of weeks, Wilson received a message telling him that his friend "Frenchy" was "working on it". According to the account his wife later gave, this was a great relief to Wilson, since he trusted his French friend implicitly. The pair had planned various robberies together including the Great Train Robbery itself, and during the Second World War, Frenchy had worked for the Resistance in France, helping to release captured Maquis from the hands of the Gestapo.

Rather than take the risk of being moved from Winson Green, Wilson elected not to travel to the Court of Appeal in July for the hearing of the case. He was quite happy to wait at Winson Green until Frenchy made his move, which he expected might take anything up to a year. Instead, less than four months after the end of his trial, Wilson was a free man.

Rather like Tom Cruise in the *Mission: Impossible* films, Frenchy put together a team of six people, all of whom had the specialized skills required to carry out the task of freeing Charlie Wilson. The first two, and perhaps the most critical, were referred to as "mountain men". The pair, whose physical size also justified their title, would be scaling the outside walls of Winson Green, and also training the other members of the quartet – one of the most expert locksmiths in England, an expert getaway driver, a Belgian pilot, and a wireless radio operator – in the techniques of climbing ropes. Although the pilot couldn't see why he needed to be trained in rope-climbing, he was told to get on with it.

They trained at a deserted monastery in northern France: one of the walls was about the height of Winson Green's exterior, and Frenchy ensured that it matched the sorts of problems that they would encounter. Each time they shaved a second off the ascent time, he pointed out that that equalled "another day off Charlie's sentence". The locksmith became concerned that he was creating calluses on his hands that would make it difficult for him to carry out his lucrative trade afterwards, but he was reassured that his proportion of the fee for the escape would more than adequately compensate him for the time off work that he had to take while he healed.

The training lasted until mid-July, and then the pilot went to reconnoitre suitable landing strips; the getaway driver then worked out the various obstacles that each might present. Eventually, Frenchy decided on a disused airfield around eighty-five miles from the prison which would meet their needs. At that point, he sent Wilson a message via the same prisoner: "Keep awake on August 12. Frenchy says four soft friends will be visiting you." "Soft" in this context meant they would be using minimal violence, and not carrying guns, something about which Wilson had been concerned. If firearms were involved in the escape, then it could have serious repercussions.

On the designated day, Wilson went through his normal nightly routine, eating his supper of bread and cheese and drinking a cup of cocoa. After lights out at 9.30 p.m., he waited patiently in his cell – the same one that had been used by KGB spy Gordon Lonsdale before he was traded with the Russians. Frenchy and his team were assembling outside the prison in a Ford Zodiac car and a converted petrol tanker.

Shortly before 3 a.m. on 13 August 1964, the two mountain men and the locksmith ran across to a builder's yard that adjoined the walls. With dark-blue raincoats hiding the ropes they needed, black trousers and trainers, they were as invisible as they could be. Using a small ladder borrowed from the yard, they quickly scaled a low iron fence beside the wall, dropped their equipment and donned black stocking masks. A rope with a grappling iron was thrown to the top of the wall, and once it was secure, the locksmith ascended. After checking all was clear, he hauled up a special mountain ladder on the end of the rope, then fixed a second rope to the wall, which he dropped on the inside. The two mountain men followed to the top of the wall, and secured a second ladder and third rope to the top. The radio operator then climbed the wall, and pulled up all of the apparatus that was on the outside.

While Frenchy monitored the police wavelengths for any signs of the alarm being raised, the two mountain men, the locksmith and the radio operator ran across the prison yard to the bathhouse door at the end of Wilson's wing. It was the work of seconds to pick this and get inside. The quartet hurried down to the main door into the prison wing, went through, and then hid in an alcove. As soon as the guard on duty, Mr Nichols, passed them, he was disabled, tied up and gagged by three of the team while the locksmith went to Wilson's cell. It took him eight minutes to crack the lock, rather longer than he had anticipated.

Wilson could hear the work, and was ready for his visitors. He only had prison uniform, so he was provided with a black sweater, a balaclava helmet, dark trousers and running shoes, which he quickly donned, and followed the four men back out into the yard. A few minutes later he was over the wall, and was being ushered through a flap in the side of the main tank of the petrol carrier. Waiting for him were mattresses, pillows, blankets and an electric torch.

The trip to the airfield took about an hour and a half. From there Wilson was flown to a villa in northern France. Frenchy took the mountain men, the radio operator and the locksmith away in his car, and paid them off. A couple of days later, Frenchy joined Wilson in Paris, and the two of them began a peripatetic existence around France.

In England, the authorities were baffled by the escape. "This is so abnormal that you just cannot cater for it," said the secretary of the Prison Officers Association. Roadblocks were set up on the three motorways running through the Midlands; Liverpool airport was especially watched for any sign of the fugitive. Hundreds of police officers and tracker dogs tore the city apart looking for him. But there was no sign – although that didn't prevent Chief Superintendent Tommy Butler, who had been responsible for the arrest of the Great Train Robbers, from following any lead.

Wilson and Frenchy spent some months together before eventually parting company in Italy. Wilson was anxious to be reunited with his wife and family, and after travelling around the world looking for a new home where they could be safe, he settled on a place near Montreal, in the Canadian province of Quebec. The family spent sixteen months in Rigaud before Butler caught up with them. Wilson was taken back to Britain and remained in prison until 1978. He was shot dead at his Marbella villa in 1990.

*   *   *

One man who was greatly cheered by Charlie Wilson's escape and subsequent evasion of the hunt was his fellow Great Train Robber, Ronnie Biggs. He had been sent to the prisons at Lincoln and Chelmsford between the trial and the appeal, but the day after the Court ruled that his sentence should stand, Biggs was transferred to Wandsworth, which he described as "Britain's answer, at the time, to Alcatraz", a place in which he had been imprisoned before.

According to Biggs' final volume of autobiography, he refused various offers of help to escape from Wandsworth, which began arriving as soon as he was moved there. Security, though, was tight on Biggs, and it was increased after Wilson's departure, as well as an attempt four days later to free another of the Robbers, Gordon Goody, from Strangeways. (Friends tried to get Goody out shortly after Biggs' escape as well, but were foiled.) Biggs was moved from cell to cell, to prevent intruders from breaking him out as they had Wilson, and in the end the pressure of the intensive security measures pushed him to ask for help in escaping.

Biggs laid his plans with fellow prisoner Paul Seabourne, who was coming towards the end of his four-year sentence, and other robbers, Eric Flower and Roy Shaw. Shaw backed out when he realized how much money he would need to stay on the run, and, as events transpired, was transferred to Parkhurst Prison on the Isle of Wight shortly before Biggs escaped. Flower, Seabourne and Biggs examined all the possibilities of getting over the twenty-five-feet-high prison wall, and came up with the idea of using a furniture removal van with some sort of platform on the top – if they could come up with a way of disguising it so it wasn't very obvious what was happening as the vehicle approached the prison.

Special Watch prisoners such as Biggs were exercised in a yard next to the main prison wall; on the far side was a service road which led to the main road. They would either go from 2 till 4 p.m., or 3 till 4, and it was down to the senior prison officer in charge that day who went when. The plan, therefore, was for Biggs and Flower to ensure that they were in the latter shift so timings could be agreed; Seabourne would arrive at 3.10, and the men calculated that it would take them half a minute to get into position by the main wall. A wristwatch was smuggled in to ensure that everything was coordinated properly.

Before Seabourne's release, plans were fully laid. Another prisoner, Brian Stone, who owed Biggs a major favour, agreed to help distract the guards, and brought another prisoner in to act as a fellow minder. Once Seabourne was on the outside, he set the rest of the plan into motion, and through messages passed to Flower, the date was agreed: Wednesday 7 July 1965.

Although the weather looked bad, everything started off according to plan. Biggs avoided the first exercise shift by claiming he had a bad stomach and needed mild treatment in the sick bay; Flower spent time with visitors so wasn't able to join the shift; the two minders had kept out of the way. At 3 p.m., all four were sent out to the yard, but within minutes it started to pour heavily. Despite the prisoners' protestations, they were taken back onto the prison wing for indoor exercise.

Although annoying, this wasn't catastrophic, as the team had planned for weather problems, and agreed simply to try again the next day. This time, it was sunny, and the plan went like clockwork. Biggs, Flower and their minders went to exercise at 3 p.m. and this time, they heard the sound of the furniture van outside the walls. A moment later, they saw Seabourne's head covered in a nylon stocking, and then rope ladders coming over the wall. Biggs and Flower ran to the ladders as the two others stopped the guards from getting too close. With Stone's cry of "You're too late, Biggsy's away!" ringing in his ears, Ronnie Biggs dropped onto the roof of the furniture van.

A hole had been cut in the roof to allow access for a hinged platform to come out, to give Seabourne the height he needed to reach the top of the wall. Inside the van were mattresses for Biggs, Flower and Seabourne to jump down onto. Two other convicts, Robert Anderson and Patrick Doyle, followed Biggs and Flower over the wall and into the van. All of them raced out of the back of the van into a waiting getaway car. They used this to go round the service road, then abandoned it in a quiet cul-de-sac near the prison, and took a second car. Biggs, Flower and Seabourne headed to Dulwich, and left the car for Anderson and Doyle.

The three men celebrated as they watched the news of the escape. Because there was no direct line between the prison and the local police station, it had taken time for the news to get to the police, so the search for them didn't begin for twenty minutes. Biggs and Flower changed location frequently; Seabourne was arrested quite quickly after the escape, and received a four-and-a-half-year jail term for the escape. The two minders had an extra year added to their sentences.

Biggs and Flower were smuggled out of the country in October 1965 and underwent painful plastic surgery in Paris. They both headed for Australia, and Biggs ended up in Brazil. He returned to the UK voluntarily in 2001, after 13,068 days on the run. He was arrested and returned to prison, this time at HMP Belmarsh in South London. Ronnie Biggs was finally released from prison on compassionate grounds on 6 August 2009.

Sources:

Montreal Gazette, 6/13/20 April 1968: "My Husband, The Master Criminal"

Birmingham Mail, 24 January 2012: "CrimeFiles Prison Break Special: The Great Train Robbery"

Biggs, Ronnie with Christopher Pickard: *Odd Man Out, The Last Straw* (Bloomsbury, 2011)

Steubenville Herald, 18 August 1964: "Attempt to Free 2nd Robber Seen"

Salt Lake Tribune, 13 July 1965: "Britain Thwarts Escape of Train Thefts Convict"

The Camper Escape

The reporter for ITN's *Reporting 67* programme was determined to leave no stone unturned in his quest to discover what had happened to the treacherous Russian spy George Blake after his escape from Wormwood Scrubs prison in October 1966. For an overview of the case broadcast early in the new year, he worked out how long it took to drive from the jail in central London to Heathrow airport, and diligently checked to see which flights would have left for Communist countries within a few minutes of Blake's hypothetical arrival – taking into account the half-hour time required in those days between check-in and flight departure, and allowing for the fact that someone else could have checked in for him, and just handed him the ticket when he arrived at the airport. He noted that a Lufthansa flight to Germany was ten minutes late that evening so the Russian agent could have just made that with time to spare. Alternately, he could have headed for the docks, where there were around a dozen Communist-run ships, two of which were out of commission because of strike action. Or he could have hired a small boat to take him out to a Communist ship waiting in the English Channel. Or he might have headed for the embassy of the USSR, or one of the satellite states, and waited there until the pursuit had died down.

What almost certainly didn't cross the reporter or his team's minds was that Blake's escape had been masterminded by a group of peace activists, and carried out by an Irishman who despite all instructions to the contrary, had used his own car as a getaway vehicle! Yet, as was first reported in an interview with the Irishman, Sean Bourke, in 1969, that's exactly what happened – and Blake's progress to East Germany was not exactly the most dignified, hidden inside a camper van.

Blake, whose real name was George Behar, had joined the British Secret Service in 1948, after studying Russian at Cambridge university. He was posted to Seoul in South Korea the following year but was captured by the invading North Koreans. Blake was interrogated by officers from the Russian MGB (a forerunner of the KGB), who were allowed access to prisoners of war by Chinese intelligence, and by the time he was repatriated to Britain at the end of the Korean War, he was a Soviet agent. Whether he changed sides because of natural antipathy to the British system or because he was a true Manchurian Candidate and was brainwashed by the Chinese is open to debate: in 2007, he said he wasn't a traitor: "To betray, you first have to belong. I never belonged."

Blake's importance to the KGB can be judged by the fact that even though he warned Moscow about a major British and American wire-tapping operation that was being carried out in Berlin, they allowed that to proceed rather than risk blowing his cover. He was posted to Berlin, where he was in a position to betray numerous British and American operatives, as well as helping to identify the CIA's man in Russian Army intelligence. Blake would later admit that he didn't know exactly what he handed over to the KGB "because it was so much".

However, his luck ran out in 1961. Polish Lieutenant Colonel Mikhail Goleniewski was working as a triple agent, reporting back to both the CIA and MI6, and he reported that the Russians had a key man inside British intelligence. Blake managed to avoid suspicion initially, but when Goleniewski defected, it became clear that Blake was the traitor. He was summoned back to London from a training course in the Lebanon and arrested.

Blake was tried in secret at the Old Bailey, and charged with five separate offences. He was found guilty of them, and sentenced to fourteen years' imprisonment for each – three of the terms to run consecutively. This forty-two-year sentence was the longest ever handed out by a British court and, according to the headlines in the newspapers at the time, represented a year for every agent he had betrayed. (This seems highly unlikely as it probably underestimated the damage that Blake caused, no matter what Blake may claim.)

The forcibly retired spy was sent to serve his sentence at
Wormwood Scrubs, which had stood in West London since its
completion in 1891. According to one of the men who helped
him escape, anti-nuclear campaigner Michael Randle, Blake
was held up to other prisoners as an example of how to do your
"bird": if Blake was dealing with a forty-two-year stretch with
equanimity, those with much less time to go should behave.

The Home Office were genuinely concerned that Blake
might try to escape: papers recently released under the Freedom of Information Act show that warders were told to listen to
his conversations with visitors, and a letter from his wife discussing the colour of the carpet was regarded as a potential code.
"We are wondering whether this is an attempt to pass a message,"
a prison report in 1963 noted. "From our point of view clandestine communication between the Blakes might well be very
damaging indeed." MI5 were supposed to be keeping an eye as
well: when one scheme came to light in May 1964, then-head of
MI5 Roger Hollis noted that the source was someone with "a
history of mental instability" who was "incapable of dissociating
fact and fantasy".

In 1965, there were claims that a plot was under way to land
a helicopter in the prison grounds to rescue Blake, more than six
years before this method of jail-break was successfully tried.
The prison governor who looked into it commented, "Blake's
letters to his wife tend to continue to be forward-looking and
uncomplaining and he devotes himself energetically to academic
studies. The whole thing is somewhat James Bondish." Blake did
complain about some of the stories that were run in the papers
about him: "Am I throughout my prison sentence to remain at
the mercy of anyone who for reasons best known to himself,
spreads stories about me?" he wrote to the Home Office after an
article had appeared in the tabloid *The People* which stated that
another prisoner had nobly foiled an attempt by Blake to escape.
On this occasion, his complaint was backed up by one of the
prison governors.

Although there was general revulsion at Blake's activities – or
at least, those which the government permitted to be reported in
the papers – there were some who felt that the forty-two-year
sentence was too harsh and savage for a man who was

apparently acting patriotically, even if his patriotism was directed towards a foreign country. "I do not see why this should be a crime in itself, to go against patriotism. Should a German have hesitated more than any other nationality to assassinate Hitler?" one correspondent wrote to the Home Office, requesting Blake's sentence be reassessed.

Those feelings were shared by some of those who served their prison time alongside Blake, including Michael Randle, Pat Pottle and Sean Bourke. Randle and Pottle were founders of the Committee of 100, a British anti-war group set up in 1960 after discussions between members of the Campaign for Nuclear Disarmament and the Direct Action Committee to foment civil disobedience and non-violent resistance against nuclear bombs. The Committee had been seen as a threat by the government, and after a protest at the US Air Force base in Wethersfield, Essex, six of the leaders were sentenced to eighteen months' imprisonment for conspiracy and incitement under the Official Secrets Act. Bourke was serving a seven-year term for "using Her Majesty's mails for transporting an infernal device" – sending a bomb to a detective sergeant who had accused Bourke of an unnatural relationship with a young man.

During their time inside, they had come to know Blake – Bourke edited a prison magazine to which the spy was a regular contributor – and came to feel that his sentence was unjust, and that trying to help him to escape was simply a decent human response. Blake himself, despite the attitude he was displaying to the authorities, had not given up on the idea of escaping: in his autobiography, he notes that he regarded himself as being like a POW, with a duty to escape.

Contrary to the belief of many in the immediate aftermath of the escape on 22 October 1966, the KGB played no part in the escapade. Blake claims that this was because he knew they wouldn't risk a major international scandal if it went wrong; the others concerned stated that they didn't want any involvement with the hated Soviet Union. They were helping George Blake, human being sentenced to rot inside a British prison, not George Blake, KGB agent. While they served their terms, Pottle and Randle offered to help Blake in any way they could, and kept in touch after their release.

Bourke himself was coming towards the end of his sentence at the end of 1965; he had behaved himself while behind bars, and was under consideration for the hostel programme. This meant he would spend the last nine months of his term working in an ordinary civilian job, and sleep in the hostel, connected to the prison. Blake approached Bourke and asked if he would help him escape. The Irishman didn't care that Blake was both an Englishman and a Communist; Blake was his friend, and he told him he would do his best.

A good line of communication was vital between Bourke, who would no longer be able to go inside the prison, and Blake, stuck on D Hall with the rest of the lifers. Since work was being carried out on the hostel by inmates from D Hall, a trusted friend was used as a go-between. Almost immediately Bourke's unreliability began to become obvious: he was also communicating with another prisoner, Kenneth de Courcy, and at one point the messages became mixed up. De Courcy got a letter with details of the escape attempt, but agreed to keep quiet, as long as he was kept in the loop about developments. To Blake's eternal gratitude, de Courcy never breathed a word, even though he could have probably gained some valuable time knocked off his own sentence if he had betrayed the spy.

To prevent a repetition of the error, Bourke arranged for a walkie-talkie to be smuggled into the prison, which operated on a frequency that wouldn't be monitored by the police. The only problem with that, as Blake found out when another prisoner came in to warn him urgently, was that it could be picked up by the ordinary radios that some of the other inmates had in their cells. "Fox Michael" and "Baker Charlie" had to be very careful about their conversations after that.

Around the same time, Bourke got back in touch with Michael Randle and Pat Pottle, and told them that he needed some financial help in order to arrange George Blake's escape. They were happy to help. With the money, Bourke bought a second-hand car, and found a small flat near the prison. When Bourke had completed his prison term, and was released from the hostel, he returned to Ireland, apparently for good – but then returned to the UK under a false name.

The escape was set for a Saturday evening, when the majority of prisoners and guards would be away from the Hall, watching the weekly film show. Blake had taken advice from one of the experts on breaking and entering at the Hall, and chosen to leave through one of the large gothic windows which overlooked the yard. These windows were comprised of small panes of glass, divided by cast-iron frames. Every other panel swivelled open to act as an air vent, but on their own, were too small for a man to squeeze through. However with the iron strut removed, a gap eighteen inches by twelve was created, just about enough room for Blake to squeeze through. Once through there, it was a short jump to the roof of a covered passageway, from which Blake could jump to the ground. Then it was a fifteen-yard dash across to the outer wall; Bourke would then throw a rope ladder over for Blake to climb. Once out, they would drive away before the prison guards had a chance to catch up with them.

There was little time to lose: after six prisoners escaped from Wormwood Scrubs earlier in 1966, extra precautions were being taken, with thick steel netting added to the windows. They were already installed in A and B Halls, and Blake knew that once these were in place, his plan was foiled. A couple of days before the escape, the panes of glass were removed, and the iron crossbar broken then put back in place with tape. All Blake had to do was kick it.

The weather started to turn bad on the afternoon of 22 October, but although this would make conditions on the roof and the wall more treacherous, the reduced visibility would be very helpful. At 5.30 p.m., Blake answered his name on the evening roll call. At 6.15, he spoke to Bourke on the walkie-talkie and confirmed that the Irishman was set; another prisoner then kicked out the bar, and Blake slid out through the window, just as the prisoners started to return from watching the film. Blake reached the roof of the passageway, and let himself carefully down to the ground.

Hiding in the shadows, well aware that an inspection and headcount were due very soon, Blake started to worry when Bourke told him to hang on, as he had hit a snag. (It turned out that it was a courting couple who had chosen exactly the wrong place to grab some privacy; Bourke put his headlights on them until they went.) A few minutes later, he sent the ladder over. It was made of rope with size 13 knitting needles strung together to form the rungs: strong enough to take Blake's weight, but light enough to be easily thrown. Blake scurried up the ladder to the top of the wall, unnoticed by the prison officers in their observation booths at its end. Beneath him he could see Bourke's car, and the Irishman there with his walkie-talkie hidden incongruously inside a pot of pink carnations. Blake lowered himself until he was hanging by both hands, and then when Bourke told him to drop, having put his flowers down by the side of the wall, Blake let go, moving in mid-air to prevent himself from landing on top of his rescuer. Unfortunately that meant that he landed badly, and as he hit the ground, he broke his wrist. Bourke bundled him into the car, and headed off down the road at high speed – and hit another car!

Blake's escape was spotted at 7 p.m., although there wasn't initially the massive outcry that might have been expected. The deputy governor called the nearby Shepherds Bush police station to let them know that they had lost "one of their chaps" over the east wall of the jail, that it was probably Blake, and he was in prison grey uniform. However, by nine o'clock the hunt was on: ports and airfields were being watched; police teams with dogs were searching the area around the prison; the embassies for countries from the Iron Curtain were under increased surveillance.

The papers went wild with speculation, with everyone from the KGB to the IRA to the British Secret Service themselves suspected of responsibility. Reports came in that Blake had been spotted on a plane landing in Sydney, Australia; he was also "seen" in the South of France and Bermuda. The government, stung by the various escapes, set up an independent inquiry into prison security, headed by Lord Mountbatten of Burma. This would eventually lead to major changes within the prison system. Help was even offered by the Institute of Psychical Studies, who thought they could find him in a couple of days: "It would be of interest to our research into a process of locating individuals by a method of map divination (akin to water diviners) if we might include the case in our current programme of readings," their letter said. "Should you feel disposed to give the method a trial please could you forward us the necessary sample (a few hairs from the man's hairbrush or a well-worn shower cap)."

George Blake must have wished that he had insisted on his rescuers approaching the Russians for help. It very quickly became apparent that Sean Bourke had no real idea what he was doing. The day after the escape, Blake's picture was plastered everywhere, and the "safe" house that Bourke had set up was nothing of the sort: in fact it was a single room in a house with shared facilities, where the landlady came in to clean weekly. When it was obvious that Blake needed medical attention for his wrist, Bourke suggested going to the local casualty department, not really thinking through the consequences of the country's most wanted man turning up in an A&E department. However, Michael Randle was able to find a doctor who would help a man who was "allergic to hospitals"!

Quickly moving from the not-so-safe house, Blake went from one temporary home to another. One friend of Pottle and Randle's was willing to host the fugitive, but after a few days pointed out that his wife was having therapy. Since she was under instructions to tell her therapist everything, she had talked about Blake staying there. Unsurprisingly, he got out speedily.

Within a few days, it wasn't just Blake who had to be kept hidden: the police were also looking for Sean Bourke, who having used his own car as the getaway vehicle, then left it where it could easily be found (and if the police had any difficulties, incredibly, Bourke rang them himself to say where it was). Bourke was desperate for people to know what part he had played in the great escape: he even went in to a police station at one point to check that his picture was displayed. Blake, Pottle and Randle realized that they would need to get not just the KGB agent but his erstwhile helper out of the country.

Bourke had originally promised that he could get hold of passports, but now with the police on his tail, he wasn't able to get in touch with his underworld contacts to do so – if indeed they even existed. Pottle and Randle had come up with an intriguing idea: change Blake's skin pigmentation, using a drug called meladinin, so that he could leave disguised as an Indian or

an Arab. Blake wasn't that keen on the plan, as he wasn't sure
that once changed, his skin would revert to its natural hue; there
were also potential side-effects from the painkilling medication
he was taken for his broken wrist. The idea was dropped, as
were discussions of smuggling Blake into the Soviet Embassy.

Eventually Pottle and Randle decided that the only way to
get Blake out of the United Kingdom was to smuggle him
inside a vehicle. With some money given by a woman in the
anti-nuclear movement, who had inherited £1,200 and wanted
to donate it to a worthy cause, they bought a Dormobile
camper van, and started to make the necessary amendments,
creating a compartment in the back of a small kitchen
cupboard. Blake would need to remain cramped in the space
for some time, and there were concerns about what would
happen if he needed to urinate. After Randle approached a
clinic for people with bladder problems, and they told him that
they could provide a device if they were told Blake's penis size,
the traitor decided that he could hold his water as long as was
necessary! In the end, he took a rubber hot-water bottle, just in
case, although he quickly got rid of it when the smell became
unbearable during the journey.

After discounting Egypt, Yugoslavia and Switzerland as
potential destinations, Blake chose to head for East Germany.
This would mean that his friends wouldn't need to have any
dealings with communists: they could drop him on the auto-
bahn that linked West Germany with Berlin, and be within the
Western sector before Blake made contact with the East German
authorities. Randle was the only person with a valid driving
licence, and he and his wife decided to bring their two young
sons along too, providing a perfect cover.

They set off on 17 December 1966, heading from Dover to
Ostend and then across Europe, arriving at Berlin early in the
morning of Monday 19 December. The Randles let Blake out of
the van not far from the checkpoint; although he wasn't greeted
with quite the exuberance he had hoped for by the guards when
he presented himself, Blake was made welcome the next morning. Two weeks later Sean Bourke joined him in East Berlin: he
had used Pat Pottle's passport, suitably amended to feature his
photograph, to travel to Paris, fly to Berlin, and then go through

Checkpoint Charlie into the Russian Sector, where he reported to the Soviet headquarters.

Blake has remained in Russia for the rest of his life; he was awarded an Order of Friendship by former KGB head Vladimir Putin in 2007, and at that stage was still contributing help to the KGB's successor, the SVR. Sean Bourke didn't enjoy his time in Moscow: he was keen to return to Ireland. He wrote a book about the escape, which made clear the identities of Michael and Anne Randle as well as Pat Pottle, but died in his early forties. In 1989, Michael Randle and Pat Pottle wrote their own book; two years later they were tried for their part in the escape and despite the judge giving clear directions regarding their guilt, their plea that they helped Blake because his sentence was hypocritical swayed the jury and they were acquitted.

Michael Randle still has no regrets: speaking to a BBC World Service documentary in 2011, he made it clear that he had no sympathy with what Blake did. But was it right to sentence him to death in prison for doing what both sides in the Cold War were doing?

Fact vs. Fiction

The Blake escape is fictionalized in Desmond Bagley's novel *The Freedom Trap*, which was turned into the 1973 movie *The Mackintosh Man*, starring Paul Newman. It suggested that a highly organized gang called The Scarperers were responsible for the prison breaks – a world away from the reality of Bourke's mismanagement! Simon Gray's play *Cell Mates*, about the relationship between Blake and Bourke, is perhaps more famous for Stephen Fry's departure from the original production than its content.

Sources:

Camden New Journal, 11 September 2008: "George Blake – The 'Red spy' who slipped over the prison wall"

Randle, Michael and Pat Pottle: *The Blake Escape: How We Freed George Blake – and Why* (Harrap 1989)

Blake, George: *No Other Choice* (Jonathan Cape, 1990)

Ealing Gazette, 5 September 2008: "Blunders by MI5 opened escape route for Russian spy"

Simpson, Paul: *A Brief History of The Spy* (Constable & Robinson, 2013)

Life Magazine, 24 January 1969: "The Irish 'Who' in a British Whodunit"

Hansard, 24 October 1966: "George Blake (Escape from Prison)"

ITN: *Reporting 67*, 1 January 1967

BBC World Service: *Witness: Michael Randle*

Sean Bourke: *The Springing of George Blake* (Mayflower, 2nd edition 1971)

Nothing to Lose

He's now a respected journalist, who lectures to prison inmates about the futility of the path they're following. But for two years at the end of the 1960s, John McVicar was deemed "Public Enemy No. 1" with newspaper headlines screaming "Wanted Dead or Alive". His biggest crime: not the armed robberies for which he had been sent down, but his escape from the supposedly impregnable E Wing at Durham Prison.

McVicar had a history of escaping before he arrived in Durham. He had been able to get away from a coach taking him to Parkhurst Prison on the Isle of Wight in 1966, while serving an eight-year sentence for armed robbery. After he was recaptured and sentenced to a further twenty-three years, he led a breakout from Chelmsford Prison, which only failed – at least according to his own autobiography – because he refused to listen to advice he was given about how to prepare the rope and hook that was going to be thrown over the wall. If he had done as suggested, he and eight other prisoners would have made it, after getting through a trapdoor in the roof of one of the bathrooms and down into the yard. Instead they carried out a protest on the roof. As a result, McVicar was sent to Durham.

Durham Prison had a pretty good record for keeping its inmates where they should be. In March 1961, when Ronnie "Houdini" Heslop dug his way out of his cell into the unlocked one beneath, using a teaspoon and a kitchen knife, and then fled into the night over the prison wall, there hadn't been any escapes for six years. Shortly after that, Durham was designated the home for the country's most difficult prisoners, and those deemed most likely to make a break for it.

During his comparatively short time in Durham, McVicar was involved in both a riot and a hunger strike, before fellow prisoner Wally Probyn alerted him to an oddity in the shower room. Probyn had escaped sixteen times from prisons during his career, and, according to McVicar, was always alert to the possibilities inherent in any situation. One of the corners of the room had been cut off – a diagonal piece of wall ran in front of where it should have been. As Probyn pointed out, nothing was ever done in a prison without a good reason: maybe it was hiding a shaft of some sort.

Because the corner was hidden from view when the door of the showers was open, the chances of discovery were comparatively low, and Probyn dug through the bricks to discover a shaft about a foot across behind the wall. With the help of another prisoner, Tony Dunford, they then began to extract the bricks properly, using papier-mâché as makeshift mortar when they were replaced at the end of each day's excavations. It took three weeks before they removed a complete path through to the shaft, at which point they realized they would have to descend into whatever lay beneath, since the shaft got narrower the higher it went.

As their digging progressed, the men were approached by crime boss Charlie Richardson, who was serving a twenty-five-year stretch on E Wing. He blackmailed them into letting him be part of the escape attempt. (Richardson made a half-hearted start on a tunnel in the same showers, which was bound to get caught; if it was, the authorities would tear the showers apart, and find McVicar and Probyn's work.) Ironically, they had been considering bringing Richardson into the scheme, since Dunford didn't want to escape.

They disposed of the rubble down the toilets – although Richardson came close to blowing that by trying to flush too much at one time – with the larger pieces thrown out of their windows. One close shave nearly saw the whole plot discovered: a random headcount was called when Probyn was deep within the hole, and it was only because the prison officer who eventually located him, (after he had got out, and hidden within a shower stall), didn't notice that he was still wearing his overalls while supposedly taking a shower, that the escape wasn't brought to a premature end.

By the early part of October 1968, the hole was big enough to see that the shaft led into a cellar under the showers, and on

20 October, Probyn was able to drop down to have a reconnoitre around the room. After twenty minutes, he returned to explain that the cellar led to an external ventilation shaft, which ran to the indoor exercise yard. All that stood in their way was a grilled window, and a padlock on the grid at the top of the shaft in the yard. There was even a broken stepladder in the cellar that they could use to get up the shaft.

To throw Richardson off the scent, since Probyn and McVicar no longer had any intention of allowing him or his cellmate Tony Lawrence to join the escape, he was told to get hold of a hacksaw blade to use on the bars, although Probyn in fact already had one. Probyn also prepared a rope and a hook to use for going over the wall. McVicar made a hole in the perspex in the library cell's outer wall, which they would need later.

On Sunday 23 October, Probyn cut through the bars and broke the padlock, leaving it looking intact. During that week, they were joined on E Wing by Joey Martin, a robber serving life. McVicar decided to invite Martin along, and the con agreed with alacrity. On the Tuesday evening, 25 October, McVicar and Martin dropped a rope from out of the hole in the library, tied to a table. After dinner that night, Martin, Probyn and McVicar went to the shower room; Richardson and his cellmate were oblivious to the imminence of the escape.

The three men dropped down into the cellar, and made their way along the tunnel, up the shaft and into the yard. They had previously hidden dark clothes in the cellar to eliminate the chances of being spotted. They went up the rope, but running across the plastic roof gave away their presence – notably to Richardson, who realized he had been betrayed, and started to cause a commotion within the prison, alerting the guards to the escape.

After dropping down from the roof, they ran along by the wall, although most of it was topped with barbed wire. When they reached the end of the remand wing and started to climb up onto the roof of the courthouse, next to the main gate, Martin was caught by one of the guards. McVicar and Probyn kept going, but realized that they still couldn't get over the wall, as it was covered with barbed wire at this point. The part of the courthouse they were on was only a single storey high, but the portion next to it was ten feet higher. Knowing that they were very close to being caught, the two men desperately used spikes halfway up the wall to pull themselves up.

Probyn and McVicar were now on a flat concrete roof, and made their way towards a section that overlooked the outside. When they were spotted by the warders, they separated. McVicar jumped from roof to roof, ending up outside the prison grounds. When he could, he descended to ground level and began running.

McVicar stayed on the run for 744 days in total. He made his way across Durham, despite not really knowing the geography of the city, and swam across the river on two separate occasions to evade his pursuers. He headed north and eventually found himself in Chester-Le-Street, around ten miles away. After calling a former girlfriend for help, he was picked up by friends from London, although not before he was chased around the streets by a couple of detectives who thought he was behaving shiftily.

Once back in London, he reverted to his criminal ways, with Detective Chief Inspector Tom Morrison doggedly on his heels. Adopting the alias Allan Squires (the name of the first detective who arrested him), he rented a flat in Blackheath, which is where he was arrested on 11 November 1970, along with two women. He had become a well-known figure in the area, buying champagne and brandy at the local off licence and not worrying about the police Panda cars which parked nearby regularly to keep an eye on troublesome teenagers.

McVicar was sent back to Durham, where he received a further three years added to his sentence. He was paroled in 1978 after studying sociology, and co-wrote and consulted on the film *McVicar*, starring Roger Daltrey, based on his time in Durham. Probyn was caught on 29 October, ninety miles from Durham prison. He was released in 1975, but later served a three-year term for having sex with underage girls.

Sources:

Glasgow Herald, 12 November 1970: "'Phone Call Led Police to McVicar"
Evening Times, 30 October 1968: "'Danger Man' McVicar Still Free"
Edmonton Journal, 4 March 1968: "Prison Mutiny Continues"
McVicar, John: *McVicar By Himself* (Revised edition Artnik, 2002)

Swooping Down to Freedom

The world's first helicopter escape wasn't, as you might think from numerous books and TV programmes, the descent in October 1973 into Dublin's Mountjoy Prison to liberate three members of the Irish Republican Army who were being interned there. It in fact took place on the other side of the world, in Mexico, two years earlier. This daring raid inspired the movie *Breakout*, featuring Charles Bronson and Robert Duvall, and because of various elements involved with the case, has featured in a number of examinations of conspiracy theories over the years.

On 18 August 1971, Joel David Kaplan was in the middle of his tenth year in prison after he had been accused of and then convicted of the murder of his business partner Luis M. Vidal Jr. He was serving out his sentence at the Santa Martha Acatitla prison, in Mexico City, a harsh facility out of which, to the surprise of many who knew the corrupt ways of the Mexican judicial system, he seemed simply unable to bribe his way.

Kaplan was the heir to a fortune in the molasses industry – his uncle, Jacob M. Kaplan, controlled the J.M. Kaplan Fund of New York (and the $100 million that went with it), and the younger Kaplan was convinced that he had been framed by his uncle, or alternatively by the CIA, for the murder. This wasn't as far-fetched as it might sound: Joel was definitely involved in some questionable dealings in Mexico and Central America, during a period when the CIA were at the height of their quests to destabilize what they perceived as hostile governments. Two years after Joel was found guilty of Vidal's murder, a Texas congressman stated that he believed that the J.M. Kaplan Fund was acting as a conduit for CIA funds, in contravention of proper practice.

The relationship between Kaplan and Vidal was stormy. According to evidence presented at the trial of Evsey S. Petrushansky, who was also accused of the murder, Kaplan told Luis deGaray Jaimes that Vidal was "a very dangerous individual, with whom he had had serious differences in the past, and he had been informed through other channels that he planned to eliminate him; for this reason, he thought that the day was not far off where either of them would do it, that is to say, commit a murder between themselves."

On 18 November 1961, blood-stained men's clothing was found by the side of the Mexico-Acapulco highway, along with personal effects belonging to Luis Vidal and a room key for the Continental Hilton Hotel. Four days later, a corpse was found two miles from the clothing, buried by the side of the road, riddled with four bullet wounds. This was identified by Mrs Teresa Vidal as her husband's – although apparently the body was that of a balding elderly man, whereas Vidal had a full head of hair and was in his thirties. The eye colour was wrong as well; Mrs Vidal allegedly suggested that someone had switched his eyeballs! Oddly, too, on 21 November a man answering Vidal's description used his passport to cross the border into Guatemala. And to add a further layer to the mystery, a US State Department official also positively identified the corpse as Vidal.

Evidence was given that implicated Kaplan in the murder. He had met Vidal on his arrival in Mexico on 11 November and helped him check in at the Continental. That night, he had told Jaimes that the rental car he had hired had broken down and needed collecting. When Jaimes did so, he saw holes in the window and blood stains on the front seat and door, which Kaplan couldn't adequately explain. The hotel staff stated that Kaplan had checked Vidal out of his room on 12 November.

In his own deposition, Kaplan stated that he met with Vidal late in the evening of 11 November along with Petrushansky and another man, Earl Scott, alias Harry Kopelson. Kaplan had been dropped at another bar, and then when Scott and Petrushansky came to collect him later, was told that Scott had killed Vidal because he "had not fulfilled his part of the deal". Kaplan denied knowing where Vidal's body was buried, but admitted checking Vidal out of his room.

Kaplan was arrested in Spain and extradited to Mexico to stand trial. After a year's imprisonment, he was tried and convicted of concealing evidence, and since he had served the sentence for that already he was freed – only to be rearrested. He claimed he was told that if he paid $200,000 he would be freed; if not, he would be charged with murder. Kaplan didn't have access to that sort of money; his uncle Jacob refused to help. After a further year of delays, Kaplan was tried for murder and found guilty.

Throughout the rest of the 1960s, Kaplan's sister Judy Dowis tried to buy or bribe his freedom, but without success. She believes that her uncle was successfully offering even more money to keep Kaplan locked up – after all, while Joel was languishing in a Mexican jail, Jacob held the purse strings for the foundation. Joel himself kept coming up with new schemes for escape: as his biography notes, "for five years, escape plans would roll off his fecund brain like symphonies by Mozart". He realized that there was no point overplanning: "A plan can be brilliant in thought and just as brilliant in execution," he told his biographers, "but pure old-fashioned luck will be the determining factor." He watched every aspect of his life within the jail: from the personal tics and foibles of the different guards, to the little changes in routine that might afford an avenue.

One such came during a period he spent in Santa Marta prison hospital. A prisoner suffering from a bleeding ulcer couldn't be treated within the prison walls, so would have to be transferred to the Mexico City General Hospital. Kaplan watched as the ambulance taking him away drove through the front gate, exactly as he himself wanted to be doing. He decided to fake an attack of appendicitis, and read up on all the symptoms; he approached the ambulance driver, who was quite happy to assist, as long as he was paid. Through Judy, he made contact with a Canadian named Dempsey who would help once he was on the outside, meeting the ambulance about three miles outside the prison. Dempsey would pretend to mount an assault on the ambulance and "force" Kaplan to depart at gunpoint, which would save the ambulance driver from being charged with conspiracy. They would then change cars and meet up with two women who would pose as the two men's wives, as they headed out of Mexico at the end of their vacation.

All seemed to be going okay; Kaplan was even willing to pay out a fee to a hospital attendant who insisted that his help would be needed, and therefore compensated. But Kaplan's machinations fell apart: the ambulance driver had gone on a drinking spree, and been fired for turning up for work drunk!

Another plan involved faking his own death: for $100,000 Kaplan was convinced that he could "persuade" a load of doctors and health officials to certify him dead. When his body was taken out to a funeral home, Kaplan would miraculously resurrect, and another dead body put in the coffin in his place. There was a certain grim appropriateness to this idea: as far as Kaplan was concerned, the identity of the corpse in his own case had been switched. However, Jacob refused to release the necessary money.

Some of the plans suggested by others seemed idiotic, even to Kaplan, who was willing to do pretty much anything to get out. Judy was living in Miami, at a time when that city's underworld included many refugee Cubans and out of work mercenaries, as well as others who were involved (whether legitimately or only in their minds) with covert plots to destabilize Communist countries. She got to know a group known as the "Soldiers of Misfortune", who appeared willing to help her with her quest to free her brother from prison.

One scheme saw a flamboyant former CIA operative, Jack Carter, drive down to Mexico City (borrowing Judy's Jaguar for the ride), with a plan that would see Kaplan rescued by a pair of Cuban exiles. They would drive a phony linen-supply truck into the prison, ostensibly to refill a storage room that Carter would have arranged to be set fire to; Joel would depart with them, and be placed in the hands of a professional Austrian mountaineer who would take him across the hills to a plane hidden in the distant mountains. Unsurprisingly, this one didn't get past the drawing board, although Carter sold Judy's car claiming that he needed it to finance the plot.

After Judy moved to Sausalito, she encountered "Lewis", the leader of a group known as the Big Sur Ranchers. Over time she came to trust him, enough that when Kaplan whispered to her during one of her visits that he had found a sure-fire way to escape, and just needed someone he could trust in Mexico City to handle things there, she asked Lewis to deal with the arrangements. Kaplan had learned that the governor of the prison was willing to drive him out of the prison and hand him over to friends, as long as he was paid around $30,000. If the warden did that, then Lewis would get him out of the country. Lewis therefore created a homemade armoured car, customizing a 1969 Pontiac with bulletproof glass, and flack-jacket insulation. If the warder decided that his best bet was to try to prevent his escape and make himself out to be a hero, at least they would be prepared. A retired Air Force colonel in San Diego agreed to fly into Mexico to collect him.

Ten thousand dollars was paid to the warden, and everyone involved was kept on standby, waiting for the warden to give a three-day warning. That went on for four months, before Lewis went to visit Kaplan, who finally agreed that it was clear the warden didn't have the guts to go ahead with the plan. The whole scheme had cost a further $12,000 in expenses and equipment; all of it went to waste.

The next idea was to tunnel into the prison; there was no way that a tunnel out would be feasible, given the concrete floors. But if someone were to dig their way beneath the fence, disguising their entry point as a chicken shed, then they could come out in the middle of the courtyard without too much of a problem. Kaplan had married Irma, a Mexican girl, without bothering to divorce his New York model wife Bonnie Sharie; he claimed that being married was the only way he could receive visitors, and Bonnie wasn't going to travel to Mexico. Irma got hold of an engineer, who advised that it would take about four weeks to dig the six-feet tunnel. Six days in, though, they hit a thick vein of lava rock. That plan also came to nothing – although it did provide Kaplan with a cooked chicken supper!

All the avenues seemed to finish like that tunnel, in a dead end, until Dowis was put in touch with Victor Ellsworth Stadter, a self-confessed "legitimate smuggler", suspected by the US Customs Service and the Drug Enforcement Administration of being a very devious and clever narcotics trafficker, no matter how much he might protest that he "never fooled with narcotics".

Stadter was intrigued by the case, claiming when he talked about the escape in 1991 that "the United States government is the only government in the world that doesn't do a damned thing to help get its own citizens out of prison. Guys like me have to do it." The potential State Department and CIA involvement meant that Stadter might be giving the US government a metaphorical two-fingered salute if he could help bring Kaplan out.

It clearly wasn't going to be easy, and Stadter used various different ruses to try to get Kaplan out of the prison, but none of them was successful. It didn't help that another factor now entered the equation: Kaplan was seriously ill, and potentially dying. Inside prison he had become an alcoholic, and was knocking back a bottle a day of spirits – which, because of his situation, had to be home-made. The rum was reacting badly with his liver, giving him recurrent bouts of hepatitis, and a bad infection. If Stadter didn't get Kaplan out of there quickly, he would be coming out in a box.

At one stage, they considered using a make-up artist to disguise Kaplan so he could exit looking like one of his own visitors; that was foiled because his health recovered sufficiently for him to be moved out of the hospital to his prison cell – although that didn't last for long, and when they tried to reactivate the plan a few days later, they discovered that someone had betrayed them. Every person leaving the jail who wasn't bald was going to be checked – and the disguise relied on Kaplan adopting the distinctive hairstyle (i.e. the wig) of his visitor.

It was at this point that someone came up with the idea of using a helicopter. According to the book he co-wrote about the escape, *The 10-Second Jailbreak*, Kaplan suggested it. Stadter has stated that it was his idea but since Kaplan "[is] dead now he can have that one". As far as Stadter was concerned, it was the answer to the problems. He purchased a high-powered Bell helicopter in Wyoming, and flew it down to Houston, Texas, where he stripped everything non-essential from the frame. Because Mexico City sits 7,200 feet above sea level, the air is thin, which makes piloting a helicopter considerably harder than it would be for many of the pilots who were to emulate the feat. The helicopter was painted blue, to match the one used by the Mexican Attorney-General, Julio Sanchez Vargas, and the doors were taken off.

At this point another obstacle presented itself. Kaplan refused to leave the prison without his cellmate joining the party. Carlos Antonio Contreras Castro, a Venezuelan counterfeiter, was a non-negotiable addition, and reluctantly, Stadter agreed.

Although he considered learning to fly the chopper himself, and initially arranged for a friend, known only as Cotton, to start lessons, in the end Stadter hired a Vietnam veteran, Roger Hershner, to fly the mission. On 17 August, Cotton visited the jail, along with Kaplan's wife. Cotton told Kaplan to wander around the prison basketball court at 6.30 p.m. on each of the next three evenings, and to carry a newspaper under one arm.

Luck, for once, was on Kaplan's side. On the evening of 18 August, for the first time in two years, a movie was being shown for the benefit of the prisoners. *The Altar of Blood* attracted most of the inmates, as well as the guards; only Kaplan and Castro were out in the yard in the rain.

Stadter had estimated that the critical phase of the escape would last merely thirty seconds. During the first ten seconds, the guards would hear the helicopter approaching, and hopefully be confused sufficiently not to react. The next ten would see Kaplan and Castro climb on board. The final ten would see the chopper have time to fly out of rifle range. The middle ten, unsurprisingly, were the most dangerous, and Stadter ordered Hershner to wait for no longer than ten seconds on the ground. If Kaplan and/or Castro didn't board during that time, it would be their bad luck.

At 6.35 p.m., the Bell helicopter came in to land on the basketball court – to be greeted not by rifle fire, but by salutes. The guards believed for the critical few moments that they were receiving a surprise visit from the Attorney General. By the time they realized their error, Kaplan and Castro were on board, and flying into the history books.

It still nearly all went wrong. As the helicopter came in to land nearly an hour later, a pickup truck with Mexican federal agency insignia was waiting – totally unconnected to the prison escape, but a worry for Stadter, who was waiting with further getaway vehicles. For a horrible moment, Stadter thought that Hershner believed that he should land by the truck, and even the dimmest-witted Mexican official might be surprised to see two men in prison outfits descending from the helicopter. He flashed the landing lights of his Cessna light aircraft, and got Cotton, who was driving the Cadillac beside it, to do likewise with his head-lights. Hershner brought the helicopter down in the right place. Kaplan raced from the chopper to the Cessna; Castro tried to follow but was directed, forcibly, by Stadtner to the Cadillac. Stadtner then took his seat behind the Cessna's controls, and piloted himself and Kaplan to La Pesca airport, near the Texas border, where they changed planes again. When Kaplan passed through US Customs at Brownsville, Texas, he used his own name.

According to the contemporary *Time* report, Castro accompanied Kaplan to La Pesca, and was then put on a plane to Guatemala, but in *The 10-Second Jailbreak*, it says that Cotton dropped Castro at the Hotel Panorama in the medium-sized town of San Luis Potosi, around 200 miles from the jail. He eventually made his way back to Venezuela, where he claimed that he was the mastermind behind the helicopter escape, and that Kaplan had paid him $100,000. Nobody took him seriously.

Unusually, the Mexican government didn't start extradition proceedings. Although Sam Lopez, the Chief of Police in Mexico City, wasn't best pleased by the news Kaplan had escaped ("That dirty f***ing gringo has crossed the border," he apparently shouted when he found out), little was done. The Mexican Foreign Ministry knew that there would be consider-able resistance to an extradition request for Kaplan, and didn't pursue it with any vigour.

All 136 guards at the prison were arrested and interrogated about the escape; no action was taken – some claimed that the alarm system had failed to work, or that the machine gun in the main watchtower had jammed. Others said they had been told the helicopter had landed because of mechanical problems. At one point the Mexicans tried to claim that the helicopter escape never happened at all. Kaplan's other cellmate, Jose Guadalupe

Olvera Rico, told interrogators, "Tomorrow, a submarine is to arrive for me." According to the press, "the most spectacular search in all Mexican criminal history" got under way. One paper suggested that Kaplan and Castro had been treated by a plastic surgeon when they arrived in Mexico City; another "assumed that the helicopter pilot was able to hypnotise the guards at Santa Marta".

Stadter developed a reputation for helping others in trouble south of the border, occasionally tapping Kaplan for cash to fund his projects. Kaplan himself died in Miami in 1988, fifteen years after cooperating in an account of his escapade. The Attorney General resigned the following day – but although many accounts link this to the escape, it seems more likely that it was a result of the investigations into a massacre on 10 June, and a breakdown in the relationship between Vargas and Mexican President Echevarria.

Fact vs fiction

The Charles Bronson film *Breakout* plays fast and loose with the facts of the Kaplan case. It doesn't pretend to be a biopic: its tagline was "Sentenced to 28 years in prison for a crime he never committed. Only two things can get him out – a lot of money and Charles Bronson!" Bronson plays a character who both plans and carries out the raid on the prison; he's hired by the prisoner's wife, rather than his sister, and considerably more difficulties are thrown in their way (including the prisoner's cellmate being the real killer, rather than an accountant!). With a disturbing marital rape scene, it's not particularly pleasant viewing – and they don't even get the make of helicopter right.

Sources:

Time magazine, 30 August 1971: "MEXICO: Whirlaway"
United States Court of Appeals Second Circuit, 30 December 1963: "UNITED STATES of America ex rel. Evsey S. PETRUSHANSKY, a/k/a Peter Green, a fugitive from Justice of the United Mexican States, Relator-Appellant, v. Anthony R.

Marasco, United States Marshal for the Southern District of New York, Respondent-Appellee."

New York Times, 31 December 2007: "In Prison, Toddlers Serve Time With Mom"

US Department of State Telegram, 20 August 1971: "Resignation of Attorney General Sanchez Vargas"

Houston Chronicle, 8 September 1991: "A Smuggler's Tale"

Asinof, Eliot, Warren Hinckle and William Turner: *The 10-Second Jailbreak* (Holt, Rinehart and Winston 1973)

The Longest Hunt

Watch interviews with members of the US Marshals office after they've caught a fugitive, and you can be pretty sure that at some point they will trot out a line warning any other escapees who are watching that the Marshals service never gives up looking for them, and that they will be caught eventually. Even if it takes decades. Linda Darby is living proof that this isn't a trite cliché: they mean every word of it. She escaped from the Indiana Women's Prison in 1972, and she was recaptured thirty-five years later, after making a completely new life for herself. And now, following the dismissal of her attempt to appeal against her sentence in April 2012, she could well be in prison for the rest of her life, serving a sentence that would otherwise have left her eligible for parole some years ago – under the Indiana code, because her offence took place before 1977, she has to serve ten years of her sentence before clemency can be considered.

Linda Darby was convicted of the murder of her second husband in 1970. She has steadfastly maintained her innocence, but the jury in Lake County, Indiana, didn't believe her. Her husband Charles, from whom she was estranged at the time, was hit with a shotgun blast, and then their Hammond home was set on fire. At the trial, her nine-year-old daughter, from her first marriage, said that her mother had left the motel room in Valparaiso on the night of the murder. A similar gun to the murder weapon was found at the motel; a gas station attendant said he sold her fuel that night. There were no witnesses to the killing. The defence tried the risky strategy of not presenting any witnesses on her behalf at the trial, but simply attacked the state's case. It was a gamble that didn't pay off.

The mother of five (four from her first marriage; a son from her second) lost her children and her liberty in one fell swoop.

She was sentenced to life imprisonment on 1 October 1970, and immediately tried to appeal on technical grounds. This was turned down in August 1971. She applied to the court for a "pauper" attorney to be brought in to help with an appeal; counsel was appointed on 14 March 1972. However no appeal was ever filed during the twentieth century, because the day before the court gave Linda Darby the chance to rectify what she saw as the wrong done to her, she escaped from prison.

In 1972, the Indiana Women's Prison was a year away from celebrating its centenary. It was the first prison specifically for women in the country, and the first maximum-security female correctional facility. It didn't just house murderers and other maximum-security prisoners – within its walls were many convicted of lesser offences, such as drunkenness and prostitution. Darby, who by all accounts was an obedient and docile prisoner, was not regarded as a particularly high escape risk, and was allowed to move around the prison confines on her own.

On 13 March, she decided to leave. Whether she wasn't aware that the wheels of justice were slowly turning, and believed that all her avenues of appeal were now closed, or she simply had had enough of life without her children, is open to question. After her eventual recapture, she maintained that she had fled the prison because she didn't want to serve time for another person's crime – and certainly since then, she has tried her hardest to prove her innocence.

Around 7.30 in the evening of 13 March 1972, Linda Darby didn't follow the guard's instructions to go to recreational time; instead, she ran to the fence, climbed over it and took off into Indianapolis. Not knowing the area, and fully aware that she had taken an irretrievable step by escaping, she first thought of trying to locate her children. However, she quickly realized that the police would immediately check there, so, instead, she turned for help to a stranger.

Knocking on the door of a local house, she told the woman who answered that she was on the run from her boyfriend, who had knocked her about – explaining the cuts and bruises she had sustained during her escape. It was there that she met Willie McElroy, with whom she fell in love. Although they never officially married, she took his last name, becoming known as Linda Joe McElroy, and moved with him back to his home town of Pulaski, Tennessee, around seventy-five miles south of Nashville.

They had two children, and eight grandchildren, and she became a respected member of the local community, running an antiques shop with her husband, and later working as a cleaning lady. No one there could quite believe it when the marshals knocked on her door: this was someone they had known their whole lives; she had babysat for their children. She could not possibly be a murderer. As former FBI agent Brad Garrett, consulting for ABC News on the case, pointed out, "It's actually quite easy [for fugitives] to be absorbed if they cut all ties from their previous life, which appears the case in this situation."

Darby hadn't quite cut all her ties. She didn't go "off the grid" as some escapees do, not using credit cards, or anything else that might identify them. She was registered in various databases, but with her date of birth and social security number slightly altered – sufficiently changed that a quick check wouldn't correlate with her original information, but similar enough that if she slipped and gave the original by mistake, it could be excused as a silly slip. And that was her downfall.

In 2007, the Indiana State Police started up the Indiana Intelligence Fusion Center, a new taskforce whose mission is to "collect, integrate, evaluate, analyze and disseminate information and intelligence to support local, state and federal agencies in detecting, preventing, and responding to criminal and terrorist activity." Working with the Indiana Department of Corrections, its Fugitive Apprehension Unit's aim was to recapture long-term fugitives. Using a new computer system set up by the Department of Homeland Security, which used fuzzy logic (i.e. a computer's equivalent of a best guess rather than absolute strict yes/no answers) as well as correlating data from every American's contacts with the police over the years, they were able to match Darby with McElroy. Photos and fingerprints from her time in the Indiana correctional system were sent to Pulaski police; they confirmed that the two were one and the same. On 12 October, police cars were sent to Darby's home in Pulaski, and she was brought out in handcuffs.

Asked by a reporter for the local *Eyewitness News* if she felt as if she had been living a lie, Darby replied, "Uh huh. But when do you stop? Where do you go back to?" The answer was simple: you stop when you're caught. And you go back to jail.

Sources:

Valparaiso *Vidette-Messenger*, 6 March 1970

Valparaiso *Vidette-Messenger*, 7 March 1970

Court of Appeals of Indiana, 19 April 2012: "Opinion – for Publication: APPEAL FROM THE LAKE SUPERIOR COURT The Honorable Salvador Vasquez, Judge Cause No. 45G01-7003-MR-41743"

WHTR.com, 24 October 2007: "Female fugitive back in Indiana after 35 years"

The Indy Channel, 17 October, 2007: "Woman Caught 35 Years After Escape Speaks Out"

USA Today, 20 October 2007: "Fugitive has support of longtime friends"

Daily Independent (Ashland), 24 October 2007: "Woman's arrest brings relief to victim's family"

New York Times, 22 October 2007: "Neighbor's Hidden Criminal Past Stuns a Tennessee City"

Indiana Intelligence Fusion Center website: http://www.in.gov/iifc/

IIRC annual report 2007: http://www.in.gov/dhs/files/07_Annual_Report.pdf

WHTR.com, 24 October 2007: "New technology was key to arrest of fugitive for 35 years"

Bird in the Sky

It may not have been the first time that a helicopter was used to assist prison inmates with an escape, but the incident at Mountjoy Prison in Dublin, Ireland, at Halloween 1973 was certainly the first one to inspire a song. Popular Irish rebel band, The Wolfe Tones, whose songs regularly include references to the struggle for freedom by the Irish against their oppressors, wrote and released "The Helicopter Song" ("Up like a bird and high over the city / 'Three men are missing' I heard the warder cry") straight afterwards, and despite being banned (or perhaps because it had been) by the Irish government, it went straight to number one in the Irish charts and remained there for four weeks.

It wasn't the only song inspired by the events. According to *Time* magazine's article from less than two weeks later, within hours "a new little ditty" was being sung in Catholic pubs all over Northern Ireland: "The length and breadth of Ireland / No finer sight to see, / The day the Provie birdie / Released the Mountjoy three." It was an unmitigated disaster for the Irish government, and a stunning propaganda coup for the Irish Republican Army (IRA) – particularly since it may not even have actually cost them a penny to carry out.

The situation in Ireland had deteriorated over the preceding five years. Although the IRA had abandoned its campaign to unite Northern Ireland and the Republic into one country in 1962, violence had flared once more in 1969, and the arrival of the British Army in Northern Ireland marked the start of a troubled period for the island which would last for most of the rest of the twentieth century. The Provisional wing of the IRA had begun an armed campaign, and as a result, a policy of internment without trial was introduced in the North, while the

Republic's coalition government, led by Fine Gael's Liam Cosgrave, tried to keep a check on IRA activity. Membership was illegal under the Offences against the State Act, with a one-year-minimum mandatory sentence imposed on those found guilty at sessions of the Special Criminal Court (SCC).

The IRA's Chief of Staff Seamus Twomey was one of those brought before the SCC in 1973. He had helped to reorganize the IRA in Belfast after the creation of the Provisional IRA in December 1969, and had been part of the group negotiating with British Secretary of State Willie Whitelaw in 1972 during a brief truce. He became Chief of Staff in late 1972 after the arrest of Joe Cahill, and held the post until his arrest in September the following year. Refusing to recognize the authority of "this British-oriented quisling court", Twomey was sentenced to five years' imprisonment. Senior IRA member gunrunner J.B. O'Hagan had been arrested in May 1973 and sent to Mountjoy for a year; he had been imprisoned on previous occasions, and had tried to escape twice from internment at the Curragh camp (see chapter 29). Kevin Mallon, another top man in the IRA, had been cleared of the murder of RUC Sergeant Arthur Ovens in 1957 but given fourteen years for arms and conspiracy charges. Now one of the commanders of the IRA units stationed on the border between Northern Ireland and the Republic, he too had been sent to Mountjoy.

Based on the design of Pentonville prison in London, Mountjoy opened its doors to inmates in 1850, and had the distinction of having its in-cell sanitation removed in 1939 when a civil servant decided that prisoners were using too much water! By the time that Twomey was sent there, the IRA had ensured that they had a great deal of control within the prison – when the authorities had tried to impose prison uniforms and to abolish segregation of the Official and Provisional IRA members, O'Hagan and seven other prisoners had gone on hunger strike. After three weeks, the governor backed down, allowing the IRA escape committee to carry on plotting without fear that they would be overheard or betrayed by non-political, ordinary criminals housed within the prison.

The first priority was getting the senior IRA members out of Mountjoy and back on the outside where they could plan more campaigns against the hated Brits. Although in the end he didn't participate in the helicopter escape (which, as it turned out, was probably for the best, given how precarious the situation became during the escape itself), Joe Cahill, Twomey's predecessor as Chief of Staff, was originally going to be one of those sprung, and according to interviews with some of the prison warders subsequently, was annoyed that he hadn't gone.

Subtlety wasn't the order of the day for the first attempt. The plan was for the three senior men to flee up a rope ladder that would be waiting to help them get over the outer wall. Explosives would be sent into the prison which they could use to blow through a door into the exercise yard. All seemed to be working according to plan: the explosives were infiltrated to Mountjoy, and a group of volunteers – under strict instructions to sacrifice their lives if necessary to ensure the senior men escaped, but specifically banned from shooting any members of the Garda (the Irish police) – threw the rope ladder over from a house adjoining the prison. But for some reason, the plotters hadn't managed to reach the exercise yard, and the rope ladder was spotted. The volunteers were lucky to escape without being arrested, and interned, themselves.

Serendipity – the art of making discoveries by accident – often plays a key part in escape-planning. The guard dog who always needs to urinate at a particular point, thus slowing down the patrol by a vital fraction of a second, perhaps; or the vagaries of television scheduling. One Sunday in October, Irish television was airing a movie that included a particularly daring feat – a helicopter swooped into a prison compound and collected a group of inmates before disappearing into the middle distance. (It's sometimes said that this was the movie *Breakout*, featuring Charles Bronson; this would be a little difficult since that film wasn't released until 1975, although it was inspired by actual events, as shown in chapter 35.) One of those charged with coming up with an escape plan for Twomey and his colleagues was idly watching the film, and it occurred to him that this might be the right time to use this particular escape route.

It wasn't the first time that the IRA had considered using helicopters, but previous plans had been put on hold because of the superiority of the choppers used by the British armed forces.

It was all very well breaking someone like Gerry Adams out of the Long Kesh internment camp, but pointless if the British could scramble faster machines and recapture him almost immediately. However, that wasn't a consideration with Mountjoy, in the middle of Dublin. The plan was discussed by the IRA's General Headquarters staff, and given the seal of approval. There was a certain aptness to the choice of exit route: the Irish Minister for Defence Paddy Donegan was well known for travelling by helicopter. As the leader of the opposition would point out the day after the escape, "It is poetic justice that a helicopter is now at the heart of the Government's embarrassment and in the centre of their dilemma. Indeed, it was hard to blame the prison officer who observed that he thought it was the Minister for Defence paying an informal visit to Mountjoy Prison yesterday because, of course, we all know the Minister for Defence is wont to use helicopters, as somebody observed already, as other Ministers are wont to use State cars."

Halloween was chosen as the date for the raid, and eleven days earlier, on 20 October 1973, the IRA approached Irish Helicopters, a private hire firm based out of Dublin Airport. American businessman "Mr Leonard" wanted to charter a chopper for use by himself and his friends to photograph locations in County Laois. He needed a helicopter that would be big enough to carry him, his driver, and all of their heavy photographic equipment. The obvious choice was the French-made Alouette 2 machine, which could seat five people, and it was agreed that Mr Leonard would hire the helicopter on the afternoon of 31 October at a rate of £80 per hour of flying time. Irish Helicopters didn't normally ask for a deposit – leading to *Time* magazine's claim that the escape didn't cost the IRA anything – but the manager recalled that Mr Leonard insisted on paying upfront. No doubt the IRA middleman was worried in case something should go wrong on such an important operation, and he was held liable if Irish Helicopters double-booked!

Word was passed to the men interned in Mountjoy, and although the plot was kept hidden from the majority of the prisoners, their help was needed to keep the guards distracted. A game of Gaelic Rules football was therefore set up for

Halloween afternoon, which had the added advantage of presenting a nice circle in the middle of the yard as a guide for the pilot.

It all nearly went wrong because of the weather – not because the conditions were so bad that the helicopter couldn't fly, but because the manager of Irish Helicopters thought that there was no way that Mr Leonard would want to take his photographs on such a dull day. He therefore didn't hurry his lunch, and was more than a little surprised to find Mr Leonard impatiently waiting for him at the airport when he returned. Leonard explained that his cameraman and the equipment was waiting at a rendezvous en route, and he needed to get going. He was introduced to Captain Thompson Boyes, and explained that not only were they picking up equipment, but they'd also be removing the doors from the chopper to allow better filming.

In Mountjoy exercise yard, the potential escapees were beginning to worry that once again everything had fallen through. Joe Cahill, alongside some of the other prisoners, gave up watching the game and returned to his cell, thereby ensuring that he couldn't take part. Twenty-three prisoners were left there, watched over by eight unarmed guards. At 3.40 p.m., the sound of a helicopter filled the air.

Fifteen minutes earlier, Captain Boyes had landed, as instructed, in a field near Stradbally. However, instead of collecting a cameraman and his equipment, he was faced with two masked gunmen. They told him very politely and firmly that if he followed the instructions he was given, he would not be harmed. Boyes was canny enough to recognize that he was caught up in an IRA operation, and, reassured to a small extent by the gunman's mask, he did as he was told, and with one of the gunmen seated beside him, started to follow the path of the Royal canal into Dublin.

When he was told about the plan, Boyes raised his concerns: three extra passengers would make taking off very tricky, as would the enclosed walls of the exercise yard, if he couldn't get sufficient upswing on the helicopter. He was told to get on with the job.

Hearing the arriving chopper, Kevin O'Mallon began signalling with white strips of cloth. The other prisoners started to surround the guards to prevent them from taking action as the helicopter came in to land. Mallon, O'Hagan and Twomey ran for the machine and started to board. For a moment, the guards thought that it might be a visit from Minister Paddy Donegan using his usual mode of transport, but the sight of the three IRA men getting into the helicopter soon disabused them of that notion.

Captain Boyes struggled with the overladen machine, as O'Hagan pulled Twomey up into the helicopter. A fourth IRA man tried to get on too, but was dissuaded rapidly by the chopper passengers from taking his escape attempt any further. Even so, the turbulence caused by trying to take off within such an enclosed area, combined with the weight of the helicopter, meant that it took much longer than anyone had anticipated before it rose over the walls of Mountjoy. To the evident amusement of the IRA prisoners left behind, one of the guards shouted out possibly the most useless instruction ever: "Close the gates! Close the f***ing gates!"

The volunteers who had managed to evade the authorities after throwing the rope ladder over the walls of the prison a few weeks earlier had been tasked with getting hold of a getaway vehicle and meeting the helicopter at Dublin racecourse at Baldoyle. They eventually commandeered a taxi, putting the driver out of harm's way, but had to move away from the rendezvous when a Garda officer started to become suspicious. By the time they got back, the helicopter had landed, and the escapees were in the middle of hijacking a vehicle. They abandoned that in favour of the already-stolen taxi, and headed off.

To his intense relief, Captain Boyes was released unharmed; he had realized during the flight that he knew one of the men – O'Hagan – and he had been reassured by the IRA men that he wasn't going to be harmed, and he would be paid. That turned out to be the case.

Although the Irish government were convinced that the men were smuggled out of the country, they had in fact simply been moved to various safe houses. The IRA released a statement: "Three republican prisoners were rescued by a special unit from Mountjoy Prison on Wednesday. The operation was a complete success and the men are now safe, despite a massive hunt by Free State forces." Over 300 Garda detectives began a manhunt in vain, as bonfires of celebration were lit in Belfast. Within Mountjoy, one prisoner recalled, "One shamefaced screw apologised to the governor and said he thought it was the new Minister for Defence arriving. I told him it was our Minister of Defence leaving." Eventually one of the largest security operations ever carried out on Irish soil got under way, with over 20,000 security personnel involved in the search for the three terrorists.

The consequences were immediate for the IRA men left behind in Mountjoy. Ten days after Twomey, O'Hagan and Mallon escaped, they were transferred to the maximum-security facility at Portlaoise. The perimeter was guarded by members of the Irish Army, and wires erected to ensure that no other helicopters would make unauthorized landings within the prison walls.

All three men were eventually recaptured. Seamus Twomey remained on the outside for the longest, evading capture until 2 December 1977, when he was spotted by Special Branch in Dublin during a raid on an arms shipment. After a short but high-speed car chase through Dublin, he was arrested, carrying with him highly sensitive IRA documents about the reorganization of the movement. He was sent to Portlaoise, and served the remainder of his term. He was released in 1982 and died in 1989.

J.B. O'Hagan was rearrested in early 1975 in Dublin, and sent to Portlaoise to finish his sentence, and then a further two years for his part in the escape. He continued to be involved with IRA activity until the peace process in the 1990s; he died in 2001.

Kevin Mallon, however, masterminded a second escape attempt, this time from Portlaoise. He was only free for six weeks after the helicopter escapade: he was arrested in the town of Portlaoise on 10 December 1973 and sent to the prison there. On Sunday 18 August 1974, he and eighteen other prisoners were able to blow their way out.

Three months before the successful breakout, the IRA prisoners' hopes had taken a battering after an eighty-foot-long tunnel was uncovered. However, the Portlaoise Escape

Committee were undeterred and decided to exploit a weakness
near the laundry area of the prison. The laundry led to an
outside stairway, which went down into a courtyard where the
Governor's House and the Warders' Mess were located – as was
a doorway which led out onto the streets of the town! If they
could only break through that door, then they would be free.

The GHQ gave its approval to the plan, and arranged for
explosives to be smuggled into the prison. The inmates began to
make ersatz prison officer uniforms so that when the escapees
were running through the courtyard, the troops stationed on the
roof of the jail wouldn't be sure whether they were prison
officers or inmates, and therefore would hold their fire.

At 12.30 p.m. on 18 August, prisoner Liam Brown asked if
he could collect an item from the laundry that he claimed he
had inadvertently left there. When the guard gave permission,
he was rushed by a group of prisoners, and the key to the laundry taken from him. The escapees then ran through the laundry
and down the stairs into the courtyard. The fake uniforms
served their purpose – the troops didn't open fire, worried that
they would be hitting prison officers, giving the IRA men
sufficient time to reach the door to the outside, set the bomb
and detonate it. As soon as that went off, of course, the soldiers
knew what was happening and began firing over the heads of
the escapees trying to persuade them to stop. However, they
had to cease fire when genuine prison officers rushed into the
courtyard!

There was confusion for some hours over how many men
had managed to flee: in order to give those who had made it the
maximum amount of time, the other prisoners refused to cooperate with the prison authorities, and wouldn't allow them to
carry out a headcount. Only when they were threatened with
riot police did they relent. At that point, it was discovered that
nineteen men – including Kevin Mallon – had made it, five
more than the prisoners themselves had anticipated.

A massive manhunt began, with every outhouse in County
Wexford searched, and the navy put on alert. But not one of the
men was recaptured during the week-long searches. A further
tunnel was masterminded by IRA man Eddie Gallagher after
the success of the August escape but it wasn't completed. "We

tried to free others by tunnelling from Portlaoise hospital under the Dublin–Limerick road and into the jail. Sean Treacy, myself and two others were removing foundation stones from beneath the outer jail wall on the night Special Branch and [the] army raided our billet nearby and arrested the day shift who were asleep in the house," he recalled in 2005. Kevin Mallon was recaptured in Foxrock in January 1975 and returned to Portlaoise; after the Good Friday Agreement in 1998, which was designed to mark the end of the conflict in Northern Ireland, he became a breeder of greyhounds.

Fact vs fiction

The *Real Prison Breaks* version of the helicopter escape states bluntly that this was the first time that such a breakout was attempted; this was not the case. It also implies that a helicopter pilot would knock back a pint of Guinness before a flight!

Sources:

Time magazine, 12 November 1973: "Ireland: The Canny Copter Caper"

Sunday Journal, 23 October 2005: "Herrema's kidnapper explains motive"

An Phoblacht, 26 August 2004: "30 years on: The Great Portlaoise Escape"

An Phoblacht, 10 September 2009: "Remembering the Past: IRA Chief of Staff Séamus Twomey"

An Phoblacht, 27 August 2009: "Remembering the Past: 19 prisoners escape from Portlaoise"

An Phoblacht, 1 November 2001: "Remembering the Past: Chopper Escape from Mountjoy"

Hayes, Paddy: *Break Out! Famous Prison Escapes* (O'Brien Press, 2001)

Real Prison Breaks, Discovery Channel, 2008: Archive news interview with Captain Thomas Boyes

Hearing the Foxes Bark

Since the vast majority of prison breaks end with the inmates' recapture, a wide variety of different items have been cited as the benefits of being on the outside. Sometimes it's something as simple as being able to have a drink in a bar; other times, it's a little more poetic. Dale Otto Remling, a conman who was the first American to be freed from a prison on domestic soil by helicopter, was good-humoured when he was captured in a bar not that long after his flight: he told reporters that he was glad he'd had a chance to be on the outside, since he could hear "some birds sing, water trickle, and a fox bark". It was the sort of charming statement that had bamboozled some of his victims and led him to Jackson Prison in the first place.

In 1951, aged twenty-five, Remling had a stroke of luck, on which he based much of his career: he found a wallet belonging to James J. Mangan, then a bellhop at a hotel in Wichita, Kansas. Rather than return it, Remling decided to adopt Mangan's identity, and over the next twenty-two years built up a whole new life for Mangan in parallel with the real man's career working for the US Forestry Service. The ersatz Mangan was considerably less scrupulous: he would issue bad cheques to buy merchandise, and then sell it on to raise cash. He was arrested in California in 1955 and sent to Soledad Prison; he escaped from there but was recaptured after three days. After serving his time, he continued his larcenous career, adding arrests for cattle theft, and then grand larceny in connection with the theft of an airplane in 1971. This landed him back in Soledad.

Remling made a fresh bid for freedom, this time from a prison farm at Sonora, California – and on this occasion he was successful. He headed east and found himself in Crystal, Michigan in 1972. Over the following year, he established his identity as a major cattle baron, with a range in Colorado, and wooed and wed Kay Petersen, the daughter of Crystal's wealthiest man, after presenting a sob story suggesting that his first wife had passed away after suffering for months in an iron lung. Remling's new bride and her father-in-law covered some of his bad debts, but time was running out for the conman. An attempt to steal 383 hogs at gunpoint from a family in Nebraska foundered when Remling and his accomplice forgot to obtain the health records for the livestock; without them, the pigs were unsellable, and worthless.

Remling eventually wrote over $50,000 worth of bad cheques, and was arrested and charged with fraud. He was sentenced in August 1973 to a maximum term of six years and eight months to ten years for attempting to purchase a $2,440 car with a bad cheque. His marriage was annulled, and the real James J. Mangan was horrified to learn what had been done in his name (including a dishonourable discharge from the US Navy!).

From the moment he arrived in Jackson Prison, Remling intended to escape. "I think cages are for something other than people," he pointed out. "You talk about problems with people: the prison system breeds it into you." However, this time he wasn't going to go over the wall. "I didn't have enough nerve to try the wall," he admitted after being returned to jail following his escape. "I'm getting a little old for that."

At that stage officially known as the State Prison of Southern Michigan, Jackson prison sat three miles north of the town of Jackson. Thirty-four-feet high walls surrounded the nearly sixty acres of prison grounds with twelve watchtowers looking after around 6,000 cells, making it the largest walled prison in the world. In 1975, there were 3,245 prisoners housed at Jackson. "The place is so damned big something could happen at one end, and you wouldn't know about it until you read about it in the newspaper," admitted one prison officer in the aftermath of Remling's escape.

Jackson's imposing edifice didn't immediately offer any obvious signs of an escape route, but Remling wasn't discouraged. Although there was a lot of publicity at the time of his eventual escape bid connecting it to the release of *Breakout*, the Charles Bronson film which was itself inspired by the escape of Joel

David Kaplan from a Mexican prison (see chapter 35), Remling was adamant that he had come up with the idea of using a helicopter long before publicity for the film began. Certainly the most that he might have been able to see in the run-up to the movie's release was the brief television trailers (which did include the scene where the chopper lands in the yard), but *Breakout* wasn't screened for prisoners, nor did Remling have any access to seeing it outside. It's more likely that Remling may have read some of the publicity that surrounded Kaplan's escape at the time, and the idea stuck at the back of his mind.

On the morning of 6 June 1975, he put his plan into motion. At 11.05 a.m., a helicopter landed on a spot in the yard of Jackson prison which had previously been marked with a red handkerchief. The pilot, Richard Jackson, a Vietnam combat veteran, had been hired at the Mettetal Airport in Plymouth to take a businessman by the name of Donald Hill to a meeting at Capitol Airport in Lansing, Michigan. However, ten minutes into the flight, Hill had pulled a knife on him and ordered him to fly to the prison. Jackson tried to make a Mayday call, but Hill pulled the microphone jacks from their sockets. Seeing that the other man was nervous, the pilot therefore decided to comply with his kidnapper's demands, and brought the chopper in to land at the prison on the second attempt (he overshot the landing point the first time). Dale Remling, who had been waiting beside the licence-plate manufacturing building, promptly ran across and jumped inside. Since the area was supposed to be under electronic surveillance, the guard towers were unmanned. That meant there weren't any guards within easy reach of the helicopter, and Jackson was able to take off unimpeded. He had been on the ground for no more than twenty seconds.

"Let's get the hell out of here," Hill told Jackson and instructed him to fly in a north-easterly direction, following state highway 106. As they approached a junction, Jackson was ordered to land the helicopter, but as soon as they were on terra firma, Hill sprayed mace in his eyes. He couldn't tell which of the various cars that had been at the drop point the escapees had disappeared in.

As soon as his eyes cleared from the stinging liquid, Jackson radioed the airport, and went in pursuit of the fugitives.

Noticing another car nearby, he passed on its information to the police, who stopped and then questioned its occupant. Jolyne Lou Conn was one of four women who had been hired as a decoy to attract attention away from Remling and Hill. They were all meant to be meeting up at a motel in East Lansing, but when the others heard that Conn had been arrested, they went their separate ways.

Donald Hill was arrested later that day – and police realized that he had nothing to do with the case. The hijacker, Morris Eugene Colosky, had taken a leaf out of Remling's book, and implicated a completely innocent man. Colosky was eventually arrested in Garden City, Kansas, along with another conspirator, mother of eight Gertrude Woodbury, and charged with kidnapping and aircraft piracy. In all, seven accomplices were arrested over the escape.

However, in the confusion at the rendezvous, Remling had missed his ride! The man whom all the fuss was about was left to run for cover. He spent the night hiding in a barn, before heading for the town of Leslie as police officers carried out a house-to-house hunt for him around northern Jackson County. Local residents spotted the stranger in their midst, and called the police (although one report suggests that Remling was turned in by a former cellmate who refused to help him).

Remling entered Huffie's Bar but before he could even order a drink he was faced with a state trooper bearing a gun. The conman grinned, then surrendered without a fight. "There was no use for me to shed tears," Remling said later. "He had the cannon on me, I didn't have it on him." He had been out of the prison for a mere thirty hours. At a press conference held by the state police, he said that he probably wouldn't try to escape again. The FBI agent in charge of the investigation, Neil Welch, was scathing about Remling's planning: "Remling spent a couple of years getting this ready," he said the day after the conman was recaptured. "And his total plan apparently ended with his getting over the wall. The whole thing just fritzed." State Corrections Chief Perry Johnson gave Remling a little more credit: "In terms of adventurousness and bizarreness, I'd say it was one of the strangest," he told reporters.

Hardly surprisingly, the prison authorities looked at ways of preventing other people from using a helicopter. Chief Johnson said that he didn't "want to have an unsightly scarecrow arrangement on one hand or act precipitously and cost taxpayers several million dollars in the next decade". A system of poles and cables that could shear off helicopter propellers was seriously considered.

Remling kept to his word; he was released from prison in 1993 after serving twenty years, and died six years later.

Sources:

Waterloo Courier, 8 June 1975: "Helicopter escapee is captured"

NBC Evening News, 8 June 1975

Palm Beach Post, 16 June 1975: "Take a Bow, Dale Remling"

Big Spring Herald, 8 June 1975: "Hunt Copter Hijacker, Con He Plucked From Prison Captured"

Provo Daily Herald, 8 June 1975: "Copter-Escape Prisoner Nabbed"

Florence Times, 7 June 1975: "Two Charged in Daring 'Copter Prison Escape"

Argus-Press, 9 June 1975: "Chopper Hopper Comes A Cropper"

The Morning Record, 19 June 1975: "Pair arrested for roles in 'copter caper"

Lawrence Journal-World, 18 June 1975: "Copter escape duo arrested"

Tuscaloosa News, 18 June 1975: "Helicopter caper gang rounded up"

American as Apple Pie

Garrett Brock Trapnell may not have been consciously trying to get his name into the history books, but his criminal career saw him become one of the first American citizens to hijack an aircraft – and very nearly one of the first Americans to escape from a domestic American prison by helicopter. "If I had made it in that helicopter," Trapnell said later, "the American public would have loved it. Escaping from prison is as American as apple pie." His slightly flippant comment hides the truth of the events of 24 May 1978: it cost the life of a woman who loved him, and ruined the life of her seventeen-year-old daughter who hijacked an aircraft in an attempt to get the authorities to release him.

On one occasion, authorities described Trapnell as "a bizarre character who often carried an attaché case, affected a James Bond role, trained two German shepherds to be vicious, and boasted that he could beat any criminal charge on an insanity plea". The cover of the book about his career, written by Eliot Asinof, co-author of the book about the very first helicopter escape (see chapter 35), boasts that Trapnell was a "Skyjacker! Supercon! Superlover! The true story of the man who used the system to beat the system and almost won . . .".

By the time that Barbara Ann Oswald tried to free him, Trapnell had been in Marion prison for around five years, and Asinof's book, first published in 1976, had given him some notoriety. He had spent time studying the law on insanity and managed to find ways around jail terms – he'd be sent to a hospital of some description, from which it was comparatively easy to escape. Charges against him for robberies in the Bahamas and in Canada had been dismissed on the grounds that he was not mentally competent. "A lawyer came to me and said,

'Trap, you are going to prison for 20 years, or you can go to the state hospital,'" he recalled in an unpublished 1971 interview that was quoted at his trial as evidence that he was playing the system. "So I went to the state hospital and I dug the whole action. I read more damned books on psychiatry and psychology than probably any psychology student will in any school in the world."

Trapnell's criminal career came to an end when he hijacked a TransWorld Airways flight from Los Angeles to New York in January 1972. Although he spent part of the time during the hijack talking to Dr David G. Hubbard, a Dallas-based psychiatrist who had written a book about what motivates hijackers, demanded the release of black activist Angela Davis from prison, and requested a personal talk with President Nixon, his real motivation seemed to be getting a fellow prisoner, George Anthony Padilla, out of jail, and receiving $306,800. When he was shot by an FBI agent, he was arrested, and promptly claimed that he could not be held liable for the hijacking. He claimed that he had a Jekyll/Hyde personality, and the crime was committed by his wicked alter ego, Greg Ross. "I have committed all these crimes and have never gotten a number for any of them," he had said a year earlier. "If Gregg Ross commits a crime, then Gary Trapnell is not responsible. It's the fallacy of your legal system." Although one jury member was swayed by this at his first trial, Padilla turned on Trapnell at his second trial, and related how he had been taught how to feign madness. Trapnell was found guilty and sentenced to life imprisonment.

In 1974, there was a bizarre attempt to secure Trapnell's release. Twenty-two-year-old Maria Theresa Alonzo, a former member of the Manson family, was arrested for conspiring with Trapnell and her boyfriend, prisoner Robert Bernard Hedberg, to kidnap a consul general. Intriguingly, the FBI weren't sure which country he would come from: the options ranged from Paraguay to Canada, even though the Paraguayan consulate in Los Angeles had recently closed. Alonzo would then hold him to ransom for $250,000, asylum in Sweden, and the release of Hedberg and Trapnell, who at the time was being held in Los Angeles while he stood trial for a robbery in LA in 1971. The plot seems to have fallen apart because Alonzo developed a boil and had to go for treatment rather than kidnapping the consul general! The FBI arrested her the next day and simultaneously charged Trapnell and Hedberg.

The publication of Asinof's book about Trapnell two years later created a buzz of publicity around the conman turned hijacker, including an interview on news programme *60 Minutes*, in which he expressed his fascination with the story of Henri Charriere, aka Papillon. One of those attracted to him was Barbara Ann Oswald, who seemed on the surface to be an ordinary housewife and mother of five. In fact, she had been a prostitute in her teens before enlisting in the US Army. She started writing to Trapnell, who was now at Marion prison, from her home in Richmond Heights, St Louis, Missouri, around 120 miles away. Telling friends that she intended to marry the convict (the source of some accounts which claim that she was his wife), she knew that they could only truly be together if prison walls weren't between them.

Marion prison, however, wasn't a place that was easy to escape from. Although it is now a medium-security institution, after being downgraded in 2006, at the time it was a maximum-security facility, built and opened in 1963 initially to take the prisoners from Alcatraz who were transferred there (and not lost in time as a recent TV series would have you believe!). Ten years after the prison began functioning, control-unit cells were introduced: prisoners would spend no more than one hour a day outside these one-man cells which were designed to prevent their contact with other people. Two years later came the first escape in the prison's twelve-year history, when five inmates were able to release the doors of the cells using a radio remote control. Rather stupidly, a prisoner who had been an electrician outside was allowed to work on the lock mechanisms of all the doors – inevitably he used his knowledge to find a way around the system. They were all eventually recaptured.

That wasn't going to deter Barbara Oswald. By spring 1978, the forty-three-year-old was regularly visiting Trapnell at Marion, and during these sessions the plot was hatched. As well as freeing Trapnell, the plan was to get his fellow prisoners James Kenneth Johnson and hijacker Martin J. McNally out from Marion at the same time. The idea of a helicopter flight topped the agenda, possibly arising from Trapnell's biographer's earlier book *The 10-Second Jailbreak*, about the escape of Joel David Kaplan from a Mexican prison in 1971. Around $5,000 was needed to sort out the various expenses involved. After the plan failed, Trapnell explained to a fellow inmate that there hadn't been time to send Oswald to somewhere far away from Illinois so she could safely learn to fly a helicopter herself, rather than risk taking a hostage. He had learned that a new tower was being constructed in front of the institution, and he was concerned that it would be up and running before Oswald would have time to complete a course of lessons.

They therefore decided that Oswald would hire a helicopter from St Louis International Airport, and then hijack it, bringing it in to land in the prison yard – an area that was strictly out of bounds to the prisoners. The three escapees would be waiting there, with one of them wearing a yellow jacket so the pilot would know exactly where to land. Oswald would be carrying handcuffs for use on the pilot if they needed to use him as a hostage. They would then take off, and head to a nearby airport, where guns, changes of clothing, and a car would be waiting for them. They would drive to Kentucky, and fly down to New Orleans, where they planned to carry out some robberies. What they didn't factor into their plans was thirty-year-old Allen Barklage, the helicopter pilot. The former Vietnam combat pilot had no intention of participating in the plot.

In the late afternoon of 24 May 1978, Oswald hired a Bell Jetranger II helicopter from Fostaire Helicopter Company, apparently to fly to look at some real estate in Cape Giradeau in Missouri, about thirty-five miles beyond Marion prison. They had been flying for just over half an hour when Oswald produced the .44 calibre pistol, pointed it at Barklage and ordered him to fly to the prison. At point-blank range, Barklage wasn't going to argue, and set course. During the flight, Oswald told him that they would be landing in the exercise yard, and that one of the people they were collecting would have a yellow jacket. She showed him the handcuffs she had brought with her, and said that they would be used on him.

Barklage knew that the chances were that he would be picking up desperate men, and that the odds of him surviving the next few minutes were not great. When they were less than three miles from the prison, he took advantage of a momentary lapse on Oswald's part. As she tried to open the door of the helicopter, she switched the gun from her left hand to her right, and put her finger on the trigger guard, rather than on the trigger itself. Barklage let go of the helicopter's controls, knowing that it would begin to pitch and turn wildly, and grabbed for the gun. A ten to fifteen second struggle ensued between the combat veteran and the Missouri housewife. Knowing it was a life-or-death situation, Barklage fired the gun repeatedly, but the helicopter was moving around so much that only one bullet hit its mark. It was enough: Oswald was dead.

Barklage quickly regained control of the helicopter and brought it down to earth outside the administration building. Not thinking too clearly, he started looking for a guard, and nearly found himself on the receiving end of a fusillade of bullets from them. He quickly explained the situation, and the three escapees were rounded up. In later life, Barklage commented, "The dominating thought that I have when I think back on that is there may have been a way to do that without shooting the person . . . Could I have talked her out of it?" He was killed while flying an experimental helicopter in 1998.

The three escapees were charged with various offences, and although Trapnell tried his usual torturous legal defences, he was found guilty.

If Oswald's daughter had had her way, though, he wouldn't have been around to answer to the charges. Seventeen-year-old Robin Oswald was devastated by her mother's death, and dropped out of high school. She kept in touch with Trapnell, whom friends said she regarded as a "father figure", and in the week that Trapnell went on trial for charges relating to the incident, Robin took matters into her own hands, apparently at Trapnell's instigation.

Eighty-three passengers and six crew were on board TWA flight 541 from Louisville, Kentucky to Kansas City, Missouri on the morning of 21 December when she claimed that she had three sticks of dynamite strapped to her body underneath a bulky sweater, and wanted Trapnell released. The plane was diverted to Williamson County Airport, near Marion, and was quickly surrounded by the FBI. Robin commandeered the back rows of the aircraft and sent notes via the flight attendants.

"She kept talking about how her mother died in the helicopter and her family had disowned her," one witness recalled. However, after negotiations, the passengers and crew were released unharmed (while many others escaped through a door that Robin couldn't see), and Robin was taken into custody. At pretty much the same time, the jury found Trapnell guilty. The "dynamite" proved to be railroad flares wired to a doorbell. She spent twenty-two months in a treatment program, after being tried as a juvenile, and then turned her life around.

Although Trapnell would continue to brag that he would eventually escape from Marion, it never happened. In 1993, Garrett Brock Trapnell died of emphysema while still being held prisoner.

Sources:

http://www.youtube.com/watch?gl=GB&v=HsBv5SIICIY   Alan Barklage look back

St Louis Magazine, February 2012: "Historic and Harrowing St. Louis Prison Escapes"

St Joseph News-Press, 21 December 1978: "Plane hijacked"

St Louis Today, 25 June 2011: "Airline hijacking at Lambert in 1972 turns bizarre"

Lakeland Ledger, 22 December 1978: "Passenger –'Beautiful Girl' Was Serious"

New York Times, 16 January 2005: "The First Hijackers"

Los Angeles Times, 11 March 1974: "Manson 'daughter' arrested in diplomatic kidnap plot"

United States Court of Appeals, Second Circuit, 10 April 1974: "United States of America, Appellee, v. Garrett Brock Trapnell, Appellant"

Time magazine, 29 January 1973: "Return of Dr. Jekyll"

Time magazine, 1 January 1979: "Skyjack sequel"

Kansas City Star, December 2003: "Hijacking family"

Kentucky New Era, 22 December 1978: "17-Year-Old Hijacks Plane to Free Hijacker"

San Francisco Sunday Examiner & Chronicle, 30 January 1972: "Another skyjacker shot"

United States Court of Appeals, Seventh Circuit, 30 December 1980: "UNITED STATES of America, Plaintiff-Appellee, v. Garrett Brock TRAPNELL and Martin Joseph McNally, Defendants-Appellants"

San Francisco Chronicle, 22 December 1978: "Girl, 16 (*sic*), Surrenders in Airline Hijacking"

Waterloo Courier, 25 May 1978: "Hijacker killed in aerial drama near penitentiary"

Journal of Prisoners on Prisons, 1993, Formatted Online Version 2006: "Breaking Men's Minds: Behavior Control and Human Experimentation at the Federal Prison in Marion"

Altoona Mirror, 25 May 1978: "Pilot Kills Female Hijacker, Prevents 3 Inmates' Escape"

Checking Out of the Hilton

Highly successful Australian drugs smuggler David McMillan is back behind bars, following his arrest in the usually quiet London suburb of Orpington in spring 2012. But as the *Australian Times* pointed out in its feature on his conviction in September 2012 (for heroine (sic) smuggling), McMillan had quickly "become infamous for his miraculous ability to evade imprisonment," and wondered whether the fifty-six-year-old criminal would attempt to escape, this time from a British cell.

McMillan featured in two escapes – one which he maintains was a scam set up to fleece him; the other in what was described by no less a person than the former Australian Attorney General Robert McClelland as "quite exceptional and athletic circumstances". The first, in 1983, would have been from Australia's Pentridge Prison in Melbourne; the second, thirteen years later, saw him become the first man to get out from the infamous Bangkok Hilton in twelve years.

The smuggler had come to Britain after many years as a feared member of the Australian underground, apparently to retire in comfort, and write books based on his adventures. He was born in London, but his family moved to Australia when he was very young, and he became widely known as a reporter while still only twelve years old, on the Nine Network's *Peters Junior News*. A continuing interest in the world of film and television – possibly derived from reading about his father, who was the controller of one of the early independent television networks in the UK and had remained behind when the family moved – led him to the fringes of the underworld in Melbourne. McMillan thrived in these environs, and soon became one of the leading drugs smugglers, reluctantly stopping bringing the drugs in himself as he was certain he would be arrested.

McMillan became involved with Lord Tony Moynihan, the disgraced British peer who had left England for Spain after facing fifty-seven criminal charges. He had ended up in the Philippines, where he ran a brothel and became involved with the drugs trade. Moynihan tried to con McMillan into rigging the cockfights in Manila, but McMillan saw through him, although this meant he created a dangerous enemy for himself.

In January 1982, McMillan, his wife Clelia, his business partner Michael Sullivan and his wife, were all arrested at the end of a major operation by the Australian state and federal police. What McMillan refers to as "The Great Helicopter Escape" in his books (although he gives no details, and didn't discuss it during a lengthy TV interview with actor Danny Dyer) would have seen a former SAS corporal, Percival Roger Hole, then living in the Philippines, bring a helicopter down onto Pentridge Prison's tennis court to collect McMillan, Sullivan and a third member of the gang, Supahaus Chowdury. They would then be deposited next to a van fitted with side panels that would allow them to hide as they were driven from Melbourne to Sydney; from there, a yacht would take them to freedom in Manila.

According to some reports, Moynihan got wind of the scheme and reported it to Australian authorities, who ran it as a "sting" operation; McMillan himself, in an online blog, called the whole plot "a scam to fleece the accused as well as help the prosecution fluff an otherwise evidence-thin case." McMillan was charged with the attempted escape, and authorities carried out a dummy run to check whether such an escape would be viable, and if so, what measures should be taken to prevent it. According to John Eacott, who was part of the Victoria Police Air Wing, writing on an internet forum in 2007, "it was prudent to prove that a helicopter could be used as implied, so on a Wednesday sometime in June 1983, Dave A. flew a 206 into the exercise yard, doors off, and picked up 3 Sons Of God who were milling around looking lost. In and out in [less than] 30 seconds, case proved." As a result, prison authorities were advised to string marked wires over all the walls, but it seems as if they didn't carry this out.

Hole was arrested on 19 January after police bugged the hotel room in which he was staying, and he was heard discussing the plan with accountant Charles Maxwell McCready. Contemporary newspaper reports suggest that he was paid $US397,000 to collect McMillan, Sullivan and Chowdury; he was sentenced to four and a half years in prison. By this point, though, McMillan had far worse things to worry about. Clelia and Sullivan's wife were killed in a prison fire at HM Prison Fairlea on 6 February while being held on remand; McMillan was sentenced to seventeen years in prison.

Beyond the helicopter getaway, it seems as if McMillan didn't try to escape from his prison sentence, although he claims that he assisted "half a dozen" others with their various attempts, without giving details. He waited for the various appeal stages to work their way through, and by the time that happened, he would have been near to release. He was freed in 1993 on parole, and promptly flew to Thailand. One policeman who worked on the original arrest told Australian paper *The Age*, "We let him go to Thailand and get picked up there because we thought he might get hanged."

He may not have been hanged but McMillan was quickly arraigned on further drugs charges. He was travelling on a false passport in the name of Donald Westlake, and was nearly arrested at Bangkok Airport. It wasn't long before a group of policemen walked into a travel agency and arrested him; and, as he told the BBC in 2007, from that moment he began planning his escape.

McMillan was sent to the notorious Klong Prem Central Prison in Bangkok. Known ironically as the Bangkok Hilton, Klong Prem was originally established in 1944 as a temporary prison during the Second World War, but after the main prison became overcrowded in 1960, the prisoners were transferred there. Around 12,000 inmates were housed there when McMillan arrived in 1993, with around 600 foreigners. Although these were mainly kept in Building 2, McMillan bribed his way to ensure that he was housed in Building 6: after a check of the various bars, walls and electric fences around the prison, he chose it because it had the thinnest bars in the windows.

Although the Bangkok Hilton was still heavily overcrowded, with some cells about the size of a family garage containing up to twenty-five convicts, McMillan was able to bribe his way into some degree of comparative luxury. By the time that he escaped in 1996, he had set up an office, had a cook and a cleaner working for him, and was in a first-floor cell, with only three other prisoners for company. He even had a light switch installed – something of a necessity given that he was planning on cutting through the bars with a hacksaw blade. Everything that he had put in his cell was there for one reason, and one reason only: to help with his escape.

Escape may have been the goal of many of the Bangkok Hilton's inmates, but most were put off by the fate of any who tried. McMillan recalled that five men had tried and failed: they had got as far as the outside wall before they were recaptured. They were then put in the punishment cells – steel boxes about five-feet long and two feet wide – and then every day they were brought out in elephant chains and beaten. Four of the five died. It was discouraging to learn that even if prisoners managed to get over the electrified fence without being thrown back by the current, chances were that the monks in the monastery next door would be as likely to turn an escapee in.

McMillan considered using one of his court appearances to effect an escape, but was counselled against it. A previous attempt had seen a group of Chinese prisoners rescued by friends, but they had been tracked down after one of their number hesitated and didn't go along on the escape. He knew where the escapees were planning to meet, and gave up the information after being tortured for four hours. The special police unit had killed everyone in the safe house.

McMillan was certain he had to get out sooner rather than later. "I knew I was going to get the death penalty and I had to move before being sent to the Bangkwang Prison, known as The Big Tiger, which holds Thailand's death row," he recalled in 2007. He obtained photos of the outer wall, showing there was a metre of barbed wire on the top, with an electric cable running through it, connected to insulators. There were no footholds to be had.

Shortly before 3 a.m., using hacksaw blades that he had arranged to be smuggled into the prison inside the rods holding up a poster, McMillan managed to cut through one of the bars, and then, with the aid of a Swedish fellow convict, pulled the remainder apart, so he could squeeze himself through. A disassembled bookcase provided a plank to get to the courtyard, and he then used a rope formed from shower curtains to lower himself to the ground level. He then had to get over six walls to reach the outside.

Breaking into a hobby room, McMillan retrieved a homemade ladder, formed from picture frames and bamboo poles, then stealthily crept past the sleeping guards. This enabled him to get over the other walls, slowly but surely. He cut through barbed wire (which he hadn't expected to encounter), crawled under razor wire and crossed the open sewer (known affectionately as "Mars Bar Creek") on the ladder.

The final fence was electrified, and he had to hope that the rubber soles of his trainers and the rubber gloves he was wearing would insulate him. They did. He reached the top of the wall as dawn was breaking, and rapidly slid down his makeshift rope – burning the skin off his hands – to land outside the prison. Then, with the sort of audaciousness that the Australian police had come to expect from him during their long hunt, he opened up a compact umbrella, and nonchalantly walked off to hail a taxi – after all, who would expect an escaping prisoner to be carrying an umbrella?

After collecting a passport from a safe house, and a change of clothing from another hideout, at 10.20 a.m. he was on a plane to Singapore. The following March, Robert McClelland gave his unexpected testimonial. "A prisoner . . . escaped from the Thai jail in quite exceptional and athletic circumstances. In terms of mere escape, it was really quite an achievement. He took the opportunity after his escape of dropping a note to the Australian embassy to thank them for all their tremendous work and said that he hoped he had not caused them any embarrassment."

McMillan's jail exploits didn't finish there, although his propensity for escape did. He was arrested in Pakistan, but released; he later served a two-year term after being caught at Heathrow Airport in 2002. He is still a wanted man in Australia for breaching his parole in 1993, and in Thailand for the escape, but as he is now a UK resident, he cannot be extradited to a country that might put him to death. McMillan appeared on the Bravo TV series *Deadliest Men 2: Living Dangerously* in 2009, interviewed by British actor Danny Dyer, in which he seemed to have changed from his criminal ways. However, although he wrote three books about his exploits, and sold the film rights of his escape from the Bangkok Hilton, McMillan was still active in the drugs trade: in April 2012, a joint operation between Bromley Police and the UK Border Force arrested him for importing and distributing heroin from Pakistan. In September that year he was sentenced to a further six years inside.

Sources:

New Strait Times, 21 January 1983: "Police foil jailbreak plot"

Australian Times, 19 September 2012: "Notorious Australian drug smuggler David McMillan jailed in London"

BBC News, 1 March 2009: "How to plan a successful jailbreak"

The Age, 12 September 2009: "There was a crooked man . . ."

Metro, 10 May 2011 "How I made my escape from Klong Prem prison"

The Independent, 16 July 1996: "Queen's Proctor v Moynihan sons; Fugitive baron's dissolute lifestyle to be kept secret"

Neos Kosmos, 9 March 2009: "Diatribe: Prison Break"

Blog: Escape with David McMillan: http://escapedavidmcmillan. blogspot.co.uk/2009/07/see-danny-dyer-and-david-mcmillan-tv.html

Bravo TV: 2009: *Deadliest Men 2: Living Dangerously*

Pro Pilot Forum: A Gun To You (sic) Head: December 2007

Sydney Morning Herald, 29 June 1984: "Jail for escape plan man"

London Evening Standard, 14 September 2007: "Drug dealer who escaped Bangkok jail is on the run in London"

McMillan, David: *Escape: The True Story of the Only Westerner Ever To Break Out of Thailand's Bangkok Hilton* (Monsoon Books Singapore, 2007)

McMillan, David: *Escape: The Past* (Monsoon Books Singapore, 2011)

Escaping *into* Prison

For most fugitives, the last place that they want to see while they're on the run is the inside of a jail. The whole point of their flight is to get away, either from what they perceive as a major injustice or from their just desserts. The thought of voluntarily going inside a prison cell would be anathema. But sometimes, hiding in plain sight is the simplest way to stay away – or at least, it was in the time before databases of fingerprints and other identification marks became automatically checked whenever someone was arrested. Cuban refugee Orlando Boquete discovered that adopting other people's identities was the best method of remaining off the radar – but sometimes that meant doing a short stint inside.

Unlike many of the other prison escapees in this volume, Boquete wasn't just convinced of his innocence; he really was not guilty of the crime for which he was imprisoned, as would be proved with the advent of DNA testing. He wasn't a squeaky clean innocent: when he left Cuba in 1980, at the age of twenty-five as one of the Marielitos that Fidel Castro permitted to depart that year, he had already served time in a Cuban jail as an Army deserter. He also left behind him two marriages, and a son.

Boquete's life changed for ever on 25 June 1982. He had spent the past two years working in various jobs, and was living with his uncle in a trailer in Key West. He had shaved his head because of the heat, leaving a full black moustache as his only facial hair. That evening he sat watching a baseball match and then the World Cup football matches, which were being held in Spain at the time. He and his cousin then went to buy some cigarettes and beer – and Boquete was arrested, after being identified by a woman who had been assaulted in a nearby apartment block. Two Latino men had entered her apartment;

one stayed in the living room, the other entered her bedroom, fondled her and masturbated on her. She had told police that her assailant had a shaved head, and no facial hair, but despite Boquete's moustache, she told the police officers unequivocally that he was the man involved. The fact that she was twenty feet away, sitting in a police car in the middle of the night did not shake her conviction.

Prosecutors tried to get Boquete to agree a deal, turning evidence against the second man in the burglary. Boquete refused, explaining in court that "If my freedom depends on my falsely stating that I'm a culprit or guilty, I would rather go to jail. I'm conscious of the fact that if the gentlemen of the jury and the ladies of the jury, if they vote against me, they are going to destroy my life, and I'm not afraid to stand here." The assaulted woman was shown a picture of Boquete the night before the trial, which showed his prominent moustache; for the first time, on the witness stand, she said that her assailant had facial hair. The defence's only hope was that Pablo Cazola, who had also been arrested for the attack and had pleaded guilty, would testify that Boquete was not involved. He had signed an affidavit to that effect, but he wasn't willing to enter the witness box. Perhaps unsurprisingly, given that Boquete's alibi was that he was with family members, the jury chose to believe the victim. Boquete was sentenced to fifty years for the burglary and five years for attempted sexual battery.

He was sent to the Glades Correctional Institution (GCI), near the small town of Belle Glade in Florida. The thousand-bed prison, closed down in December 2011, had been built in 1932, and had its fair share of escapes over the years before Boquete decided to depart from the facility. Four men, including William Barbre, had sawn through a window in July 1980 and made their escape; three were quickly recaptured, but Barbre stayed on the run for nearly six years (he was recaptured after working in the area under an assumed name – he was recognized and arrested). In December 1984, convicted murderer Crawford Lee Grooms used a pair of wire-cutters to escape from the prison, after hiding in the athletics field. He was picked up by police nine days later in Miami on a vagrancy charge.

GCI's security was pretty standard: there were two fences, with a ten-feet boundary area between them. This was filled with pressure detectors that would set off alarms as soon as they were touched. The outer fence was around fifteen-feet high, and covered with razor wire. Guard towers were dotted around the perimeter, and a van patrolled the outside of the wall on a road near the fence. Beyond that were sugar-cane fields, in which some of the prisoners worked, and an irrigation canal, which was filled with the local fauna including snakes and alligators. This made for a very effective moat beyond the fields – no one in their right mind would risk tangling with an alligator unless they absolutely felt they had to.

Boquete was inspired by the tale of Papillon (see chapter 53); Henri Charriere's account of his various escapes from French penal colonies may well err on the side of fiction, but Boquete knew it contained important lessons for anyone wanting to get away from false imprisonment. Patience wasn't simply a virtue – it was a necessity. And observe everything that is going on around you: in the words of the Biblical book of Ecclesiastes, keep your ears open and your mouth shut. Boquete took in all the little details and realized that to get over the fences and escape successfully, he would need some assistance.

Through a contact within the prison, he was able to get hold of a map of the surrounding area, vital if he was to stay on the loose for any length of time. Without making it appear too obvious, he checked out the routine of the patrol van, and estimated that from the time an alarm was triggered, he would have approximately one minute before the van returned from the farthest part of its journey. And he enlisted help from another inmate, robber George Wright (not to be confused with the hijacker George Wright, who escaped from Leesburg State Prison in 1970), while they were jogging in the yard (at least according to Boquete). The two men were both assigned to the cannery plant in the prison, and it was from there that they made their getaway on 6 February 1985.

The machinery at the cannery tended to malfunction, and when it did, the four guards' attention was focused far more on arranging to get the forty or so prisoners back working than on thoughts of escape. Boquete and Wright took advantage of this and when the machine went wrong for the third time in a week, they simply slipped away while the guards were distracted. Using a door frame which had been left out for them, they went over the first fence, pulled the frame after them, sprinted across the pressure-pad-filled strip (activating the alarms, they believed), and then leaned the wooden block against the outer fence, and scrambled up it to the wire-covered top. Jumping from the outer fence, and with the prison van still not back in sight, they raced towards the canal.

At the time, the prison authorities suggested that the first they knew of the escape was when one of the other prisoners in the cannery told them that Wright and Boquete had disappeared, but whether that or the activation of pressure pads was the cause, within minutes the search dogs had been called out. For the next three hours, a helicopter, tracking dogs, sheriff's deputies, Belle Glade police and the Florida Highway patrol all combed the area searching for the men.

By that point Boquete and Wright had separated. Both men had risked jumping into the alligator-infested canal, but while Boquete remained in the water as long as he dared, Wright had headed swiftly for the main road. The dogs were able to follow the scent as far as Highway 715, but the prison's Assistant Superintendent Willie Floyd had to tell reporters that "somewhere along the highway, they lost their scent". Wright may have been picked up by an accomplice; he refused to explain what happened to him when questioned later. He was on the run for about eighteen months, and was captured in the Pacific North West.

Boquete spent two nights hiding very close to the prison, attacked by ants but aware that the intensive search for him wouldn't go on for too long. On the third morning, he crossed the sugar-cane fields and the canals until he reached the railroad tracks. He knew from the map he had purchased that there was a truck depot not far away. However, when he reached it he realized that he was too exhausted to go much further, and after an abortive attempt to get help from his family in Miami, he asked some Mexican labourers for assistance. He joined them, working in the fields, until they all pooled their earnings, bought a truck, and headed for Miami.

For the next ten years, Orlando Boquete lived an incredible life, adopting many different identities, and staying one step ahead of the law. He kept pieces of sandpaper in his wallet, so he could rub his fingertips and make his fingerprints just that little bit different. He trained himself not to respond to his original name if called by a stranger, which saved him from recapture on more than one occasion. His good looks and charm got him into and out of many dangerous situations, up and down the eastern seaboard of the United States.

Using fake social security numbers, or adopting those of dead people whose decease hadn't yet registered with the authorities, Boquete was able to work. Occasionally these people were wanted for something, and he'd serve brief terms for drunk and disorderly, or driving under the influence. He worked on a construction crew inside a prison, and took clothing and other items to a fellow Cuban refugee who had been arrested and was being held in a central Florida prison on drugs charges. He spent some time working in Illinois and Arizona, disappeared to North Carolina for a time when he was warned that he needed to get away from Florida. But he kept coming back to the Cuban community, known as Little Havana, in Miami.

He was arrested repeatedly for minor offences, but in March 1995, the charge was more serious. Boquete was using the name Hilberto Rodríguez and was found with an illegal firearm. He was sentenced to a year imprisonment, but soon absconded from a work party, gaining help from a drug-dealer friend, Ulises, who he had known since he first returned to Miami after breaking out of the GCI.

Boquete stayed with Ulises, but this proved to be a mistake. When the Florida Drugs Enforcement Agency took an interest in his friend, it was Boquete who ended up arrested for possession of two pounds of marijuana. And once in the police station, the increased computer networking between jurisdictions marked his downfall. Palm Beach County were after someone with those fingerprints, and the law enforcement officers realized that Hilberto Rodríguez and Orlando Boquete were one and the same.

Given an additional year and a day to his sentence for the escape (and the time on the original award starting to run once again), Boquete faced the prospect of many more decades in prison for a crime he didn't commit. But he was to benefit from a change in the law covering DNA testing in the state of Florida, following the case of Frank Lee Smith, an innocent man on death row whose conviction was only overturned when he was terminally ill.

Boquete applied to the Innocence Project, set up in 1992 as "a national litigation and public policy organization dedicated to exonerating wrongfully convicted people through DNA testing and reforming the criminal justice system to prevent future injustice". On 23 May 2006, three years after his application, he was exonerated, his conviction fully vacated by the state of Florida. There was no way that Boquete could have produced the semen which was found on the victim's underwear, and indeed the evidence that was available in 1983, which showed his blood type excluded him as a possible perpetrator, should have been made clearer to the original court. "No words spoken by this court today . . . would do justice to the penalty that you have been required to pay for offenses that now we know conclusively that you were not guilty of committing," Judge Richard Payne said. "You are hereby ordered to be immediately released from the custody of Florida."

The only problem was that Boquete didn't have permanent residency status in the United States, so was detained by the Immigrations and Customs Enforcement Agency. Was he a danger to society? The crimes he had committed while escaping – and even the escape itself – were initially held against him, but eventually, after three months, he was released.

Even then, Boquete's story wasn't over. He eventually was granted full American residency status on 16 November 2010, but while this lifted a threat from over his head, it didn't help him with other problems. He should have been eligible for compensation for the time he spent wrongly incarcerated, but a loophole in the 2008 Victims of Wrongful Incarceration Compensation Act meant that a convicted felon can't receive the $50,000 a year recompense. In February 2011, Boquete told the *Orlando Sentinel*, in broken English, "That's a terrible law . . . The people who wrote it, they're tricking. They're bad people . . . I had a clean record before I went to prison." As at the time of writing, this situation has not yet been resolved, and a man who only committed crimes after being found guilty of a much greater one that he was not responsible for, lives on the poverty line, ironically in a much worse situation than he would have been had he remained inside jail.

Sources:

Twitpic: 16 November 2010: http://twitpic.com/37fs14
New York Times, 11 February 2007: "Fugitive"
The Innocence Project: About Us: http://www.innocenceproject.org/about/Mission-Statement.php
The Innocence Project of Florida: http://floridainnocence.org/
The Innocence Project: http://www.innocenceproject.org/Content/Orlando_Boquete.php
Orlando Sentinel, 12 February 2011: "Only two of 12 Florida inmates cleared by DNA have collected money from state"
The Innocence Project, Press Release 23 May 2006: "23 Years After Conviction Based on Eyewitness Misidentification, DNA Proves Orlando Boquete's Innocence"
Florida Sun Sentinel, 8 February 1985: "Police Lose Track of Escapees Who Fled Glades Correctional"

Back to Badness

At the end of his latest spree in Australia, which culminated in a siege that had officers fearing that he was planning "suicide by cop", Christopher David Binse – who had given himself the nickname "Badness" some years earlier – had escaped, or tried to escape from Australian jails eight times. He had appeared in the *Real Prison Breaks* television series in interviews counter-pointed with his nemesis in the police, making it clear that he didn't regard escaping as anything other than something that he would do when the circumstances demanded it. At that point – in 2008 – the inference was that he had "gone straight", and the leopard had changed his spots to a degree (a metaphor he used himself). Very obviously that wasn't the case, and with Binse back inside, a close watch is being made to ensure that he doesn't go for escape number nine.

Binse's first major escape came from HM Prison Pentridge, a maximum-security facility in Melbourne which had been built in 1850 – and from which the first escapes (a party of fifteen convicts) were recorded the following year. It was infamous for being the last resting place of famous Australian bushranger Ned Kelly, after his remains were moved there in 1929 from Melbourne Gaol, where he had been hanged in 1880. It was also the site of the last hanging in Australia: Ronald Ryan was executed in 1967 for shooting a prison officer during an escape from Pentridge two years earlier (see chapter 31). Pentridge was closed down in May 1997.

Christopher Binse was in "the College of Knowledge", as it was known to its inmates, in August 1992 as just part of a long criminal career. He had been declared uncontrollable nine years earlier, at the age of fourteen, and he was sent to a boys' home in Turana. He knew Pentridge wasn't going to be an easy place to get out of: 1,500 prisoners guarded by 250 officers, six guard towers, surrounded by razor-wire covered fences. He was there on remand for armed robbery, something for which he admitted he had a passion: after one of his arrests, he told Melbourne police he carried out raids "for the excitement, the rush. Lifestyle, you'd have to know what it feels like. It's like you on a raid, you're in control, your blood starts rushing, you feel grouse, you're hyped up. F--k the money. It's more than excitement, it's an addiction. I don't know what it is."

He may not have seen it as such at the time, but Binse got lucky on the evening of 28 August. Taking a shower, he felt as if he had been punched a couple of times, but in fact he had been knifed with a shiv – an ordinary implement sharpened by prisoners to form a lethal weapon. He was rushed to the nearby St Vincent's Hospital in a critical condition and kept in a locked ward under armed guard; even though there was a good chance that he wasn't going to survive the incident, the Australian prison bosses weren't taking any chances.

Binse was in the locked-down ward on the seventh floor of the hospital for ten days, but at some point on the evening of 8 September, he received a female visitor, who apparently gave him a gun which she had smuggled onto the ward inside her boot. (It has never been proved that this was the case, but the alternative – that one of the guards provided him with the firearm – is not one that the Australian authorities cared to contemplate). Once she had left, Binse waited until the guard's back was turned, then slid out of bed, and pointed the gun at his captor. After a brief discussion, the guard elected to be cooperative, and opened the first deadlocked door. The threat to his colleague persuaded the guard in charge of the control room to open the other door, allowing Binse access to an elevator. From there it was easy to get to the ground floor, and then exit the hospital through the emergency department – even if he was only dressed in a hospital gown! He stole a van from a nearby car park and made his getaway.

While Victoria police searched for him, using dogs, helicopters, car and foot patrols, Binse had escaped to New South Wales, reaching Sydney the day after his flight from the hospital, despite still bleeding from his wounds. After a week of holing up, though, he turned to his only source of finance: armed robbery. He raided the Commonwealth Bank at Chatswood, firing his way out through a glass door, but he was betrayed by an informant, who tipped off the police. Binse was arrested and the process of extradition back to Victoria was begun. In the meantime, he was held at Parramatta Correctional Centre in Sydney, which had the distinction of being the longest-running and oldest jail in Australia, founded in 1798 (it closed in 2011 after some embarrassing escapes).

Binse had no intention of waiting around to be sent back to Pentridge, and within a week of arriving at Parramatta, he had worked out a way of escaping from the prison. As with his flight from St Vincent's Hospital, he used outside help, this time arranging for a hacksaw blade to be thrown over the wall at a specific point where he could collect it without being noticed. He created a rope out of his bedsheets and then he patiently sawed through the bars of his cell window. On 25 October 1992, he let himself out through the window, down the rope and onto a roof, which was covered with razor wire at its edges. He leaped over that and a further twenty feet to another roof which he just managed to grab (he claimed in 2008 that his imprints on the tin roof were still visible at that point, over fifteen years later), then, despite being fired at by a prison guard, he swung his rope so that he could abseil over the inner perimeter fence. Unfortunately for him, his rope broke and he fell to the ground, breaking his wrist.

That wasn't going to deter Badness. He was caught in the sterile zone between the inner and outer walls. There were guard towers to either side of him. From the catwalk between them, he made an easy target. But he was determined that he was going to get out, and so, even though there were bullets whizzing past him (and one has to assume that the guards were shooting to try to persuade him to stop, rather than actually shooting to kill), he climbed over the perimeter fence. His accomplices were waiting for him, and he disappeared once more.

He managed to stay hidden for six weeks, but on 5 December 1992, he was arrested in the aftermath of the shooting of notorious criminal Edward "Jockey" Smith. Disguised in a false moustache, sunglasses and a cap – clothing that he donned regularly during his bank raids – Binse had raided another branch of the Commonwealth Bank, this time in Doncaster, Victoria, on 23 November, stealing $160,000 and using his shotgun to blast open a glass door that prevented him from reaching the money, then escaping in a car driven, police believed, by his girlfriend, Laura Skellington. By 3 December, he and Skellington had teamed up with Jockey Smith – who was on the run once more, following various incidents in November in New South Wales. They rented a room in a farmhouse which was being looked after by Guiseppe Corso and were planning an armed robbery on an Armaguard security truck somewhere in the northern suburbs of Melbourne. The police tracked Binse to Corso's farm, and they took up surveillance on the property.

On the evening of 5 December, Binse and Skellington disappeared for a short time, but returned to the property by 6.20 p.m. After the three robbers had dinner with their landlord, Smith headed out around 8.20. As he was driving through the small town of Creswick, he was stopped by a police officer, and after a tense four-minute stand-off, there was an exchange of gunfire. At the end of it, Jockey Smith lay dead.

Knowing that Binse was in possession of radio scanners which would within minutes pick up the many reports flying around from police officers describing the death of Smith, the Armed Robbery Squad moved on the farmhouse, arresting Binse and Skellington.

Binse would spend the next thirteen years in jail, but not for want of trying to escape. The year following his double escape, he planned on getting out of Pentridge, along with thirty other convicts taken from the prison's top-security H Division. Rather oddly, most of the information about the plan was derived from Binse's own diary, seized shortly before the escape was due to take place – quite why he was keeping such detailed notes has never been explained.

According to the reports, Binse was one of four inmates in charge of the escape plan. Double murderer John William Lindrea had already managed to get out of Pentridge; another of the plotters, Robert Chapman, had done a runner from an amusement park while on day leave; while convicted car thief and escapee Paul Alexander Anderson acted as a "consultant". The idea was that one of the inmates would overpower the single guard on night duty, take his gun, and then open the cells of the thirty escapees. After that, they could either get hold of the keys for the separated-off area of H Division, get out into the main part of the jail, and then scale the outside wall behind the prison – or they could use the guard as a hostage, and use him to bargain their way out through the main gate. Along the way, a bit of revenge would be dealt out: Julian Knight, who had killed seven people and injured nineteen others during a killing spree in Hoddle Street, Clifton Hill, in 1987, was regarded as an informer by a number of the escapees, and he was going to be either seriously injured or killed as a by-product of the escape.

Whereas good luck aided Binse to get away from Pentridge in 1992, he suffered from the reverse the following year. On 25 October, a day before the escape was going to occur, Pentridge prison officer Les Attard was stabbed seventeen times with a pair of tailor's shears. Unsurprisingly, the prison authorities cracked down and carried out an intensive sweep of the entire jail. To their annoyance, the guards discovered that Binse's cell door had been compromised: the lock had been neatly cut with a hacksaw blade. They also found a home-made prison officer's uniform, which had been completed using Binse's civilian shirt. As well as confiscating Binse's diary – and discovering the details for the plan – they got hold of two home-made daggers, six ersatz Office of Correction shirt insignias, and a hacksaw blade.

A blade also featured in Binse's next attempt, two years later. Rather than getting involved with a large group, Badness worked solo on the bars in his cell. After carefully removing them, he made his move, but was recaptured in the prison grounds; according to some reports, John William Lindrea was with him when he was found.

The following year, by which point he was spending all but one hour a day in leg irons and handcuffs, he was sent to New South Wales to face the charges arising from his crimes in autumn 1992. A further six and a half years were added to his sentence, and the judge advised him to change his lifestyle, or he would rot in jail. He tried to bring legal action against the state for the restraints, but the Court of Appeal threw out the action.

In 2001, Binse was one of the first prisoners sent to the new Supermax facility at the Goulburn Correctional Centre, marking him as one of the elite one per cent of offenders within the Victorian prison system – the psychopaths and the ingenious escapers. Nicknamed the HARM-U by the inmates (from its original name, the High Risk Management Unit), it has all the lack of pleasant facilities and the high presence of security of the American Supermax. Prisoners are rarely let out of their cells; they get little time with other inmates. If they are moved around, they are in leg irons and handcuffs. And Christopher David Binse did not get out of there until he was permitted to do so in 2005.

Binse didn't stay out of jail for long. He was rearrested for threatening a security guard and a receptionist at a strip club in November 2005, and other firearms and drugs offences, returning to prison until April 2008. At that point, he was interviewed for the *Real Prison Breaks* series, and intimated that he was gradually learning the error of his ways. The former prison guards and police officers interviewed evidently didn't believe it for one moment – with good cause. Binse was apprehended just before Christmas 2008 with a loaded pen pistol, a Taser stun gun and a spray canister by members of the Special Operations Group.

Around now, it seemed as if Binse was losing the easy charm that had characterized his actions. He had pulled a gun on three officers in May 2012 when they were checking the registration of his motorbike, and had raced to his girlfriend's house where he barricaded himself inside. By the end of the two-day siege, even his girlfriend had walked away from him, worried about his state of mind; officers involved in the situation were seriously concerned when he exited the house still carrying a gun. Would Binse's story end with "suicide by cop"? In the end a gun that fires small beanbags was used to bring him down – and Christopher David Binse was arrested to face trial yet again . . .

Fact vs. Fiction

The account of Binse's arrest following Jockey Smith's death is highly misleading in the *Real Prison Breaks* instalment, implying that police had no idea that Binse was involved with Smith. In fact, as discussed, they were simply biding their time to ensure that they had sufficient evidence to arrest all three perpetrators.

Sources:

Sydney Daily Telegraph, 9 May 2009: "Inside the walls of Super-Max prison, Goulburn"

Real Prison Breaks, Discovery Channel, 2008: Christopher David Binse interview

Melbourne Herald-Sun, 24 May 2012: "Christopher Dean Binse charged with multiple offences"

The Age (Victoria), 22 May 2012: "Born to be Badness: the criminal behind the East Keilor siege"

Silvester, John and Andrew Rule: *Tough. 101 Australian Gangsters* Floradale Productions & Sly Ink, 2010

The Age (Victoria), 23 May 2012: "Meet Badness, the man behind the siege"

Melbourne Herald-Sun, 19 December 2008: "Armed bandit Christopher Dean Binse arrested"

Haddow, Peter "Jockey Smith's Last Stand" contained in: *On Murder 2* (BlackInk, 2002, edited by Kerry Greenwood)

The Lucky Escaper

As he was being handcuffed and leg irons applied, leaning up against a police cruiser, a tired-looking Tony Artrip was pressed by reporters who were keen for answers from the man who had just led their local cops on a merry chase through the town of Marmet, West Virginia, after robbing a bank. When he finally gave his name, one reporter recognized it, and asked him what the secret of his regular escapes was. "I don't know, man. Just luck, I guess," Artrip drawled before asking a cameraman if he could pass his love on to his daughter, Cierra.

This incident in 2009 marked the end of Artrip's third escape from custody, twelve years after he first made a daring bid for freedom from the Boyd County Detention Center in Cattlets-burg, in the north-east part of Kentucky. In April 1997, Artrip was being held in Boyd County, awaiting transfer to a state prison to serve a ten-year stretch for a burglary in Scioto County, Ohio, as well as being a persistent felony offender. The prison was comparatively new at that point, completed in 1991, and the ninety-three-bed facility was built in a podular style, with the cells circling a centralized control room. The theory was that the inmates would be visible at all times to the guards – as long as the guards were paying attention, of course. Like so many insti-tutions constructed around that time, the prison authorities believed it was escape-proof. To the average offender this was probably true, but Tony Artrip had no intention of remaining in the Kentucky lock-up.

Alongside Artrip in Boyd County were Alan Scott Williams and Donald Tipton, who were awaiting a retrial for the armed robbery of a supermarket in Westwood, Kentucky. They decided to use a different mode of exit from the prison than the usual jail breakers: a tunnel wasn't practical, so rather than go down, they went up – into the ceiling of the prison itself. The men noticed that the panels in the false ceilings in their cells weren't welded together particularly well, and if a sufficient degree of pressure was applied, they could be loosened. Lying on the top bunk in Artrip's cell, they were able to push at the panel until it came free.

As a reward for keeping their cells clean, inmates at Boyd County were allowed special privileges, including movie nights, and during a screening of the Mel Gibson historical epic *Braveheart* on 29 April 1997, Artrip and his accomplices made their move. As Gibson's William Wallace was noisily telling the Scottish army that the English might take their lives, but they'd never take their freedom, Artrip, Williams and Tipton kicked the ceiling panel out of the way, pulled themselves up into the space above, snapped the welding around a grating beneath an air-conditioning unit, pushed that aside, and went out onto the roof. They then leaped the twenty feet over the fence, and ran into the night.

Tipton and Williams split away from Artrip, heading to Arizona, where they were eventually arrested after they carried out a hold-up in the city of Winslow. They served their sentences for that, and the escape, in an Arizona prison. Williams was later sentenced to life imprisonment for the armed robbery of the Citizens National Bank branch in Ashland on Christmas Eve 2009: because of his record he was tried as a persistent felony offender, and the jury recommended the maximum term.

Artrip headed back to his home town of Ashland, six miles north of Boyd County Jail, where he had family and friends. Although the police received various tips regarding his whereabouts, he always seemed to be aware when they were coming for him, and he managed to remain out of the law's clutches for nearly six weeks. His luck deserted him on 3 June when he was caught in a routine traffic stop in Ironton, Ohio, a few miles on the other side of the Ohio river. He was sentenced to fifteen years for the escape, but after remission for good behaviour, and despite reports that he attempted to escape from the federal facility in which he was being held in 2000, he was released in 2002.

He didn't stay out of jail for long. In 2005, he was arrested for three armed robberies and in the early summer of 2007 was being held at Grant County Detention Center at Williamstown,

Kentucky, awaiting sentence after pleading guilty. Contemporary reports indicate that he had been there for about two and a half months, held in solitary confinement for all but one hour a day, when he made another daring escape, once again going up into the ceiling to get to an air vent, the roof and freedom. This time, rather than go from his cell, Artrip was more brazen: around 11.30 p.m. on the night of 24 June 2007, he scaled a basketball backboard in the prison gym recreation area, leaped to the wire mesh behind it all the way to the ceiling, then wormed through the ductwork to reach the vent. By the time the guards had reacted, he had jumped the eighteen feet off the roof and escaped into the woods surrounding the prison, evading a cordon of guards that was quickly set up.

The US Marshals, Kentucky state police and local police agencies all began another manhunt anticipating that he would repeat his pattern from before, and return to Ashland, in part so he could visit his daughter Cierra. John Schickel, US Marshal for the Eastern District of Kentucky told reporters that Artrip had "a history of escapes and bank robberies, and we consider him dangerous".

However Artrip went straight back to work – his kind of work, robbing banks, and brought his cousin Chris along to help. On 30 June, he entered a bank in Princeton, West Virginia (three hundred miles south-east of his last confirmed location at the prison), handing the teller a note reading, "Give me all the money or I'll start shooting". He shoved the $1,600 into a McDonald's bag, and drove off, later abandoning the car. Two days later, continuing to travel south-east, he hit a bank in Raleigh, North Carolina, using a gun to gain access to the tellers' drawers, emptying them of cash. He then spent around $57,000 on a vacation to Panama City, where it was reported he and Chris (called a nephew in some reports at the time) partied.

On the night of 27 July Chris and Tony were spotted in a red van, along with a female passenger. The girl was arrested on drugs charges but Chris and Tony fled into a nearby wood (something Tony Artrip was very good at doing). The Kentucky State Police, along with the US Marshal's Office, the Kentucky State Police Response Team, the K-9 unit from the

Enforcement Special Investigation, the Boyd County and Greenup County Sheriff's Departments, and the Ashland Police Department all scoured the woods for some hours but to no avail. The next morning at 11 a.m., Chris was arrested at a roadblock on Route 5. There was no sign of Tony. (Chris continued a life of crime: he and his cousin Randall Artrip were fought off by a machete-wielding home owner Grant Lambert when they tried to rob him on 13 May 2010 using a toy gun. They were charged with first-degree robbery, as was their driver Amy D. Sturgill. Chris, who was seriously injured in the attack, was sentenced to twelve years, Randall to ten. Sturgill got a five year term.)

Tony's next reported robbery came at the start of August, when he headed north, and visited a bank in Monroe, Michigan, making an unauthorized withdrawal at gunpoint. On 21 August he went to another Monroe bank, but was nearly caught by police, who had tracked him down to the place in Frenchtown Township where he had been staying, apparently trying to establish a new life for himself, furnishing the house and buying a new television. Slipping out of a window, he managed to elude them in a stolen red pickup truck. He returned to North Carolina, where marshals received a tip that he was in the Asheville area, and started distributing posters there on 10 September. Once again, luck was with Artrip: although he was spotted by a marshal the next day, he was able to lose his pursuers in nearby woodland. Three days later, he was caught on camera during a raid on a bank in Mount Airy, North Carolina. By this point, law enforcement officials reckoned, he had stolen around $93,000 since escaping from prison.

At this point, the US Marshals put Artrip on their "15 Most Wanted" list. "Anthony Ray Artrip is exceptionally dangerous. He is a federal fugitive who is not laying low, but continuing to commit violent crimes while on the run," said United States Marshals Service Director John Clark in the press release announcing this. "By placing him on our 15 Most Wanted list, I have directed our investigators to use all resources to find and apprehend this dangerous criminal. From what we've seen since his escape, there is no indication that Artrip's criminal activities are going to end. We need to put a stop to his crime spree." The publicity from this – which included a feature on the TV programme *America's Most Wanted* – brought Artrip's latest escape attempt to a moderately swift close.

A robbery in Calhoun, Georgia, netting $20,000 was the last one that police believed he carried out before he was recaptured. That wasn't easy: it came after a major stand-off at the Knights Inn motel in South Fayette, Pennsylvania, on the south side of Pittsbugh on 8 October, during which, as US Marshal John Schickel pointed out when announcing his arrest, Artrip tried to "pull off one more vanishing act". Acting on a tip-off, the marshals had tracked him down to room 106 at the motel. Alongside the Allegheny County SWAT team, as well as police from sixteen local departments, they surrounded the building and broke down the door at 9.30 a.m. – only to find no apparent sign of Artrip. No sign, that is, until someone remembered his usual method of escape and looked up – and there, in the ceiling of the bathroom, a tile had been removed. Artrip continually moved around in the crawlspace for the next four hours, as attempts were made to negotiate with him, which he ignored.

Around 1.45 p.m., the marshals began to lose patience, and fired a concussion grenade into the area, but this still failed to dislodge Artrip. Eventually, about an hour later, they started to pump pepper spray into the confined space. That was enough, even for Artrip. Screaming, "Shoot me! Shoot me!" he tried to escape from the pepper spray, but it filled the area, and after fifteen minutes, he broke through the ceiling of room 123, and was promptly arrested.

"It is great news that we have finally managed to bring Tony Artrip in," Marshal Shickel said. "This was likely one of the most brazen and elusive criminals we have ever pursued and all of us are relived [sic] that his crime spree has come to an end without further violence or injury."

He would only remain behind bars for eighteen months. In April 2009, he was up to his old tricks once more, this time making his escape from the Edgecombe County Detention Center in Tarboro, North Carolina. It would be the shortest of his times on the run – within twelve hours he was back in custody. He still found time to rob another bank!

After his robbery spree in 2007, Artrip was sentenced to seven years at the Supermax prison in Florence, Colorado, with the judge in charge warning that Artrip was likely to take advantage of laxer security if he was taken around the country to stand trial for the various offences he committed in different jurisdictions. During his trial in Kentucky, he was held in shackles, with marshals all around to ensure that he didn't escape. The problem was that the North Carolina detention centre (described as a "podunk jail" by Artrip's lawyer) wasn't anywhere near as secure as it needed to be to hold someone as determined as Artrip.

While awaiting trial, Artrip sought help from David Lee Cox, accused of felony conspiracy, and James Butler, held on firearms charges. This time, there were no devious plans involving air ducts or ceiling panels. On 16 April 2009, the three men simply broke open a fire door at the prison leading to the outside, ran across the open space to the fence, and then used a mattress to help get over the razor-wire-topped obstruction. Stealing a van from a nearby house, they sped off, heading 400 miles towards West Virginia.

The next morning at 9.15, Tony Artrip walked into the City National Bank in Marmet, West Virginia, just off the West Virginia Turnpike. Demanding money, he then vaulted over the counter, and grabbed $53,000. Cox and Butler were waiting in the stolen truck and the trio headed for Charleston. However, when the truck was spotted at a Shop N Go gas station, a chase ensued, at speeds of up to ninety miles per hour through the streets of Charleston. The men dumped the truck, and tried to escape on foot, jumping over a fence. It was too late – police officers apprehended them. When he was asked why he had robbed the bank by a local journalist, Artrip claimed it was for "gas money"; Cox claimed that he didn't know a bank robbery was planned. They hadn't even had time to change out of their jail outfits.

Another Edgecombe County inmate tried his luck the same weekend as Artrip made his abortive getaway. Seventeen-year-old Chamone Diggins, being held for breaking and entering, larceny, felony, conspiracy, robbery, assault on a female and assault with a deadly weapon, overpowered guards around 9.30

p.m. on 18 April and was able to escape from the jail annex. He was rearrested at lunchtime the following day in Farmville, twenty-five miles from Tarboro. With four escapes in the space of seventy-two hours, Sheriff James Knight noted that "procedures were not followed".

On 4 August 2010, Tony Artrip was sentenced to two consecutive life sentences, and three twenty-year sentences to run concurrently with the forty-year sentence imposed in 2008. He will not be eligible for parole. "Today's sentencing puts an end to the criminal career of a man who brazenly made his way across half of the United States robbing banks and terrorizing citizens, and brings justice and closure to the many victims of his crimes," US Attorney Sally Quillian Yates said.

But when he was asked by a reporter in 2009 whether the break from Edgecombe would be his last, Tony Artrip said, "Probably not." And even though he's now an inmate of the Supermax at Terre Haute, Indiana, no one would be in the least surprised if Tony Artrip somehow finds a way out.

Fact vs. Fiction

Although the *Real Prison Breaks* series filmed a lot of its material at the sites of the various activities, note that the Grant County Jail footage was shot in 2011, and the reconstruction of the recapture of Artrip at the Knights Inn Motel suggests that the gas was thrown into the room, which brought him out – telescoping the events considerably.

Sources:

Boyd County jail design/history: http://www.cmwjustice.com/projects/BoydCountyDetentionCenter.html

The Independent (Ashland, KY), 26 June 2007: "Tony Artrip still at large"

The Independent, 27 September 2011: "Williams gets life for bank robbery"

US Marshals Service, 18 September 2007: "U.S. Marshals Add Convicted Bank Robber To '15 Most Wanted' List"

The Kentucky Enquirer, 26 June 2007: "Man awaiting trial for bank robbery escapes from Ky. jail"

America's Most Wanted Online Hotline's Blog, 23 September 2007: "Dramatic Escape From County Jail"

Pittsburgh Post-Gazette, 9 October 2007: "'Escape artist' corralled"

US Marshals Service, 8 October 2007: "U.S. Marshals End Bank Robbing Spree Of '15 Most Wanted' Fugitive"

The Independent, 28 July 2007: "Chris Artrip arrested; Tony still at large"

The Independent, 14 May 2010: "Boyd machete-wielding home-owner fights back"

The Independent, 22 January 2011: "Would-be home invader sentenced"

The Herald-Dispatch, 17 April 2009: "3 NC Fugitives caught near W. VA. capitol."

WSAZ.com, 18 April 2009: "3 NC Escapees, Including Tony Artrip, Caught After Robbery"

WSAZ.com, 5 August 2010: "Tony Artrip Gets Two Life Sentences for Bank Robberies"

Real Prison Breaks, Cineflix Productions, 2011

The King of Escapers Takes Off

"Fool me once, shame on you; fool me twice, shame on me." So goes the Chinese proverb. It doesn't say how you should feel if you're fooled a third time – but that's what the so-called King of Escapers, Pascal Payet did to French authorities when he used a helicopter to escape from jail in both 2001 and 2007, and to add insult to injury, organized for others to get out using the same method in 2003.

Luynes prison in the south of France was the target on two occasions; the jail was only opened in 1990, and its 600 inmates included many who were classified as DPS (*détenus particulière-ment surveillés* – prisoners under particular watch). Payet, a habitual criminal who had convictions for aggravated assault and conspiracy, had been sent there following his arrest for murder during an armed robbery on a security van in November 1997, during which he had used his favourite weapon, a Kalashnikov AK47 automatic rifle, to shoot a guard who subsequently died. He had been on the run for fourteen months before being arrested in Paris in January 1999.

Helicopters had been used in a number of escapes in France during the 1990s – at least ten had been successful – so it's a little surprising that somewhere as new as Luynes wasn't better equipped to deal with the possibility. (After the escape, the governor pointed out that the unions had been calling for better security ever since the prison had been opened but had been ignored because of the cost implications.) Payet, who at the time was being held under the name Paillet, could see the obvious possibilities, since there wasn't anything to prevent a chopper from landing in an open part of the prison yard which couldn't be monitored properly from the guard towers. He therefore arranged with an accomplice on the outside to hire a helicopter from a local airfield.

As soon as the chopper was in the air, shortly after 4 p.m. on 12 October 2001, Payet's friend drew a weapon and threatened the pilot and co-pilot. He ordered them to head towards the prison, and as they flew over the prison yard, he threw a bag of tools out of the door to Payet, who was wearing a distinctive fluorescent-yellow T-shirt for easy identification. He and another prisoner, Frédéric Impocco, who was serving a life sentence for murder, then used wire-cutters and pliers to get through the mesh fence that separated the yard from the open area. The helicopter landed, and the two jumped on board.

Their destination was the small town of Bouc-bel-Air, about ten miles north of Marseilles, where they returned control of the helicopter to the pilots. A Peugeot car was waiting for them; they abandoned that a few miles away and stole a Volkswagen Golf before vanishing apparently without trace – they evaded the special police cordon, codenamed Sparrowhawk, that was thrown up around the prison without difficulty.

Payet successfully avoided arrest for two years, although not without some run-ins with the police along the way during various armed robberies that he carried out to keep himself financed. Impocco wasn't so fortunate. He was picked up by police in Paris less than a week after the escape. The authorities at Luynes learned their lesson, and made sure that there were security lines across the whole yard.

That didn't stop Payet, when he decided to get two of his friends, accused of running an international drug ring, out from the prison. As far as he was concerned, that's what friends did for one another. On 14 April 2003, he put his plan into action.

Once again, a helicopter was hijacked, but instead of bringing the chopper in to land, the pilot was ordered to hover over the prison yard, taking advantage of exactly the same blind spot as before. While one of the hijackers kept the pilot at gunpoint, the other dropped down on a rope ladder, and used a power saw to cut through the steel security netting. All that Michel Valero and Eric Alboreo had to do was grab hold of the rope ladder, and they were flown to safety. This time someone else came along for the ride: another drug trafficker, Franck Perletto, known as Lucky Luke, who later told a court that he was playing Scrabble when he saw the rope descending from the helicopter, and took advantage of the situation. Once again, the pilot was released unharmed.

The escape prompted outrage from the newspapers, with *Le Parisien* running the banner headline, "Yet Another Escape". Future French president Nicholas Sarkozy, then the Interior Minister, promised that "Teams are mobilized to find them and put them back where they belong – in prison." He was able to live up to his promise: three weeks later, all three were back under lock and key – as well as Payet, who was acknowledged to have masterminded their escape.

The group hid in plain sight in the country area of La Baume-de-Transit, in the Drôme department in south-eastern France, eighty or so miles from the prison. They rented a charming house in a small village, apparently based on its recommendation in the Routard travel guide, and as far as the locals were concerned, they were simply there for a holiday and to take part in various sports, as they trained for an upcoming biathlon. They went for drinks with the neighbours, but otherwise kept themselves to themselves, doing their own cleaning, and cooking steaks in the vineyard gardens of their home.

They did travel from time to time back to some of their old haunts, and this was to be their undoing. Michel Valero was spotted by the Swiss police near a bar in Geneva, driving a car that had been used in an attempted robbery on 5 May by Payet, whose hood had slipped during the abortive theft. The surveillance was taken over by the Lyons police, and a group of forty officers was assembled. At 6 o'clock on the morning of Friday 9 May, they swooped on the house in Richerenches and arrested the four men smoothly, without any shots being fired. There they found a stash of weapons and money in different currencies.

The French authorities learned their lesson, and didn't allow Payet, or the others caught with him, to remain in any one prison for any length of time. Payet made a big fuss about this, publicly complaining about the many different prisons he had been incarcerated within – at one stage, he was transferred nine times within thirty months. In January 2005, he received a thirty-year sentence for his original murder; two years later, he confessed to his part in the 2003 operation and received a seven-year additional term, as well as six extra years for his escape in 2001. (This add-on has led some sources to believe that he was out of prison for six years; instead, the courts simply trebled the amount of time he was free to create the sentence.)

Payet wasn't going to stick it out. Bastille Day, Saturday 14 July 2007, saw his most recent escape, and once again, a hijacked helicopter was key to his plans. In the spring of that year, he sent a postcard to Alain Armato, a pimp in Marseilles, who he had known some years earlier in prison. Armato sympathized with Payet's situation; as he later told a court, Payet needed binoculars to see the end of his sentence.

Armato therefore put a team together. However, this wasn't a finely tuned team, working seamlessly with one thought. He hired young convicts, promising them large sums of cash if they were successful; three of them dropped out at the last minute, with one of them later claiming that it felt as if they were in a comedy film, not a serious criminal operation. A safe place was hired by one of them with his own name; one of the cars they planned to use was borrowed from a friend . . .

Despite all this, at least initially, it all played out as planned. Armato's team of four burst into a helicopter company at Cannes airport, and ordered a pilot to fly a chopper north to the state prison at Grasse, where Payet was currently being held. (One of them also stole €170 from the till.) Twenty minutes later, they landed on the roof, and, leaving one man behind to guard the pilot, they threatened the guards with machine pistols and sawn-off shotguns before cutting their way through a number of doors to reach Payet's cell. Hardly any guards were on duty to stop them from breaking the cell open, where Payet was in the middle of writing a letter to his wife. The hijackers hurried Payet through the prison corridors up to the roof and into the helicopter, which immediately took off and headed south-west.

The vehicle was abandoned half an hour later at a heliport next to a hospital in the town of Brignoles, twenty-five miles north of Toulon. As ever, the pilot had not been harmed, and was left handcuffed to a fence in a local cemetery. The alarm had already been raised, and within an hour of the escape, 150 gendarmes were patrolling the area, with police helicopters searching from above.

They found out who was responsible pretty quickly: the thugs involved were so amateur that they boasted about it around town. All the police had to do was keep an eye on Armato and his "lieutenant" Farid Ouassou, and they would lead them to Payet. Despite Payet's best precautions – using payphones miles from where he was hiding – he, Armato and Ousassou were apprehended in the seaside town of Mataro, eighteen miles from Barcelona, two months later. On them were four guns, a false French passport and a set of skeleton keys.

In April 2011 Payet was given an extra five years on his sentence (the prosecution had asked for him to receive twelve), while Armato got a nine-year term. Ouassou and Abd-el-Moutaleb Medjadi, Armato's other lieutenant, were given seven and six-year sentences; the drivers got three years each. The fourth man in the helicopter died between the escape and the court case.

This time the police were taking no chances with Payet: 200 specialist police and gendarmes surrounded the court. As far as they were concerned, Payet was grounded. Indefinitely.

Sources:

20 heures le journal, 4 March 2005

USA Today, 21 September 2007: "Escaped killer from French prison caught"

Daily Mail, 15 July 2007: "Killer 'Kalashnikov Pat' flees jail in audacious helicopter escape (again)" (NB numerous details in this are inaccurate)

Good Morning America, 17 July 2007: "Helicopter used in French prison break"

LibéMarseille, 8 April 2011: "Pascal Payet, as de l'évasion pas au bout de sa peine"

Le Parisien, 8 April 2011: "Evasion de la prison de Grasse : Pascal Payet condamné à cinq ans"

L'Investigateur, 10 May 2003: "Les évadés de la prison de Luynes arrêtés dans la Drôme"

Le Nouvel Observateur, 19 October 2001: "Un des deux évadés de Luynes arrêté à Paris"

AFP, 12 October 2001: "Deux détenus dangereux s'évadent par hélicoptère de la prison d'Aix"

CNN, 13 October 2001: "French helicopter jailbreak"

Liberation, 13 October 2001: "Un hélico emporte deux détenus de Luynes."

AP, 15 April 2003: "Jailbreak Revives French Prison Debate"

AFP, 4 March 2005: "Six ans ferme pour Pascal Payet, évadé de Luynes par hélicoptère"

New York Times, 15 April 2003: "French Prison System Gives Hope to Inmates"

L'Express, 13 March 2011: "L'évasion de Pascal Payet, 'une histoire d'amitié', selon les accuses"

France-Soir, 24 June 2008: "Procès sous haute surveillance pour Pascal Payet"

Florida Getaway

Steven Whitsett's escape from the Martin Treatment Center for Sexually Violent Predators in June 2000 would not normally have attracted that much attention, but for two key factors. Firstly, Whitsett wasn't an ordinary prisoner as such: under Florida's controversial "Jimmy Ryce" law, he was a "resident" at the Center, with apparently no date set for his release. And perhaps more importantly, he was one of the first prisoners to try to escape from the jail using a helicopter.

When Whitsett made his daring getaway, the Treatment Center had only been in operation for a matter of months. Prior to that the buildings acted as the Martin County jail, and it was also the home for a drug treatment programme. Operated jointly between the Department of Corrections and Liberty Behavioral Health Care, Inc., it looked like a prison, and, from the description of the security measures in place, its inmates were treated like prisoners, no matter that technically they were referred to as residents. The fifteen-feet-high fenced enclosure was protected with razor wire and barbed wire, and microphones and microwave devices could detect anything that moved between the central enclosure and the outer fence. Still, because the residents were civilians, rather than prisoners, the security level was less than at other institutions, including a smaller number of staff, who only carried pepper spray, rather than guns.

At the time of his escape, the twenty-eight-year-old Whitsett hadn't been committed to the treatment programme by the court. In 1994, he had received a six-month probation term for soliciting sex from a sixteen-year-old boy. The following year, he got too close to a fifteen-year-old patient at a treatment centre for sex offenders, and on 2 February 1995, was

sentenced to eight years in prison and fifteen years' probation
for sexual battery on a child by a person in custodial authority
and for lewd, lascivious or indecent assault on a child (i.e.
taking Polaroid photos of him). By 1999, with remission for
good conduct, Whitsett should have been on his way after
serving his time.

But by the time Whitsett became eligible for release, Florida
had enacted the Involuntary Civil Commitment of Sexually
Violent Predators Act, otherwise known as the "Jimmy Ryce"
Act, named after a nine-year-old Miami boy, who had been
kidnapped, raped and murdered by a sexual predator. Once he
had served his sentence, Whitsett had to be assessed by the
Department of Children and Families to see if he remained a
threat to public safety; if the courts determined that he was, then
he was sent for treatment, and his case reviewed annually until
such time as he was considered safe.

Whitsett was furious that he wasn't able to leave. A hearing
was scheduled for early June 2000, but Whitsett was warned by
his attorney that another molestation case was making the headlines, so it would be advisable to delay his application for release.
Whitsett couldn't wait.

To get out, though, he needed help, which came in the form
of his long-term lover, Clifford Burkhart, who was five years
younger. They had been in a relationship some years earlier, but
Burkhart had later married. When Whitsett finished his prison
sentence and was moved to Martin Treatment Center, Burkhart
became a regular visitor, divorcing his wife, and starting to plan
a future with Whitsett. In the months leading up to the escape,
Burkhart would regularly tell his co-workers at the Rainforest
Café how angry the treatment his friend was receiving made
him. When the two men chatted at the centre, it was clear to
them that the only freedom Whitsett was likely to see was a freedom that he made for himself. Burkhart therefore started taking
lessons in piloting helicopters, maxing out his credit cards to
pay for the tuition.

The two men laid their plans carefully for six months.
Burkhart would land the helicopter inside the compound and
collect Whitsett. They would fly over the fences and land by a
van hidden there by Burkhart, then head to a motel room in

nearby Okeechobee, where there was a change of clothing and hair dye (as well, according to *Time* magazine, as a stack of "porn featuring the type of boys Whitsett favoured"). From there, they were going to head for the train station and a new life in New York City. Whitsett was so confident that the plan was going to succeed that he mailed his CD player and his headphones to his home address, and went round giving away his possessions to other residents.

Burkhart had been learning how to fly for eight weeks, and had racked up around thirty hours of flight time, but only one solo flight – virtually nothing at all. On 5 June, he loaded two guns, and rented a two-seater 1993 "Robinson 22" helicopter from Fort Lauderdale. As his liberator was flying towards the centre, Whitsett was calmly having a haircut, telling Liberty staff that he wanted to look good for a job he was applying for within the prison.

At 1 p.m., the guards and the treatment staff noted that a helicopter was approaching the centre, and to their amazement, it hovered in the area between the interior and the exterior fences. Whitsett dashed over the inner fence, from which the razor wire and barbed wire had recently been removed, and started to board. (The original plan had been to land in the basketball court but with nothing stopping Whitsett from climbing the fence, the other area was easier for Burkhart to target.)

And that's where things started to go seriously wrong. Burkhart was simply too inexperienced to be able to cope with the sudden addition of a man's weight onto the skids of the helicopter and didn't compensate in time. The chopper lurched sideways, breaking the landing skid, and bringing the rotor to hit the ground. Although Whitsett clambered on board, the helicopter was too badly damaged to fly very much further, and although it was able to achieve sufficient altitude to clear the fences, it crashed a hundred yards south of the perimeter fence, near a canal. By the time that the guards reached the crash site, Whitsett and Burkhart had run for the orange groves that surrounded the prison.

Although initially amazed by the audacity of the attempt (and believing that they were being hoaxed), police and the guards quickly instituted a manhunt for the two fugitives, alarmed by the discovery of two empty holsters within the wreckage. "We do consider them armed and dangerous, and, frankly, desperate," Jennell Atlas, the spokeswoman for the Martin County Sheriff's office, told reporters, adding that the escape was "out of a Hollywood script. He landed in broad daylight and [Whitsett] ran out like in a movie, but unlike in a movie, they crashed." Atlas didn't expect them to be free for long: "They're not prepared to stay out here like we are," she pointed out. "They likely don't have food or water and come nightfall, the bugs will carry them off." Dog units were brought in to search for the men.

Whitsett and Burkhart initially just tried to find cover; they knew their firearms would see off any creatures that tried to attack them, at least during the day. At sunset, the men realized they would have to stay out in the woods – there were simply too many officers searching for them to risk moving forward. The next morning, the dogs were loosed once more into the groves, and were able to track where the men had been from the smell of their excreta.

Desperate to evade capture, the two fugitives entered an alligator-infested canal, hoping to remove any scent trail that the dogs could follow. However, this laid them open to being spotted from the air, and twenty-six hours after they fled the crash scene, Whitsett and Burkhart were arrested, a mere nine miles from the unit.

Burkhart received a four-year sentence for his part in the breakout; Whitsett was sentenced to twenty years, but after a plea bargain and other court proceedings, is set for release in 2017. It is ironic to note that it was eventually found that he wasn't a threat under the terms of the Jimmy Ryce Act. If he hadn't decided to make a break for it, Whitsett would have been a free man for nearly a decade.

Sources:

Time magazine: "The Boy Who Loved Me" 11 June, 2000

I Escaped: Real Prison Breaks: Cineflix Productions, 2011: Whitsett interview

Palm Beach Post, 8 April, 2010: "Child molester in helicopter escape could get out of prison in Martin"

Sun Journal, 6 June 2000: "Inmate escapes by helicopter"
Office of Program Policy Analysis and Government Accountability: "Escape from Martin Treatment Center for Sexually Violent Predators". Report No. 99–58 June 2000

Knoch-out Blow

There's absolutely no question. If Demonte Johnson had known with whom he was tangling on that cold day in February 2001, he might have thought twice about tackling the intruder that he found in his home when he unexpectedly returned. But he can hardly have expected escapee Lee John Knoch to have chosen his particular house in which to hide.

Knoch was one of the nastier inmates held at the Snake River Correctional Institution in Ontario, eastern Oregon, midway between Portland and Salt Lake City, which opened its doors to prisoners in August 1991, part of the state's increasingly tough stance on law-breaking which has seen seven new correctional facilities built in the past two decades. Although there was a lot of local opposition to the creation of the prison – to the extent that there was an unsuccessful attempt to oust the local officials who gave the go-ahead – it is now a valued part of the community, providing jobs and supporting the local infrastructure.

Perhaps part of that good feeling stems from the relatively low number of escapes from its doors. And perhaps that's because it's well set up: there are two sixteen-feet-high perimeter fences, as well as rows of razor wires and multiple guard towers which look out over the acres of empty land surrounding the prison.

Lee John Knoch didn't care about the local community. In February 2001, he simply wanted his freedom, something that the state of Oregon was determined to deny him. Knoch had been found guilty in 1998 of aggravated murder, assault, kidnapping, theft by extortion and harassment. At the time of the offence in 1996, Knoch was out on bail on charges of kidnap and torture: he had allegedly snatched Robert Lee Holliday, a thirty-four-year-old mentally challenged Oregon resident, and over a two-week period, he had broken eleven of his ribs and poured carburettor fluid into his eyes, leaving him with heat and chemical burns as well as internal bleeding. Knoch was indicted in January 1996 of these charges, but freed on bail. He didn't report as ordered, was caught speeding or driving recklessly on four occasions, and was stopped in the area of town where Holliday lived, contrary to a direct instruction from the judge granting bail.

Finally, on 28 March 1997, shortly before his trial was due to begin, Knoch kidnapped Holliday again. This time he and his accomplice Amanda Walker clubbed Holliday, slit his wrists and throat, and then buried him alive on Trask Mountain, one of the highest peaks in northern Oregon. Knoch was sentenced to prison without possibility of parole. (As a result of Knoch's actions while out on bail, the voters of Oregon passed Measure 40, later amended to Measure 71, which required that judges hold people accused of serious violent crimes without bail if the judge found by clear and convincing evidence that the accused was a danger to the victim or to the public.)

In 2001, Knoch was cellmates with twenty-three-year-old Aaron O'Hara, who was serving a six-year term for sodomy, sex abuse and rape. Both were set on escape, but they were aware that no one had managed to get out of Snake River in the decade it had been operational. Somehow, though, they were able to get hold of a pair of wire-cutters: although it has never been officially confirmed, prison officials believe that they may have been inadvertently left by construction workers (although given that a lot of the work on the prison was carried out by prisoners themselves, chances are that it may have been a deliberate act to enable one of their fellow inmates to get out at a later date).

Knoch was a psychopathically clever murderer, and it seems probable that O'Hara simply did what he was told. The plan was to get away from the evening work detail and head to a part of the grounds least watched by the guard towers, cut through the fence, crawl beneath the razor wire, and then cut through the perimeter fence. From there, they would have to take their chances in the open countryside evading the patrols.

O'Hara and Knoch got themselves as fit as they could, and on 28 February 2001, they dropped out of a line heading to the prison chapel, and raced across the grounds to the pre-designated point in the fence. It took them nearly an hour to cut through the toughened steel fence and then they needed a further hour to negotiate the razor wire, cutting themselves considerably in the process. By the time they reached the perimeter fence, alarms were being tripped, and the guards headed to round them out.

They expected to find the escapee long gone, and indeed Lee John Knoch had made a quick getaway. Aaron O'Hara, on the other hand, was still very near the prison, and was picked up by one of the guards patrolling nearby, who had been alerted to the escape. He wouldn't answer any questions, and it wasn't until a headcount was carried out that the prison authorities realized that there hadn't just been one escapee – two men had broken out, and they had only recaptured one of them. Oregon State Police and Malheur County sheriff's deputies began the manhunt for Knoch.

Although he was injured from the razor wire, Knoch was able to evade his pursuers, who found it difficult to track him through the open countryside littered with grain stubble and many ditches, all of which needed to be checked. He made it six miles across to the yard of Warrington Irrigation, where he was able to steal a truck that had been left overnight ready to go out, and headed east on the I-84 towards Idaho.

Knoch had managed to travel around 300 miles when the fuel began to run low in the truck, and he had to stop. He had reached the Fort Hall Indian Reservation, home of the Shoshone-Bannock Native American tribe – and Demonte Johnson and his family.

Johnson was taking his boys to visit the state basketball tournament in Boise, Idaho, but when he realized that he had forgotten the adaptor for the video recorder which they had in their van, he turned round and headed home. To his surprise, a van with Oregon plates was sitting in the driveway. Entering the house on his own, Johnson discovered Knoch rifling through his possessions, looking for food and clothing to steal. The fugitive tried to leave, but Johnson wanted him to wait for the police, the last thing Knoch intended doing.

As Knoch headed for his stolen van, Johnson grabbed a shovel, and whacked the murderer on the leg. "Took a good baseball swing and knocked him down," Johnson told reporters later. "He tried to get up again, and I nailed him again on the knee . . . I told him, 'If you get up again, I'll hit you again.'" Johnson detained him until the police arrived. They only realized who they had caught once they took responsibility for Knoch from Johnson, and according to Fort Hall Tribal Police Department Captain Gene Fenton, the fugitive was treated for minor injuries and then jailed. Johnson admitted that it was only when he learned who he had been assaulting that he was scared!

Knoch was sent to the maximum-security jail at Salem, Oregon, and in a touching coda to the story, the superintendent of Snake River Correctional Facility ordered the inmates in the sign shop to make a gift for Johnson. "We are putting together a token of our appreciation," Superintendent Bob Lambert told the *Eugene Register-Guard* newspaper. "We did want to recognize his particular heroism and actions."

Fact vs. Fiction

The *Real Prison Breaks* account includes interesting interviews with some of the law enforcement personnel, as well as Demonte Johnson, but some of its factual material is suspect (Holliday was kidnapped and tortured in 1995, not 1997 – that was when he was murdered.)

Sources:

ABC News, 1 March 2001: "Rapist, Murderer Escape Ore. Prison"

Snake River Correctional Facility website: http://cms.oregon.gov/doc/ops/prison/Pages/srci.aspx

Oregon Business, April 2008: "Prisons don't bring prosperity to rural towns"

Details of Robert Holliday's murder: http://www.crimevictimsunited.org/cases/robertholliday.htm

Real Prison Breaks: Cineflix Productions, 2011: Dick Warrington interview

Eugene Register-Guard, 18. March 2001: "Inmates craft gift for civilian hero."

The Spokesman-Review, 3 March 2001: "Escaped murderer caught in Idaho"

Slipping the Supermax

Supermax prisons, or the sections within prisons that are designated as Supermax, are meant to be escape-proof. According to the American National Institute of Corrections, a Supermax prison is "a stand-alone unit or part of another facility and is designated for violent or disruptive inmates. It typically involves up to 23-hours-per-day, single-cell confinement for an indefinite period of time. Inmates in Supermax housing have minimal contact with staff and other inmates." They are for the worst of the worst, those people who are seen as flight risks, and an absolute danger to those around them.

The H Unit at McAlester State Penitentiary in Oklahoma was constructed in 1991, as part of the on-going upgrade of the prison, following the riots that took place there in July 1973 that caused between $20-40 million worth of damage. It's a vault within the already-secure facility, which is designed to ensure that no one can tunnel out, or otherwise make a bid for freedom. Two fences as well as twenty feet of razor wire provide a deterrent. According to the official Department of Corrections website, it provides new quarters for disciplinary segregation inmates, death row, and the lethal injection death chamber. H Unit also houses Administrative Segregation and Level III general population inmates. Nearly 300 inmates from across the state are kept there. But while McAlester officials might prefer to be best known for being the home of the world's biggest "behind the walls" rodeo in 1940, the prison achieved notoriety when three desperate inmates got out from its Supermax H Unit in January 2001, the first prisoners to escape from McAlester since 1992, and the first ever to manage to get round the tight security in H Unit.

In 1997, James Robert Thomas was sentenced to life without parole for first-degree murder and 400 years for rape for an attack on his eighty-one-year-old neighbour, Jessie M. Roberts in March 1993, when he was just seventeen years old. At his trial, the prosecution maintained that she was strangled with a telephone cord, and then raped while unconscious. Before his conviction, Thomas had briefly escaped from the Oklahoma County Jail. His colleague in the escape was twenty-one-year old Willie Lee Hoffman, who was in the middle of a twenty-year sentence for kidnapping and other charges. He too had escaped from less secure jails previously, breaking out of Payne County Prison in 1998, and from the Cimarron private prison in Cushing, Oklahoma. Nathan Washington, convicted for robbery with force and fear was also part of the breakout, but he didn't get very far.

The cells in H Unit each had their own toilet, secured with steel bolts to the back wall of the cell. Thomas and his confederates deduced that the plumbing from these had to be housed somewhere, and worked out that if they could somehow remove the toilets from the walls, they could get through to the duct where the plumbing was running, and from there to the roof. This left them the problem of removing the steel bolts – but these were men with nothing but time on their hands, the downside of the Supermax regime. For anything up to twenty-three hours a day, they could work on the bolts, using whatever came to hand. In this case, it was dental floss, made more abrasive by the application of a cleaning powder, such as Ajax. Although the prison spokeswoman Lee Mann would later tell reporters that she believed that dental floss was no longer being sold in the canteen because of its use so often in escapes, it seems probable that this is what Thomas, Hoffman and Washington used. Whatever the method, they successfully managed to clear the toilets from the wall, and, some point before 5 o'clock on the morning of Monday 15 January 2001, they crawled into the maintenance space.

From there, the three men were able to use an air duct to reach the roof. They dropped to the ground, and then used ropes created from their sheets to get over the inside fence. That left them the razor wire to negotiate. Thomas and Hoffman had no problems; Washington, regarded by some as the most dangerous of the three escapers, became caught up in the razor wire. The others left him behind, and scaled the perimeter fence.

As soon as Washington was found, a headcount revealed the disappearance of Thomas and Hoffman, and the manhunt was begun. Tracker dogs were brought in, and, according to Jerry Massie, the spokesman for the Department of Corrections who briefed reporters during the investigation, "they were able to get some type of track". Roadblocks were set up, and both a helicopter and a plane from the Oklahoma Highway Patrol searched from overhead.

Around 6.15 a.m., they were spotted running through a yard belonging to John Brewer, who was feeding his horses at the time, and shortly afterwards they tried to steal a truck. That failed to start, so they abandoned it and carried on running. Realizing that they needed to hole up somewhere until they could get hold of a reliable vehicle, Thomas and Hoffman headed to the Boys and Girls Gymnastic Club on Hereford Lane in McAlester, about two miles east from the prison, and hid beneath a trampoline.

When Betty Curtis and Judy Adams arrived for their aerobic workout, the two fugitives pounced on them. Threatening the women with a knife, they demanded money and keys for a car; Adams gave them the keys to her distinctive white 1995 Oldsmobile, which had a maroon stripe down the side. After a discussion about taking the women hostage and deciding against it, Thomas and Hoffman took the $65 the two ladies had in their purses, and headed off in the car.

The manhunt continued throughout Monday, but the Pittsburgh County Sheriff's Office reluctantly had to admit that they didn't know which way the fugitives were heading. The operations were scaled back overnight, but on Tuesday morning, all the teams were once again on the ground searching for the men. Throughout that day, there was no sign of either the escapees or the car, then on Wednesday 17, the car was found abandoned in a hospital car park in Coalgate, around forty-five miles southwest of McAlester. Hoffman and Thomas were spotted by hospital staff who were able to give sufficient information to the police that they were able to track them to a house in Lehigh, five miles south of Coalgate. After arresting two accomplices who had allowed the fugitives to stay with them, police recaptured Thomas and Hoffman and returned them to H Unit.

Hoffman received an additional eight years for his part in the escape, Nathan Washington an extra five. As a result of the breakout, metal plates were installed behind the toilets in the three damaged cells, and shortly afterwards throughout the unit. "We are always certainly more vigilant when something like this occurs," spokeswoman Lee Mann said once Hoffman and Thomas were back in custody. "It brings it all to us the reality that such things occur. And all security measures that are in place are being looked at."

Sources:

Daniel P. Mears, *Evaluating the Effectiveness of Supermax Prisons* (Urban Institute: Justice Policy Center, March 2006)

McAlester history: http://www.doc.state.ok.us/facilities/institutions/osp.htm

Amarillo Globe News, 16 January 2001: "Two escape in Oklahoma"

ABC News, 16 January 2001: "Two Okla. Inmates Still on Loose"

Lubbock Avalanche-Journal, 15 January 2001: "Two escape from Oklahoma maximum-security prison"

Lubbock Avalanche-Journal, 17 January 2001: "Two escapees from maximum security prison caught"

Real Prison Breaks: Discovery Channel, 2008: Judy Adams interview

A Rubbish Escape

Some escapers work out well in advance what they're going to do once they get to the other side of the bars which are preventing them from experiencing freedom. They make sure that they have a change of clothing to put their pursuers off the scent, or a vehicle waiting to whisk them far away from the prison. Usually, of course, they are imprisoned in their own country, so there isn't a language barrier. For former Green Beret and nurse Ted Maher, getting out of Monaco's luxury prison was simply the start of his problems, since, by his own admission, he hardly spoke a word of French – not exactly the best way in which to blend into his environs.

Maher's case raised a lot of questions, as the evidence that convicted him of the arson deaths of his employer and a nurse was far from clear-cut – not helped by a claim that the court in the principality had already made up its mind to convict him before a single word of evidence was heard. According to Maher's version of events, he had been hired to work for Edmond Safra, the founder and principal stock owner of the Republic National Bank of New York, who suffered from Parkinson's disease and needed round-the-clock care. Maher's background, both within the army and as a nurse, made him an attractive prospect to the Safras, and they offered him a well-paid job, on condition he immediately moved to Monaco, where the Safras were based. Needing the money, Maher moved to the principality.

Three months after Maher arrived, Safra and one of Maher's fellow nurses, Vivian Torrente, were dead. On the morning of 3 December 1999, a fire alarm went off in the building; ten minutes later, at 5 a.m., Torrente called the head nurse from inside Safra's secure dressing room to ask her to call the police, and told her that Maher had been injured. Maher was taken to the Princess Grace hospital twenty minutes later, and five minutes after that a blaze was noticed by many residents in the building. By the time that fire fighters made their way to Safra's dressing room, he and Torrente had succumbed to the smoke.

Maher claimed that he had been attacked by two intruders in the apartment who were intent on assassinating Safra. He had nobly fought them off, receiving stab wounds to the stomach in the process. He had given his cell phone to Torrente and told her to take Safra into his dressing room, and to call for help from there. Meanwhile he had set fire to some toilet paper in a waste bin to set the fire alarms off. He had then gone down to the lobby of the building to get help, where he was found and taken to hospital.

There is no doubt that Maher set the blaze that indirectly caused the deaths of Safra and Torrente; he has never denied it. The motives behind it, though, continue to be debated. Was it, as was claimed at his trial, a mad attempt to curry favour with his boss by being seen as the hero of the hour? Did the intruders ever exist, or were they simply part of his cover story? Had he just stabbed himself in the thigh and the stomach for it all to look more realistic? Was his confession, that he subsequently repudiated, forced out of him? Given his lack of knowledge of French, did he even understand everything that was going on? Did the police really threaten Maher's third wife, Heidi, when she rushed over to Monaco after his arrest?

The debate, and subsequent trial – which took over two years to come to court – were a sensation in Monaco and around the world. But at the end of the proceedings, at which Maher's own lawyer, Michael Griffith (the same man who had represented *Midnight Express* writer Billy Hayes on occasion), was not allowed to address the court, Maher was found guilty, and in December 2002, he was sentenced to ten years' imprisonment.

Many prisoners found guilty of a crime in Monaco are sent to French prisons under an agreement signed in 1963; however the principality maintains the right to keep certain criminals within its jurisdiction. Its prison, the fifty-cell House of Arrest, high on a promontory overlooking the sea, wouldn't ever be included in a list of Top Ten Hellholes. Compared with most, it is more like a holiday destination than a penitentiary, but there are still bars on the windows, and locks on the outside of the doors. "The place is like a luxury hotel," Michael Griffith commented shortly after Maher's abortive escape. "They were eating avocado and vinaigrette for lunch. He had a TV in his cell and an en suite bathroom." The prison was believed to be totally secure – it had been fifty years since the last escape. Faced with up to a decade in total within its walls (he had already spent over two years in the prison before coming to trial), and after learning that his wife would not be allowed to visit him with their children, Maher decided to escape, even though there was a fighting chance that if he kept his record clean, he might be released on parole within a couple of years.

He was imprisoned with Luigi Ciardelli, whom he would later try to claim was the instigator of the escape bid. The forty-five-year-old Italian had already served three sentences in a French prison, and was being held in Monaco following an armed robbery at a pharmacy in 1994. Initially Maher had been in his own cell, but the plan he had in mind needed two people, so between them they persuaded the prison director that Maher was a suicide risk, and Ciardelli would be able to keep an eye on him if they were in the same cell.

The view of the sea provided an ever-present reminder of the freedom both men craved. The plan was as simple as removing the bars from the windows, climbing through and letting themselves down to ground level. Maher wrote to his sister in America explaining his situation, and she sent four small hacksaw blades to him inside a copy of the Bible which was brought in by a priest who visited Maher regularly: the House of Correction had no prison workshop that the men could use to create any form of tool, and because of recent heart surgery, the priest wasn't allowed to go through a metal detector.

Maher didn't underestimate the work ahead of the two men: they had to get through six steel bars, and two wire meshes that lay between them and the outside. It was a painstaking task, since they had to work as quietly as possible; this meant they had to use small strokes of the blade against the initial steel mesh to avoid making too much noise. Two blades were quickly rendered smooth by the cutting. Each night they would glue the pieces back together, and paint them over, using materials that Ciardelli was able to obtain from his work in the prison library, then hide the blades inside the refrigerator so they wouldn't register on metal detectors.

It took three weeks to cut through the steel mesh, but, to Maher's delight, he discovered that the bars behind them were an easier target. Once he had cut through the top, he was able to bend the bars back, creating a gap that would be tight around his six-foot-three frame, but achievable. Knowing that there was no chance that they would simply be able to remove all the bars and create a gap the size of the window, Maher practised manoeuvring his body through the rungs of the ladder on the bunk bed in his room, and kept himself fit by running in small circles in a basement area. Two weeks after starting work on the bars, he had reached the outer mesh, and could see the grass beneath the prison walls.

The next obstacle was the drop to ground level, which was over twenty-five feet. Maher therefore created a rope out of forty-six rubbish bags, which he secured with Scotch tape and braided together. The area was also overlooked by a highly effective panoramic security camera. He and Ciardelli monitored its movement, and realized that they would have half of its forty-five second arc in which to make their move.

On the night of 22 January 2003, Maher and Ciardelli made their escape. After making dummies in their beds that would fool the hourly inspection by the guards, they removed the wire mesh and the bars, and tied the rope to one of the bent bars. Ciardelli went out of the window first, quickly followed by Maher, who was horrified when the Italian decided to strike out on his own. As soon as he let go of the rope, Ciardelli raced away, heading eventually for San Remo in Italy.

Maher had banked on Ciardelli's assistance to get out of Monaco, and was now in trouble. His face had been all over the Monaco papers only two months earlier during his trial and sentencing, so he knew he had to try to avoid attention. He used a sleeve from the sweater he was wearing to create a hat, and put on a pair of Ciardelli's reading glasses to add to the disguise. Managing to use the little French he had to say good evening to a passing policeman, but realizing that he needed to get out of the principality as quickly as possible, he started to walk to Nice, twelve or so miles away over the border in France.

Four hours later, around 3 a.m., Maher arrived in Nice. Desperate for somewhere to stay to get out of the freezing conditions, he knocked on the door of a cheap hotel and spun a yarn about his car breaking down. The manager agreed to allow him to make a collect call so he could arrange for some money, but Maher then received his second major setback of the night.

When his wife Heidi answered the phone from her home in New York state, she told him point-blank that she wasn't going to aid and abet him with his escape, and was not going to give him her credit card number. Even though he and his wife had been starting to discuss divorce, Maher couldn't believe that she wouldn't help him after standing by him right the way through the trial, and angrily slammed the phone down. He then tried to ring Father Ball, who had unwittingly brought the hacksaw blades into the prison for him, telling him that he was free, and wanted access to the money that his family had been sending the priest to buy items for Maher while in jail. Ball agreed, and told Maher to ring back at 10.30 that morning. Relieved that things were starting to go his way, and reassuring the manager that money would be forthcoming later that day, Maher took a long bath and went to bed.

As agreed, Maher called the priest at 10.30 on the morning of 23 January, and couldn't believe it when Father Ball announced, "The man you want is on the phone". He hung up, realizing that the Monaco police would have liaised with their French counterparts. He got dressed quickly, but by the time he reached the lobby of the hotel, the police were waiting for him. Without making a fuss, Maher surrendered into their custody.

His calls had been his undoing. His estranged wife, who had apparently decided after hearing the evidence at his trial that he was guilty, had got in touch with the producer of a CBS documentary on the case, who had then spoken to the segment producer in Monaco. When they got in touch with the prison authorities, they were told that there had been no escape. However, when Father Ball then confirmed that he had spoken with Maher in Nice, the escape was taken seriously.

Maher was eventually extradited from France to Monaco, and a further nine months was added to his sentence for the escape. He tried to claim that Ciardelli – who had been apprehended in Pisa, Italy, after two months on the run – was the instigator of the escape, and that he hadn't taken an active role. The court didn't accept another version of Maher's earlier trial defence (which can be summed up as "It's not my fault!"), even on appeal.

The director of the Monaco House of Arrest was suspended, and the authorities announced that improvements would be made. Maher was unable to get out of the House of Arrest a second time. He was released in 2007 and returned to America, where he still maintains his story about the intruders.

Probably the best epitaph on Maher's escapade came from Billy Hayes. When they learned the connection between Maher and Hayes, the American press got in touch with the former drug smuggler. "I feel bad for the guy," he said on the day Maher was recaptured. "Everyone talks about escaping, but there is a vast space and fear between thinking and talking about it and actually doing it. It sounded like he got real stupid."

Fact vs. Fiction

The *Real Prison Breaks* account of Maher's escape makes the Monaco House of Arrest look like a medieval prison, its only nods to modernity an old refrigerator and standard-issue jail beds. In fact, as contemporary news reports show, the cell looked more like a basic American motel room!

Sources:

Court TV, 23 January 2003: "Daring Monaco escape ends in France"

Vanity Fair, 1 September 2005: "Did Someone Say Safra? Some cases just don't get cold, and the mysterious death of billionaire Edmond Safra is one. (Obituary)"

Tru TV, 20 March 2010: *Dominick Dunne: Power, Privilege & Justice – Mystery in Monaco*

La Liberation, 23 January 2003: "L'infirmier pyromane brûle la politesse à ses gardiens"

Riviera Gazette, 30 January 2003: "The Not So Great Escape"

Monaco Times, 12 July 2006: "Ted Maher gets nine months"

Monaco Times, 28 November 2006: "Ted Maher in court to reduce sentence"

Vanity Fair, December 2000: "Death in Monaco"

New York Post, 31 July 2007: "New Claim in Safra Death"

Dateline NBC, 23 March 2008: *The Mystery of the Billionaire Banker*

Real Prison Breaks, Discovery Channel, 2008

Shawshank Redux

The warders in charge of the new buildings at Union County Jail, in Elizabeth, New Jersey, were able to maintain a proud boast for eighteen years: no felon managed to escape from their grasp. In that sense, it was rather like Stephen King's fictional prison in his novella *Rita Hayworth and Shawshank Redemption*, which became the basis for one of the best prison escape movies of all time, *The Shawshank Redemption*. And prisoners Otis Blunt and Jose Espinosa looked to that film for inspiration for their escape in December 2007.

There has been a prison on the site of Union County Jail since 1811 – forty-seven years before there even was a Union County. New buildings completed in 1989 serve the community that lies adjacent to Newark International Airport. The jail is an ugly, large concrete building surrounded by barbed wire, filled with over a thousand prisoners in for everything from parking tickets to murder charges, watched over by armed guards.

In the autumn of 2007, those inmates included thirty-two-year-old Otis Blunt, accused of armed robbery and shooting a convenience store manager, although he was strenuously protesting his innocence. Like so many others, he was worried that he was about to be railroaded into a long prison sentence – anything up to twenty years, given his prior history – and he was determined to escape before that could happen. In September, he tried to whittle away at the mortar surrounding a cinder block in his cell in the hope of dislodging it, so he could wriggle through the opening. One of the other inmates betrayed him to the guards, and Blunt was moved into cell B310 in a higher security section of the jail, sealed within a concrete bunker.

His next door neighbour on the third floor, in cell B311, was Jose Espinosa, a nineteen-year-old illegal alien member of the Bloods gang, with a long criminal record, who was await-ing sentencing for aggravated manslaughter. Facing a seventeen-year prison term for his part in the drive-by shoot-ing of Hassan Jackson, a member of rival gang, the Crips, unsurprisingly Espinosa willingly agreed to become part of an escape attempt.

The plan was for Blunt to break through the wall between the two cells, allowing him to enter Espinosa's, while the younger man created a hole in the wall next to his window. From there they could get access to a small roof that Blunt had noticed, and a thirty-feet drop over the razor-wire fence to cross the railroad tracks to freedom. Since he had some experience in the construc-tion industry, Blunt was aware that the weak point of the walls was the mortar around the blocks, so he stole a towel hook, and flattened it. Once all the prisoners had been locked in their cells for the night, and the guards were slightly less attentive, he and Espinosa then started to use it to scrape away the filling on the blocks that they had respectively chosen.

It wasn't going to be a quick job, although Blunt was under time pressure since his court hearing was rapidly approaching. However, they couldn't proceed too quickly, or the work would be discovered. Each cell was checked twice hourly, and from their block of eight, three would be randomly searched each day. To keep the damage to the wall hidden from prying eyes, Blunt emulated Andy Dufresne's method from *Shawshank Redemp-tion*: in the book, he covers the hole with a poster of film star Rita Hayworth; in the movie, Dufresne uses pictures of Hayworth, Marilyn Monroe and finally Raquel Welch. Blunt didn't have access to that sort of shot: he simply used pin-up pictures of women in bikinis (prosecutor Theodore J. Romankow pointed out that in the movie, "they had better pictures on the wall"). The dust and rubble were concealed in their lockers or disposed of in the toilets within their cells.

The towel hook proved to be insufficiently strong: they needed something that would do the job much faster. Looking around the recreational area, Blunt noticed that the valve for the water supply had a small wheel on it, about the size of a saucer, which could easily be removed. This was a much more effective implement, and using that, as well as a piece of wire that prison officers believed the men found inside the wall, the pair were ready to make their move after three weeks' work.

On the night of 14 December 2007, each rolled up blankets and placed them underneath the covers on their beds, so that a quick glimpse by the guard would not reveal their departure. Blunt then squeezed through the eight-by-sixteen-inch hole that he had created between the cells. The pair made the final hole in the outside wall and stepped out through the similarly sized gap onto the roof.

The razor wire was the last obstacle. Although prison officials originally believed the two men had jumped together, then gone their separate ways once they were free of the prison, it eventually transpired that Espinosa was first to jump the ten or so feet over the wire, although he damaged his ankle on landing. His cry frightened Blunt, who waited for some time on the roof before eventually deciding to clamber down into the gap beside the perimeter fence and then climb over that. Although he injured himself during this part of the escape, Blunt was finally free.

One of the more unusual elements of the escape is the length of time it took for it to be discovered. Blunt and Espinosa were long gone from the prison by dawn on 15 December, but the alarm was not raised until 5.15 that afternoon – a good twenty or so hours since they left their cells – when guard Rudolph Zurick pulled the cover off Blunt's bunk to reveal the rolled-up blankets.

A manhunt immediately began, and at a press conference on 17 December, prosecutor Romankow showed the note that Blunt had left addressed to Zurick: "Thank you Officer Zurick, for the tools needed. You're a real PAL (sic)! Happy holidays." It was completed with a smiley face. At first glance, it appeared as if this was suggesting that Zurick was complicit in the plans, but it was very clear to all the prison authorities that "at most we're looking at negligence by corrections officers". Zurick didn't see it that way. On 2 January 2008, the day that he was due to talk to investigators regarding the escape, Rudi Zurick, who had a fourteen-year unblemished record in the prison service, committed suicide.

This added a further edge to the investigation. Espinosa was the first to be captured, after a tip-off to the US Marshals. He was arrested in a basement apartment in Elizabeth on 8 January along with nineteen-year-old Odalys Cortez; he had hobbled on his injured ankle to the train station, where he caught a cab and lain low in a motel for a few days before holing up in the apartment. Cortez was charged with resisting arrest. When Espinosa was asked by reporters about Zurick's suicide, he simply said, "It wasn't my fault."

Blunt was located in Mexico City, and civil rights activist Reverend Al Sharpton became involved with trying to persuade him to surrender. On 6 January, two days before Espinosa was tracked down, Sharpton claimed that he had been contacted by "people in touch with Blunt", possibly as a result of prominence given to the case on the TV programme *America's Most Wanted*. "I have been asked by them to help facilitate his safe surrender," Sharpton said. "I have contacted law enforcement to see if I can be helpful towards that end." The next day he issued a statement from Miami noting that he and members of his National Action Network were travelling "in regard to the request made by fugitive Otis Blunt that he would like to surrender himself ... I am prepared to move within the next 24–48 hours to personally see if I can physically facilitate Mr Blunt's request."

This grandstanding didn't go down well with the law-enforcement officials trying to find Blunt. "I am upset that Reverend Sharpton is waiting between '24–48 hours to personally see if (he) can physically facilitate Mr Blunt's request'," prosecutor Romankow said in a statement. "Meanwhile, the escapee is still on the loose."

Sharpton went to Mexico City on 8 January and spoke to Blunt that night; the next day, at 4.30 p.m. Blunt was arrested by Mexican Federal Police. According to one report, he defecated himself when he was captured. The authorities wouldn't confirm whether Sharpton's involvement had assisted with locating Blunt; Sharpton himself said, "I wish I could have been on hand to assure Mr Blunt's safety but clearly his calling me to where he was helped lead to the conclusion that it did, and I hope that justice for all parties will be served."

It was. Blunt received a five-year term for the escape; ironically, he was cleared of the charges that he was on remand for, and would have been freed. He served his sentence at the East Jersey State Prison in Woodbridge and received an extra year after it seemed that he hadn't learned his lesson: on 22 July 2010 he was spotted by one of the correction officers sketching a diagram in the sand with a stick while talking to another inmate. The guard moved closer to the two men, and said that he over-heard Blunt tell the other man how to break off a piece of metal from a cell and bend it into a tool to cut mortar from the cell wall. Blunt denied the charge, insisting that the guard misheard the conversation, and he wouldn't have taken such a risk so near to his release date. The other inmate, who wasn't identified, claimed they were discussing a sketch for a tattoo. Although he appealed against the decision, Blunt's term was increased. He became due for release on 11 May 2012.

Espinosa also was given a five-year term, which was added to the seventeen years for manslaughter. As a result of their break, security at Union County Jail was considerably increased.

Fact vs. Fiction

The *Real Prison Breaks* episode about this escape, first broad-cast in summer 2011, gives a false impression of the physical nature of the cells in which Blunt and Espinosa were housed. It also fails to mention the note left by the men, or its consequences for Rudolph Zurick. For footage shot in the actual cells, go to the *America's Most Wanted* link given below: Thomas Romankow shows reporters where the holes were.

Sources:

New York Times, 18 December 2007: "Bold Escape Not First Try for Inmate"

Union County Jail website: http://ucnj.org/government/dept-of-corrections/

USA Today, 7 January 2008: "Rev. Sharpton may help inmate surrender"

America's Most Wanted: http://www.amw.com/fugitives/capture.cfm?id=51698

New York Post, 26 June 2009: "Two in 'Shawshank' Jailbreak Sentenced"

Elizabeth Inside Out, 30 December 2011: "Otis Blunt Serves more time for helping to plan an Escape"

Real Prison Breaks, Cineflix Productions, 2011

PART III: THE BERLIN WALL

My City, My Prison

What do you do when your entire city becomes a prison? For those who were caught in the partition of Berlin after the Second World War, with relatives spread between the Western Allies' sectors and the Russian part of the city, this question became highly relevant when the political situation became more volatile, and a strictly enforced barrier was erected between the two portions.

The division of Berlin as part of the settlement following the war against Hitler was always going to cause problems. The city was its own separate enclave deep in the heart of East Germany, with Western capitalist ideology governing the American, British and French sectors, while the Russians imposed Communism on the rest of East Germany, including their sector of Berlin. Stalin tried to starve the Western powers out of Berlin shortly after the end of the Second World War, but an airlift of food into the besieged city forced the Soviet leader to back down. West Berlin became a symbol of freedom, to the Communists' increasing anger.

Eventually, on the night of 13 August 1961, they took action to prevent the flood of refugees who were crossing between East and West Berlin. As thousands of soldiers lined the border, concrete posts were erected, and barbed wire strung between them. The Berlin Wall – which would divide the city for the next twenty-eight years – had been started.

To begin with, escapes weren't as hard as they later became. The Wall itself didn't boast the defences that later generations would feature, but people who crossed it were risking their lives. One of the very first to go was East German soldier Conrad Schumann. The nineteen-year-old former shepherd was part of a brigade that was transferred from Dresden to Berlin on 12 August 1961, the day before the Wall was erected. The soldiers must have known that something major was going on: their pay was increased by nearly ten per cent for "danger money".

On 15 August, Schumann was on guard at the corner of Bernauerstrasse and Ruppinerstrassse, and watched as a small girl was refused entry back into West Berlin. Her parents were waiting for her on the western side: she had simply been visiting her grandmother in East Berlin before the Wall was erected. That didn't matter: free travel between the two sides was simply not permitted any longer. Even though the child could see her parents, the rules were strict: she was sent back to her grand-mother's house.

According to accounts that Schumann later gave, that was the catalyst for his escape. He swapped his full sub-machine gun for an empty one, as people on the West German side called for him to come over to them. By chance West German cameraman Peter Liebing was standing near the junction, and photographed Schu-mann as he hesitated for a moment, then vaulted over the barbed wire, and ran to a police car that was on the other side of the barrier. "I had him in my sight for more than an hour. I had a feeling he was going to jump. It was kind of an instinct," Liebing later explained. "I had learned how to do it at the Jump Derby in Hamburg. You have to photograph the horse when it leaves the ground and catch it as it clears the barrier. And then he came. I pressed the shutter and it was all over." The still photograph – as well as cine footage of the escape – became an iconic image, representing the desire of East Germans to flee the country.

Schumann's family were not impressed by his defection, and he received numerous pleas from them to return to the East, which he declined. The East German secret police, the Stasi, would have loved to use him as a poster boy to show the failings of the West, but Schumann refused to cooperate, remaining in the West, where he worked for car manufacturers Audi. When the Berlin Wall fell in 1989, he was able to return home, but was still regarded as a traitor by some. Suffering from depression, he hanged himself on 20 June 1998.

While East Germans were finding holes in the barbed wire and desperately making their way through to a new life in the West – around 12,000 people managed to escape during the latter part of 1961 before the Communists tightened security at the Wall – some gave their lives in the pursuit of freedom. Nine days after the Wall was erected, on 22 August, the East German police and army were told that anyone "violating the laws of our GDR is to be called to order, if necessary by use of weapons". Two days later, Günter Litfin was the first escaper known to be shot.

The tailor, who had worked in West Berlin until the Wall, decided to try to cross the border near the Reichstag building just north of the Brandenburg Gate. When he was spotted, Litfin dived into the Spandauer boat canal that separated the two parts of the city, and swam desperately for the Western side. He was within a few inches of the bank when a border guard fired his sub-machine gun; Litfin was hit in the head, and sank underwater. His corpse was fished out from the canal later that day.

One of the few watchtowers that wasn't destroyed in the aftermath of the fall of the Wall has been preserved near the Invalidenfriedhof, the invalids' graveyard that sits beside the canal, close to the site of Litfin's death. It has been preserved as a memorial to Litfin.

In the very early days of the Wall, there were still many buildings abutting the barbed wire, and while the interiors of the buildings may have been within East Germany, their exteriors were in the West. This meant that people would jump from the windows and as the Communists began emptying the houses of tenants and bricking up the windows of the lower levels, so potential escapees had to take ever increasing risks. The West German fire brigade would often assist jumpers: on 24 September, seventy-seven-year-old Frieda Schulze tried to make the leap but was held back by East German soldiers before she was finally able to free herself from their grasp and fall into the firemen's arms below. Eighty-year-old Olga Segler wasn't so lucky, dying of internal injuries caused by her fall.

Graduate student Leslie Colitt was desperate to bring his fiancée out from the East. They had met the year before, when travel between the two sectors wasn't a problem. He was on holiday in France with his parents when the Wall went up, but was determined to bring Ingrid across. Westerners were still allowed to cross into the East, but their movements were being watched far more carefully. Colitt's original plan was to travel with Ingrid by train, with her using his sister's American passport. She learned sufficient English phrases to deal with the questioning she might receive, and prepared for her escape.

All seemed to go well initially, but to Colitt's horror, on the day they chose to implement the plan in late September 1961, an astute border guard noticed that he had entered East Berlin three times within one day. Although he was able to come up with a suitable story to placate the East German, Colitt knew that going back through Friedrichstrasse station with Ingrid at his side would be too risky. The only route was via the border crossing on the south side of the city at Zimmerstrasse, which would eventually become known as Checkpoint Charlie, the scene of a tense confrontation a few weeks later between American and Soviet tanks. To Colitt's relief, the guard on duty at the crossing waved them through the barbed wire and the tanks to enter the West. In common with all refugees, Ingrid was interrogated by West German and Allied intelligence, in case she was a plant by the Stasi. Her father was demoted from his post at the East German state engineering company as a result of her escape, even though he knew nothing of it; her parents were eventually allowed to travel to West Germany when they were pensioners.

Train driver Harry Deterling used the transport system to great effect on 5 December 1961, as he brought his wife, four children – and a trainload of other passengers, many of whom were unaware of what was going on – over to the West. The railway crossed the border at Staaken, and when Deterling learned that the line was going to be blocked off, on 3 December he and his family decided that they had to act now.

According to the press conference he gave after reaching the West, Deterling persuaded officials that he wanted to "improve his technical qualifications" and was thus allowed to run an extra train that wasn't on the schedule. This became what he described as "the last train to freedom, departs today at 7.33 p.m.". The train – initially with hundreds of passengers on board, the vast majority of whom departed before the terminus

– ran to Albretchtshof station as planned but instead of stopping, Deterling, with his friend Hartmut Lichy acting as fireman, kept the steam engine fired up and headed up the single track that crossed the border. Although the two men hid in the coal tender, and the passengers who knew of the escape ducked to the floor, in case they were fired upon by the guards, the audacity of the plan seemed to amaze the border patrols, and not a single shot was aimed at them.

Of the thirty-two passengers on board, seven decided to return to East Berlin of their own accord. Deterling celebrated his twenty-eighth birthday the day after the escape, and told reporters, "Freedom is my happiest birthday present." The train was pulled back over the border by an East German locomotive, and the line was shut the next day. It was reopened eventually in 1995. Deterling's plan became the basis of the 1963 West German film *Durchbruch Lok 234*.

By this stage, the East German authorities were trying to plug every possible gap in their Wall. Houses beside the border became derelict, and access to the sewerage system was blocked off with gratings. This meant that those seeking to help people escape had to find alternate routes, and some would pay the ultimate price for their willingness to assist those in need. One of the most famous of the escape-helpers to be killed was Dieter Wohlfahrt, who was killed on 9 December 1961.

The twenty-year-old student had Austrian citizenship, and therefore was allowed to cross the border between East and West without restrictions while growing up. When the Wall prevented his East German friends from free movement, he decided to find ways to help them get to the West. As part of a group of students, he was able to come up with various ways to evade the security forces, initially through the sewers. His Austrian passport allowed him to enter East Berlin, and he would act as "cover man" for the escapees, opening the manholes that led down to the sewers. However, when the sewers were blocked he was as happy to assist with more blatant crossings, and in early December 1961, he agreed unhesitatingly to help Elke, a seventeen-year-old student fetch her mother across the barrier not far from where Harry Deterling had broken through the border on his train.

Wohlfahrt, his friend Karl-Heinz Albert, and Elke drove to the agreed crossing at the corner of Bergstrasse and Hauptstrasse, with Elke remaining in the camper van on the Western side. Wohlfahrt and Albert climbed over the rope marking the border and started to cut through the three layers of barbed wire. However, according to Albert, Elke's mother started to call out for her daughter, which alerted the East German border patrol. They barked an order for everyone to stop, but rather than wait for them to obey, they opened fire. Albert crawled back to West Berlin, but Wohlfahrt was hit, lying about twenty feet from the border. Although West German police and British military police tried to go to his aid, their East German counterparts made it clear that they would fire on anyone who approached him – and they themselves had no intention of giving any aid to the dying man. He was left there for an hour before being carted off.

The East Germans tried to make a propaganda coup from Wohlfarht's death, claiming that the young Austrian and his friends had opened fire on the state police, but this was vehemently denied. "The Communists' claim that the young men had pistols and plastic bombs with them was clearly made up out of thin air. It is their old method of saying, 'The deceased is guilty.'" The guard who shot Wohlfarht didn't face legal proceedings after the reunification of Germany, apparently because he might have been acting in self-defence.

Wohlfahrt's death and the lack of action by the police and the British military prompted fierce criticism from the mayor of Berlin, who pointed out that "the reserve demonstrated from our side will only encourage the Eastern ruling powers to continue to show no consideration for human life". The influential *Der Spiegel* magazine also pointed out that Wohlfahrt "was a victim of the bitter realization that, now all other escape holes have been sealed, the only way out is to break through the walls or the barbed wire by force."

The deaths of Günter Litfin and Dieter Wohlfahrt, among many others during that first year that the Wall existed, including Lutz Haberlandt, Axel Hannemann and thirteen-year-old Wolfgang Glöde, did not serve to deter those who wanted to reach the

West. As the Berlin Wall became literally more concrete, with materials from the Second World War bombsites contributing to the more permanent barricades that were now erected from breeze blocks and concrete slabs, people sought other routes, and the most obvious one was underground.

According to Dietmar Arnold, the head of the Berlin Underworlds Association, between 1962 and 1972, the authorities are now aware of seventy-one different tunnel projects that were begun, with around twenty per cent being successful. Occasionally construction work on the roads in the vicinity of the Wall will reveal others. One of the more unusual was the Seniorentunnel, which was masterminded by an eighty-one-year-old man, who made it clear that he didn't even want to be buried in East Germany. Together with a dozen fellow senior citizens, he spent sixteen days digging a tunnel with very unusual dimensions: while its 160-feet length meant it passed from beneath a chicken coop on Oranienburger Chaussee on the Eastern side to Frohnau in West Berlin, it was six feet high, rather than the usual few inches. This meant that considerably more earth had to be moved, but, as one of the escapees explained when they reached the West on 5 May 1962, "We wanted to walk to freedom with our wives, comfortably and unbowed."

A good proportion of the tunnels were begun from the Western side, often by those who had already escaped and wanted to be reunited with their loved ones. East Germans had to be extremely careful when discussing any plans: the Stasi built its reputation on its formidable army of informants, and Berliners intending to travel were always on the lookout for eavesdroppers. Many tunnels, such as one dug from Heidelbergerstrasse in the Western district of Neukölln in mid-September 1962, were betrayed to the secret police, but others, like Tunnel 29 which stretched from Bernauerstrasse to Schönholzerstrasse, enabled many East Germans to escape (sometimes to find themselves filmed on their arrival in the West by camera crews from American network NBC who helped finance Tunnel 29 in exchange for the rights!).

The interest of the West in the plight of the Berliners sometimes led to difficult publicity for the East German authorities. By mid-1962, the infamous death strip had started to take shape, with a second wall behind the border Wall. Over the years, between these two could be mines, tripwires, or dogs. On 17 August, Peter Fechter, a nineteen-year-old bricklayer, was shot near the Wall while trying to escape with his friend Helmut Kulbeik. They hid out in a carpenter's workshop near the wall in Zimmerstrasse and once the border guards were out of sight, intended to cross the death strip and then climb the far wall. They were shot at as they reached the boundary with the West; Kulbeik was able to clamber over, despite the barbed wire and glass at the top. Fechter was shot in the hip, and lay for a long time in front of hundreds of witnesses, bleeding out slowly in full view of the TV cameras.

As with Wohlfahrt, the Western authorities felt unable to give assistance (a *Time* magazine report suggested that a US Army officer was given specific instructions not to do anything) and Fechter took two hours to die. However, unlike in Wohlfahrt's case, Fechter's death did lead to some positive action – four days later, an ambulance was stationed at Checkpoint Charlie. Two of the guards who shot at him were convicted of manslaughter in 1997; a third had subsequently died. A memorial stands at the spot where Fechter died.

A documentary produced around the time of the first anniversary of the Wall's erection in 1962 by the Berlin Film Unit, simply titled *The Wall*, demonstrates many Berliners were gradually becoming used to the scar on their city. That didn't mean that everyone had given up. In fact the following year saw many highly unusual methods of escape tried, starting with East German acrobat Hans Klein who decided to use his natural talents to cross the border.

On the night of 27 December 1962, the thirty-six-year-old anti-Communist acrobat climbed a steel pylon and leaped to the porcelain insulator on a 110,000 volt high-tension cable, which ran sixty feet over the heads of the guards – if he had touched both the tower and the cable at the same time, he would have been turned to ashes. "I could hear humming and had a tingling sensation in my seat," he admitted to the Associated Press, describing how he slid seventy yards then jumped to a second tower. Two guards were patrolling the wire barricades facing the Teltow Canal, but Klein was above the reach of their searchlights.

After sliding a further thirty yards, Klein hooked his legs over the cable and started to pay out a rope he had coiled over his chest, hoping to sling it over the cable, and then climb down it into the West. The temperature, though, was seven degrees Fahrenheit (nearly minus fourteen Celsius) and his hands had numbed. He missed the rope and he fell forty feet to the towpath, breaking his arms. When he recovered consciousness three hours later, he called for help, and the West German police and fire brigade came to his assistance.

On 17 April 1963, nineteen-year-old Wolfgang Engels tried to break through the wall in a novel way, using a Soviet armoured personnel carrier. As a young soldier he had helped to put up the barbed-wire barriers in August 1961, and now, employed by the National People's Army as a panel beater, he decided to liberate a personnel carrier from the garage where he was working. Engels drove straight at the Wall, but unfortunately the Wall was rather stronger than the personnel carrier. However, the impact was sufficient to create a hole, through which the young German could scramble, only to find himself enmeshed in barbed wire. At that moment, a border guard approached him, and, as he told a History Channel documentary in 2009, "I found myself standing in the middle of the rolls of barbed wire. I didn't even feel the bullets hitting me."

Engels was saved by the new rules of engagement that followed Fechter's death. A West German policeman provided covering fire and Engels pulled himself over the Wall, with the assistance of some West Berliners, who took him to a local bar. "I came to on top of the counter," he later joked. "When I turned my head and saw all the Western brands of liquor on the shelf, I knew that I had made it." Although seriously injured, Engels survived.

Possibly emboldened by Engels' actions as well as previous successful escapes by this method in December 1962 and February 1963, a group of young East Berliners stole a bus on 12 May and tried to break through the cement barriers at the Invalidenstrasse border. They so nearly made it, too – but the 138 shots fired by the border guards stopped the bus a mere three feet from the final barrier, and it skidded into the anti-tank wall. Driver Gerd Keil and two of the passengers were seriously injured; all eight on board were arrested and sentenced to prison terms ranging from three to ten years.

Cars were an obvious way of transporting people across the border, but the guards tried to be rigorous in their searches. They couldn't anticipate that someone would simply try to drive underneath the barriers that they had set up – but when Hans Meixner did exactly that a few days after Keil's failed attempt in May 1963, the guards acted quickly to prevent anyone else following suit.

Meixner had noticed that a sports car stopped at Checkpoint Charlie had nearly slipped beneath the barrier when the young woman driving it lost her concentration and let go of the handbrake. The twenty-two-year-old Austrian student was able to mark the exact height of the barrier, and then searched for a car that would be able to pass beneath. The British Austin Healey Sprite fit the bill, and even came with a detachable windscreen.

Like Leslie Collitt a couple of years earlier, Meixner had fallen in love with an East German girl and wanted to live with her in the West. He therefore planned to bring her and her mother through in the car. Of course, it wouldn't be as easy as accelerating up to Checkpoint Charlie and cheerfully driving under the barrier. The East Germans had built four-feet-high walls around which the cars had to drive as they approached the border. Meixner practised assiduously at driving round these at high speed, creating a mock version of the border crossing in a deserted space in West Berlin using oil drums and piles of bricks to simulate the obstacles.

On the chosen day, Meixner drove into East Berlin and collected his fiancée and future mother-in-law, hiding them behind the seats and removing the windscreen. When he reached the start of the inspection point, rather than meekly going into the bay to allow his papers and vehicle to be checked, he floored the accelerator and shot round between the walls, exactly as he had practised. The guards were too astonished to open fire, and Meixner reached the final straight without a shot aimed at him. Pointing the car directly at the barrier, Meixner ducked his head and slammed the accelerator pedal to the floor. The Healey Sprite sprang forward, and passed beneath the barrier, exactly as planned.

Double metal barriers were erected by the East Germans within days. No one was going to emulate Meixner's feat. They'd just have to think of something different – as Horst Breistoffer did a few years later, removing the battery and heating system from a 1964 Italian Isetta car to create a compartment inside which an escapee could hide. Nine East Germans were brought across before Breistoffer's pimpernel activities were brought to a close when he was caught with the tenth refugee.

Jockey Michael Meyer felt claustrophobic within the German Democratic Republic (GDR), and determined to escape in the late summer of 1964. On Sunday 13 September, he decided to swim for it across the River Spree, but after thirty minutes in the water he realized that he hadn't reached the Western side. At 5.20 a.m., he approached the barbed-wire fence close to Checkpoint Charlie, but as soon as he went beneath it, the border guards started firing at him. The Stasi claimed that they fired 300 shots during the incident, some of which, as the US Ambassador noted to the East German commandant in a sharply written note the following day, penetrated the American sector, risking the lives of residents and US Army personnel in the area. At least five of the rounds hit Meyer, but he struggled on. US Sergeant Hans-Werner Puhl went to Meyer's aid, even though East German border guards were trying to pull him back. Puhl threw a gas grenade, which forced the Communists to retreat, and Meyer managed to cross the wall, with assistance from a rope that Puhl threw him. Although he lost a large amount of blood, Meyer recovered in hospital, although one of the bullets remained in his back.

Events three weeks later were to have long-lasting repercussions for those wishing to escape from Berlin, when East German guard Egon Schultz was shot during the shutting down of what became known as Tunnel 57 (the tunnel titles derived from the total number of successful escapees). The West German students responsible for the tunnel were held accountable for the shooting in the East German propaganda that followed – and it was only many years later that the truth came out. In the meantime, many East Germans became wary of involvement in such attempts, and escapers lost public sympathy.

The tunnel was the brainchild of Peter Schulenberg and engineering student Hubert Hohlbein, whose mother was in the GDR, as well as future Skylab astronaut Reinhard Furrer. It ran from 97 Bernauerstrasse on the Western side of the Wall for 145 metres, coming out in a courtyard at 55 Strelitzerstrasse. Although only seventy-five square centimetres wide, the tunnel took six months to dig, with the students working in two-week shifts underground, not coming up for air during that time and risking their lives in the hot, cramped, and scary conditions – if any part of the tunnel roof or wall collapsed, the digger would be lost for ever. Hohlbein was the first to enter East Berlin from the tunnel, after they realized that the soil through which they were digging had become softer, and they could smell air.

Schulenberg collected the first batch of escapees, who travelled through the tunnel on the night of 3/4 October. One of the first through was Hohlbein's mother. In total, fifty-seven East Germans fled that night. Unfortunately, a second batch weren't so lucky. Although the tunnel-diggers believed that one of the potential escapers betrayed them, Stasi records suggest that two of their operatives had spotted Furrer and the other students who were guarding the tunnel entrance at Strelitzerstrasse and thought they were suspicious. The students thought that the plain clothes Stasi men were really civilians looking for the escape route, and didn't demur when they said they wanted to fetch a friend who would also want to come along. Instead the Stasi brought back the border guards, including twenty-one-year-old Sergeant Schultz.

When faced with the guards' machine guns, the students knew they needed to retreat rapidly, and student Christian Zobel fired a warning shot to alert those who were down the tunnel. This provoked a wave of firing, during which Schultz was hit by ten bullets. The students dived back into the tunnel, and hurried as quickly as they could back to the West, fearful that at any moment a hand grenade could be thrown in behind them, bringing the walls crashing down to entomb them. Probably because they were tending to the fatally injured Schultz, however, the guards didn't pursue the students, and all of them reached safety.

Schultz's death became a political cause célèbre, with the East German authorities making great play of the "treacherous murder" and "assassination" of the border guard. The students admitted that a shot had been fired, but there was no proof that the bullet had hit Schultz. They sent balloons over the Wall near Checkpoint Charlie stating that "The causative murderer is the East German secret police. These men, with great acting skill, first pretended to be fugitives. Reluctant to intervene themselves, they instead fetched the soldier and had him clarify the situation. But the real murderer is the system that addressed the massive flight of its citizens not by removing the cause of the problem, but by building a *wall* and giving the order for Germans to shoot Germans."

East Germany demanded the students' extradition; instead the West German public prosecutor closed the case. More than a hundred different institutions were named after the martyr in the following months. In 1992, an investigation proved beyond a doubt that Schultz had been killed by bullets from a Kalashnikov, fired by one of his colleagues. Zobel's bullet did hit Schultz, but lodged in his lung and wasn't the cause of death. The damage to the escapers' cause, though, was long-lasting.

While many of those who wanted to flee had to risk the death strip, the barbed wire and the border guards' machine guns, various groups found unusual methods of exit during the mid-1960s, as the defences at the Wall started to be made even stronger. In January 1965, six people, including a seventeen-year-old girl, hid inside wooden cable drums that belonged to the Berlin Electricity Works, and were transported to West Berlin by haulage contractors.

The Holzapfel family, complete with their nine-year-old son, used a zipwire to cross from the roof of the East Berlin House of Ministries (the home now of the German Finance Ministry) to the West on the night of 28 July 1965. The guards charged with watching for such manoeuvres, after Hans Klein's escape three years earlier, assumed that the Stasi were responsible, and were using an unorthodox method of infiltrating agents into West Berlin!

A year later, five East Germans bulldozed their way through the border at Staaken. Knowing that they would be fired upon when they approached the wall in their stolen vehicle, the escapers stuffed rags into the cabin, since they couldn't accumulate enough steel plate in time. But they did think of a back-up plan if they didn't succeed: "My friend had a lot of pepper with him," the driver later explained. "And if a border guard had come along and caught us, he would have thrown it in his eyes."

The driver, a twenty-four-year-old professional bulldozer operator, was accompanied by his pregnant wife and their four-year-old son, as well as another married couple. According to the interview he gave with the Associated Press, they had originally intended to break through the day before, but hadn't had time to weld steel plates to anything beyond the fuel tank and the windows.

On the morning of Sunday 11 September 1966, they knew they needed to go, or risk discovery. They bulldozed their way through the four barbed-wire fences before ploughing into a tree. More than a hundred bullets were fired at them, but they only received slight injuries. However, they knew they had to get out of the bulldozer before the sub-machine guns could inflict any more damage, so they went under a garden fence and ran into the house, with the boy crying, "Are we in the West? Are we in the West?" The East Germans pulled the bulldozer back and repaired the fence.

With the Wall becoming ever-harder to cross directly, people started to find ways around it altogether. Bernd Boettger's way of crossing the border was unique to him: he actually devised his own new method of transport, which then went into production around the world. His escape in 1968 necessitated the creation of the aqua-scooter.

The chemical technician had spotted the lightship, the *Gedser*, anchored in the North Sea fifteen miles or so off the beach at Mecklenburg over eighteen months before he finally clambered aboard the Danish ship in September 1968. Although he was a strong swimmer and former lifeguard, Boettger quickly realized that he wouldn't be able to battle the currents and temperature of the water, so would need some form of mechanical assistance. However, when he first tried out his prototype, he was noticed by the marine patrols, and arrested. Although he was sentenced to three months in jail for an illegal attempt at border crossing, the term was suspended because he worked in an essential industry. He was even allowed to remain based near the sea.

Boettger worked on the second machine for a year, knowing that the tenacity of the guards meant that he would only have one shot at this. If he was caught again, then the East German authorities would have no option but to throw the book at him. His craft had to be quiet, efficient, and reliable. The final machine lived up to all his requirements, and would give him around fifteen miles' range.

Late in the evening of 8 September 1968, he entered the water at Warnemuende, just a few hundred metres from the guard post. Immediately submerging to a depth at which the guards couldn't spot him, Boettger spent ninety minutes underwater before surfacing and heading for where he hoped the lightship would be. Three hours after spotting the light he was picked up by the crew, after a total of five hours in the water.

As a result of the publicity given to his escape by the European press a few weeks later, Boettger's invention came to the attention of Rockwell International, who developed it for commercial use. Sadly, Boettger himself died in a diving accident off the coast of Spain in the early 1970s.

The East German authorities regularly added to the perils of the death strip. Dogs, mines automatically firing weapons – all were present to prevent anyone from treacherously trying to leave the Democratic Republic. And not everything was immediately obvious to the naked eye, as Miriam Webber discovered.

The sixteen-year-old student had been arrested for sedition in the autumn of 1968, after preparing posters complaining about the police reaction to protests in Leipzig following the demolition of the old University Church of St Paul on 30 May that year. She and a friend had been kept in solitary confinement for a month until they broke down and confessed. When she was let out to await her trial, Webber decided to flee the country.

Heading to Berlin from her hometown on New Year's Eve 1968, Webber naively looked for weaknesses in the Wall, discarding the Brandenburg Gate because the Wall was too high, even though there didn't appear to be any other barriers there (in fact they were all on the far – Western – side of the Gate, within the hemispherical section of the Wall at that point). She believed she had found what she was looking for when travelling by train near the Bornholmer Bridge.

As fireworks were celebrating the New Year in the West, Webber started to make her way through the gardens that abutted onto the death strip, by chance not encountering any of the guards who normally patrolled them, and climbed a ladder to look over the hedge at the strip. She managed to get through the barbed wire, cutting her hands to shreds in the process, and started to cross the death strip on hands and knees, all the while expecting the guards to spot her. To her surprise, despite the fact that the strip was constantly illuminated, no one spotted her. She froze when a giant German Shepherd guard dog seemed alerted to her presence, but it didn't raise the alarm.

Webber crossed the final barbed-wire fence, and thought she was going to make it. She was actually at the border Wall itself, looking across into West Berlin – and as she moved toward the final railing, she activated nearly invisible tripwires, which now criss-crossed the entirety of the area in front of her. She had been so careful, but was caught because of yet another security measure.

During her interrogation, the Stasi were keen to discover exactly how Webber had known the way to evade the security measures. How did she know how to cross barbed wire? Who told her about the proximity of the gardens to the Wall at the Bornholmer Bridge? How did she persuade the highly trained guard dog not to raise the alarm? When they didn't believe her, Webber made up a story that should have set off as many alarm bells for her interrogators as the tripwires on the Wall. She claimed that she had met men in a bar who had given her handy hints for Wall-jumping – something that in the atmosphere of paranoia and suspicion that permeated Berlin in the Cold War days would simply never have happened. The Stasi followed up her "lead" and eventually realized they had been fooled. Webber was sentenced to eighteen months' imprisonment and told that she had nearly started World War III – if the guards on either side had fired at each other during her flight, the situation could easily have escalated!

US General George S. Patton once said, "Never tell people how to do things. Tell them what to do and they will surprise you with their ingenuity." East Germans wanting a new life in the West knew they had to come up with as many diverse ideas as possible to evade the Stasi and the border patrols. Although a *Milwaukee Journal* feature from 1969 suggested that an average of 500 refugees were still crossing the border each month, the true figure seems to be more like a fifth of that. Some were audacious, borrowing Soviet Army uniforms and taking advantage of the rule that allowed uniformed military personnel complete access to the city. At one point, Playboy club membership cards were waved towards the guards; they looked sufficiently like the passes allowing free access that the border soldiers were fooled. Photographer Horst Beyer persuaded a group of attractive athletes into posing with guards at Freidrichstrasse, then kept backing up to get the "perfect photo" until he had crossed the line into West Berlin.

And while Bernd Boettger devised a completely new mode of transport, a group of escapees in 1969 looked back to history for inspiration – back around 3,000 years, in fact, to the Trojan War. The siege of Troy had gone on for ten years before the Greeks pretended to depart, leaving a huge wooden horse outside the gates of Troy apparently as a peace offering to the gods. The Trojans duly dragged the surprisingly heavy object within the gates – and that night the Greeks who had been hiding within let themselves out and put the town to the sword.

The Germans didn't have a wooden horse available. They did, however, have a cow – or, more accurately, a bull, a display item that was transported between East and West. By July 1969, it had already been used on two occasions to bring escapees over the border, but on 7 July, the border guards directed the van in which it was being carried from the back of the queue at the Drewitz border crossing. Opening the rear of the van they found the wooden crate, with the cow inside – and inside that was an eighteen-year-old girl, only identified as Angelika, from

Karl-Marx-Stadt who was travelling to meet her fiancé. He had paid 5,000 DM for the escape, and would owe a further 5,000 when she reached the West. Angelika was imprisoned for two years and ten months, although a ransom was paid by the West German government after four months to ensure her release; the professionals responsible for the cow received three years in prison each.

During the 1970s, the border between West and East became easier to cross – so long as you were West German. In 1971, it was decreed that West Berliners could visit the GDR once or several times for up to thirty days a year "for humanitarian, family, religious, cultural and tourist reasons" while the following year, those who fled to the West before 1 January 1972 lost their East German citizenship but could re-enter East Germany without fear of prosecution. East German citizens under retirement age could make trips to the West (provided there were hostages left behind to ensure their return). A Basic Treaty, signed at the end of the year, normalized relations even further.

That didn't halt the flood of escape attempts from East to West Germany. According to official GDR figures, there were 2,699 in 1972 and 3,004 in 1973, of which 242 resulted in successful "border breakthroughs (it's worth noting that figures compiled after unification suggest that there were really 1,245 successes in 1972, and 1,842 in 1973, 144 of these in total through Berlin itself). Border troops were reminded of their responsibility to call, "Stop! Border guards! Hands up!" before firing but told that weapons were to be used "ruthlessly" to prevent escapes.

Some of these escapes were the work of Hartmut Richter, who had fled to the West in 1966, by swimming across the Teltow Canal dividing Berlin. His motto was very simple: "The first one who comes over helps the others to escape." When the transit rules were relaxed, Richter crossed over the border regularly and realized that once the border guards started to recognize faces, they weren't so stringent in their security checks. In 1973, he was asked by an acquaintance if he knew of anyone who might assist with helping an escapee; Richter decided to do it himself, and the young woman was the first of thirty-three East Germans who Richter smuggled through in the boot of his car, after picking them up from a shed on his parents' property near the village of Glindow, or from a bus stop near Finkenkrug.

As Richter learned later, the Stasi began to cross-reference the transit lists with the number of defectors and realized that every time he went from East to West, someone went missing. It was highly unfortunate that the occasion they decided to search his car was the time that he was carrying his sister and her fiancé across the border. Richter was sentenced to fifteen years in prison, although he was ransomed after four.

Some of the most successful escapes have formed the basis of movies, many released solely in German-speaking territories. One, however, captured the imagination of executives at the Walt Disney Company. The daring feats of Peter Strelzyk, Günter Wetzel and their families were immortalized on celluloid in the 1982 Disney feature film, *Night Crossing*, which gave a pretty faithful account of the Germans' balloon passage over the border (although Wetzel has since set the record straight with a detailed account on his own website www.ballonflucht.de).

The inspiration for the flight came from an article that Wetzel's sister-in-law showed him during a visit she made to the family from her home in America during March 1978. The report from the International Balloon Festival in the American town of Albuquerque gave Wetzel the idea of using a hot-air balloon to cross the border. It was pretty much silent and would rise well over the border fortifications. Wetzel and Strelzyk and had discussed their mutual desire to get their families to freedom in the West, and on 7 March 1978, the two families agreed to work together to get the four adults and four children away by balloon.

None of the people involved had any experience with ballooning, so they weren't sure exactly how to go about making one. They decided to make the balloon itself with a lining fabric used for leatherwear, which they could obtain in sufficiently large quantities, and created their own burner from a propane gas cylinder, stove pipe and a valve. The "basket" was a sheet of metal with guard rails and flat steel bars to which the balloon could be fixed. However, after trying to test a prototype, they realized that they needed to rethink a number of elements.

After burning all evidence of the first balloon, Strelzyk and Wetzel began work on its successor, after evaluating various potential fabrics. Umbrella fabric, tent nylon and taffeta were the eventual choices and a second balloon was constructed, although it too presented problems with fuel supply and inflation. Disheartened, the Wetzel family decided to pull out of the project. While Günter Wetzel considered building a glider, the Strelzyks pursued other avenues of escape via the foreign embassies, but none of their plans amounted to anything.

The Strelzyks then tried to flee using their own balloon, but their flight on 3 July 1979 was unsuccessful, and they crash-landed in woods still on the East German side. A couple of weeks later, the Stasi had found the materials left by the Strelzyks at the site, leading them to be more vigilant for anyone buying the kit required for the escape. Knowing that they were running out of time, Wetzel and Strelzyk agreed to work together again. Using some ingenuity, and travelling as far as they dared, the families were able to purchase what they needed – using bedding as an alternative where absolutely necessary – and by 15 September 1979, the new balloon was ready to go. Weather conditions were ideal, so the families agreed that there was no time to test this third attempt. It would have to work first time.

At 1 a.m. on the morning of 16 September, the two families arrived at the launch site, between Oberlemnitz and Heinersdorf, and within ninety minutes, the balloon was inflated. After problems with the launch, in which one of the flyers was injured, they got under way, but a hole in the top of the balloon meant they had to use the burner continuously, jeopardizing how long they could remain in the air. Still, they were able to ascend to a height above the reach of the searchlights at the border. (Contrary to the impression given in the movie, the East German police weren't hot on their heels, but it makes for a more dramatic sight on screen.)

Although they didn't know it at the time, they had already crossed into West Germany when the burner packed up, and they were forced to land in fields, which they later discovered were at Finkenflug near Naila. Heading south to get further away from the border, they came upon a farmhouse with West German implements, and then encountered a car, containing two policemen. The pair were surprised to be asked if they were in the West, replying, "Of course you are, where else would you be?" The tense relationship between the Wetzels and the Strelzyks meant that after they arrived in the West, the two families went their separate ways.

As Günter Wetzel explains in his account of the flight, one of the biggest concerns that the families had was that someone would betray them to the authorities. They ensured that a friend from the West knew what they were doing in case they suddenly disappeared into the harsh East German prison system, and they were worried that their purchases would attract undue suspicion. Even being stopped for driving the wrong way down a one-way street was enough to make Wetzel believe that the Stasi had come for him.

Their fears were justified. By the start of the 1980s, the web of informants run by the Stasi meant that over ninety per cent of escape attempts were foiled at the planning stage, and only five to eight per cent were successful. No one could have dreamed that by the end of 1989, the Wall would be no more: those who wanted to escape still looked for ways around the restrictions placed on them by the Communist authorities, and hoped that they could trust those around them.

Twenty-four-year-old Kerstin Beck found herself embroiled in a much larger month-long adventure than she had anticipated when she decided to use her time studying languages in Afghanistan as a way of escaping from the GDR. The daughter of a diplomat, she had some experience of the world outside the Communist sphere of influence, and she wanted to see all the world, not simply the "one corner" that the East Germans allowed.

In March 1984, shortly before she was due to return to the GDR after a six-month study-visit to Kabul, she met a member of the Mujaheddin resistance to the Soviet occupation of Afghanistan, who took her to her mother's house. When she revealed that she didn't want to return to the Communist state, they agreed to help her cross over into Pakistan. Wearing the burqa adopted by Muslim women, Beck accompanied the Mujaheddin, pretending to be a relative of the men from Tajikistan. Even as the alarm was raised in Kabul by loyal fellow East German students, and planes searched in the hunt for her, Beck was getting through the various Soviet checkpoints and closer to the border.

Her luck nearly ran out when the four armed men who were going to take her into Pakistan ran into another group who realized that Beck was a westerner – they didn't care whether she came from the Communist East or capitalist West: she was a white woman, a symbol of what they were fighting. Even though she was wearing the burqa, the way she walked set her apart from ordinary Afghan women. Although they took her across the border, her fate was undecided: one group thought she was a Soviet spy, another wanted to ransom her, while one Mujaheddin leader wanted to marry her. Eventually she was taken by a member of an exiled Afghan family to their house in Peshwar – and from there, she was finally able to head to the airport to board a plane to Frankfurt in West Germany.

An attempt by a thirty-seven-year-old to escape using a home-made motorized glider on 20 December 1986 came to nothing when he lost his bearings and ended up exactly where he started from, near Potsdam. He might have got away with it if various residents who saw his flight hadn't reported him to the authorities.

A flight by a light plane, piloted by an eighteen-year-old on only his second solo sortie, was rather more successful on 15 July 1987: flying beneath all radar detection, the young man flew to the British military airfield in West Berlin. The British Army kindly returned the plane to the East Germans at the Glienickie Bridge, scene of various handovers during the Cold War period including U-2 pilot Francis Gary Powers and Soviet human rights campaigner Anatoly Sharansky.

The bridge was the setting for two other escape attempts – one failed on 9 December 1987, when two men tried to break into the military lane, and only succeeded in detaching the closed entrance gate from its hinges before skidding into the gatepost. Four months later, on 10 March 1988, Bernd Puhlmann drove a truck with two friends, Gotthard Ihden and

Werner Jäger, on board, at high speed through the steel barriers. Unlike many of their fellow refugees, the three men hadn't spent ages planning their route – they were drinking beer around midnight and decided it was time to go!

Perhaps surprised by the attempt, which would turn out to be the first successful breaching of the border at this point in the twenty-seven-year history of the Wall to date, the border guards didn't fire – although Puhlmann suspected that the propane tanks on the back of the 7.5 ton truck were a good deterrent as well (they were actually empty). The flatbed truck destroyed the two metal gates on the East German side, as well as a chain-link fence before coming to rest in West Berlin, taking off another steel gate in the process. The three men were not injured, but the truck was a write-off. The West German authorities considered prosecuting the men for destruction of property and dangerous driving!

Families were split by the Berlin Wall, in the first instance in 1961 by the erection of the barrier itself. If you were in the West when it went up, there you stayed, and vice versa. The numerous escape attempts meant that generations could be divided: youngsters were often more daring, and participated in the various schemes, while their parents remained behind, often suffering as a direct result of their children's activities. One particular family was determined to be reunited on the Western side of the Wall, although it would take fourteen years for all three of the Bethke brothers to achieve that.

"Life in freedom is impossible without risk," Holger Bethke told *Popular Mechanics* magazine after his daring flight from Berlin in 1983. He was the second of the three to escape: his brother Ingo had preceded him eight years before. Ingo had been drafted into the army, and was posted along the border between East and West Germany, near the river Elba, an area regularly patrolled by border guards. The fast-moving current was usually sufficient deterrent to those wishing to cross, even without the death strip containing mines, barbed wire and trip-wires leading to automatic weapons that fired pellets at anyone caught within range.

Four months after returning to Berlin, and now working as a street sweeper, the twenty-one-year-old Ingo rented a car and on 26 May 1975, he drove back to the location he had chosen to cross with a trusted friend. The two men edged forward, using a small paddle to pat the ground in the minefield, in case Ingo's memory of where the mines were laid failed him. The theory was that if the paddle caused a mine to explode, they might be captured, but at least they wouldn't get all or, worse, part of their legs blown off. All went well, and they weren't spotted by the guards. Reaching the bank of the Elba, they inflated mattresses, and floated out on them into the water. It was pitch black, and the two men paddled as quietly as they could across the 150-metre-wide river towards the Western bank.

When they pulled themselves on shore, they were surprised to find a West German border patrol van. According to Ingo, when he tapped on the van window, one of the officers told him it was a cold night to go swimming; Ingo disagreed. "Not when you're swimming out of the East."

Ingo's escape had repercussions for his family. His parents had both been high-ranking officials within the East German administration, and were forced to quit their jobs. The youngest of the three brothers, Holger, was constantly followed by the Stasi, putting him under intolerable pressure. However, he too outwitted the border patrols and the secret police.

By 1983, the fourth generation of the Berlin Wall was in full operation, complete with death strip, lights, automatic weapons, beds of nails, brushed sand which would show up footprints, and tripwires. Trying to cross it was regarded as little short of suicide, even though there were some who still tried. If he couldn't go through it, and he couldn't go under it because of the vibration sensors and the tunnels that the border patrols themselves had created, Holger would have to go over it.

The plan was the brainchild of a friend of Holger's, Michael Becker, a plumbing and heating fitter, who first tried to escape during a holiday in Hungary in 1979. He made it across several barriers that partitioned Hungary from Austria, and had only one ten-feet-high fence left to climb when he was spotted by a border guard, arrested, and sentenced to twenty months' imprisonment. On his release, he was even more resolved to get away, and took inspiration from a West German magazine article about earlier escapes – which included details of the Holzapfel family's zipwire run from the top of the House of Ministries back in 1965. What worked once could work again, albeit in a revised form.

When Becker approached Holger with the idea in November 1982, the youngest Bethke was delighted, even if Becker only gave his plan an eighty per cent chance of success. The odds were improved when Holger brought Ingo in on the scheme using letters with fake return addresses, cryptic telephone calls and messages via third parties. (In the account given to *Popular Mechanics* shortly after Holger and Becker reached the West, Ingo's identity was kept secret, presumably for fear of further reprisals against his parents and other brother.)

Becker made some wooden rollers, supposedly for a cart for his father's garden, and obtained 297 feet of quarter-inch steel cable from a friend who worked at a crane-making factory. He and Holger scouted out a suitable location, choosing a house on the corner of Schmollerstrasse and Bouchestrasse. Its top floor was a storey higher than the building opposite it on the Western side, and in all their visits, neither man saw a border guard near (after their escape, a new watchtower was built at the spot!). Practising their manoeuvre in a local park, Holger and Becker pretended they were training for the circus.

They needed to get the cable over the wall to the far side, where Ingo would be waiting, which meant learning how to shoot a bow and arrow. But by 30 March 1983, the two men were ready to make their getaway. Dressed as electricians, they lugged their equipment to the top floor of the house, and waited for darkness.

At 3 a.m. on 31 March, they made contact with Ingo via walkie-talkie, and then shot the arrow across to the West. The guard in the nearest watchtower seemed to be asleep, and didn't stir, even when the arrow fell short and landed in a tree. The second arrow landed on a flat roof. The third missed the target but landed in the courtyard of the building where Ingo was waiting, although it took him an hour to find it, lodged in a tall bush. Ingo attached his end of the line to his BMW, to provide maximum tension, after the other two wrapped theirs around the chimney. Even though the chimney started to buckle under the strain, no one was alerted – not even the little old lady (a genuine small elderly person!) in the apartment beneath them. Holger went first, but ended up two yards from their target balcony. He therefore swung his legs up onto the cable, and shimmied down. Becker followed and the two men were safely in the West.

That left just Egbert, the middle brother, in the East, and unsurprisingly the Stasi made his life hell after Holger's escape. They watched his every move, and ransacked his apartment. At one stage, they tried to entice him with a free ticket to the West, but he maintained his love for the GDR, knowing it was a trap. In Cologne, Ingo and Holger ran a bar called the Al Capone, and tried to think of ways of reuniting with their brother.

The answer came courtesy of *Playboy* magazine. Membership cards from Hugh Hefner's club had once upon a time been able to fool the guards, and now a feature on a baby helicopter within the magazine's pages inspired Ingo. When he went to an air fair in Hanover to examine it, he discovered it was only a prototype, but a chance conversation with two French pilots alerted him to the existence of "ultralights" – miniature planes, of the type used at the start of the James Bond film *Octopussy* to enable 007 to escape from danger. Five metres long, with a ten-metre wingspan, they could seat two people and fly at around eighty miles per hour.

Ingo and Holger not only had to buy the planes, but learn to fly them as well. After numerous scrapes – including losing three propellers, burning out engines and even breaking a wing – they eventually felt confident that they could pull off their plan: fly over the Wall into East Berlin, swoop down and collect Egbert, and then fly back to the West.

On 25 May 1989, they were ready to go. Egbert had established a pattern of jogging in Treptower Park early each morning, so when he received the coded message from his brothers, he was equally prepared. Now veterans at evading the border guards, the brothers had chosen their time carefully: they knew that the guards were forbidden from firing at aerial targets without permission, and at 4 a.m., the odds of a guard gaining that permission from his battalion commander (who would probably have to refer it up the chain of command anyway) and firing at them in the few seconds that they would be noticeable were negligible. They didn't take chances though: in what was probably the cleverest part of their plan, they affixed huge red stars to the underside of the planes' wings. Even if a guard was suspicious, he would think twice, if not considerably more times, before risking using his initiative and firing on a Soviet plane.

Flying over the Wall from a sports park in the West, Ingo and Holger piloted their planes to Treptower Park, where Egbert was waiting. Ingo came in to land; Holger stayed at altitude, watching for any signs of the guards. Egbert raced to the plane, and Ingo took off again, following his brother over the Wall. As they had hoped, the red stars were sufficient precaution to avoid an attack, and once they were safely in the West, they brought the planes in to land on what was at that time a field outside the Reichstag building, which had previously served as the seat of government for the united Germany. Abandoning the planes, they had a rapturous reunion.

The Bethke brothers admitted that had they known the Wall would be coming down within six months, they would probably have still gone ahead with the rescue, but there was no way that anyone could have foreseen the speed at which Communism collapsed. Across the summer of 1989, the Iron Curtain that had separated Communist Europe from the West since 1947 started to unravel, and on 9 November 1989, East Germans were given permission to travel to the West unconditionally. It wasn't what the East German government had meant to do, but once the announcement was mistakenly made, it proved impossible to stem the tide.

The honour of being the last known escaper via Checkpoint Charlie went to Hans-Peter Spitzner. The teacher's wife Ingrid had been granted permission to visit relatives in Austria, and Spitzner was determined to follow her with their seven-year-old daughter Peggy. Relying on the rule that military personnel's vehicles were not searched when they went through the border, Spitzner tried to find an American soldier who would help him and Peggy. For two days, his search was fruitless but on 18 August 1989, just as he was on the point of giving up, a young serviceman, Eric Yaw, agreed to assist.

Persuading Peggy that this was just an adventure on their way to see her mother, Spitzner and his daughter squeezed into the boot of Yaw's Toyota Camry. After an agonising half hour, during which the car was stopped at Checkpoint Charlie, the boot was opened and they were in the West. Although the border patrol used infra-red cameras to check for escapers – at one stage they had even used X-rays without thought of the consequences to those exposed to them – Spitzner believed that the car's black paintwork, already hot in the August sunshine, masked their presence. All that remained was to stop Ingrid from returning to the GDR, and a hastily dictated note to the receptionist at her hotel ensured that the family was reunited.

Official figures suggest that there were at least 5,075 successful escape attempts from Berlin during the twenty-eight years that the Wall stood. No one knows how many plans were foiled by the Stasi. At least 136 people died trying to flee from the GDR. The watchtowers and the death strips may have been dismantled, and some of those who committed state-sponsored murder found guilty, but there are still many in the city who remember the time when escaping was worth anything – even losing your life.

Fact vs. Fiction

Disney's *Night Crossing* is one of the few English-language fact-based films about escaping from East Germany. It takes some liberties with the facts (the Stasi were nowhere near as close on the families' heels as the movie indicates) but the story itself was dramatic enough that it didn't need much spicing up. The 2001 German film *Der Tunnel* is based on the creation of Tunnel 29; the 1963 West German film *Durchbruch Lok 234* takes the 1961 train breakthrough as its source.

Spy thrillers of the 1960s used the Wall as a backdrop: the end of John Le Carre's *The Spy Who Came In From the Cold*, both the original novel and its film version starring Richard Burton, sees Alec Leamas choose not to complete his escape from East Berlin. *Funeral in Berlin*, the second movie featuring Michael Caine as British agent Harry Palmer (unnamed in Len

Deighton's original book) is centred on an escape attempt; the 1972 TV series *Jason King* deliberately used a similar plot in the episode "A Page Before Dying" by Tony Williamson.

Sources:

Beck, Kristin: *Verschleierte Flucht: Mein Weg in die Freiheit* (Ullstein Taschenbuchvlg, 2006)

Berlin Film Unit documentary: *The Wall* (Berlin Film Unit, 1962: http://www.youtube.com/watch?v=nch5MbnvTqY)

Der Spiegel, 28 March 1962: "DER DRITTE MANN WARTETE IM GRAB"

Des Moines Register, 12 September 1966: "5 Bulldoze Way Into West Under Hail of Red Bullets"

Funder, Anna: *Stasiland: Stories From Behind the Berlin Wall* (Granta, 2003)

Hertle, Hans-Herman: *The Berlin Wall Story* (Christoph Links, 2011)

http://www.ballonflucht.de/html/englisch.html: Günter Wetzel's own account (translated by Gary Holland) of their flight. Note, where this contradicts other accounts, this has been followed.

National Geographic documentary: *The Berlin Wall: Escape to Freedom* (Michael Hoff Productions, 2006)

Palm Beach Daily News, 8 December 1961: "Sensational Escape Story Told by Harry Deterling"

Salt Lake Tribune, 15 September 1964: "Sharp US Note Protests Gunfire at Berlin Wall"

Taylor, Frederick: *The Berlin Wall: 13 August 1961-9 November 1989* (Bloomsbury, 2009)

The Florence Times, 30 January 1963: "Trapeze Artist Makes Slide to Freedom" from an AP report

The Milwaukee Journal, 24 November 1969: "German Escapees Devise New Tricks"

AP News: 10 March 1988: "Three East Germans in Truck Smash Border Barriers at 'Bridge of Spies'"

Popular Mechanics, November 1983: "Daring High-Wire Ride to Freedom"

PART IV: GETTING OFF THE ISLAND

PART III: THREATS TO THE ISLAND

The Hour of Need

In the twentieth and twenty-first centuries, daring prison breaks have inspired films and television series. But escapes from imprisonment have always been a muse for writers, painters and poets, and the bid for freedom by Mary Queen of Scots from Lochleven Castle in the Scottish Highlands has been a fruitful source for many across the years. Eighteenth-century poet Robert Allan evokes the dangerous conditions on the loch in his poem "Put Off, And Row Wi' Speed" (also known more prosaically as "Queen Mary's Escape from Loch Leven"):

> Put off, put off, and row with speed,
> For now's the time, and the hour of need!
> To oars, to oars, and trim the bark,
> Nor Scotland's queen be a warder's mark!
> Yon light that plays round the castle's moat
> Is only the warder's random shot!
>
> Put off, put off, and row with speed,
> For now is the time, and the hour of need!
> Those pond'rous keys shall the kelpies keep,
> And lodge in their caverns dark and deep;
> Nor shall Lochleven's towers or hall,
> Hold thee, our lovely lady, in thrall;
> Or be the haunt of traitors, sold,
> While Scotland has hands and hearts so bold;
> Then, steersmen, steersmen, on with speed,
> For now is the time, and the hour of need!
>
> Hark! the alarum-bell hath rung,
> And the warder's voice hath treason sung;

The echoes to the falconet's roar,
Chime swiftly to the dashing oar.
Let town, and hall, and battlements gleam,
We steer by the light of the tapers' beam;
For Scotland and Mary, on with speed,
Now, now is the time, and the hour of need!

In June 1567, Mary Queen of Scots was imprisoned in Lochleven Castle, which dominated a small island in the centre of the twelve-mile-wide Loch Leven. She was taken there, supposedly for her own safety, following an encounter at Carberry Hill in which her forces deserted her, and managed to escape ten months later – although her freedom would be short-lived.

Mary had become queen when aged only six days old, and her reign had seen considerable infighting among the nobles of Scotland. Brought up in France while regents ruled in her place in Scotland, her first marriage was to Francis, Dauphin of France, and for a brief time, she was French Queen until Francis' death in December 1560. She returned to Scotland, and eventually married Lord Darnley, but it was a difficult union. He was killed in February 1567, and his house destroyed; the man many thought responsible for it (although he was acquitted) was the Earl of Bothwell, who Mary married in May 1567.

Neither of Mary's marriages had gone down well with the Scottish nobility, or indeed with the English Queen Elizabeth. Darnley's Catholicism meant that Mary's half-brother, Earl of Moray, joined with other Protestant lords openly rebelling against her. The marriage to Bothwell amazed many who couldn't believe that Mary had wed the man who may well have been responsible for the death of her child's father. Eventually twenty-six peers, known as the confederate lords, raised an army against Bothwell and Mary; a meeting at Carberry Hill on 15 June became one-sided, as Mary's troops deserted her during the discussions. Bothwell was allowed safe passage from Carberry, and vanished to Scandinavia, hoping to raise an army to save Mary. However, he was imprisoned in Denmark, and held in jail for ten years, during which time he gradually went insane. He died in 1578.

Mary was taken to Edinburgh, and was horrified by the reaction of the crowd: they branded her a whore and called for her to be drowned. She was imprisoned at the lord provost's house at Craigmillar and tried to call to the crowds through the windows. That worried her jailers, who thought she might be able to swing them round to support her, so without even letting her finish the first meal she had eaten since the abortive battle at Carberry Hill (she had been worried about being poisoned while at Craigmillar), she was taken out for the journey to Lochleven, fifty or so miles north of the city.

Just over a month after Mary arrived at Lochleven, in the care of Sir William Douglas, the Earl of Moray's half-brother, she miscarried twins, and shortly after that she was forced to abdicate the crown of Scotland in favour of her son, James VI – with the Earl of Moray placed as regent. James was crowned on 29 July, but, even as she regained her health following the miscarriage, Mary was resolute that her story was not yet over.

She still had some supporters, not least Queen Elizabeth of England, who was keen to ensure that Mary wasn't executed in case it gave any of her own opponents bright ideas about the way to handle arguments with the reigning monarch. Sir Nicholas Throckmorton, who had been sent in a vain attempt by Elizabeth to prevent Mary from marrying Darnley in 1565, was now dispatched from the English court to try to help, although he was unable to secure Mary's release – it didn't help that Mary refused to turn her back on Bothwell. Throckmorton was recalled to England before he could provide any more practical assistance, although he believed that his presence had been enough to stop the Scots from dealing with Mary in a more permanent way.

During the autumn of 1567, Mary considered various avenues of escape. Two young men – George Douglas, the younger brother of her keeper, and teenager Willie Douglas, believed to be his orphaned cousin – fell under her spell, and passed on messages to the mainland for her supporters. Assorted plots were dreamed up, including smuggling Mary out in a box, but before any of these could be put into effect, winter fell, and any idea of escaping across the loch became impossible.

Mammoth Book of Prison Breaks

Mary's first serious escape attempt came in late March 1568. She disguised herself as one of the washerwomen who came over from the mainland to work at the castle. Wrapping a muffler around her face, she came close to succeeding, but the boatman rowing her back became suspicious, and went to pull the muffler down. Mary put a hand up to stop him, and the boatman realized her fingers were "fair and white", hardly those of someone whose hands were submerged in water all day. He turned the boat round and took the queen back to her imprisonment. Some reports suggest that as much for his own safety as hers, he said nothing about it, but George was banished from the island around this time, and continued coming up with schemes.

Matters weren't helped by an odd wager laid by Sir Archibald Napier, Laird of Merchiston that "by the fifth of May Her Majesty would be out of Lochleven". This made William Douglas all the more suspicious, and the guard around Mary was increased. This didn't curtail her freedom more than it already was – she was allowed out on boating expeditions on the loch, for example, during which her servants pretended that she had been able to flee – but meant that any escape activity would have to be very clandestine.

Queen Mary's trusted maid Mary Seton became one of the cornerstones of the eventual plan that was laid. She was to remain behind at Lochleven, posing as her mistress for the short period that might prevent a hue and cry from being launched too precipitously. Her father, Lord Seton, was one of Mary's staunchest allies, and worked with George Douglas on the plan. Mary would write her instructions on a handkerchief using a piece of charcoal, since she was prevented from using pen and paper, and young Willie would take these with him over to the mainland to pass to George and Lord Seton.

Although further ideas were considered – including a suggestion that the queen could perhaps go to a part of the perimeter wall that wasn't as well watched, climb over it, and drop the seven feet to the far side, which was abandoned when a maidservant badly sprained her foot trying it out – in the end, it was decided that Mary would simply walk out through the main gate. Willie therefore suggested that for the Mayday weekend, he should act as the Abbot of Unreason (a figure more usually associated with the Christmas revelries, rather than May), which gave him licence to behave in an apparently drunken and mad manner. Under cover of this, on Sunday 2 May 1568, he was able to damage all bar one of the boats on the island. William Douglas found this suspicious, but there were no obvious other signs that his charge was trying to escape. At the same time, George Douglas, Lord Seton and friends were waiting on the far side of the loch, their horses saddled up, ready to whisk Mary off to safety; William Douglas apparently noticed their presence but didn't connect it to Willie's actions.

To further allay Douglas's suspicions, Queen Mary pretended to feel faint, and went back to her room. Once there, she changed clothes with her servant, and waited for Willie's signal. William Douglas usually kept the castle keys safely with him, but in his apparently drunken state, Willie was able to cover them with a handkerchief and purloin them. As soon as he had them, he went out to the courtyard, and signalled to Mary. She descended, along with another of her servants, and Willie used the keys to let them out of the main gate, then locked the gate behind them and threw the keys in the loch, where they were found centuries later when the loch was drained.

The journey across the loch was unremarkable, although it was clear that some of the washerwomen had recognized Mary as she departed from the island, and Mary was greeted with elation by George Douglas, Lord Seton and a party of fifty men. They sped south on horseback to North Queen's Ferry, crossed the Firth of Forth on the ferry, and landed at South Queen's Ferry before heading to Lord Seton's home at West Niddry. It was a brief respite of freedom before Mary's further imprisonment began. After she raised an army of around 6,000 men, the forty-five-minute long Battle of Langside followed on 13 May, which culminated in Mary's defeat. She rode to seek refuge in England, and was taken into protective custody. She never regained her liberty: she became the figurehead in numerous plots, and eventually was convicted of treason. Mary was beheaded at Fotheringay Castle on 8 February 1587.

During her exile and restrained liberty in England, she didn't forget those who had helped her escape from Lochleven Castle. She provided money so that George Douglas could marry a

French heiress who had taken his fancy; "services like his ought never to be forgotten", Mary wrote to his uncle. Willie Douglas stayed in her service until the very end, and was remembered in her will. The Seton family enjoyed favour under Mary's son, James VI, when he became James I of England under the Act of Union following the death of Queen Elizabeth.

Sources:

www.marie-stuart.com "Lochleven Castle & Mary, Queen of Scots"

Harper's Monthly, December 1850: "The Escape Of Queen Mary From Lochleven Castle"

Fraser, Antonia: *Mary Queen of Scots* (Weidenfeld and Nicolson, rev. 2009)

Escaping the Gentlest Jail

In 1814, many of the allies in the sixth coalition believed that the greatest threat to peace in Europe was finally under lock and key – or at the very least, on an island where he could cause no more trouble. The man himself, Napoleon Bonaparte, said, "I do not think of anything beyond my little island. I could have sustained the war for twenty years if I had wished it. I exist no longer for the world. I am a dead man. I am occupied in nothing but my family and my retreat, my house, my cows, and my mules."

He was lying. On 26 February 1815, the French Emperor escaped from the island of Elba and travelled back to France. For the next hundred days, he proved that he had lost none of his ambition, until his forces were routed at the battle of Waterloo, and he was sent into an exile from which there was no escape.

The Corsican general had risen to prominence during the French Revolution, becoming First Consul in 1799, and crowning himself Emperor on 2 December 1804. The tide turned against him after his attempted invasion of Russia in 1812, and by spring 1814, his army was massively reduced in size, and the coalition forces had even taken control of Paris. When he decided to march on the capital, his marshals confronted him, and Napoleon realized he had lost control. He tried to abdicate in favour of his son but the allies would not accept this, so on 11 April 1814, he declared that since he was apparently the "sole obstacle to the restoration of peace in Europe . . . he renounces, for himself and his heirs, the thrones of France and Italy, and that there is no personal sacrifice, even that of his life, which he is not ready to do in the interests of France." In return, under the Treaty of Fontainebleu, he was given "free possession and the peaceable enjoyment in full sovereignty of the island of Elba, and of the Duchies of Parma, Placentia, and Guastalla". It might sound like a generous assignment of territory. It wasn't: it was just creating a jail cell on a rather larger scale than the usual six foot by six foot garret commonly given to prisoners.

And like many prisoners sentenced to life imprisonment – because regardless of whether he was allowed to keep his title of emperor, or receive a hefty pension as laid down in the treaty, that's what this was – Napoleon considered ending it all rather than endure many years' confinement. He tried to commit suicide using a pill that he had kept with him since the retreat from Moscow two years earlier, but it had lost its efficacy.

Napoleon knew that he would come to be regarded as a museum curiosity – "let them stare, then they can go home and amuse the gentlemen by distorting my words and gestures" he wrote – but he was charm personified to those who visited him. He flattered the captain of HMS *Undaunted*, the ship that transported him to Elba, to the extent that within a month of embarkation, Captain Ussher was accepting gifts of wine and a diamond-encrusted snuffbox from the emperor. A throne was prepared for him on board another vessel, HMS *Curagao*, on 4 June, and it seemed that any Englishman or woman who visited Napoleon came away with a heightened regard for the man.

The emperor then tried to convince himself that life on Elba represented a temporary exile and that before the end of 1814, the sovereigns of Europe would need to call upon him. However, he learned from a magazine forwarded by Lady Holland that plans were afoot to exile him much further away – to St Helena, an island in the South Atlantic, from where it would be nigh on impossible to escape, or to answer the call if the French people or army demanded his return. He considered taking the offers made by some of his English visitors of asylum in Great Britain, assured that the enmity that had been directed at him previously had dwindled now the two countries weren't at war.

But returning to France seemed like a much better prospect. Napoleon had to keep the British commissioner on the island, Sir Nicholas Campbell, from suspecting anything. Campbell had been instructed by the British Foreign Secretary, Lord

Castlereagh, to give "every proper respect and attention" to Napoleon, and at the end of 1814, he noted in his diary, "It is universally supposed in Italy, and publicly stated, that Great Britain is responsible to the other Powers for the detention of Napoleon's person, and that I am the executive agent for this purpose. Napoleon believes this."

Napoleon was quite happy for Campbell to believe this, and didn't demur when the British Commissioner spent time with his mistress in Florence when he began to bore of the post. Indeed, Campbell spent the ten days away from Elba before Napoleon absconded from the island, despite being asked by His Majesty's Minister in Florence, Lord Burghersh, to return to his duties.

During the nine months leading up to his escape, Napoleon had spent time developing the iron mines on the island, while keeping an eye on political developments in Europe at the Congress of Vienna, which was sorting out the shape of countries in the aftermath of the Napoleonic Wars. At the start of February 1815, he judged that it was time to stop concentrating on the smaller-scale issues, and to return to the larger stage. There was obvious dissatisfaction with the restored Bourbon monarchy in France, and Napoleon felt that he would be by far the better ruler. He also heard that a plot was under way in France to overthrow Louis XVIII.

On 13 February, Napoleon ordered his brig, the *Inconstant*, to be painted like an English vessel, and three days later was delighted to hear that Campbell was heading to Tuscany for a break taking the main Royal Navy ship, HMS *Partridge*. Captain Adye unwisely told one of Napoleon's men that he was going back for Campbell ten days later, making that the ideal day for Napoleon to make his move.

On the evening of 26 February, with Adye out of the way, Napoleon set sail from Portoferraio on board the *Inconstant*, accompanied by five smaller vessels carrying a large contingent of his volunteer troops. Their progress was very slight for much of the next day, as the winds fell – although equally that meant that Campbell's return was delayed. On the 28th, Campbell discovered that Napoleon had fled; a day later, the emperor and his 600-strong army was back on French soil.

On the afternoon of the 27th, the winds had started to pick up again, and the *Inconstant* was hailed by the *Zephyr*, a ship from the French Navy, representing the restored Bourbon monarchy. Its master, Captain Andrieux, asked after the emperor, to be told he was marvellously well. (Tradition has it that Napoleon dictated this response.) Andrieux asked no further questions, and allowed the *Inconstant* to pass.

Perhaps not surprisingly, questions were asked about the ease with which Napoleon was able to set sail. French minister Tall-eyrand said there was a "negligence [the English] will be hard put to explain", while there were plenty of rumours that Napoleon had been allowed to escape so he could be recaptured and dealt with more severely. It was pointed out that Elba was hardly a suitable place to keep a man who, in Admiral Sir Sydney Smith's words, "has marched from one end of Europe to the other", and there were some who considered that Napoleon had only agreed to be exiled there because he knew it would be so easy to return to France.

Whether Napoleon planned his escape earlier than the start of February is unlikely ever to be known for sure; what he certainly didn't anticipate was the speed with which his return to France would be routed. Although he started to put in place reforms that would alter the constitution of the empire, he immediately had to face a fresh coalition of allies ranged against him. Following the Battle of Waterloo on 18 June 1815, Napoleon abdicated for a second time, and on 15 July, after considering trying to escape to the United States, the defeated emperor formally requested political asylum from the British.

Napoleon was exiled to St Helena, and lived there for the last six years of his life. Although there were numerous plots to rescue him – one involving a primitive version of a submarine – none ever came to fruition. In addition to the difficulties anyone would face trying to retrieve him caused by the island's remote location, St Helena also received an extra garrison of troops, and a naval squadron patrolled the nearby waters. Napoleon died in 1821, and his remains were eventually returned to France in 1840.

Sources:

Brown University Library Center for Digital Scholarship: "Time-line: The Congress of Vienna, the Hundred Days, and Napoleon's Exile on St. Helena"

History Today, Vol 44. #2, February 1994: "A Sympathetic Ear: Napoleon, Elba and the British"

Gates, David: *The Napoleonic Wars, 1803–1815* (Pimlico, 2003)

McLynn, Frank: *Napoleon* (Pimlico, 1998)

The Real Papillons

"Devil's Island penal colony is one of the world's sore spots, and it breeds more social pestilence than one can imagine. The aftermath of imprisonment is sometimes worse than continued confinement or death." That was the headline story in the *Virgin Islands Daily News* in October 1937 when Captain Raymond Vaude and three other fugitives from Devil's Island arrived on the island of St Thomas, and it made clear that although they would be treated for injuries after their homemade canoe hit a reef, "these convicts will not be permitted to remain longer than Tuesday". Even though Vaude told reporters that "we know not what to do next", they were forced to leave. Unless escapers from possibly the worst prison in the world managed to reach Venezuela, chances were that all their efforts would be for nothing – but, as they told officials, "they preferred the perils of another ocean voyage in an open boat rather than return to the convict settlement".

Technically, Devil's Island refers only to the actual Île du Diable, the smallest island at the north of the Îles de Salut (the Islands of Salvation), where the political prisoners, such as Captain Alfred Dreyfus, were kept, but the name has become used in English to signify the entire prison area in French Guyana. The prisoners themselves had a very different name for it: *la guillotine sèche* – the dry guillotine.

Although it was promoted as the true story of a daring escape from the clutches of the terrible regime on Devil's Island, the events described in Henri Charriere's book *Papillon* – and even more so, the subsequent movie – were highly unlikely to be true. One Devil's Island survivor, who died in 2007, lived through events that were very similar to those that Charriere claims were his own experiences, and there is even some doubt as to whether

Charriere was even sent to the Îles de Salut at all, or whether he was kept in one of the mainland camps in French Guyana. There is no question, though, that the horrendous world that Charriere describes in the book is true to life, and it paints a picture of a prison unlike any other. (Charriere responded to criticisms of his book's veracity, from other prisoners as well as guards, by saying that he didn't "go into that hell with a typewriter".)

Devil's Island was established by Louis Napoleon, himself an escaped prisoner (as related in chapter 52), in 1852, to get rid of those who had opposed his coup d'etat the previous year, as well as common criminals who the French didn't want polluting their society. The prisoners were transported by ship from Marseilles to the prison, at the tip of South America, in France's only colony on the continent. Those that survived the journey faced dreadful hardship in the prison, where they were constantly watched. Escape was feasible – if you could get to the mainland, and travel north through the jungle to Dutch Guyana, or somehow create a craft that would survive the rough seas and the sharks that patrolled the waters to reach Venezuela, or go even further north to Cartagena or other ports on the northern shores of Colombia. Escape attempts were punished severely. Solitary confinement, on the Île du Joseph, left men craving death.

Alfred Dreyfus, the French Army captain who was framed for treason and espionage by anti-Semitic colleagues, was kept on the actual Devil's Island, and even though there was no possibility of escape, was kept in almost total isolation. When a rumour arose that he had tried to flee, he was strapped to his bed each night, unable to protect himself from the vampire bats that attacked him. The publicity over Dreyfus's case, which included an impassioned plea by writer Emile Zola headlined "J'Accuse" published on the front page of Paris newspaper *L'Aurore*, brought details of conditions in the prison to the public's attention, but people really didn't want to know.

Not long after Captain Dreyfus was returned to France for a fresh trial, pardoned and eventually exonerated, anarchist Clement Duval managed to escape, one of the first recorded successes. Born in 1850, Duval had served in the Franco–Prussian War of 1870–71, but then succumbed to smallpox, which left him unable to work. He was convicted of theft and served a year in prison, before joining anarchist group The Panther of Batignolles. During the course of another burglary in 1886, he set fire to the house, and the following year he was sentenced to transportation for life, and because he was an anarchist, his sentence was to be served on Devil's Island itself.

Duval tried to escape from the island on more than twenty different occasions, building rafts that were found, or trying to stow away on the ships that called at the islands, but each time he was caught, and sent for punishment. Although he didn't realize it at the time, Duval was lucky during one of these: other anarchists on the island began a revolt on 21 October 1895, and instead of simply quelling the disturbance, the authorities decided to use the opportunity to rid themselves of the nuisance of the anarchists. The guards were allowed to get as drunk as they wanted, and then were let loose on the prisoners. At the end of the massacre that followed, eleven of the key anarchists were dead, and their bullet-riddled bodies were simply thrown into the sea for the sharks to devour.

Six years after the abortive revolt, on the night of 13 April 1901, Duval and eight others successfully managed to steer a flimsy canoe they had built away from the island. Their absence wasn't spotted until the next day, by which time they had rowed a considerable distance and after surviving a horrendous storm, during which they nearly capsized, they reached the port of Paramaraibo, in Dutch Guyana, the next day. Aware that the French could request their extradition, they adopted false names. Duval made his way to New York, where he later wrote a rather self-serving book about his time as an anarchist in the penal colony.

By the early 1930s, escapes from the colony weren't that infrequent. In 1928 the Marseilles poisoner Dr Pierre Marie Bougrat and two other criminals managed to get away using a hollowed-out tree trunk that they had secretly obtained from a Chinese merchant. They made their way down the Guyanan coastline, eventually arriving in Venezuela in the middle of an epidemic, which the doctor immediately set to work to deal with. He survived there until his death in 1936.

Regular large-scale escapes in 1931 from the mainland camp led to reports around the world that the French had "definitely" decided to abandon Devil's Island and to find a more secure prison. Two hundred convicts had headed towards Dutch Guyana because they had heard inaccurate rumours that a new railway was being built, and they were desperate for jobs. When they discovered the truth, they surrendered to authorities and were returned to the prison.

According to the *Milwaukee Journal*'s substantial story on the proposed change, the islands themselves were still regarded as pretty much escape-proof ("although escape from the isles is by no means impossible", the paper noted), the metaphorical walls of the mainland prison were porous. "Competent critics have declared it to be doubtful if any other penal settlement in the world presents the same chances for escape and the same high percentage of successful breaks for liberty ... Hundreds have won their way through to the broad Orinoco in the Venezuelan hinterlands and then followed it through to the settlements." Once in Venezuela, they were safe: since there was no extradition treaty with France, many chose to stay there and build new lives.

The prisons weren't closed. The "inescapable pit of hopelessness and despair" was to remain in operation for a further twenty-two years, although it would certainly have shut down earlier had it not been for the outbreak of the Second World War. The catalyst for the government's decision wasn't a sudden change of heart about the way the convicts were being treated, but the public approbation that followed the publication of the book *Dry Guillotine*, by former Devil's Island inmate René Belbenoit.

Before that, during the 1930s, those who did manage to cobble together some form of raft, and head towards the Virgin Islands, received a poor reception, as the reports from the local press indicate. Others, who made it as far as the Dutch territory of Aruba, did rather better, particularly as there were around 1,200 Americans based there with the Lago Oil & Transport Company. One party of escapers reached Aruba in 1934 or thereabouts, providing a snapshot of life on Devil's Island at the time. The captain of the group, Jean Duvernay, had been imprisoned on the Îles du Salut, and was part of a group of ten who had bribed a local fisherman to allow them to use his dugout canoe, "about seven metres long and a metre and a half wide".

They had braved the seas "realizing we might be sacrificing our lives for the sake of the liberty we loved so much". With help from the crew of a British freighter who set them on the right course, they reached Trinidad, where the majority of the party continued on to Colombia – where they were caught and returned to Devil's Island. Duvernay was taken ill so didn't join them, but teamed up with two other groups of escapees, both from the mainland prison colony. They had set out for Haiti, but ended up shipwrecked in Aruba, where the Americans had a whip-round, and bought them a new boat, as well as supplies. The ten men made it to Colombia, where seven of them headed off inland; Duvernay and two others were sent to Baranquila prison until they could show they had a valid way of leaving Colombia. The rest of their fate is not known.

A year or so later, René Belbenoit escaped for the fifth, and final, time from Devil's Island. During the period he was a fugitive, he made contact with Ernie Pyle, a freelance journalist who arranged for his story to be published in the *Los Angeles Times Sunday Magazine* in August 1936. "As this is published," an editorial informed the reader with rather more hyperbole than accuracy, "he is living like an untamed animal in the jungles of Colombia – unless the police have captured him. If they have – it means his end." Sentenced to eight years hard labour in 1921, after committing a burglary following his demob from the army, Belbenoit eventually arrived in Guyana in June 1923. At the start of July, he made his first escape, crossing the River Maroni into Dutch Guyana but was arrested by the authorities there and returned. After a three-month punishment spell, he was sent to work in the jungle – and promptly escaped again with six other convicts, stealing a canoe and paddling frantically to get to Georgetown in British Guyana. The authorities there also sent him back.

Perhaps to his surprise, although he was declared "incorrigible", Belbenoit wasn't immediately sent to the Îles du Salut. Instead, he was put in a punishment camp, where the prisoners had to work naked in the jungle to prevent escape. During that time he got to know an American writer, Blair Niles, who used his story as background for two of her novels. After nine months, Belbenoit planned to leave with Niles and her husband; Niles provided him with money, and he bought a suit, but the Dutch authorities were suspicious of a man walking in ordinary clothes through the jungle. They returned him to the French, who this time took his escape attempts seriously, sending him for a six-month stretch on Devil's Island.

Belbenoit was brought back to the mainland after serving his term, and kept out of trouble for a few months. However, the desire to escape was too deeply ingrained, and he and six others set out for Brazil. This time it was the Brazilian police's turn to send him back. A further six months in Devil's Island followed, at which point Belbenoit decided he might as well serve out his term, and then go back to France. He worked conscientiously as the governor's secretary during this time, and was horrified when he was told that, on completion of his sentence, he was not allowed to go home. He would have to stay in Guyana for the rest of his life – a condition that was imposed on all the French prisoners who were sentenced to seven years or more in the colony.

After some begging, Belbenoit was allowed to spend a year in Panama, on condition that he didn't try to escape, but he did, on board a freighter bound for France. However, on landing at Le Havre, he was arrested, and sent back to Guyana for a further three years, all of which he spent locked up on Devil's Island. On 2 November 1934, he became a "free man" once more.

There was no possibility of Belbenoit accepting that he had to stay in Guyana for the rest of his life, and on 2 May 1935, he and five others set out in a canoe to paddle to Trinidad. They reached there in a pitiful state, after nearly losing their lives on many occasions. The British authorities didn't arrest them, or try to send them back to Guyana – instead, because their canoe was so badly damaged, they provided them with a new lifeboat, with sail, oars, a chart, food, water and a lamp! They planned to head for Florida, but got caught in currents, and ended up in Colombia, where they were arrested and taken to Barranquilla prison. The French ambassador wanted him to be returned to Guyana; the Colombians refused, and, Belbenoit believed, passively assisted him to escape. The others with him, who were still prisoners, rather than freed like Belbenoit, were returned. Belbenoit made his way through Colombia to Panama City, where he met Pyle and told his story.

At this point Belbenoit's story becomes rather puzzling. According to most accounts, Belbenoit travelled from El Salavador to Los Angeles, and with help from Blair Niles, had his account of life on Devil's Island published. He lived on and off for the next twenty years in America – he attracted attention from the immigration authorities, and served a term for false entry, but eventually gained American citizenship. He died in 1959, and received an obituary in the *Los Angeles Times*.

However, an article published in Brazil in 2005 claimed that Belbenoit never went to the US. Instead, another prisoner went in his place, and pretended to be Belbenoit. The real Belbenoit remained in Brazil and invested heavily in gold and diamond mines. He also wrote accounts of his life in prison and afterwards, which found their way into Henri Charriere's hands and became his bestsellers *Papillon* and *Banco*. Charriere was one of the five others who fled from Devil's Island with Belbenoit; according to them, Belbenoit died in 1978. (The inconsistencies in this account with Belbenoit's original version, let alone the story as related in *Dry Guillotine*, make it dubious, although it does provide one explanation for where Charriere derived his material.)

Dry Guillotine, subtitled "Fifteen Years among the Living Dead", caused a storm and went through fourteen printings in its first year in a translated edition. The French government issued a decree in June 1938 preventing any further prisoners from being dispatched. But before too much could be done by the authorities to deal with conditions on Devil's Island, France was overrun by the Nazis. It was during this time that the later events of Henri Charriere's *Papillon* are set.

If Charriere's story is taken at face value, then he was wrongly convicted of the murder of a pimp, and sent to Devil's Island. He quickly escaped, sailing to Trinidad but was then arrested when he reached Colombia. He managed to get away from that prison, and spent time living with an indigenous tribe. Unfortunately, he was recaptured, and despite many attempts to escape from Barranquilla prison, he was returned to French Guyana. He spent years in solitary confinement after various tries to flee from the island, but when the authorities decided to support the quisling Vichy regime after the conquest of France by the Germans, the penalty for escaping became death.

Charriere therefore tried to feign madness, and was sent to the prison asylum, which wasn't as well guarded. A flight by sailboat ended with the death of his fellow fugitive, and the boat smashed against the rocks. Apparently cured of his illness, Charriere asked to be sent to Devil's Island, where he studied the wave pattern, and deduced that every seventh wave could carry a large object out to sea so it could drift to the mainland. He and another prisoner tried this, using coconuts as a make-shift flotation device, and succeeded in reaching land, only for his fellow to succumb to quicksand. Charriere eventually made his way to Venezuela where he found freedom.

The title *Papillon* (butterfly in French) derives from a tattoo that Charriere had; he also had a deformity on his hand. Oddly enough, so did another convict from Devil's Island, who defi-nitely was imprisoned there: Charles Brunier, who had the tattoo of a butterfly on his arm, and an atrophied left finger.

Brunier came to media attention in 2005, aged 104, when there were a number of articles in the French press about him after the then-minister of tourism wanted to see if Brunier recalled the minister's grandfather, who had also been incarcer-ated in Guyana. (He didn't.) He had been sent to Devil's Island in 1923 for an attack on a pimp and the murder of an old woman. Once there, he adopted the name of Johnny King, and tried hard to escape. On one occasion, he reached Venezuela and spent several months there before being recaptured in a manner very similar to Charriere's supposed adventures; after the outbreak of war, he finally made it to the coast of Mexico, and enlisted as a fighter pilot. He fought with the Free French Army in North Africa, but at the end of the war, he was returned to Guyana. On 12 June 1948, he was given a complete pardon "because of his skilled conduct during the course of the hostilities".

After entering the nursing home in 1993, Brunier would often tell staff that Charriere stole his story. "From time to time Monsieur Brunier tells us stories from his life. He certainly served in the 'bagne' with Henri Charriere, and knew him quite well. And he is utterly convinced that Charriere stole the idea for *Papillon* from him," Isabelle Mesureur-Cadenel, the director of his retirement home, said. Brunier died in 2007, the last survivor of Devil's Island.

Charriere was certainly held prisoner in French Guyana, and he escaped from the prison in 1944. But it seems certain that it wasn't by jumping from Devil's Island holding onto a string of coconuts. "Far from being one of the outstanding tough guys in the penal colony, he was a comparatively well-behaved convict, who was contentedly employed for a long time on latrine duty. He never escaped from Devil's Island, and the heroic confrontation with the commander of the camp never occurred," Gerard de Villiers commented in the *New York Review of Books* after carrying out a detailed investigation into Charriere's story, published as *A Butterfly Pinned*.

Whether he conflated many people's stories into one or not, Charriere's *Papillon* and the movie starring Steve McQueen and Dustin Hoffman taken from it, both ensured that the name of Devil's Island will remain remembered for many years to come. The prison itself was finally shut down in 1953 (although some of those who had gone insane lived out the remainder of their lives there), and although most of the Îles de Salut are now a tourist resort, boats don't go to Devil's Island. Those brave few who venture across unanimously report that it feels haunted . . .

Sources:

Duval, Clement with Michael Shreve, Marianne Enckell: *Outrage: An Anarchist Memoir of the Penal Colony* (1929; PMP 2012)

Canberra Times, 7 September 1928: "Prisoner's Escape"

Sabotage Times, 7 September 2012: "Return To Devil's Island: The Toughest Penal Colony Of All Time"

Mail & Guardian, 26 June 2005: "Papillon alive and well in a Paris retirement home"

Le Parisien, 17 December 2005: "The real Papillon"

ISTOE Independent, 17 August 2005: "A verdadeira história de Papillon"

Belbenoit, Rene: *Dry Guillotine* (Blue Ribbon Books, 1938)

Los Angeles Times, 3 March 1959: "Death of a Fighter"

Los Angeles Times, 23 August 1936: "Fugitive from Devil's Island"

Murderpedia: Dr Pierre Marie Bougrat: http://murderpedia.org/male.B/b/bougrat-pierre.htm

Black Flag Quarterly, Vol 7, Number 5 (Winter 1984): "An Anarchist on Devil's Island"

Pittsburgh Press, 17 October 1937: "3 Fugitives Spend 77 Days in Canoe" (note: error in number of escapees)

Virgin Islands Daily News, 18 October 1937: "Four Fugitives from Devil's Island Here"

The Victoria Advocate, 19 October 1937: "Four Devil Island Men Float 77 Days"

Milwaukee Journal, 28 November 1931: "France to Abandon 'Devils (sic) Island' as Prison; Too Many Men Escape"

The Lamp (probably 1934): "Escaped from Devil's Island" (posted at http://www.lago-colony.com/DEVILS_ISLAND_ESCAPE/escape_from_devil.htm with lots of photographs from the time)

Charriere, Henri: *Papillon* (HarperCollins, 1970)

Farewell to the Rock

One of the best-known prisons in the world is Alcatraz, the maximum-security penitentiary that was built on the island of that name in the middle of San Francisco Bay. Its location meant that there were considerable natural forces opposing anyone who wished to flee from its not particularly welcoming shores, and although most people only think of the federal penitentiary featured in the 1996 Sean Connery movie *The Rock*, or the recent short-lived J.J. Abrams TV series *Alcatraz*, there were prisons on, and escape attempts from, the Rock long before Joseph Bowers tried to leave in 1936.

The Rock first became a long-term prison in 1861. There had been a guardhouse on the island as part of the Army outpost that was stationed there but on 27 August 1861, four months after the outbreak of the American Civil War, the Rock became the point for collecting military prisoners on the west coast. Civilians were also incarcerated, although there aren't adequate records of the period to indicate how many. The Rock's usefulness was noted in a report by Colonel De Russy in 1865: "the only locality in this Harbor suitable for such a purpose is Alcatraces (sic) Island, where the guard house and prison are of a good size and well guarded by sentinels, added to that, the difficulty of escape from the Island is rendered extremely difficult on account of its size as well as the formation of the high banks or bluffs which surround it."

That hadn't prevented John D. Wood, of the 2nd Cavalry Volunteers, who was under sentence of death for trying to kill his captain, from getting hold of a small boat and disappearing on 21 June 1862, making him possibly the first person ever to escape from Alcatraz. The first massed escapes from the Rock occurred soon after De Russy's death in 1867 when prisoners from Alcatraz were moved over to work at Fort Point, situated beneath where the Golden Gate Bridge now runs. They took advantage of being on the mainland and scarpered. The remaining prisoners were returned to Alcatraz in early 1868.

Prisoner numbers increased in the early 1870s, necessitating further building work which went on throughout the rest of the nineteenth century. Alcatraz prison had deplorable sanitation, even by contemporary standards, and the hole in the floor in the privy which allowed the sanitary waste to flow into the bay was so large that on one occasion in around 1890, an intoxicated civilian fell through it.

Attempted escapes were frequent, mostly from work details on the mainland, rather than from the Rock itself. In the mid-1870s, deserter James Wright of the Fourth Artillery caused some scandal by taking a fifteen-year-old girl to a hotel bed while on the run after escaping from a work party at Point San Jose. In 1877 nine prisoners escaped from such work parties, and one fled from the post hospital on Angel Island. May 1878 saw two prisoners commandeer a boat, and row to freedom from the Rock itself; similar such escapes are noted in the records in both 1884 and 1890. On these occasions, the guards didn't try to shoot the prisoners, but in 1892, an Alcatraz inmate was shot when trying to escape from a work detail at the Presidio, on the mainland. A further prisoner was killed while trying to flee in 1900.

The coming of the twentieth century saw some ingenuity enter the prisoners' planning. In 1898, some blatant nerve meant that three men were able to escape. Edgar M. Sweeney, H.R. Beale and John Meredith were working as stage managers for a prisoners' concert, and escaped through a door at the back of the stage in the prison chapel (or possibly the library – the newspaper reports vary). They headed for the wharf, and stole a boat under the nose of the sentry on duty. Although they muffled the oars, the sentry heard them, and opened fire. The fifth shot hit one of the prisoners, who dropped to the bottom of the boat and started groaning.

At that point Sweeney called out, "Don't shoot any more. Don't you see we've got no oars?" (and possibly claimed that they were fishermen). The guard stopped firing, and began to explain the situation to his superiors, and while his attention was elsewhere, Sweeney and his comrades started rowing again. By the time that the prison boat set off after them, Sweeney had too much of a head start, and they reached the mainland.

In early April 1906, four prisoners thought that a butter vat might provide suitable transport across the bay, and liberated one from the bakery. Unfortunately, Arthur Armstrong, George W. Davis, Thomas Stinnatt and George W. Brossman had no way of controlling the vat to counter the effects of the wind and the tide, and they soon found themselves back on Alcatraz, and very soon after that, in irons. In February 1907 three men tried the same trick using a dough-kneading trough, but encountered similar problems. They had managed to keep the trough hidden for a month after stealing it from the bakery, while making some oars, but it wasn't seaworthy, and pitched them into the sea when they were only a few feet from the shore.

A deserter from the 5th Cavalry used a log as a flotation device later in 1907 and very nearly made it to shore; unfortunately for August Stilke, just as he approached the Union Street dock on the night of 22 October, he was hit by a ferry steamer. The crew brought him aboard, bringing his escape to a premature end.

One daring prisoner simply forged his own release papers while on the island in 1910. He presented them at the office, and departed the Rock on the San Francisco ferry, never to be heard from again. He was following in the footsteps of Joseph White, John L. Moore, Cornelius Stokes and James Darling, who used forged pardons to escape from the prison in 1903 – in Stokes' case only five days before a genuine pardon was heading his way. The forgeries were probably compiled on Alcatraz, and then mailed to the prison by an accomplice on the outside, a messenger who deserted as soon as he came under suspicion.

Two prisoners, both of whom had been transferred from Fort Leavenworth with a wealth of convictions behind them, tried to escape from the island on 16 November 1912. According to the report in the *San Francisco Call,* Thomas V. Frayne (or Frayney) had been court martialled thirteen times, Michael Mullins five, while between them they had been tried 234 times by executive officers. Although some accounts suggest that they disappeared successfully on a raft, a report in the *Call* on 20 November says that "[w]eakened in flesh and spirit by two deadly foes, hunger and thirst" both men had been recaptured three days later. After somehow getting out of the dungeon beneath the main corridor of the prison, they had hidden under a pile of driftwood, and had been able to file off their heavy ball-and-chains. What they hadn't bargained on was being unable to find food or fresh water, and Mullins was found, covered with slime and nearly famished on 19 November.

Another pair disappeared from a work party on the island into the heavy fog in 1916, and stole a log each from the flotsam washed up on the Rock. One was initially believed to have drowned, but hid in a boathouse hoping to escape later; the other made it to safety on Little Alcatraz Rock, to the north-west of the mainland, but had to call for help from the prison. Two years later, a brace of cheeky inmates who had worked their way up to become trusties, and thus not watched so closely, managed to purloin guard officers' uniforms, probably from the prison laundry, and simply boarded the ferry to the mainland. Their audacity wasn't rewarded with liberty: they were arrested two days later at Modesto.

The same government tug, the *General McDowell*, was used by four conscientious objectors who tried to leave Alcatraz without permission in August 1919: they had managed to get hold of civilian clothing, but two of them were queried by the captain of the ferry, who wondered why they had wet trousers. He also asked for their passes, which they claimed they had been told they wouldn't need. Although Captain Hornsman seemed to accept their explanations, he told the officer of the day on Angel Island that he had suspicious persons on board. All four were found and returned to Alcatraz.

"I believe the men attempted to escape in the belief they could secret (sic) themselves on board with the members of a visiting baseball team which came to the island on Sunday," Colonel Joseph Garrard, the Commandant of the island told the *San Francisco Examiner*. "There is little possibility of men getting away from the island without proper credentials. Everyone coming and going is required to display a pass. Lack of this was responsible for the apprehension of these men."

However, five years later a similar ruse worked for Edward Lay, Basil Mann and Roy Kennison. The trio apparently took overcoats and hats belonging to guests attending a reception on Alcatraz on 8 October 1924, and then simply mingled with them as they returned to San Francisco. There is no record of the men being returned to the island.

Planes assisted with the search for two escapees in 1927, but their plank-paddling exploits were brought to an end by the astute Captain K.V. Anderson of the *Redwood Empire* ferry, who additionally captured himself a $100 reward. Two men clinging to a ladder in 1929 only managed to get a few hundred yards from the Rock before the tides prevented them progressing. A trio of escapees a year later tried to sail across to Berkeley on large planks of wood, after prising the bars off the barber shop window, but they soon realized that their chances were slim, so yelled for help. They were located by the large searchlight on the island and brought back, one of them in a seriously exhausted condition.

The final recorded escape from the military prison took place on 23 June 1930. Jack (or Jasper) Allen simply stripped off, greased his body and dived into the bay, or at least, that was Colonel G. Maury Cralle, the Alcatraz commandant's opinion. Since Allen's corpse was never discovered, he may have been one of the few to make it off alive, but like the 1912 escapees, there was never any trace of him alive either.

According to an editorial in the *San Francisco Chronicle* in 1933, seventeen military prisoners escaped from the island either using boats or by swimming across the bay, and six fled by other means during the Rock's seventy years as a military prison. As a percentage of the total number of prisoners incarcerated there during that time, it wasn't that many, but it alarmed the good people of San Francisco who objected strongly to the Justice Department's plans to house "desperate or irredeemable" types on the Rock.

Their protests were to no avail. Even attempts to prove how easy it was to escape were ignored – including the demonstration by Doris McLeod and Gloria Scigliano that it was perfectly possible to swim from the Rock to the shore safely. Security in the prison was tightened up considerably, with the new inmates confined to a much smaller part of the island than had been used by the military prisoners. Doors were placed across tunnels, new metal window guards were installed, and tool-proof gratings added around ventilation shafts. The Justice Department wanted Alcatraz to be escape-proof. Guards tried to saw through the bars, but could only make an impression on the softer outer metal – the inner core defeated them.

On 19 June 1934, the US Army officially departed from the Rock, leaving thirty-four prisoners behind; on 11 August, the first batch of new civilian prisoners arrived on Alcatraz. Of those fourteen, half had escaped from or been involved in attempts to escape from previous jails; nearly all were described by the Warden as "desperate" and quite a few, it was noted, would be prepared to kill in order to get away. Not one of them is listed in the successful escapes from Alcatraz that followed over the next thirty or so years. According to the Bureau of Prisons report on the first year of operations, "The establishment of this institution not only provided a secure place for the detention of the more difficult type of criminal but has had a good effect upon discipline in our other penitentiaries also. No serious disturbance of any kind has been reported during the year."

It didn't really surprise Alcatraz's warden to learn that there were rumours of escape plans from the Rock right from the start. As he explained to his superiors, prisoners automatically checked their surroundings for weak spots. They came up with plans that would work if only they had a gun, or access to a speedboat or airplane. He refused to allow such rumours to give him the jitters.

The first acknowledged escape attempt from the Federal Penitentiary was carried out by Joseph "Joe" Bowers, who was one of the first prisoners transferred to Alcatraz, aged roughly thirty-seven, in September 1934. His crime: a post office robbery that netted the grand total of sixteen dollars and thirty-eight cents. His sentence: twenty-five years' imprisonment.

Bowers claimed that he had been raised in a travelling circus, and had visited multiple countries acting as an interpreter as he spoke six languages. He had been arrested for transporting stolen vehicles across state lines in 1928, and driving while drunk two years later, before graduating to robbery in 1932. While imprisoned in the Washington state McNeil Island federal penitentiary, he was described as "unpredictable and at high risk resulting from being emotionally unstable". His period at high-security prison Leavenworth was marked by violations of institution rules, a practice he continued when he was transferred to Alcatraz.

Within six months of arriving on the Rock, Joe Bowers tried to commit suicide, cutting his throat by breaking his spectacles and using a piece of glass to inflict a three-inch-long wound. The Alcatraz authorities didn't take the attempt on 7 March 1935 seriously: the prison psychiatrist Edward W. Twitchell observed Bowers and reported to his superiors that "the recent attempts at suicide have been theatrically planned and have resulted in very little damage to him . . . Bower, while an abnormal individual, is not truly insane in my opinion and is pretending a mental disturbance for some purpose."

A year passed, during which time Bowers failed to cope well with the tough regime at Alcatraz. Prisoners were only allowed to communicate with each other on rare occasions, and then usually only to the extent required (such as in the mess). For a man who claimed that he had made his living by speaking to others, it was a torment. In March 1936, he was assigned to the incinerator detail, one of the worst assignments on the Rock, sorting out metals and burning the prison waste. On 26 April 1936 Joe Bowers came to a premature end of his sentence when he was shot down by Junior Custodial Officer E. F. Chandler.

Some inmates thought that Bowers was trying to retrieve a piece of rubbish that had become lodged in the fence. Others said that he was trying to feed a seagull that he had spotted. There is a school of thought that he simply cracked and committed suicide. Whatever his motive, it is certain that at around 11 a.m. that morning, Bowers climbed the wire fence, and refused to listen to warnings from guard Chandler to get down. In his official report the next day, Chandler wrote:

> He ignored my warning and continued to go over. I fired two shots low and waited a few seconds to see the results. He starded (sic) down the far side of the fence and I fired

one more shot, aiming at his legs. Bowers was hanging on the fence with his hands but his feet were pointing down toward the cement ledge. After my third shot I called the Armory and reported the matter. When I returned from 'phoning the body dropped into the bay.

His report was corroborated by another junior guard, Neil S. Morrison, who said that he heard two shots and saw Bowers "bare-footed, with his pants rolled up, climbing up the fence with his back and part of his right side towards me. I ran along the fence toward the incinerator in hopes I could get there in time to stop him if he got stuck on his way over. There was one more shot before I got to the rock crusher ... When I reached there, I saw his body on the rocks through the incinerator grating."

Chandler was certain that Bowers' actions were deliberate. "He knew what he was doing and I couldn't go get him without wings," he told a Coroner's jury panel. Even if he didn't mean to escape, though, Bowers' last moments after being shot in the lungs, were spent sixty feet below the walls of Alcatraz – on the free side.

The first confirmed escape from the island came in December 1937, although its perpetrators, Theodore Cole and Ralph Roe, were never heard from again. Cole was serving a fifty-year term for kidnapping, Roe a ninety-nine-year sentence for armed robbery. The two men answered their names for the 1 p.m. count on 16 December, but had vanished by the next count half an hour later. They were working in the industrial buildings on the north-west side of the island, which posed some security problems for the authorities, since its waterside aspect couldn't be seen by the guards in the watchtowers. The warden had made the Justice Department aware of this problem, but funds hadn't been available to rectify the situation. Somehow Cole and Roe had broken two panes of glass on that side of the mat shop, then jimmied a lock on the wire fence surrounding the building.

There were few places for them to hide, particularly as it was high tide and the caves under the north-west end were flooded, so it was assumed that they must have made a swim for it – choosing a very picturesque way to commit suicide, according to Director of Prisons James V. Bennett. Alcatraz Warden James A. Johnston firmly believed that they tried swimming. As he explained to the *San Francisco Chronicle*, "Serving terms tantamount to life imprisonment, it is my belief they decided to take a desperate chance and that they had no outside aid. I believed they drowned and that their bodies were swept toward the Golden Gate by the strong ebb tide." Despite this, a wave of hysteria flooded San Francisco with eventual sightings of the felons near Petaluma, in Arkansas, Oklahoma, and even South America. The San Francisco police warned the citizens that the two men might well try to carry out further robberies.

However, Johnston's theory is the most likely, and he was backed up by a report from assistant city engineer Floyd C. Whaley, who knew the local tides and eddies. Whaley was sure that it was impossible for the two men to reach the mainland since the tides had been exceptionally high that day. There was a very heavy fog, and it was just possible that a vessel might have been able to come closer to the shore than the usual 200-yard cordon, and pick the men up, but it seems pretty certain that, like Bowers, Cole and Roe achieved their liberty, but paid the ultimate price.

As a result of their breakout, the Public Works administration agreed to finance a new watchtower which would have eyes on the rear of the industries building, which itself was renewed as part of a modernization of the prison.

Five months after Cole and Roe disappeared from the Rock, three prisoners tried their own breakout. One of them, James C. Lucas, already had a claim to fame, after stabbing Chicago gang boss Al Capone in the shower room. He and Rufus Franklin were both serving thirty-year sentences; their accomplice Thomas R. Limerick, a bank robber and kidnapper, was in for life.

The three men were all engaged in the woodworking shop in the industrial building and on the afternoon of 23 May 1938, they decided that they had had enough of the brutal regime in force at Alcatraz. Carrying with them a hammer, some lead weights and pieces of iron, they resolved to escape over the roof. What they had in mind after that never became clear, since they never got as far as the edge of the island. "They probably figured they could seize the prison boat and make their getaway from the island," Warden Johnston suggested to the *San Francisco Chronicle*, but this was never confirmed by any of the men.

In their way on the top floor stood the unarmed senior custodial officer Royal C. Cline, who was quickly despatched by a blow to the head with a hammer, leaving him lying on the ground fatally injured. The three men climbed through a window out onto the roof, but before they could go any further, they were spotted. Franklin had inched around the wall of a raised portion of the roof, but the guard apparently sensed something was wrong, and turning, shot him in the shoulder. Lucas and Limerick tried to throw the pieces of iron at the guard to put him off, but only one piece went through the shatterproof glass in the guard tower, slightly injuring the guard in one leg. Limerick was hit in the head, and Lucas managed to hide behind a wall, but soon realized the futility of his actions and surrendered. Both guard Cline and prisoner Limerick died within twenty-four hours.

Lucas and Franklin were tried for first-degree murder, and received life sentences; their defence that they had been beaten, kicked and pushed around by the prison officers was ignored.

The administration paid the price for not upgrading the bars across the whole prison in January 1939 when a group of five prisoners made their bid for freedom. They had all been involved with a "strike" action in September 1937, and as a result they had been held in the isolation cells. Unfortunately these still had the original soft iron bars from the prison's time under the control of the US military, which were considerably easier to get through than their counterparts in the main prison.

The five men included Arthur "Doc" Barker, a member of the Ma Barker crime family. He had been arrested by FBI Special Agent Melvin Purvis in January 1935 on charges of kidnapping, and sentenced to life imprisonment. After his transfer to Alcatraz, he was assigned to the mat shop, where he quickly took control of the other inmates, and was believed by the authorities to be instrumental in organizing a general strike over prison conditions. According to a fellow prisoner, Alvin

Karpis, though, Barker was "more interested in escape than confrontation. We join the strike to avoid suspicion; if we refuse to strike the officials will ask themselves why and it will make our escape plans more difficult." No matter the extent of his involvement, Barker was sent to the isolation cells in the old military dungeons and realized that here was a perfect place from which to escape.

Barker became embroiled in various other potential escape plans before putting his own into operation: Al Karpis suggested breaking out of the isolation cells, overpowering the guards, stealing their uniforms, heading over to the family compound, where the prison guards' and officers' wives and children lived, and taking the warden and his wife hostage. They would then commandeer a launch that would come to pick up the warden's wife, who they would claim was ill. Barker, not too surprisingly, felt that this was too complex.

Instead, Barker arranged for a crew of five – himself, murderer and kidnapper Dale Stamphill, and robbers Rufus Roy McCain, Henry Young and William Martin – to get themselves placed in isolation for infringing the rules. There they started using hacksaw blades which had been smuggled into the prison to cut through the bars of the cell, evading the metal detectors by keeping the blades near their feet, where the crude metal detectors weren't effective.

Although the cell bars were easy enough to get through, the window bars were of the stronger quality found elsewhere on the Rock. To get through these the men devised a small-pressure jack, which was strong enough to bend the bars back and forth and eventually break the strong core. The breaks were filled with putty and painted with aluminium paint, matching the colour of the bars.

On Friday 13 January 1939, the Barker gang were ready to make their move. They let themselves out of their cells, and spread open the bars of the windows, squeezing through. The heavy morning fog prevented the guards from spotting them as they made their way to the base of a cliff and prepared to swim across the bay. They lashed together pieces of driftwood and lumber and started out, only for McCain to point out that he couldn't swim!

By this time, the alert had been sounded, after the floor officer had spotted their departure on an informal roll call around

3.45 a.m. Patrol boats were launched by the coastguard and the prison guards, and spotlights used to illuminate the coastline. Although the accounts of what happened next are contradictory, it's clear that Doc Barker was hit in the leg and the head, and Stamphill was also injured. Young and McCain were arrested after surrendering immediately the light was turned on them, although McCain had apparently suggested that they run towards the prison officers' houses, because they wouldn't be shot there. Martin was at large for the longest of the fugitives, but after he fell down the cliff at the south end of the island, he surrendered to prison officers. According to Warden Johnston's book about his time on the island, Barker said he had been "a fool to try it" and succumbed to his wounds twelve hours after the escape attempt. A guard commented, "Well, he's a lot better off now where he is than where he was."

As a result of his death, a Coroner's jury was empanelled, and decided that:

> ... the said Arthur R. Barker met his death attempting to escape from Alcatraz Prison by gunshot wounds inflicted by guards unknown.
>
> From the evidence at hand, we the jury, believe that this escape was made possible by the failure of the system for guarding prisoners now in use at Alcatraz Prison, and we recommend a drastic improvement by those in authority.
>
> Further, that a more efficient system be adopted for illumination of shore and waters immediately surrounding the prison; and that the citizens of San Francisco unite in an effort to have a more suitable location chosen for imprisonment of the type of desperadoes at present housed at Alcatraz.

A year later, funds were apportioned so that the isolation block could be modernized. No one else was going to leave Alcatraz from there.

The industrial building was the scene of another attempted escape a couple of years later, shortly after Henry Young was placed on trial for murdering Rufus McCain, whose inability to

swim he probably blamed for the failure of the 1939 escape and
the death of Doc Barker, as well as his unwillingness to use the
wives of guards as shields during the break. Four felons, brothers-
in-law Joseph Paul Cretzer and Arnold T. Kyle, Floyd H. Barkdoll
and Sam R. Shockley took four prison guards, including future
Alcatraz Warder Paul J. Madigan, in the mat shop hostage and
then tried to pull apart the steel bars over the windows.

Warden Johnston described events to the *San Francisco
Examiner* for their 22 May 1941 edition:

Right after lunch the four men lured Stoops into one of the
rooms of the mat shop on the pretence that a machine was
out of order. Then they fell upon him, bound him hand and
foot with heavy bundle twine, and gagged him.

Then they herded other convicts into a separate room
and went to work on the window, using a piece of pipe to
pry off the reinforced inside casement.

They had worked at it about half an hour when Manning,
who wasn't expected, entered the shop on a routine inspection tour. They had a lookout posted. When Manning
entered one grabbed him on each side and one from behind,
and they hustled him into the room with Stoops, binding
him but not gagging them [sic].

Then they went back to the window. By this time they
had pried off part of the casement. They dragged over a
small motor-driven emery stone and began grinding away
at one of the toolproof bars.

One of the convicts remained posted at the door as a
guard, and when Officer Johnston entered he was hustled in
with the other officers. So far as I can gather they at no time
used any weapons on the officers, just overpowering them
by surprise and strength of numbers. Barkdoll is a big,
husky man and took the lead.

Finally Captain Madigan entered the shop. They overpowered him too. But Captain Manning pointed out to
them that it was time for the officers to ring in to the administration building, and that an alarm would be sounded if
the officers failed to ring in. They were about ready to give
up anyway. They had to cut through at least probably three

of the bars before they could drop down to the outside and they hadn't even cut through one.

So they freed Madigan. He phoned the administration building, and by the time we got there he was leading them away.

This wasn't the last time that at least two of them were going to try to get away: Cretzer and Shockley were key figures in what would have been the most daring attempt, which culminated in the Battle of Alcatraz in 1946.

Before then came three other thwarted prison breaks. Twenty-five-year-old bank robber John R. Bayless was caught on the point of swimming away from the island by prison guards, after he had absconded from a garbage detail, taking advantage of a thick fog that had settled over the island. Some reports suggest that he surrendered when he realized how cold the water in San Francisco bay was on that September afternoon in 1941, others that he was pulled from the water before hypothermia set in. Either way, it didn't prevent him from wanting to gain his freedom: when he appeared in court the following year, during a hearing to try to gain a writ of habeas corpus on the grounds he hadn't been represented by legal counsel when he was convicted, he took advantage of what he thought was lax security. He leaped over a railing and headed for the rear door of the court but was grabbed by a deputy marshal.

The mat shop was the scene of yet another group attempt on 14 April 1943. The four involved on this occasion were some of the most violent men on the island at the time: Floyd Hamilton, who had been Public Enemy Number One; kidnapper Fred Hunter; and bank robbers Harold Breast and James A. Boarman. Around 9.30 a.m. the would-be escapees overpowered, bound and gagged Custodial Officer Smith, using home-made knives that they had smuggled into the room. When the Guard Captain Henry Weinhold realized that Smith wasn't where he was meant to be, he investigated, and was also overpowered. With the two guards out of action, the prisoners jumped out of a rear window, and headed down the thirty-foot cliff to the water's edge. They had already stripped to their underwear, and greased up, to provide some measure of protection against the cold of the bay. Their intention was to use cans as floats, but in their haste, they left two behind in the mat room. These also had army uniforms inside, which they were hoping to use as disguises once they reached the mainland.

While the prisoners were working out what to do, the guards started to open fire, or, as the *San Francisco Chronicle* described it, "Fusilade after fusilade spattered the waters with deadly slugs, peppering the surface with tiny geysers." Smith had managed to work one hand into his pocket to retrieve his whistle which he then placed in Weinhold's mouth. With bullets raining down on them, the prisoners started to swim for it. Boarman was hit in the back of the head, and Breast held him up for a time. However, when the prison launch came to pick them out of the water, Breast let go of the body and it sank. If Boarman wasn't dead from the bullet, he would have quickly drowned. His body, however, was never located.

Hunter and Hamilton kept swimming. Hunter tried to find shelter in the caves underneath the cliffs, but bloodstains were spotted near the entrance, as if someone had been leaning on the rocks for support. The guards brought their boat around to the entrance and ordered him to surrender. When he didn't come out, they fired a single round into the cave, which prompted Hunter to exit rapidly.

The search for Hamilton continued, but when no trace was found, Warden Johnston confidently told the press that he was positive that the gangster had been shot, and fallen into the water. It was therefore rather embarrassing for him when Hamilton was discovered by guard captain Weinhold three days later, still in the industrial building! He had been concealed in the same cave as Hunter, but hadn't surrendered with his colleague. Instead, he had waited there considering his options before deciding to return to the prison. The *Chronicle* suggested that he was "[l]ike a bad little boy who ran away from home and came crawling back in trembling fear of a spanking". Climbing the cliff, he re-entered the mat room through the same window he and his friends had used earlier, then hid himself in a pile of material where he was found by Weinhold who was searching for further evidence regarding the escape.

*   *   *

Four months later, Arkansas bank robber Ted Huron Walters, one of Floyd Hamilton's associates, made his move, escaping from the prison laundry by sneaking through a door and over the fence. His presence was missed shortly after he had vanished, and five coastguard boats as well as the prison's own launch patrolled the waters searching for him. He was eventually found hiding on the island beach, with the warden noting that he had been "balked by the cold tide".

One of the earliest prisoners ensconced at Alcatraz thought he had found a foolproof way of getting off the island in July 1945, but ended up simply getting a tour of San Francisco Bay – and becoming an inadvertent star, after his story was told on the radio series *Gang Busters* later that year.

John Knight Giles was convicted for murder in Oregon, and while serving a life sentence there, had escaped from prison and gone on to try to rob the Denver and Rio Grande Western mail train. On recapture, he had been sent to McNeil Island, thence to Alcatraz in August 1935. Giles had bided his time, working as a prison dock stevedore for eight years before trying his escape. As he told one of the guards on his return, he "had his chance to get away – and had nothing to lose".

Before he stepped on board an Army launch at 10.40 a.m. on 31 July 1945, Giles had diligently pulled together a military uniform, probably from the large number of service items that were cleaned at the prison laundry. Although the bags were regularly checked for contraband on their way in, it seems that nobody thought of correlating the numbers of garments on entrance and exit. Giles donned his borrowed staff sergeant's uniform on the docks and stationed himself beneath the dock, armed only with a flashlight. He then joined the launch, the *General Frank M. Coxe*, by jumping through a freight hatch and proceeded to nonchalantly stare out to sea as the boat headed to Fort McDowell, claiming that he was a lineman working on the cable in that area.

What he didn't realize was that standard operating procedure meant that the number of soldiers on board was regularly checked. When one extra soldier was noted, the guard on the Alcatraz dock was told; this tallied with the loss of one stevedore that the Alcatraz guards had just noticed themselves. Assistant

Warden E.J. Miller therefore hurriedly went to the pier, and overtook the *General Coxe* in a speedboat, arriving at Fort McDowell before the Army launch.

Even before the Alcatraz authorities could claim him for their own, Giles was in trouble. The officer of the day, Lieutenant Gordon L. Kilgore, pulled him aside, because he wasn't wearing the correct uniform. When he inspected the passes that Giles had also secretly prepared, he realized they were crude forgeries. Giles was preparing to argue when Assistant Warden Miller arrived to take him back to the Rock in handcuffs. The only question remaining was where Giles obtained the dog tags that he was wearing around his neck. Giles never explained, although he did tell the warden that "time means nothing to him – that he had everything to gain by trying to escape and nothing to lose. And he also said he had been planning a getaway since his imprisonment here in 1935."

Everything that had come before on the Rock was overshadowed by events in May 1946, in what quickly came to be known as the Battle of Alcatraz. Two guards and three prisoners died; fourteen guards and one inmate were seriously wounded; two men went to the gas chamber for their involvement. It was a vicious affair, during which it was by no means certain that the prison authorities would get the upper hand. As Warden Johnston said, via telegram at 5.43 p.m. on the afternoon of the first day, "Our situation is difficult and precarious. Our officers are all being used in every place that we can man. The armed prisoners on the island are still eluding us so that at the moment we cannot control them. The Navy, coastguard and San Francisco Police Department are standing by to help when we find we can use them to our advantage."

The first Warden Johnston knew of the impending problems was when he received a call at 2.30 p.m. on Thursday 2 May 1946 from the prison armorer. "There's some trouble in the cell house. I don't know what it is, but I think it's bad," he told Johnston. He had no idea how bad it was: some of Alcatraz's worst prisoners had gained control of the gun gallery, a section that looked out over the cell block inside which armed prison officers kept watch, and therefore were in possession of guns.

Kentucky bank robber Bernard Paul Coy had carefully monitored all the various guards' movements looking for any sign of weakness. When guard Bert Burch left the gun gallery in response to a call from his colleague, Cecil Corwin in the isolation block next door, Coy, who had been floor-sweeping in the main cell block overlooked by the gallery, knew that it was time to act. When guard William M. Miller let prisoner Marvin Franklin Hubbard into the cell block, Hubbard and Coy attacked him and took his keys. They let out Joseph P. Cretzer, who was eager to make up for his failed escape five years earlier, and a Choctaw Indian, Clarence Clarnes, one of the youngest prisoners on Alcatraz at the time.

Coy then smeared axle grease all over his body, and started to climb the West End gun gallery. Between his teeth was a bag in which he was carrying a bar-spreading device, which had been put together in the prison workshops, cannibalizing toilet fixtures. At the top of the gun cage, the bars curved over into a sort of basket shape. Those bars proved the easiest to spread and once he had forced them apart, Coy had a gap of about five to seven inches, and eighteen inches between the cross-hatching to slide through. Once he had got through, Coy ran down the ladder within the gallery to the lower level. Grabbing a riot club, he hid beneath the window in the door.

Out in the cells, his accomplices started to make a racket. When Burch came to investigate, Coy slugged him, and although Burch put up a struggle to prevent Coy from gaining his weapon, the prisoner was able to get the advantage and then strangled the guard unconscious with his own tie. Then he started to pass the captured weapons – a rifle and a .45 revolver – as well as riot clubs out to the other prisoners. They captured officer Corwin, and placed him in a cell with Miller. They then freed a load of prisoners – at the time, Warden Johnston said that he believed it was as many as sixty; the official report afterwards indicated that it was only twelve. These included Sam Shockley and Miran Edgar Thompson, both of whom were extremely violent men. The one man whose help they could really do with – Rufus "Whitey" Franklin, a guard killer and escape artist – couldn't be released from his cell because they couldn't work the electrics. If he had been with them, it is possible that the prisoners could have found ways round some of the problems they encountered.

As further prison officers, including guard captain Henry H. Weinhold, entered the cell block, they were captured and locked up in two adjoining cells. For obvious reasons, they weren't armed when they went in: guns were used only within the gun gallery. Another officer, who was in the basement, realized there was trouble, and rang the armorer who alerted the warden. At the same time, Associate Warden E.J. Miller went to investigate, and was faced with Coy wielding the rifle. Coy fired twice, setting fire to a gas canister that Miller was holding, leading Miller to believe that Coy had a machine gun – an assertion Johnston initially repeated in his notifications of the revolt to the mainland. The distress sirens began blaring out across San Francisco Bay, telling the world outside that there were major problems at the prison. Coastguard officers as well as Marines were despatched to Alcatraz to help the guards keep the other prisoners under control.

Using the weapons they had liberated, the prisoners started firing at the gun towers. They knew that if they could knock out two of them, they would have a clear run to the boats through the back door that led into the yard. However, they were still stuck inside the cell block: they hadn't found the key for the outside door. Although they believed that Miller had given them all his keys, he had kept the most important one from them; he hid it in the toilet of the cell where he and the other guards were held hostage. When they realized that they hadn't got the key, the escape attempt turned into a battle for control of the prison itself. "Well that does **** it up," Cretzer was heard saying when he knew he didn't have either the key or the benefit of Rufus Franklin's experience. "San Francisco is just as far away as ever." At that point, goaded by Thompson and Shockley, Cretzer started firing into one of the two cells containing the prison guards, shooting Captain Weinhold, fatally wounding Miller, and injuring junior guard Ernest Lageson.

Determined to regain control of the prison, and rescue his captured men, Warden Johnston prepared a strike team. Led by Lt Phil Bergen and Lt Frank, they managed to reach the first storey of the gun gallery, with various guards trying to provide covering fire against the barrage coming from the prisoners. During this exchange, guard Harold Stites was shot, as were three others. After the guards retreated carrying Stites, he was pronounced dead. The others were sent to hospitals on the mainland. The electricity was cut off within the prison.

Bergen and four other guards returned to the gun gallery, from where they could report back to the warden, who ordered a further assault. At 10 p.m., a group of fourteen officers led by the associate warden burst into the cell block. Although they managed to close the door between the cell block and the isolation wing, they came under heavy fire.

At this, the Marines started to bomb the isolation block, believing that that was where the majority of the ringleaders were hiding. Holes were drilled in the ceiling and tear gas grenades were thrown in. Eventually, after Robert Stroud – who would become famous as the "Birdman of Alcatraz" – managed to persuade Bergen that there were no weapons inside the block, nor were the men they were seeking there, the barrage was better aimed.

Things were quieter on the second day, and there was even a brief attempt by some of the prisoners to cut a deal with the warden; he wasn't in the mood to negotiate. They either surrendered, or he continued with the assault. They didn't surrender.

It became clear that the prisoners were holed up in a utility corridor in the main cell block, described by the *San Francisco Chronicle* as "a tunnel-like passage with a door at either end of an almost impregnable spot". A pattern began: one guard would jerk the door to the corridor open, and another would fire a shotgun blast down the corridor. Then the door would be slammed shut. In-between shotgun rounds, fragmentation grenades were dropped in from above. On the third morning, squads of guards kept rushing into the cell block firing repeatedly into the narrow corridor, and at 9.40 a.m., they were finally able to enter it without resistance. There they found the bodies of Cretzer, Coy, and Hubbard: Cretzer and Coy probably died the night before, Hubbard that morning. A handful of convicts, who only ever had one rifle and a pistol between them, had held the prison authorities at bay for two days. No one had escaped.

Although Thompson and Shockley had retreated to their cells on the first night, after realizing that they were in over their heads, they were prosecuted for the murder of prison officer

William Miller, alongside Clarence Carnes. Thompson and Shockley – whose IQ was said to be 54, just over half the average – were sentenced to death, and were executed side by side in the gas chamber at San Quentin on 3 December 1948. A prison guard who witnessed their execution simply said, "That makes it five to two. It's a little more even now."

Apart from a short-lived abortive escape by Arkansas bank robber Ted H. Walters to abscond from the new prison laundry in August 1948 – he got as far as the shore on the south-west corner of Alcatraz Island but couldn't summon up the courage to risk the waters – there weren't many notable attempts at escaping from the Rock during the decade following the Battle of Alcatraz. Warden Johnston retired in 1948, and was succeeded by Edwin Swope, who served until 1955. The third Warden was someone who already knew the problems of the prison, because he had come up through the ranks: Paul Madigan.

There were two key escape attempts during Madigan's wardenship. Murderer Floyd P. Wilson – who killed the manager of a food store he was holding up to try to get the $17 he needed to buy some coal for his freezing wife and five children – was initially believed to have tried to get away on the prison's water barge, which brought fresh water supplies over to the Rock. On 23 July 1956, he was working on the docks, and was present at 3.25 p.m. in a line-up carried out when the water barge was due to be towed; twenty minutes later, he was gone. Two young boys claimed that they had seen a man in shorts swimming across a cove not far from where the water barge docked on its return to the mainland, but careful inspection of all the small boats in the area revealed nothing.

That wasn't too surprising. Wilson was no luckier on Alcatraz than he had been in the outside world. During his abortive robbery, he had left $10,000 in the car next to the man he murdered. On the Rock, he simply slipped away from the gang he was working with, apparently under cover of smoke from a rubbish-burning fire – the departure of the barge was a complete coincidence. He didn't get far: he was found by the water's edge at 2.45 a.m. on 24 July, wet and shivering, near the foot of the cliffs on the south end of the Rock. When asked whether it was true that Wilson was captured because he couldn't swim, Warden Madigan simply said: "We don't know. How could we?"

The other escape that Madigan had to deal with did look for a time as if it had been successful. Although one of the pair of prospective fugitives was captured quickly, the fate of the other wasn't known for some time, and newspaper reports were considering the first "impossible" escape from the Rock.

The FBI's former Public Enemy Number One from 1949, Clyde Johnson teamed up with gunman Aaron Walter Burgett. Both men had been working on the rubbish detail outside the prison for about six months; shortly after 3 p.m. on 29 September 1958 Burgess grabbed their guard, Custodial Officer Harold Miller by the shoulder and swung him round. Johnson held a knife to his chin.

Although they had planned the escape some time earlier, the two men had waited for Daylight Savings Time to end, so darkness would fall earlier; they also wanted the cover of fog, which fell for the first time that season.

Telling Miller that if he behaved, he wouldn't get hurt, the two prisoners covered the guard's eyes, lashed his wrists and gagged him, then guided him down the hill, tying him to a eucalyptus tree. Perhaps in an effort to put pursuers off their scent, they also explained that they had a getaway launch waiting out in the fog in the bay, outside the 200-yard cordon, ready to spirit them away.

Their absence was spotted at 3.40 when Miller's colleagues realized that he hadn't returned. They found him lying in the bushes behind the guards' houses on the south-east side of the island, and raised the alarm. Thirty sets of two-man teams were formed from the guards, who began a thorough check of the shoreline; coastguard boats circled the island looking for the getaway launch or any sign of the two men, while a helicopter circled overhead watching in case the launch broke out of the fog bank. Within an hour of Miller's discovery, a crewman on a coastguard patrol boat spotted Johnson, standing just off shore, up to his waist in water on the west side of the island. "We made a good try, and it just didn't work," Johnson commented, and apologised to Associate Warden Joseph B. Latimer – although the warden noted, "I think Johnson's sorry he failed."

Despite an intensive search, there was no sign of Burgett. Most believed he had perished – even a friendly priest in his hometown of St Louis, Missouri, noted, "I don't think he had either the physique or the mental drive" to swim across the bay. The prisoners were kept locked in the cells while the search continued, let out only for mealtimes, for a week until Warden Madigan was satisfied that Burgett wasn't on the island.

He wasn't. Burgett's body, partially decomposed from thirteen days immersed in the cold waters of San Francisco Bay, was spotted about a hundred yards from the east side of the island on 12 October. Identified by his clothing and a thumbprint, Madigan was satisfied that they had found their missing man.

Perhaps the greatest escape to take place from Alcatraz happened on 11 June 1962: it warrants the superlative not just for the ingenuity of the escapees, but also because it seems quite possible that, government protestations to the contrary, the three men may well have got away.

The basis of the 1979 Clint Eastwood/Don Siegel film *Escape from Alcatraz*, the plan saw professional villain and armed robber Frank Lee Morris, and robber brothers John and Clarence Anglin dig through the concrete walls of their cells, head over the roof, and off the island by a raft that they had stitched together from raincoats. It took months of planning and preparation but Morris, who boasted an IQ of 133, within the top three per cent or so of the population, had a long history of escaping from prisons, and regarded Alcatraz as the last challenge.

The press reports at the time concentrated on the way in which the men escaped from their cells: "Out of Alcatraz – By A Spoon" noted the *San Francisco Chronicle* on the day after their departure. That story featured this wonderful statement of the obvious from Paul Madigan's replacement as warden, Olin G. Blackwell, "With spoons it takes more time than if you had a jackhammer."

The first that the prison staff knew of the escape was at 7.15 on the morning of 12 June. During the night, prison guards patrolled the floors of the cell blocks, confirming that each prisoner was sleeping in his cell by the simple method of looking through the bars at him. However, the first roll call of the day required the prisoners to stand up at the front of the cell for a full visual inspection. Morris and the two Anglin brothers failed to get up, and when the prison guards entered their cells to find out why they were being so blatantly disobedient, they received a shock: in all three cots, beneath the blankets, were bodies made from pillows, topped by heads made from plaster, with painted faces and some form of hair. Somehow three men had managed to get out of the cells, apparently under the noses of the guards.

In fact, they had exited from the back of their cells, via the mesh-covered air vent at the base of the cell. The vents were about six inches by ten inches, and using teaspoons that they had taken from the kitchen, the three men had chipped away at the concrete around the vent until they were able to remove it. They then replaced the real vents with cardboard replicas which they had made and smuggled into their cells, and continued to remove the concrete from around the vent to allow sufficient room for them to be able to squeeze through into the utility corridor that ran behind the cells. It was from there that they could reach their ultimate goal: a vent in the ceiling of Block B, which, for some reason, hadn't been concreted over. It was an exit route onto the roof.

Although only three men escaped this way, a fourth – car thief Allen Clayton West – was part of the preparations and was meant to accompany them. He may even have been the mastermind behind the plot. However, fearful that they would get caught, West had apparently re-cemented some of the hole around his vent. When Morris and the Anglins moved their plans forward by a few days, West didn't have time to complete his work. He did try to follow them, but when he realized that they had gone without him, he returned to his cell. The information that he provided later would prove invaluable to the authorities when piecing together how the escape had been planned.

The preparation for the escape had begun as early as December 1961, more than eighteen months before the trio would eventually break out. Not only did they have to make their way through the concrete vents, but they needed to prepare the fake heads and the false ventilator grilles, create a life raft and get all the tools together that they'd require to open the vent.

The Anglin brothers were in adjacent cells; West and Morris were also nextdoor neighbours. One of each pair would work on the holes around the vents in their cells each evening for about three and a half hours before lights out while the other kept watch. The Anglins also worked on the dummy heads, which they nicknamed "Oink" and "Oscar"! They were made from a homemade cement mixture formed from soap and toilet paper, and then painted with flesh-tone paint taken from the art kits provided for the prisoners. The hair was actual human hair, swept up from the prison barbershop.

Men serving life imprisonment understand the meaning of patience. If they were going to get away successfully from the Rock, everything had to be done carefully, methodically and properly. By May 1962, over a year before they would make their getaway, the men had removed the vents, made their way into the access corridor, and were working on the vent at the top of the cell block. They also created a workshop and storeroom in the area around the vent, where their contraband could be stored, above the cells, and out of reach of the guards.

Although the Alcatraz authorities would initially deny that the men had been able to use rubber raincoats to create lifejackets or a raft, prisoners on the Rock confirmed that Morris and the Anglins would borrow or steal them – a prisoner might wear his raincoat outside during recreation. One of the escapees would be in shirtsleeves at the start of the break, but by the time the prisoners went inside, he was the one with the coat.

The team stole glue from the prison glove shop to stick the raincoats together, while West was able to get hold of an electric hair clipper and drill bits to use as a makeshift drill. This wasn't powerful enough for the men's needs, so West sought permission to repair the prison vacuum, which had recently broken. To his pleasant surprise, he discovered that it contained two motors, but would work effectively with just one. The other became the motor for the drill, although in the end, the gang weren't able to use it to drill through the roof ventilator, since it was simply too noisy.

To inflate the raft once they got outside, Anglin created a valve assembly, and Morris altered a concertina to form bellows. West created the lifejackets and wooden paddles for the raft, but didn't anticipate that the others would be ready to go as quickly as they were.

On 11 June 1962, Morris decided that it was time to leave. The top ventilator was loose enough to be pushed from beneath, so there was no time to waste. He brought the dummies from their hiding place above the cell block, and he, the Anglins and West placed them in their beds. The Anglins joined Morris in the utility corridor, but West couldn't get through the hole. Clarence Anglin tried to kick the ventilator from the corridor side, but it wouldn't budge. Morris and the others left him behind.

From there, they climbed the drainpipes to the top of the cell block and they knocked the ventilator from inside, and it fell to the ground (the sound was apparently heard by a guard, but nobody thought anything of it). They had already pried off the bar, so all they had to do was squeeze through the twelve-inch-wide hole onto the roof.

They were lucky. They were in view of the Number 1 gun tower, and they had to slide down a kitchen vent near the recreation area, in a part of the prison that was brightly illuminated by a searchlight. The guard was looking in a different direction, and didn't spot them. From there they scaled the fences – both twelve-feet high, topped with barbed wire – and headed for the north-east section of the island. From there, officially, the trail runs cold.

When their disappearance was noted the next morning, the prison went into its usual lockdown mode. The prisoners were fed but otherwise kept in their cells while all the guards and officers searched the island, with sniffer dogs and helicopters all playing a part. It was at this point that West started to talk, breaking the usual prisoners' code of silence. He told the FBI that the plan had been to head to Angel Island, and from there swim across Raccoon Straits to Marin County on the mainland, steal a car and some clothing and then head their separate ways.

Based on this information, Bureau agents, working with the prison authorities and the coastguard, stepped up their searches, looking on Angel Island. According to most contemporary reports, they found nothing, nor were there any cars stolen in the part of the Bay area at a time that would correlate with the prisoners reaching there. When two makeshift life-jackets were found in the water – one in the bay, the other outside the Golden Gate – as well as oars, and a plastic wallet with letters and photographs belonging to the Anglins wrapped up tight inside (including contacts that would have been helpful if they had made it to the mainland), it seemed certain that, like so many before them, Morris and the Anglins had succumbed to the water. The final evidence seemed to come when a Norwegian freighter spotted a body in the water a few weeks later, dressed in what looked like prison clothes. Although they didn't retrieve it, it seemed likely that it was one of the three men. Officially, therefore, the three were declared missing, believed drowned.

Officially, but perhaps not accurately. The responsibility for the search for the men was passed to the US Federal Marshals office, who will continue to look for them until their hundredth birthday – in Morris' case, 2026. In the course of their re-assessment of the case files, they noticed something very unusual. Although it was "accepted" that no evidence was found on Angel Island, and no cars were stolen, paperwork from the time suggests that that wasn't strictly true.

On 12 June 1962 at 11.10 a.m. an APB (all-points bulletin) was issued for the three fugitives. After giving detailed descriptions of the trio, it states:

> Fugitives believed attempting to effect escape through Marin County. All subjects are convicted bank robbers.
>
> Should be considered extremely dangerous.
>
> Last known to be clothed in blue denim trousers and shirts. Raft believed used be (sic) escapees located on Angel Island.

On its own that wasn't too odd: there were contemporary reports of a raft being found on Angel Island, but according to the *San Francisco Chronicle*'s article on 13 June: "What appeared from the air to be a raft turned out to be an old fish net."

But what caught US Marshal Michael Dyke's eye was a second report, dated 13 June. The previous day, the California Highway Patrol had placed an All-Points Message to local police in the area to lookout for a blue 1955 Chevrolet. The message continued:

According to information received by the Stanislaus County Sheriff's Office, a raft had been found on Angel Island; foot prints were found leading from the raft, and it was (sic) being assumed that the escapees had come ashore at that point on Angel Island. In addition, the Marin County Sheriff's Office had furnished information that the car, described above, had been stolen in Marin County, date and time of theft unknown to the Stanislaus County Sheriff's Office. At approximately 11:30am, 6/12/62, according to [name redacted], an unnamed complainant had called the California Highway Patrol, Stockton, California, advising that agency that he had been forced off the road by three men in a blue 1955 Chevrolet.

So much for the "no cars were reported missing" evidence used to counter claims that Morris and his colleagues had survived. It's not the first time that important evidence regarding crimes has become buried in FBI files: a report on the state of his car that would have destroyed James Earl Ray's alibi for the time of the murder of Dr Martin Luther King in 1968 only resurfaced in 2002 when the files were re-examined. Is it possible that the three men beat the system, and then somehow managed to keep themselves out of trouble?

The body spotted by the Norwegian freighter may well not have been any of the three men. A corpse, which may well have been the same one spotted by the crew, was washed up at Point Reyes a few months later; it was buried under the name "John Bones Doe", and exhumed by Marshal Dyke. Although the pathology report on the corpse indicated that it was of a man of Morris' height and approximate age, DNA testing on the remains against a member of his family proved negative.

There are reports that the Anglins masqueraded as women to attend a family funeral; there was another claim that they had been picked up, but then shot for their possessions. Neither of these can be substantiated.

Whatever the truth, the Marshal service will continue to hunt them – albeit not with the same urgency that they track sex offenders and current murderers. "I think there's still a decent chance they made it," Dyke told the *San Francisco Chronicle* around the fiftieth anniversary of the escape in June 2012. "I can't prove it. Well, nothing I can tell you anyway." And as US Marshal Don O'Keefe added, "The ongoing U.S. Marshals investigation of the 1962 escape from Alcatraz federal prison serves as a warning to fugitives that regardless of time, we will continue to look for you and bring you to justice."

The final breakout from Alcatraz took place on Sunday 16 December 1962, twenty-five years to the day after Theodore Cole and Ralph Roe took their – probably fatal – swim and proved that, no matter what successive wardens and officials in the Justice Department had maintained during the Federal Penitentiary's time on the Rock, it was possible to swim from Alcatraz to the mainland and live to tell the tale.

Bank robbers Darl Lee Parker and John Paul Scott took advantage of a long-brewing escape scheme that was centred around a storage room below the prison kitchens in which a twenty-eight-man detail worked. Although Scott would claim later that they had used a piece of string dipped in abrasive kitchen cleaner to saw through the bars of the window, Federal Director of Prisons James V. Bennett told reporters that prison officials found a spatula, suitably knicked to produce a sawtooth effect, hidden in a drainpipe inside the room after the escape.

The cutting had been started by a prisoner over a year earlier. The man surreptitiously began sawing at the double bars over the high window, and the project had been continued by at least four other prisoners, who would climb on a table, then clamber up the inner bars to reach the sawing point. If a guard was heard approaching, then they jumped back down: prisoners were often locked in the storeroom for periods to get on with their work, giving them ample time to work on the bars, and ensure that they would pass a cursory examination.

Bennett believed that Scott decided to make a break for it, because he knew the bars they were sawing through were due for inspection, and if he didn't go at that point, then all the work would be wasted. He completed the work, then called out to Parker to join him. They then went up an outside drainpipe to the roof of the main cell block, crossed it, then used a fifty-foot length of electrical cable to lower themselves to the ground, fleeing to the cliffs at the island's west side. Using stolen surgical gloves, inflated to act as flotation devices, the two hit the water. (The original theory was that they had simply climbed the cyclone fence, and slid down to the water.)

Their absence was spotted at 5.47 p.m., seventeen minutes after they had last been checked in a routine prisoner count. Parker only made it as far as Little Alcatraz, a hundred yards west of the prison island. The coastguard was notified and at 7.40 p.m. teenagers found what they thought was a body on the rocks at Fort Point. It was Scott, who had successfully swum to the mainland. "His condition is not too serious," Colonel James Mackin of the Letterman Hospital Staff told the *San Francisco Chronicle*. "You might just say that he's damn cold." At 10.45 p.m., Scott was on his way back to Alcatraz. If he had only managed to go a few more feet, he would have reached a sandy beach – and quite possibly become the first absolutely certified escaper from the Federal Penitentiary.

Scott and Parker's unorthodox departure from their workplace was the last time anyone fled from the Rock. By the time that they made their move, plans were already in action to close the prison down. Morris and the Anglins' escape had highlighted the dreadful state of the buildings – figures of $5million were bandied around at the time to bring it up to a high standard of security – and the people of San Francisco were becoming increasingly vocal in their opposition to the Rock being used this way. In December 1962, only 206 remained of the prison's 336 capacity, the others having been "phased out", leading Warden Blackwell to comment ironically, "Apparently we weren't phasing out fast enough." With the completion of the maximum-security prison at Marion, Illinois, Alcatraz Federal Penitentiary was closed down, its inhabitants shackled hand and foot and moved to other prisons (no matter what fanciful TV series might like to believe!).

Unlike many of the other former prisons that are featured in this book, you can still go to visit Alcatraz (a tour is shown at the start of the feature film *The Rock*). "Come experience the beauty, history and infamy of Alcatraz on the San Francisco Bay" says the cruise website. It may not have been escape-proof, but Alcatraz tested the mettle of all those who were there.

Fact vs. Fiction

The visual attraction of a bleak prison stuck on a rock in the middle of San Francisco Bay has pulled film-makers over the last century. Burt Lancaster's *Birdman of Alcatraz* was based on the life of Robert Stroud, although he was not the model of sweetness and light that the film makes him out to be. His role in the 1946 Battle of Alcatraz is considerably overplayed, according to those who knew Stroud.

The most famous escape film, of course, is Clint Eastwood's 1979 movie *Escape from Alcatraz*, based on events in 1962. Eastwood plays Frank Morris, with Fred Ward and Jack Thibeau as the Anglin brothers. Veering away from the facts, Patrick McGoohan plays a (sensibly) unnamed warden, and the real Allen West became the fictional, cowardly Charlie Butts, played by Larry Hankin.

The 1995 film *Murder in the First* also maintains that it's based on truth, but turns bank robber Henri Young into a thief forced by circumstance to steal $5 to feed himself and his sister. It plays fast and loose with the events of Young's 1939 escape, and then claims he died on the Rock in the mid-1940s. He actually jumped parole in 1972.

Fictional escapes from Alcatraz form the basis of the short-lived US TV series *Alcatraz*, which claimed that the last inmates from the Federal Penitentiary were not sent to other prisons, but instead somehow disappeared before returning in 2011 to cause trouble. It lasted thirteen episodes before being cancelled.

Possibly the best fictional escape is seen in the Michael Bay 1996 movie *The Rock*, with Sean Connery as a forcibly retired British spy (sound familiar?) who was imprisoned there because he knew secrets that the American government didn't want revealed. He was the only man who had ever escaped from the

Rock, and the government (and more particularly Nicholas Cage's chemical weapons specialist Dr Stanley Goodspeed) need to know how, so they can infiltrate the prison, where an armed force is holding hostages and threatening San Francisco with chemical weapons.

Sources:

Thompson, Erwin N., The Rock: A history of Alcatraz Island, 1847–1972, historic resource study, Golden Gate National Recreation Area, California, Denver: National Park Service, 1972 (available at www.alcatrazhistory.com)

Johnston, James A., *Alcatraz Island Prison and the Men Who Live There* (Scribner's, 1949)

Karpis (Karpowicz), Alvin and Robert Livesey, *On the Rock: Twenty-five years in Alcatraz* (Beaufort Books, 1980)

San Francisco Chronicle, assorted dates

Catching the Midnight Express

Prison breaks are one of the staples of Hollywood movies. Think of films like *The Great Escape* or *The Shawshank Redemption*: although sometimes, as in the former case, they're based on real events, the necessities of condensing a story into two hours or so running time means that many factors can be changed – sometimes removing what some would consider more "filmic" moments.

That happened in the case of one of the most famous prison films of all time: Alan Parker's *Midnight Express*, which tells a version of the story of Billy Hayes, a young American drug smuggler, who was caught and thrown into prison in Turkey. A harsh, gritty film, it ends with Hayes escaping from jail by killing a cruel jailer who was about to rape him. Ironically – given that "Midnight Express" is the term given to an escape from prison within the film – Hayes' escape was nothing like that at all. (When Hayes asked Alan Parker why it was changed, the director replied, "What forty-five minutes of this film do you want to cut out to put in your escape? They'd had enough, get the audience out of the bloody theatre.") The film was based on Hayes' own autobiography, written with William Hoffer in 1976; however, he had to bear in mind various considerations while writing that, so the full story of his escape had to wait until 2010.

Hayes was arrested at Yesikoy International Airport in Istanbul on 7 October 1970, literally as he was about to step on a plane, carrying four pounds of hashish. On his first night in prison, he learned the way of life in Turkish jails: he took a blanket from another cell, and was beaten up by the guards, including Hamid, a sadist who took great pleasure from making Hayes' life a misery. (In the movie, Hamid is the guard that Hayes kills; in reality, Hamid was already dead by this point: a former prisoner recognized him outside the jail, and shot him eight times.) Hayes was sentenced to four years and two months in prison.

In Sağmalcılar prison, escaping was known as "taking the Midnight Express", referring to the train that ran from Istanbul into Greece, from which escapees could jump off to freedom. Even though he had a comparatively light sentence, Hayes knew that he needed to escape, and learned that prisoners who were deemed to be criminally insane were moved to Bakirkoy Mental Hospital. Compared with Sağmalcılar, Bakirkoy was an easy place from which to escape. Being given an official "crazy report" might also assist with getting him freed legitimately. Hayes discussed his plan with a visiting friend, Patrick, who agreed to pick him up and drive to the border, providing false papers and a change of clothing. All Hayes had to do was convince the Turkish authorities that he was crazy.

Hayes succeeded in being sent to Bakirkoy for observation in 1972 – and discovered that he had swapped the frying pan for the fire. Bakirkoy only housed the criminally insane but Hayes was sure that he could survive while Patrick raised the necessary cash to arrange the papers. The plan fell apart when Patrick got on the wrong side of the wrong people; Hayes was informed in a telegram from his father that Patrick had been found dead in his hotel room with a bayonet in his chest. Hayes lost all hope at that stage, blaming himself for his friend's death. Giving up on ideas of escape, he was returned to Sağmalcılar and resigned himself to serving out the remaining years of his sentence. (Hayes only revealed this part of his escape plans in recent times – his original account in *Midnight Express* only mentions his time in Bakirkoy, not the escape plan, or its unfortunate consequences. Patrick's death is mentioned, but isn't linked to the escape plan.)

With just fifty-four days left to go, Hayes received a visit from the American Consul and was horrified to learn that the High Court in Ankara had decided that they wanted to change the charge in his case. Instead of convicting him of possession of drugs, they were now convicting him of smuggling, an offence that carried a life sentence – or possibly just thirty years. Unsurprisingly, Hayes' resolution to escape came back to life. A brief attempt to file his way out through the prison bars came to nothing when children spotted Hayes and a colleague at the window and reported them.

The US authorities tried, in vain, to persuade their Turkish counterparts to allow Hayes to be returned to America to serve out his sentence there. The Turks pointed out that the Americans couldn't give the absolute guarantees that they required, so refused permission. The Foreign Minister suggested that the Americans try to make an appeal on the grounds that "Hayes' health, physical and/or mental, was deteriorating as a result of his incarceration in a Turkish prison". There was no guarantee that it would be successful, but privately, he indicated to the American Ambassador that he would do all he could to assist.

Billy Hayes refused to allow his countrymen to go down this route. According to the telegram from the American Ambassador to the State Department, "his experience in submitting to mental and physical examination at Bakirkoy mental hospital in 1972 was apparently highly traumatic for him. He does not like the hospital and based on this earlier experience there he does not believe that hospital staff will certify that state of his health warrants early release. (It will be recalled in this connection that in 1972 Turkish psychiatric authorities decided he was not psychotic and dismissed earlier efforts of his attorneys to play up Hayes's psychological problems.)" He hoped to be transferred to a "half-open" prison, and that various amnesties that were being discussed might benefit his situation.

Hayes was moved to ımralı Prison on 11 July 1975; three months later he was in Greece. ımralı island lies seventeen miles off the coast of Turkey, and had been used as a prison since 1935. (A newly constructed building now houses terrorist Abdullah Ocalan, serving a life sentence for treason.) After the deprivations of Sağmalcılar and Bakirkoy hospital, this was like paradise for Hayes – but he was still locked in, working in a canning factory during the day.

The factory was served by boats which normally returned to the mainland overnight; however on 2 October, a storm whipped up so rapidly that the boats had to remain tied at anchor for the evening. And, as Hayes had noticed, all of them had little dinghies, complete with oars, tied to their side. If he could get out from the prison after bed check and swim out to the boats, he could relieve one of the owners of their dinghy, and row to the mainland. The prospect of the swim didn't faze him: he had been a lifeguard and a surfer in his time.

Screwing up his courage, Hayes slipped out after the bed check, and crawled across the rocks, knowing that at best if he was caught, he would be returned to Sağmalcılar; at worst, he could be shot by the guards. As unobtrusively as possible, he entered the water, and began swimming quietly towards the moored boats, hoping that the searchlights manned by the guards wouldn't be turned in his direction. He reached a dinghy, and was in the process of cutting it loose, using a knife that he had liberated from the canning factory, when he was nearly discovered by the owner of the boat. Narrowly avoiding being seen, Hayes cut through the rope, and rowed himself past the rest of the boats, and the end of the island.

His muscles strengthened from yoga and carrying large sacks of beans around, Hayes was able to row through the night, and hit the beach around the time the next morning that the guards realized that he had escaped. His initial plan had been to ask a favour from a former prisoner friend and hide in his hotel in Istanbul; however when he got there, he learned that his friend had just gone to Afghanistan. Hayes' hopes of remaining in a basement till the hue and cry died down faded.

If he couldn't stay out of the way then Hayes knew he had to cross into Greece as quickly as possible; he reasoned that the hatred between Greece and Turkey meant that it was unlikely he would be returned to Turkey unless he committed murder. For three days, he ran through Turkey, dying his hair, and even inadvertently travelling through a minefield on the Greek/Turkish border. He had close encounters with border guards, and tried his best to evade the dogs on his scent by removing his shoes and socks. Eventually reaching the Maritsa river that divided the two countries, he swam across and once on the far side, he was intercepted by a Greek soldier and arrested – he had arrived in a heavily restricted military zone. For nearly two weeks, he was interrogated about everything he had seen, both at the prisons, and on his journey across Turkey to the Greek border.

On State Department advice, Hayes didn't remain in Europe, in case the West Germans or others decided that they would return him to Turkey. He caught a flight via Frankfurt, remaining in the transit lounge just in case, and Amsterdam to New York. It was more than thirty years before he would visit Turkey again: the film of *Midnight Express* had a noticeable anti-Turkish bias, which Hayes himself did not share, and he eventually went back, as he described it, to heal the breach. In the meantime, he became a film-maker, actor and director. He hasn't been tempted to smuggle since that day in 1970.

Sources:

Hayes, Billy with William Hoffer: *Midnight Express* (revised edition, CurlyBrains Publishing, 2012)

Crave Online, 28 June 2010: "Billy Hayes Reveals 'The Real Midnight Express'"

Time magazine, 13 April 1970: "Americans Abroad: The Jail Scene"

Tete de Turce: "Midnight-Express Phenomenon" www.tetedeturce. com

National Geographic TV, 2010: *Locked Up Abroad: The Real Midnight Express*

US Department of State, 25 May 1974: Telex from American Consul, Istanbul to American Embassy, Ankara

US Department of State, 19 March 1975: Telex from American Embassy, Ankara to Secretary of State, Washington DC

US Department of State, 9 May 1975: Telex from American Embassy, Ankara to Secretary of State, Washington DC

US Department of State, 21 October 1975: Telex from American Consul, Thessaloniki, to Secretary of State, Washington DC

PART V: PRISONERS OF WAR

Where the Wind Blows

He survived torture at the hands of the infamous Klaus Barbie, and was one of the few people ever to escape from the dreaded Fort Montluc prison in Lyon, but one thing was too much even for French resistance hero André Devigny. After he retired from the Army, he considered a career in politics, but decided that it wasn't for him when he realized that "the backstabbing was far worse than anything I'd ever encountered in secret warfare".

Devigny was working as a spy within occupied France during the Second World War when he was captured and sent to Montluc. In May 1940, the former school teacher had been commanding French troops in Belgium, battling against the advancing Germans, working behind enemy lines; unfortunately, he was the victim of "friendly fire" from his own side, and he was hospitalized back to Bordeaux, and then sent to recuperate at his family's farm in the Savoie region, in the French Alps.

In 1942, Devigny became one of the undercover operatives run by Colonel Georges-André Groussard out of Geneva. Groussard was working with British Intelligence – both MI6 and the Special Operations Executive – as well as Allen Dulles, representing the American Office of Special Services, and was fomenting anti-Nazi resistance within France as part of the "Gilbert" network. Lieutenant Devigny, codename Valentin, was exactly the sort of young officer he needed.

In April 1943, Devigny's Resistance cell based out of Annemasse, near the Swiss border, was infiltrated by a spy for the Gestapo. Robert Moog had worked at a gunpowder factory near Toulouse that had been sabotaged by Devigny's cell, and he was determined to take revenge. He betrayed one of Devigny's key colleagues, Edmee Deletraz, to the Gestapo, and she was forced to identify her leader. On April 14, Devigny and another member of the Resistance killed an Italian counter-espionage agent who was in the pay of the Germans. Three days after this execution in Nice, Devigny was arrested after Deletraz met him at the railway station at Annemasse.

Devigny was taken to Fort Montluc, a nineteenth-century prison which had been taken over by the Gestapo in November 1942 to act as a prison, interrogation centre, and internment camp for those awaiting transport to concentration camps. During the twenty-one months it was in operation, it is estimated that over 15,000 people were imprisoned within its walls; over 900 of them were executed there. In charge was Klaus Barbie, known as the Butcher of Lyon for his extreme methods of interrogation and torture, many of which he carried out himself rather than leave it to his assistants.

From 17 April to 25 May, Barbie and his men interrogated Devigny but he didn't break, and gave them no useful information. He did his level best to escape from the prison, but each attempt was unsuccessful, and only resulted in ever more severe punishment. During one try, while he was being transferred, he was shot. In the end, on 20 August 1943, he was sentenced to death by a German military court; he would face the firing squad on 28 August.

Three days before he was due to be executed, Devigny escaped. Although the Germans thought that they had kept him firmly under lock and key during his incarceration, Devigny had been able to move around the prison. He knew how to remove his handcuffs using a safety pin, and had then ground down a soup spoon on the concrete floor of his cell to create a tool. He used this to push out the wooden slats at the bottom of his cell door, and found that he could squeeze through the opening. At night, when the guards were confident that their prisoners were secure for the night, Devigny moved around the cell block, talking to the other inmates. He would then return to his cell, and wedge the slats back into place.

The frame of an old lantern that he discovered in the hallway gave him the idea for his means of escape – he knew he would need some sort of grappling hook in order to get over the walls. He took the lantern apart and created hooks from it, which he fixed to a home-made rope, formed from a mattress cover and a blanket, with pieces of wire.

After his appearance before the German military, Devigny knew he had to put his plan into effect quickly, but the day before he was going to flee, the Germans put another prisoner in with him. Devigny realized he had two options: take the rather dim-witted Gimenez with him, or kill him. He decided on the former course.

As soon as the clock chimed ten on the night of 24 August 1943, Devigny sprang into action. He knocked out the wedges which held the slats up, and removed the wooden boards from the door, passing them to Gimenez, who stacked them in the corner of the cell out of the way. He then checked the corridor was empty, and helped Gimenez to squeeze through the gap.

A skylight gave some meagre light into the corridor, and it was through this Devigny and Gimenez planned to exit. Devigny tried to climb up to it but his strength had been sapped by his days of solitary confinement following his previous escapes. Knowing that if he stopped now, he would be a dead man, Devigny summoned up all his energy and managed to boost himself up to the ceiling, and push the skylight open. After a few minutes' rest, he let a small rope down to Gimenez, who passed up a bundle containing the large rope that they needed to get over the walls, as well as their clothing. Devigny then helped Gimenez to ascend.

The pair had to wait for trains to pass nearby the prison to mask the noise of their movement across the roof of the fort, but since the stretch of line near the fort carried trains between the two main stations of Lyon, there wasn't too long a gap between them. Covered by the sound of a slow goods train making its way through the night, they managed to reach their goal, the side of the roof opposite the infirmary, slightly quicker than Devigny had anticipated.

Leaving Gimenez while he checked out the lie of the land, Devigny spotted a pair of guards smoking near the wash house, but from his initial position he couldn't see the stretch of wall they would need to climb down. With infinite patience, he slowly made his way around the roof and checked whether it was safe to proceed.

Although it seemed that the coast was clear, Devigny double-checked, and was very pleased that he had: his second inspection revealed a sentry sleeping on the steps, who would be in exactly the right position to see the two escapees as they came down into the courtyard. At midnight, the guard was changed, and Devigny watched his movements carefully. He then went back to Gimenez, and told him that they would be descending when the next train approached.

Just before 1 a.m., the two men heard a whistle in the distance which increased in volume. Telling Gimenez not to worry about the man patrolling below, Devigny slid down the rope into the courtyard, raced across to a low wall, threw the rope with the makeshift grappling hook over, hauled himself up and then dropped down the other side. Leaving the ropes for Gimenez, Devigny killed the sentry, then signalled for Gimenez to follow.

The two men raced across the next courtyard to the inner wall of the perimeter as quickly as they could, since they could easily be visible if anyone happened to look out of the infirmary windows, or from the central block. Devigny's strength was sapping, and in his memoirs, he admitted that he probably would have had to give up at this point if he had been on his own. Gimenez however, was able to ascend the wall without any trouble, and helped Devigny to reach the top. They then had to get across another roof before they reached a point which looked out at the outer wall.

They got up there, dislodging a couple of slates along the way that were luckily not heard, but when he saw what they faced, Devigny wondered if the attempt was doomed to fail. He had been unable to see the exact layout of the perimeter area between the walls from the roof before, and hadn't realized how brightly lit it was. They could hear voices coming from the perimeter – if there was a sentry box nearby, they wouldn't have a chance.

Devigny refused to give up, and craned his neck out to look at the area. To his relief, he saw that there was in fact only one sentry, who was patrolling the fifteen-feet-wide perimeter strip on a bicycle. The "voices" they had heard was the man talking to himself to relieve the boredom. At three o'clock, Devigny decided it was time to try. Waiting for the sentry to pass them by, he threw the rope with a grappling iron onto the top of the wall. It held fast the first time, and he then attached the rope firmly behind him.

The Resistance leader was exhausted by this stage, and encouraged Gimenez to go first, since he was lighter. If the rope snapped under Devigny's weight, at least Gimenez would have escaped. However the younger man lost his nerve, and refused to go.

Dawn was fast approaching, and Devigny realized that it was now or never. As soon as the sentry cycled past once more, passing beneath the rope, Devigny gripped the rope in both hands, swung himself out into space, and then pulled his legs up into position. Then, hand over hand, he made his way across to the far wall, and pulled himself up. As soon as the sentry passed by again, Gimenez followed suit. They then made their way along the outer wall to an area where it was much lower, and dropped to the ground. At 5 a.m., they were free men: the only two to escape from Fort Montluc while it was under Gestapo control.

The escape was nearly short-lived. Gimenez and Devigny were stopped by German patrols a couple of days later, but Devigny was able to escape from them by diving into a nearby river, and staying submerged in the mud for five hours. With help from his Resistance colleagues, Devigny made his way to Switzerland, and became active in the war effort again – he was captured in Spain later in the conflict, but after two months in prison, he managed to escape again. His escape came at a cost. As a direct result, Barbie ordered the arrest and deportation to the death camps of two of Devigny's cousins.

Devigny served with distinction for many years after the Second World War, becoming a leading figure in French counter-intelligence. He retired in 1971 and died in 1999.

Sources:

The Independent, 25 February 1999: "Obituary: General Andre Devigny"

Ordre de la Liberation: "André Devigny, alias: Valentin"

The New York Times, 27 February 1999: "Andre Devigny, 82; Escaped from Gestapo Prison"

Devigny, André: *Un condamné s'est échappé* (A Man Escaped, translated Peter Green) (Hachette, 1956; Lyons Press, 2002)

The Greatest Escapes?

Some of the most famous escapes from prisons took place from the prisoner-of-war camps operated by the Germans during World War II. These have inspired films, novels and TV series, and names and phrases like 'Colditz' and 'The Great Escape' have entered the general language. But as with so many of the escapes recounted in this volume, the true stories are often very different from the screen versions – the 1970s BBC version of *Colditz* needed an American star, so a character was created for Robert Wagner who would not have been imprisoned at Oflag IV-C for as long as he was in the series. The Cooler King played by Steve McQueen in the movie of *The Great Escape* wasn't part of the real escape, and the fate of the fifty men was markedly different in real life to the dramatic conclusion of the movie. In this section we look at a couple of famous cases, and a pair that aren't so well known.

One movie that did steer close to the facts of the case was *The Wooden Horse*, based on events at Stalag Luft III, the same camp from which The Great Escape would take place in March 1944. Three men – Lieutenant Michael Codner, Flight Lieutenant Eric Williams, and Flight Lieutenant Oliver Philpot – escaped after digging a tunnel whose entrance was out in the yard of the camp.

The first compound at Stalag Luft III was opened in March 1942, and RAF navigator Eric Williams arrived there the following year after being shot down in December 1942 and proving to be a difficult POW for the Germans. He and Michael Codner escaped from the first camp in which they were being held, so were sent to Stalag Luft III since it was meant to be escape-proof. It had the standard German security measures, including guard towers, searchlights, barbed wire, fences and armed guards, and a few refinements, such as microphones in the soil which could detect the sound of tunnelling. The camp's location benefitted the Germans as well: the ground in that part of the former Poland had a grey topsoil, but a very distinctively yellow-coloured stratum underneath that made tunnelling harder, since it was so fine that tunnels were likely to cave in. As far as the Germans were concerned, this was the most secure facility that they possessed.

To make things harder for any escape-minded prisoners, which was the majority of them, the huts were built on stilts (except for concrete foundations around the stoves and the washrooms), and were around a foot off the ground. To reach safety, a tunnel would have to be dug underneath the entire yard, beneath the fence, and then for some further distance before it reached the treeline. In total, as the escape committee discovered very quickly, a tunnel would have to stretch for nearly a hundred yards. This, of course, did not deter the British soldiers from attempting to escape since tunnelling was the only way of getting out, and it was their duty to try.

But if they did manage to get out, they still faced other difficulties: the camp was built in the middle of a huge pine forest, about 400 miles from the Swiss border, or 175 miles from the Baltic coast.

Williams and Codner considered the problem, and reasoned that if they couldn't move where the tunnel finished, then in order to shorten the length, they would have to move the starting point closer to the treeline. Something of the sort had been tried before: some POWs had tried to dig a tunnel in the open ground area simply using their hands and covering the hole with bed-slats and sand, hiding the sand in their pockets. This hadn't got very far, but Williams thought that there must be a way of hiding the trapdoor into the tunnel out in the open. Ideally it should be right underneath the noses of the Goons (the nickname that the POWs gave to the German sentries). Codner was not enthusiastic about the idea until Williams had a brainwave. What if they could find something that could cover the trapdoor which would not attract suspicion?

What Williams was thinking of was a wooden vaulting horse, like the ones that they had used in school gymnasia. The horses were about three feet high, two feet wide at the base, and tapered as they went up, to around a foot width at the top. One could easily be made from the crates that were sent to the men by the Red Cross, with cigarette-packet wrappings used to create the top. Once the Germans were used to seeing it out in the yard, a man could be transported inside it, clinging to the sides, until the horse was placed over the trapdoor. He would then dig down during the day, fill up bags with sand, and attach them to the underside of the horse. He, and his cargo, would then be carried back to the POWs' hut, and the sand dispersed in convenient places around the camp. The trapdoor would be disguised with extra grey topsoil each day so the yard would look completely clear. While he was excavating underground, the POWs who brought the horse out would carry out athletics training, thumping down onto the ground as they landed from the horse, thus deflecting the attention of the seismographic microphones from the digging. (Interestingly, in the obituary for Michael Codner in *Time* magazine, it suggests that the wooden horse was his idea "with his knowledge of the classics".)

Codner and Williams had to bring a third man, Canadian RAF pilot Oliver Philpot, into the scheme, since he was the escape committee coordinator for the hut in which they were living. Like Codner, Philpot was unsure about the chances of success, but was willing to help by organizing the vaulters and the transport of the horse, as well as overseeing the disposal of the sand. The escape committee gave the go-ahead, and the horse was constructed.

Over a number of weeks, the vaulting horse became a familiar sight: it would be carried out from the hut each day, supported by a pole at each end (when these were removed, the holes that they left provided air for the tunneller), and placed in the same spot, which eventually became very obvious. The Germans, of course, were naturally suspicious, and made regular checks to see what the British were playing at; every so often, one of the POWs would "accidentally" knock it over to show how innocuous it was.

When they judged that it was as safe as it was ever likely to be, Codner and Williams began the tunnel. First off, they had to dig a shaft down through the topsoil to the level at which they were going to head horizontally towards the trees, and they lined this with plywood panels taken from the Red Cross parcel boxes. To create the thirty-inch square, five-feet-deep shaft took four days; the trapdoor was eighteen inches below the surface and was covered daily with topsoil – it needed to be that far beneath the ground to prevent any alert German guard from hearing a hollow echo as they walked around the yard.

The next part of the tunnel was in many ways the riskiest, since it was being dug directly beneath where their POW colleagues were thumping down onto the ground as they vaulted over the horse. To ensure that there weren't any inconvenient cave-ins, the first seven feet of the tunnel were fully shored up, with bed boards on the bottom, the roof and the sides. There wasn't sufficient timber to line the entire tunnel; the Germans would certainly notice that much going missing. They had to hope that the chances of cave-in remained slim, although, as with any tunnel, it was an ever-present risk.

The digger would excavate sand at the "front" end of the tunnel and then drag it back to the bottom of the shaft, and place it in the bags for lifting and disposal. It was a slow job, and to begin with, only around twelve bags per athletics session could be lifted. When Philpot took a more active role as one of the diggers, they switched to a slightly different system: two men would dig out thirty-six bags, and leave them at the foot of the shaft, then on the next three trips, one man would lift twelve to the surface. This helped to alleviate the pressure on the vaulters who were beginning to get tired from all the exercise that they were having – these included future star of the *Carry On* films, Peter Butterworth.

The work proceeded without too many major mishaps: on one occasion, the roof gave way when Codner was digging, which actually left a hole in the surface of the yard. Luckily, one of the athletes saw the ground opening, and deliberately landed badly, so that he could fall convincingly to the ground and cover the entrance. As he lay there, Codner was able to scoop away the sand, and shore up the roof with some planks that he took from the shaft.

It was difficult to be sure that the tunnel was proceeding according to plan. The escapers used a poker to ascertain its position, and realized that it was at about the right level, but was running about thirty degrees away from the necessary course. The physical effort involved tired out all three men considerably, and Williams ended up hospitalized for almost a week from exhaustion.

Eventually, at the start of October, the tunnel had reached beyond the wire, so the trio started their preparations, sorting out their cover stories, and planning their routes to freedom. They decided to take advantage of the no-moon period at the end of the month, and set a date of 29 October 1943, 114 days after they began digging, for the escape.

That morning Codner and Philpot went to the tunnel inside the horse to collect some sandbags; Philpot was brought back to the huts, but Codner stayed inside the tunnel to finalize the digging. He ventilated the tunnel by sticking a metal pipe up through the soil to create some air holes. The POWs were adept at covering for missing officers during roll call, so Codner's absence wasn't noticed by the Germans, and once that was complete, Williams and Philpot were carried out to the tunnel entrance. With them came another POW, McKay, whose job it was to seal them in once they had got under way. Just after 6 p.m., they broke out from the far end of the tunnel.

During the preparation for the escape the three men had agreed that Philpot would make his own way once they were at liberty. He had created a character for himself called Jon Jörgensen, a Norwegian margarine salesman. Williams and Codner posed as French workmen. All three made their way to Sagan railway station and caught the train to Frankfurt. There Philpot had hoped to continue straightaway to Küstrin, but had to wait until the next morning for a train. He decided to hide in the woods rather than risk hanging around the train station and being caught. He managed to get to Küstrin the next day, and then headed on towards Danzig. Although he nearly made the classic mistake of POWs travelling across Germany and swearing in English, he successfully bluffed his way past a police officer, and started to look for a ship that would take him to Sweden. He found one, but the captain tried to make him leave in case he risked the crew's freedom; luckily for Philpot the chief engineer took pity on him, and hid him until the ship was safely at sea. On 4 November, six days after he had escaped from Stalag Luft III, Oliver Philpot was taken to the British Legation in Stockholm. He became a senior scientific officer in the Air Ministry for the rest of the war, and in later years became chairman of the RAF Escaping Society. He wrote up his experiences as *Stolen Journey*.

A number of the items Philpot used during his escape were donated to the Imperial War Museum in London by his family after his death, with the compass selected as one of the BBC's *History of the World in 100 Objects*. It shows the ingenuity of the escapers: as Philpot described in his memoir: "The bowl was a moulded gramophone record and it had a glass top measuring three inches across, and in the bowl stood an inverted gramophone needle. Two pieces of a razor blade had been magnetized by the camp electric light circuit, and had been pasted on to the underside of a circular cardboard compass card. The card had, in the middle, a press-stud from an officer's uniform into which the gramophone needle fitted neatly, enabling the card to swing freely under the glass. The card markings were large and clear, with phosphorus added from old and broken watch-faces."

Williams and Codner also made a "home run" as a successful escape to England was termed. They travelled by rail as far as Stettin, a port city now in Poland, and were able to make contact with members of the Resistance. They were sent by ship to Copenhagen, hiding in the bilge to avoid the regular searches of the vessel – it was initially checked out by SS officers with sniffer dogs before it was allowed to leave port. Once in Denmark, they were transported across to Sweden in a fishing boat. Once there they went to the British Legation, to find Oliver Philpot waiting for them.

Eric Williams was posted to the Philippines for the rest of the war; on the journey back to Britain he wrote the first draft of what became his book *The Wooden Horse* (which fictionalized some of the adventures that he and Codner experienced on their travels from the camp). After the war, Michael Codner applied to serve in Malaya, living in a village ringed with barbed wire. When guerrillas sabotaged the water pipe, Codner was killed in an ambush when he went to repair it. When Williams learned of his death, he said, "He was quite the bravest, the most gifted and the most unassuming man I've ever met." Oliver Philpot added: "It's appalling, but it's the way you might have expected him to die."

"If you see me walking around with a tree trunk sticking out of my arse, don't ask any questions, because it'll be for a damned good reason." So said Squadron Leader Roger Bushell to new arrivals in the North camp of Stalag Luft III. Bushell had been sent to the camp in 1942 after escaping from various places but never quite making it across a border to safety. When the Germans purged the camp of some of the real troublemakers, in an effort to reduce the number of escape attempts, Bushell was placed in charge of the Escape Committee. He came up with an audacious plan: to dig three tunnels simultaneously, and try to get two hundred men out of the camp, all equipped with suitable disguises, papers and cover stories. The three tunnels were codenamed Tom, Dick and Harry; Bushell himself was known as Big X.

The tunnels were begun in the spring of 1943, but in the early summer it became clear to the Escape Committee that they were going to lose some of the expertise that they were using to dig the tunnels: the United States Air Force (USAF) officers were being transferred to a new part of the camp (ironically this was being built in a forest area which had been the target for Dick). To try to get one tunnel completed before their forces were split, Bushell gave the order to press ahead with Tom. However, when the tunnel reached the perimeter fence, the Germans suddenly decided to cut down the trees around the area that those going through Tom would have surfaced. It was clear that either the Germans' surveillance microphones were considerably better than they had anticipated, or that there was a traitor among the POWs. When Bushell realized that the Germans had no idea that Tom began in Hut 123, he decided the former was the reason, but it meant that he had to divert their attention.

Digging continued, but the disposal of the earth by "penguins" – POWs moving around the camp, letting pieces of dirt slip from concealed pouches made from old socks within their greatcoats – had to be curtailed, so progress was slowed. Hut 123 was one of many barracks that were targeted, but the Germans didn't find the tunnel whose entrance was in a dark corner of the hall. When Tom was less than twenty feet from completion, the Germans got lucky during an inspection – a metal probe dropped to the floor, which dislodged the sand and cement that disguised the tunnel entrance – and the tunnel became the ninety-eighth to be found within the camp. The tunnel was destroyed.

Undeterred, Bushell ordered the men to reopen and continue work on Harry as soon as it was safe to do so. From overheard conversations, it seemed that the Germans had been fooled: they did not consider the possibility of there being another tunnel being as advanced, one of the reasons Bushell had wanted to dig three simultaneously in the first place. (It was around this time Williams, Codner and Philpot escaped from the other compound.)

After work recommenced on 10 January 1944, Harry was completed that March, with two halfway houses – known as Piccadilly and Leicester Square – ready as resting spaces for the escapers, with the second one directly beneath the perimeter fence. Despite warnings from the Germans that the punishment for escaping would be considerably more severe than it had previously been (usually a spell of solitary confinement), the escape committee resolved to continue with the plan. Some of their key members were moved to a satellite camp five miles away at the start of March, but that was not enough to deter the POWs.

A date of 24 March was chosen, and even though the weather wasn't particularly good – which would cause problems for any of the escapers who had to travel across country – Bushell decided that they had to proceed. The Germans had increased their surveillance, and it was only a matter of time before the tunnel was discovered. No trains ran on Sundays, so if they didn't go that day, they would have to wait until Monday, and by that time it would no longer be a new moon and they would lose the advantage of darkness. A huge logistical operation had been prepared to ensure that all the escapers had the necessary items, and on the morning of Friday 24, Bushell gave the order to proceed. All the forged documents then had that date (or an appropriate one as necessary) inserted.

Bushell still hoped to get 200 men out through Harry. Included in the first hundred were the group known as serial offenders, who were those with the best chance of making it back to England: they had escaped before and many of them spoke German. The other seventy or so were men who had spent the most time working underground on the tunnel. The second group of one hundred was selected by lots from the other five hundred men who had contributed to Harry; these were nicknamed "hard-arsers" and weren't expected to have a great deal of chance of making it. Their benefit was, as POW Jack Lyon later explained, "to contribute to the success of the whole operation – the more people on the loose at the same time, the more confusion and difficulties for the Germans."

The night of 24 March was bitterly cold and when the escapers arrived in Hut 104 to travel through Harry, according to some accounts they discovered that the entrance had frozen solid. It took ninety minutes to force the hatch open, and then the plan hit a further snag. When the tunnel was pushed through to the surface at the far end, it hadn't reached quite as far as they had anticipated: the exit wasn't within the treeline, but was out in the open. They quickly came up with a solution: a rope was tied from the ladder at the end of the tunnel to a nearby tree. When each man came through the tunnel, he waited for two tugs on the rope to indicate that it was clear to run from the exit into the trees; when he reached shelter, he then kept watch to advise the next escaper.

This slowed the escape down tremendously: Bushell had hoped to get one man a minute through. Instead, the rate dwindled to ten per hour. It was quickly agreed that no one with a number higher than 100 was going to be able to go through, and even that wasn't achieved – the electric lighting in the camp (and therefore in the tunnel) was switched off because of an air raid, and then there was a small collapse in the tunnel itself which had to be repaired.

Seventy-six prisoners of war managed to get through Harry before the exodus was spotted by the guards. At 4.55 a.m., the seventy-seventh man was seen, and surrendered. The alarm was raised, but the Germans took so long to reach Hut 104 that the POWs were able to burn their fake papers. The Germans were unable to find the tunnel entrance, and in the end sent one of their men through from the other end to locate it.

Only three of the escapees made a home run. Norwegian pilots Per Bergsland and Jens Müller reached Sweden; Dutch airman Bram van der Stok headed south through France, and finally gained safety at the British Consulate in Spain. Hitler was furious when he heard about the escape, and wanted all of them found and executed; in the end, when Heinrich Himmler and Hermann Goring both pointed out that this would be political suicide, since there would be no way of covering it up, he compromised at fifty. The pursuit and disposal of the prisoners was handed to the Gestapo and of the other seventy-three, fifty were executed – not all at once, as the feature film account of the escape suggested, but singly or in pairs as they were captured. Roger Bushell's death certificate was typed up as soon as he was captured at Saarbrucken, one of the first escapers to be caught – there was a small error in his travel documents.

At Stalag Luft III, Harry was pumped full of sewage, topped with sand. A few of the escapers were returned there, but on 6 April, news was passed on that "forty-one of the escapers were shot while resisting arrest or in their attempt to escape again after being recaptured." Nine days later, a list of forty-seven escapers who had been murdered was posted within the camp; a further three were added a little later. As Hitler had demanded, fifty of the POWs had paid the ultimate price. It was described by Foreign Secretary Anthony Eden as a "cold act of butchery", and post-war, various members of the Gestapo were held accountable for the executions.

A new tunnel was started by the Escape Committee, but more for morale-boosting than because they expected it to be particularly effective. Before it could be used, the Second World War came to an end.

By pure coincidence, around the same time as the seventy-six escapers from Stalag Luft III were making their way through Sagan on the morning of 25 March 1943, another trio of fugitives from the Germans were making their way through the town. John McCallum, his brother Jimmy, and their friend Joe Harkin had managed to get away from Stalag Luft VIII-B.

McCallum had been captured in France during the German invasion in 1940 and sent to the camp in Upper Silesia, close to the Polish border. VIII-B had been established to deal with the prisoners captured during the initial Nazi blitzkriegs so very quickly became a melting pot of different nationalities.

At VIII-B, McCallum was reunited with his brother – who thought he had been killed in action in France – and Harkin. Escape wasn't possible for the first year of imprisonment: McCallum's ankle had been very seriously injured during a battle, and he needed to rebuild mobility. However, escape attempts were plentiful during that time, and the three men took note of what worked, and, more importantly, what didn't.

Many of the POWs volunteered for working parties, simply to relieve the monotony of their existence in the camps. The McCallums and Harkin ended up working on a railway construction project and engineered their own departure from that in 1942, after managing to persuade the Germans that they were non-commissioned officers. They then volunteered to join a party working in a holiday village in the mountains, and were moved to a much less well-defended camp nearby.

This brought them in contact with a lot of the locals – particularly the young ladies – and in order to have some enjoyable fraternization, they built a tunnel from their quarters to an outside toilet near the barbed wire. They had no intention of using this for a proper escape: according to McCallum, in working parties, there was an unwritten rule about not escaping from a good camp, in case it jeopardized the others who were left behind. For some time, McCallum used the tunnel to go for assignations with local girl Traudl, and later some of the POWs went out to steal a radio so they could keep up with the BBC news.

In early 1944, after two years, the working party was wound up, and the men returned to Stalag Luft VIII-B. Traudl offered to help the McCallums and Harkin with an escape: she would have access to information they would need. The idea was that they would volunteer for another party, escape from there, and return to Traudl's village. However, the escape committee in

VIII-B refused to assist them, as the policy wasn't to help first-time escapers, no matter how good their plan might be.

They were sent to a factory in Jagerndorf, around ten miles from Bad Karlsbrunn where Traudl awaited them. However, this wasn't a lax regime like the camp they had been in before: they were kept in a concrete blockhouse, with iron-barred windows and barbed wire surrounding it. They had arrived on a Friday, intending to leave that Sunday, but were taken aback by the security measures.

Thanks to help from a couple of fellow Scots who had been working on an escape previously, they were able to go on the Monday: the other POWs had already cut through the iron bars in the windows. Harkin had smuggled pliers into the camp with them, and made short work of the barbed wire. That easily, they were out and heading for Bad Karlsbrunn.

While his brother and Harkin waited in a hut in the woods, McCallum visited Traudl and with her help, forged various documents. At 2 a.m. on 25 March, they made their way down to the local train station and caught a train to Sagan, arriving there around midday. They had hoped to look for help from the local Resistance. However, they weren't welcomed with open arms: Sagan was being shut down by the Gestapo following the escape from Stalag Luft III. McCallum decided that the only thing to do was continue with their journey, and head for Frankfurt. They were lucky: no one stopped them to check their documents, and they were able to leave Sagan safely. (Their papers did eventually pass muster when checked on one of their train journeys.) They arrived in Stettin, and Harkin, a former Merchant Navy seaman, found a ship on which they could stow away to Sweden. They reached Malmo, and went to the British Consulate. Shortly after D-Day, 6 June 1944, they were flown back to the UK. Although she waited for McCallum for some time, Traudl eventually married a Czech officer.

An equally daring escape was tried by another pair of prisoners, but unlike the events chronicled above, this hasn't received a lot of attention. Perhaps this is because it features German soldiers trying to flee from Great Britain?

Leutnant Heinz Schnabel and Oberleutnant Harry Wappler were being held at Camp 15 at Shap about ten miles from Penrith in Cumbria. The former Shap Wells Hotel had been set up as a prisoner-of-war camp, with around 250 naval and Luftwaffe officers held there fenced in with two rings of barbed wire, as well as searchlights, while guards lived in Nissan huts in the grounds. Wappler's Heinkel He111 bomber had been shot down over Newport and the pilot was taken to the Royal Herbert Hospital, in Woolwich, where he met Schnabel, a fighter pilot who was shot down in his Messerschmitt ME 109 on 5 September 1940.

On 24 November 1941, the two men made their escape from the camp. Some sources say that they hid in a laundry basket, others that they went for a walk, having given their word that they would return. Either way, they were equipped with identification papers they had forged using art materials supplied to them by their guards, which claimed that they were Dutch airmen.

The two Germans put flying jackets over their German uniforms – particularly at that stage of the Second World War, no one wanted to risk being accused of spying – and headed by train into Carlisle. From there they went to RAF Kingstown just north of the town, and were able to bluff their way onto the airfield.

Their plan was simple: steal a plane, and fly back to Germany. There were about fifty Miles Magister aircraft sitting on the airfield, which were being used for training flights. A ground mechanic eagerly helped them to start up, and they headed south, landing at another airfield to refuel. From there they set off across the North Sea.

Unfortunately for them, they had miscalculated. They needed to travel about 365 miles to the Dutch coast, and the maximum flight range of the Magister, in ideal conditions, was 367 miles. The margin of error was too small, and when they started to encounter bad weather, the two Germans realized that they would have to turn back. Very reluctantly, they turned around, and landed near Great Yarmouth on the Suffolk coast.

Still posing as Dutch airmen, they were taken to RAF Horsham, but their ruse was seen through there when news of the theft of the Magister arrived. They still had time to have a meal in the officers' mess before they were rumbled. For their exploits, the pair received twenty-eight days' solitary confinement. Shortly afterwards they were sent to Canada, where they spent the rest of the war.

Sources:

Gill, Anton: *The Great Escape* (Review, 2002)
McCallum, John: *The Long Way Home: The Other Great Escape* (Birlinn, 2005)

Free as a Bird

Over the course of the Second World War, there were many daring escapes from Colditz Castle, quite a few of which were ultimately successful, with the prisoners of war making "home runs". Whole books have been written charting these escapades, so rather than try to give too broad an overview, this is the tale of just one of the attempts, which, as events transpired, was never seen through to fruition. It's the story of the Colditz Cock, the infamous glider.

Colditz Castle has become synonymous with the POW camp that began there in November 1939. The movie *The Colditz Story* in 1955 was one of the first to tell the tale, based on the books by Major Pat Reid published in 1952 and 1953. A major BBC television series from 1972 to 1974 inspired a popular board game (devised by Reid himself in its early incarnations), and still attracted large audiences for cable television when it was repeated in 2011. Even now, the townsfolk are happy to cooperate with documentaries that revisit that period.

The castle sits several hundred feet above the town of Colditz in Germany, and in its long history had been used as a sanatorium and insane asylum.

Many of the prisoners who were sent to Oflag IV-C, Colditz's official designation, tried to escape. They attempted disguises; they duplicated keys; one small officer even managed to hide inside a Red Cross packing case and was taken up to the German command area, from where he was able to flee (unfortunately he was apprehended while trying to get on board a ship in Danzig a week later). There were various tunnels, and in one six-week period in 1942, twelve officers escaped from the castle, with six of them making home runs. Heinrich Himmler may have claimed that the castle was escape-proof, but the POWs were determined to prove him wrong.

The Great Escape from Stalag Luft III changed a great deal at Colditz, as it did in all the camps around the Third Reich. Previously, escaping had been, to an extent, regarded as an adventure. Of course the Germans would shoot at escapers, but usually with intent to wound rather than kill (the one fatality at Colditz came when a bullet ricocheted into Lieutenant Mike Sinclair's heart). However, after it became clear that the Nazis were now regarding escape as punishable with death, the predilection of the officers to "have a go" was reined in. MI9, the branch of British military intelligence that assisted potential escapers, advised caution.

However, one plan was still being worked on in secret: the Colditz Cock, the brainchild of Flight Lieutenant Bill Goldfinch, who had been sent to Colditz from Stalag Luft III after tunnelling out, and Lieutenant Tony Rolt, a former racing driver. In the winter of 1943, Goldfinch was standing in a room overlooking Colditz town and observed the way in which the snow drifted up and over the top of the castle. It showed that there was a really smooth flow of air, which would be perfect to use in a glider. As he explained to a Channel 4 documentary in 2000, "All the other methods of escape had been attempted by somebody. This seemed much simpler to me – to stand on the roof and jump off."

They would need to improvize a runway along the forty-foot ridge, and then use a counterweight to catapult themselves off the roof down towards a field on the other side of the River Mulde, about five hundred yards away. On the roof, they were out of the way of the searchlights, but they would need to build the glider in secret within the castle walls, and then get it into position. A bath filled with concrete would be fastened with a bed rope to the end of the glider. When it was dropped from the third floor of the chapel block, it would be enough to send two escapers on their way.

The escape committee gave their blessing to the attempt, reasoning, in part, that work on the glider would keep the officers focused. To his delight, Goldfinch found a two-volume book in the castle library entitled *Aircraft Design*, which explained exactly what was needed to build and fly a glider. A false wall was built in the attic above the chapel, which made the upper room seven feet shorter, but the POWs gambled on the Germans never measuring the rooms. A trapdoor in the ceiling allowed entrance to this new secret room, in which construction work began on 1 January 1944.

Sixteen men were directly involved with the work. The originators – Goldfinch, Rolt, RAF pilot Jack Best and Jeff Wardle – were assisted by twelve "apostles" building the glider, while forty others kept watch and diverted the Germans' attention. Thirty-two ribs had to be made for the wings and the tailplane, all of which had to be exactly accurate or the glider wouldn't fly. In the end, over 6,000 different pieces of wood were used, while electricity cable was repurposed for the control cables, and beds were taken apart for their bolts. Saws were created from the spring of an old gramophone. But the prisoners played fair: the Germans had allowed them to use tools for the flourishing theatre in the camp grounds so long as they weren't used to help with an escape. Not one of these ever went into the workshop.

The skeleton of the glider was complete by the summer of 1944. Paillasse covers were then stretched over the top of the fuselage, and painted with what the POWs called "dope" to keep it tight – although none of it was waterproof, meaning that the glider's sole flight would need to be on a dry night.

The glider never flew. It soon became clear that the tide of the war was turning against the Germans. The D-Day invasion in June 1944 saw the Allies start to march on Berlin, but those in the camps were unsure how their captors would react, particularly one group held at Colditz, the "Prominente". These were relatives of key members of the Allied forces, such as Winston Churchill's nephew by marriage, a nephew of King George VI, and the son of the American Ambassador to Britain. When the POWs learned that squads of SS soldiers were now stationed in Colditz town, probably with orders to exterminate the Prominente if necessary, it was decided to hold the glider as a potential lifeline to alert the outside world of an impending massacre.

The original glider was still in position when Colditz was liberated by the Americans in April 1945 – the only photograph of it was taken by one of the US soldiers. However, it was duplicated on three occasions. In 1993, a miniature version was constructed from Goldfinch's original designs, which he had kept since the war, and launched from the castle roof. For a Channel 4 documentary in 2000, a full-size replica was built and launched at RAF Odiham: both Goldfinch and Jack Best witnessed their dreams become reality. On 17 March 2012, a further full-scale version of the glider flew from Colditz Castle, for all of fifteen seconds before crashing into the exact field that Bill Goldfinch had identified nearly seventy years previously. Sadly Goldfinch had died five years earlier, but as the youngest member of the reconstruction team, Jess Nyahoe told the *Radio Times*, "If we got it wrong, then the world would have thought that they got it wrong. For them and their memory we wanted to get it right."

Sources:

Chancellor, Henry: *Colditz, The Definitive History* (Hodder & Stoughton, 2001)

Radio Times, 17 March 2012: "Colditz Castle glider escape plot realised more than 65 years after the war"

Daily Telegraph, 12 October 2007: "Obituary: Flight Lieutenant Bill Goldfinch"

PBS, 6 February 2001: "Nazi Prison Escape" (edited from the Channel 4 *Escape from Colditz* series)

A Christian Helper

According to official US records, only three servicemen captured during the Korean War made it back across enemy lines. Of those, just one was captured and escaped twice, and had to contend with both ankles so badly fractured that the bones had come out of the side of his feet. Major Ward Malvern Millar bore the marks of his escape until his death in January 1999.

Millar had served in the United States Air Force during the Second World War, and after being demobbed, had gone to study nuclear physics at Reed College in Oregon. However, when the North Koreans invaded South Korea in 1950, and the USAF became active in the conflict assisting the United Nations, Millar was called back to active service, flying sorties over the North Korean lines.

In June 1951, during his thirtieth mission, his plane caught fire, and he had no option: he had to bail out over North Korean territory, knowing that he would be captured and held in one of their prisoner-of-war camps. His problems were compounded by his bad landing: it was very obvious to him that he had broken both his ankles, but his Chinese Army captors either didn't understand him, or chose not to take any notice of his pleas. Instead they told him to march off to a nearby hut.

With guns pointing in his face, Millar didn't think he had any option. He stood up, but as he did so, he could hear the bones of his ankle crunch. As a direct result of the pressure of his weight on them, he ended up with a compound fracture of the bones of his right ankle. When they saw this, even the Chinese realized that he was not going to be able to go any further. He was therefore permitted to crawl on his belly to the hut – at least until some American planes started to fly over. At that point, one of his captors picked him up and carried him on his back the remaining hundred yards.

Once he was finally in the hut, Millar was stripped of all of his possessions, although he was allowed to keep his service jacket and his "Mae West", the inflatable lifejacket which USAF personnel were issued with as part of their flight gear, named after the buxom film star. Millar was pleased that they let him keep the Mae West: he figured that it would help him when he reached the coast after he escaped. And escape was what he intended to do, no matter what injuries he might have received.

Millar guessed that he was being kept not too far from the coast; if he could get there, he had a good chance of finding a boat which would take him to one of the US Navy ships. Before he could do any major planning, he was interrogated by the North Koreans, who alternately promised to release him, and then start preparations for his execution. Millar was determined that they weren't going to break him; he was simply not going to give them that satisfaction. He stayed firm, and in the end was transferred to a small hospital in a nearby village, where his injured legs were put into a cast.

Although rations for prisoners of war weren't particularly large, Millar started to stockpile a cache of food, ready for the long trek to the coast. He was aided by a seventeen-year-old South Korean boy, Ho, who was willing to go with him. Each night while the other patients slept, Millar practised crawling but he discovered that his toes were protruding from the end of the cast, and dragging painfully along the ground. He therefore developed some protection for his feet, by tying two boards to his legs to act as skids, then attached tin cans to his insteps so the boards wouldn't cut into the top of his feet, and wrapped pieces of cloth around his toes. Unfortunately, before he could test this out very much, he had two pieces of bad luck: the teenager was taken away, and Millar's cast, which had previously only extended up to his knee, was replaced with one that nearly reached up to his hips. The only upside was that this new cast meant that he was free of the lice which had crawled inside the old one and caused him almost intolerable itching. However, when he split the back of the cast down to the knee, he gained some manoeuvrability and on 27 July 1951, he started to crawl away from the hospital.

It took Millar three hours to crawl twenty-five yards. At that speed it would take him 211 hours – seventy-two days – to make the first mile. Reluctantly facing up to the reality of his plight, Millar turned back and made the equally painful and slow return trip. By sheer luck, his exploits weren't noticed.

A week later, on 5 August, the medical team at Na-han-li hospital removed the cast from his leg. But whoever had placed it on his leg had no real idea what he was doing: instead of placing the bones at the correct angle so they would heal properly, they had been set in such a haphazard manner that his toes pointed downwards stiffly at a grotesque angle – when Miller stood up, his body tilted backwards. However, as far as the staff at the hospital and his Chinese guards were concerned, the treatment had been a success. At a suitable time in the near future, he would be transferred from there to a regular prisoner-of-war camp.

Millar wasn't given any boots, despite asking for them, although his captors did allow him to use a couple of sticks as crutches, and for a time he had use of a pair of tennis shoes. Eventually he was provided with an old pair of galoshes which were designed to fit a shoe two sizes larger than Millar's feet. Although he initially thought these would be useless, he came to realize that they might be exactly what he needed after all. There was enough room in them to build a false heel, which would allow him to walk better, and if he stuffed rags around the lower part of his legs, the upper part of the galoshes would fit comfortably, and provide a degree of ankle support. With that bolstering, the galoshes allowed Millar to get up a turn of speed that he had begun to believe would be impossible again.

The airman checked that his "escape kit" was ready: he had some rock salt, a few small pieces of soap; a piece of towelling; a tin can top bent over, which could be used as a crude knife; and 200 won inside the lining of his Mae West. In better spirits than he had been in some time, Millar waited for his chance to go. The evacuation to the prisoner-of-war camp had been delayed because heavy rains were preventing trucks from getting through to the hospital, but when those dried up on 14 August, Millar knew he had to chance it now, or risk being much further behind enemy lines. He managed to gain one extra night in the hospital by faking a bad cough, but was warned that he was being sent to Pyongyang the next day.

Millar knew that he would be checked up on around 11 p.m., and as soon as the Chinese nurse had done the inspection, he made himself ready, and at midnight, he hobbled out of the hut. Rather than head immediately for the UN lines to the south, Millar decided to head north, hoping that this would put his pursuers off the scent. He managed to get a few miles before collapsing into an exhausted sleep. Over the next few days, he realized that he was nowhere near the coast, as he had first thought: Ho had told him that they were being held in the centre of Korea, around seventy miles from the sea, but Millar had dismissed the boy as being illiterate.

Recognizing that there was nothing for it but to keep going, Millar headed west. He was wracked with dysentery, irritated by lice, and in perpetual pain from the chafing of the galoshes on his skin. He had one run-in with a Korean who found him, and tried to hand him in to the local authorities, but the man was mute, and was unable to make the Chinese understand what he was trying to tell them.

After eleven days hobbling across North Korea, Miller was finally captured, after another civilian spotted him and went to fetch soldiers. The North Korean military found him hiding in the bushes, but when their leader, Kim Chal Phail, started to search Millar, he discovered a tiny cross that the airman had created from a twig. He said three simple words to Millar which proved to be the American's salvation: "Jesus, Mary, Christian?" Millar nodded: his faith and his love for his family had been all that had kept him going over the past week.

Kim carried Millar the four miles to his village on his back, and once they were alone, he explained that he too wanted to get away from the north. He hoped to defect to South Korea. Between them the two supposed enemies devised a plan of escape.

When Kim was ordered to transfer Millar up to a prison camp at Hwangju in the north a few days later, he drained fuel from the truck so that it would run out before they reached their destination. Kim took a circuitous route towards the camp, and, as he had planned, the fuel ran out when they were partway there. Finding a replacement supply would take some time, so Kim sent the four soldiers who had accompanied them off on a search, while he and Millar used a headlight and the truck's battery to flash an SOS at passing US aircraft.

For four days, they tried to attract attention, using a mirror during the day, and the headlight at night. On 10 September, the pilot of an F-80 saw the glint in his cockpit mirror, and turned to investigate. When he saw the two men, he signalled to them that they had been spotted and radioed for help. Two hours later, nearly fifty Allied planes reached them, and wiped out the surrounding villages with machine-gun fire, rockets and napalm bombs, to allow a helicopter to land safely to collect them.

The element of luck (or perhaps divine providence) that had assisted Millar throughout his escape hadn't deserted him at the last minute: the F-80 had in fact been looking for the crashed pilot of another plane who had been forced to land in the area a few days earlier.

After the end of the war, Kim Chai Phail was given a special commendation by the US 5th Air Force; Millar was also decorated. After the war, he went on to a career in medical technology. His escape and his fortitude were regularly cited in US military survival manuals, and in 1955 he wrote an account of his travels through North Korea.

Sources:

The Miami News, 25 January 1955: "Jet Pilot Tells of Escape From Korea"

Toledo Blade, 29 April 1954: "North Korean Cited; Saved U.S. Officer" (note: this report was written before full details of Millar's escape were released by the US military; a number of details are therefore incorrect)

Catholic Sentinel, 26 February 1999: "Obituaries: Ward Millar"

Millar, Ward: *Valley of the Shadow* (D. McKay Co., 1955)

So Near and Yet So Far

Very few escapees successfully managed to make their way out of North Korea during the conflict in the 1950s; when the United States became embroiled in another conflict in South-East Asia the following decade, even less men achieved every prisoner of war's aim of escape. Only one American was able to travel from North Vietnam into the south – but his freedom was exceedingly short-lived, and he would spend six years being tortured and incarcerated as a direct result of his escape attempt.

Aged just sixteen, George Everett Day, known as Bud, enlisted in the Marine Corps straight after the Japanese attack on Pearl Harbor in December 1941. He served on Midway Island during the Second World War, took a law degree in 1949, and two years later was called to active duty with the US Air Force. He had a couple of lucky escapes, including an incident when his parachute failed to open while based in England, and another time when he had to carry out a zero visibility, zero ceiling landing (effectively bringing his plane in blind). "That was as scary as it was going to get," he commented at the time, little realizing what the Vietnam War would bring his way.

On Easter Sunday 1967, Major Bud Day went out to Vietnam as a Combat Fighter Pilot and Squadron Commander. One hundred and thirty-seven missions over South and North Vietnamese airspace went without major incident; on 26 August 1967, Day and Captain Corwin Kippenham were tasked with taking out a North Vietnamese surface-to-air missile (SAM) site very close to the demilitarized zone (DMZ) between the two opposing sides. They were about to blow the Russian SAM to pieces when their F-100 was hit. The two airmen bailed out, but their parachutes were immediately spotted by the North Vietnamese members of the local militia. Kippenham was lucky: he was rescued by American forces almost as soon as he hit the ground. Day was much less fortuitous: he was looking down the barrel of a rifle in the hands of an enemy soldier. The helicopter that had rescued Kippenham tried to swoop in to collect Day, after picking up the distress signal from his parachute, with Kippenham given a rifle and told to provide covering fire. However, the pilot realized that he was not going to be able to land; Day was, very reluctantly, left to his fate.

In some ways, Day's situation was similar to that of Ward Millar a decade and a half earlier; he too suffered serious injuries during his landing, although in Day's case, it was his upper limbs that were badly damaged. He had bone protruding through the skin on his left wrist, and multiple fractures to his right arm; he had also dislocated his left knee, and was forced to march to the Vietnamese soldiers' base in a nearby village. His watch, knife, boots and flight suit were taken from him, and he was then thrown into an underground bunker, which had a log roof. His broken left wrist was tied to the ceiling, and his feet were bound. Not, as Day recognized, the easiest situation from which to escape, but, like Millar before him, he was absolutely determined to reunite with his family.

Day was brutally interrogated by the North Vietnamese, but he refused to divulge anything other than his name, rank, and serial number. This dogged attitude earned him worse torture, but Day made sure that he made its effects look worse than they actually were. The majority of the soldiers guarding him were simply teenagers, unused to combat, or the discipline of the army, and he was certain that if he could lull them into a false state of security, he would be left alone long enough to be able to untie his ropes, and escape into the jungle under cover of darkness.

His opportunity came on the sixth night after his capture, and Day was able to get a two-mile head start on the North Vietnamese. Guessing that he was approximately eighteen miles from the DMZ, Day struck out for the border, but was slowed down by his injuries and a lack of covering for his feet. To begin with, he was able to navigate by the stars, but as the jungle canopy grew increasingly thick the further south he went, he was unable to get accurate bearings, and in the end, had to rely on going along the trails that he was pretty certain ran from north to south. These, of course, were also the paths that were used by the Viet Cong as they travelled around, so he spent a lot of time hiding from passing patrols, as well as the guards and dogs who were busily searching specifically for him.

Soldiers weren't the only problem he faced: the only items of food he could find were live frogs and berries, and anyone who crossed his path was unlikely to be a potential ally. Even children had to be treated with extreme caution. His own comrades in the US forces didn't help: bombing raids were a regular occurrence, and on more than one occasion, Day was far nearer to the impact zones than he would have liked. Shrapnel became lodged in his leg, and his eardrums were ruptured by being too close to explosions on only his second night of freedom. He suffered from periods of delirium, violent nausea and dizziness as a result.

Day was never too certain how long he was wandering for – somewhere between twelve and fifteen days – but during that time he managed to cross the Ben Hai River on a bamboo log. He realized that he was getting close to the sanctuary he sought when he started to find discarded US rations wrappers on the ground, and tried in vain to signal to passing American aircraft. He wandered within South Vietnam for some time before finding the US Marine base at Con Thien, but he didn't want to approach it at night, in case the troops opened fire on a perceived enemy. He waited for the next morning, but he was hailed by a young boy who saw him hiding in the bush. Day had no intention of surrendering this close to home, and tried to make a run for it. He managed to get about a dozen yards before he was shot in the thigh and through the hand. Refusing to give up, he kept going and tried to hide in the jungle, but a couple of teenagers were able to follow the trail of blood that he was leaving, and a day and a half later, they captured him.

The next time that Bud Day saw freedom was 14 March 1973; over the intervening five and a half years, he was severely tortured and interrogated to an extent that, as he admitted in his autobiography, death began to have some appeal. He became cellmates with future Presidential candidate John McCain who later commented, "Bud Day is the toughest man I have ever known. He had an unwavering and unshakeable sense of honour that made him able to withstand physical and mental pressures of an enormous degree." He was back on active service only a short time after being released and retired in 1977.

Day was awarded the Medal of Honor for his bravery and on 14 March 1997, the Air Force named its new Survival School building at Fairchild Air Force Base in Washington State, the "Colonel George 'Bud' Day Building" in honour of his escape.

Sources:

Siouxland Lifestyle magazine, Winter 2005: "Col. George 'Bud' Day, Siouxland's Hometown Hero"

US Air Force official website: "Maj. George 'Bud' Day"

Airforce magazine, February 1984: "Valor: The Long Road to Freedom"

Vietnam magazine, June 2007: "Bud Day: Vietnam War POW Hero"

Airforce magazine, December 2005: "The Strength of Bud Day"

PART VI:
TUNNELLING FOR FREEDOM

Like Rats From a Trap

The American Civil War, which raged between 1861 and 1865 following the secession of seven states from the union to form the Confederate States of America, led to the creation of thousands of prisoners of war. Many of these were housed in dreadful conditions, and officers saw it as their duty to get back to their armies if at all possible.

One of the biggest escapes of the Civil War, and indeed from an American jail in the nineteenth century, came from the Confederate-run Libby Prison (sometimes referred to as Libey in contemporary news reports), in Richmond, Virginia. A former ship-supply shop and warehouse had been taken over at the start of the war – the owner was given forty-eight hours to pack up and leave – and hundreds of Union prisoners, as well as Confederate deserters, were stashed there. If they looked out of the windows, they risked being shot: Confederate guards would treat a head as a legitimate target, and there were numerous instances of Union soldiers being shot when they were doing nothing more than sitting reading the newspaper.

The prison occupied an entire city block, with Carey Street running along the north side of the prison, and sloped down to the south where a canal and then the James River flowed. The jail was on three floors, each divided into three rooms, with cellars beneath each of the rooms on the ground floor. Prisoners were kept on the upper two storeys, one of the rooms on the ground floor was used as a dining room, and an area in the cellar beneath the hospital was initially used as a kitchen during the day before an infestation of rats forced its closure. The ground floor also housed the commandant's office and a hospital. The middle cellar was used as a carpenter's shop – because the prison was built on a hill, there was access to it from the street to the south side. The Confederates cut doors between the rooms on the upper levels, allowing the inmates to mingle freely, but the rooms on the ground floor, as well as the cellars, were kept as separate units. To the east of the prison was a vacant lot between two buildings, about seventy feet away from the jail walls.

Although 109 men escaped from Libby on the night of 8 February 1864, they were by no means the first to do so. As early as 23 October 1862, Confederate deserters who were being held in the prison hospital, took what the *Richmond Dispatch* referred to as "French leave" – in other words, they escaped. A month later, four deserters got up to the roof, and then let themselves down to the ground using a rope made from blankets. The guards that they passed during their escape were sent for court martial. Another escaper, James Simmon, was returned to Libby in December after being arrested for drunkenly drawing a knife. Nine black slaves ran off at some point during the morning of 16 February – they were only counted twice a day, so had plenty of time to make a clean getaway. And so it went on, as hundreds of Yankee prisoners were brought through the doors, some to be exchanged for Confederate POWs, others to remain within the walls.

One of those brought to Libby following the battle of Chickamauga on 20 September 1863 was Colonel Thomas E. Rose. He had already proved that he wasn't going to submit to prison easily: on the journey to Richmond, he escaped from his guards in North Carolina but was recaptured after a day wandering around the woods. Arriving at Libby, he took stock of his surroundings and noticed that rats exited from the prison into the river when the tide was high, and that there was a sewer running beneath the street immediately between the prison and the canal. Chatting with another prisoner, Major Hamilton, Rose deduced that the best means of escape would be by a tunnel to go from the easternmost cellar down to the sewers. From there they could reach the canal, and thus to safety.

There were only two snags immediately apparent. The easternmost cellar was the one that had been abandoned because of the large colony of rats that lived there, lending it the nickname Rat Hell. And there was no easy way of getting to it. The only room on the ground floor to which they could get access was the dining room, which was in the middle.

Before they could even begin digging a tunnel, they needed to find a way into Rat Hell, and Hamilton devised the solution. They would need to cut a hole in the back of the dining-room fireplace, without breaking through the wall into the hospital room, or disturbing the ceiling of the carpenters' cellar beneath, both of which were visible to Confederate guards throughout the day. They then had to cut a way down the portioning wall so that when they did break through, they were in the rat cellar – creating an inverted S shape. The gap had to be wide enough to allow a man to get through, but small enough that its entrance could easily be hidden from guards, or, indeed, other prisoners who crowded round a stove in front of the fire from dawn until dark.

For days, between 10 p.m. and 4 a.m., Hamilton worked using only an old jack-knife and a chisel to remove the mortar from between the bricks, hiding the dust in an old rubber blanket, which he then removed and began digging at the wall behind to create the tunnel. Promptly at 4 a.m., Hamilton and Rose would replace the bricks, and throw soot at the area to hide their handiwork.

When the S-bend was complete, Rose volunteered to test it out, and nearly ruined the whole enterprise. He lost his grip on the rope which they had tied to a support in the dining room and fed down through the hole, and pinioned his arms by his side. The shape of the tunnel meant that he couldn't move either up or down, and the more he struggled, the more tightly wedged he became. As Rose began to asphyxiate, Hamilton raced to the upper levels for help, and with only seconds to spare, was able to pull Rose free. Hamilton widened the tunnel.

Once it was able to accommodate the two men, they slid their way down the rope to Rat Hell, and began to dig the proper tunnel, in what remained of the kitchen area in the south-east corner of the room. Rose was the tunneller, with Hamilton fanning air down into the hole, as well as dragging out the dirt, and concealing it in the rats' straw. However, they quickly realized that they would not be able to succeed on their own, and made a careful choice of thirteen other men to assist. To help get in and out of the cellar, they created a proper rope ladder with wooden rungs that could be pulled back up and concealed – with some difficulty – after each night's work.

The men worked in shifts, one night on duty, two off. They initially planned to dig down alongside the east wall, go beneath it, and then turn south, and head for the large street sewer next to the canal that Rose had previously seen workmen entering. From these observations, Rose had guessed that the sewer should be six feet high, and they should hopefully be able to get to the canal without a problem.

That's when they hit the next snag. Although Rose encouraged them to use their very basic tools to cut through the large timbers that had been used to support the prison on the south side, when they got through these, they realized that they had gone beneath the level of the canal. The danger of this was brought home to them when water began to seep in – slowly, at first, but then suddenly it broke through the tunnel roof, nearly drowning Rose. That branch of the tunnel was quickly blocked up.

The next attempt similarly caused a cave-in, with equally potentially hazardous results. Tunnelling towards a small sewer led to a breach in the pavement outside the prison wall, and the Yankee officers saw their captors looking at it suspiciously. However, when the word "rats" was repeatedly heard, Rose was relieved, although he deliberately took the next duty shift on his own, in case they had been rumbled; if that happened, he would be the only one held accountable. No one arrived to arrest him, so the work continued.

Another sewer was tried, but this was too small for a man to get into unless they removed the wooden planks. This the team did, although by now they were becoming very disenchanted with their lack of progress. By 25 January 1864, they believed, however, that they were about to break through to the main sewer, and everyone bar the two men on duty anxiously waited for the diggers' return the next morning. To the consternation of their colleagues, the pair reported that the final barrier to the main sewer was made of seasoned oak. The tools they had been using were worn out; it was becoming harder to keep any sort of light blazing to work by. They were ready to quit, despite having spent thirty-nine nights working. (They may also have been discouraged by the ease with which First New Jersey Cavalry soldier John Bray had simply walked out of the prison on the morning of Sunday 10 January, disguised in a Confederate Army coat he had bought from a rather dim-witted guard.)

Rose and Hamilton understood their frustration and disbanded the group. That didn't stop either man, who decided to start a new tunnel, this time in the north-east corner of Rat Hell, going east. This had the advantage that they were digging through clay, and not heading towards water, but the disadvantage that they would have to reach a shed adjoining the vacant lot, which was easily visible to the guards patrolling the south side of the prison. Rose watched the nearest guard's movements, and realized that they would have a few moments' grace while his back was turned patrolling westwards. Additionally, unless it was obvious to him that he was looking at escaping prisoners, he was unlikely to challenge anyone in the streets of Richmond.

After three tries to find a suitable place to begin their new tunnel, Rose and Hamilton began work afresh, and were able to persuade some of their former helpers to return. It was hard work getting through the very densely compacted sand that had been placed around the prison walls when the building was erected, but by sheer hard work, they were able to create a tunnel that was two feet wide in diameter, and around two feet high, set about six inches above the level of the cellar floor. Without any tools, they couldn't be sure that they were keeping the tunnel totally horizontal, but they did their best.

Teams of five carried out the tunnelling, working day and night now: one digging at the clayface, putting the dirt into a spittoon, which was taken by a second man and hidden in the straw; a third man fanned air into the tunnel using one of Hamilton's inventions: a rubber blanket stretched across a wooden frame; a fourth man deputized for the second and third men when needed, while a fifth man kept a look out, since the Confederate guards were ordered to check every part of the building regularly. If they were about to come through the south door, the lookout would give a warning, and the three men above ground would hide in the straw, nestling alongside the rats, while the digger stayed within the tunnel. The guards weren't keen on entering Rat Hell, and tended to stay down the south end, far away from the tunnelling work.

Although strict silence was maintained, Rose made sure that each man knew how much their efforts were assisting with the general escape, and it helped that progress was very clear each day. One evening, one of the diggers became overconfident, and started to dig up to the surface, convinced that they had reached their target. Instead, as he very rapidly realized when he glanced around him, he was still in the open lot, and thought he was clearly visible to a guard, if he happened to look in that direction. One of the other members of the team went to get Rose, who hurried down the tunnel to check, but realized that the situation wasn't as bad as the digger had feared: although anyone exiting there would be clearly seen, the hole itself wasn't an immediate threat. He stuffed his shirt into the hole, and covered it with dirt. (The mistake did come in handy though – the next day Rose put a shoe through the hole, and when he looked down at the lot from the prison, he saw that the tunnel had slightly deviated from its course, and got the diggers moving slightly to the left.)

Sixteen days of digging later, on Saturday 6 February 1864, it looked as if everything was lost. A party of Confederate soldiers made a detailed inspection of the cellar, although they didn't spot the tunnel entrance. Captain Johnson was the only tunneller there at the time; he had missed roll call on a number of occasions, claiming he was only "devilling the clerk" (when he was actually digging beneath the surface), but eventually he was forced to remain in Rat Hell twenty-four hours a day since his reappearance would have led to questions no one would want to answer. That night, he briefed Rose on their activities, and it caused general dismay amongst the escape party. Rose knew they were so near to success, and, once again, wasn't willing to give up so close to their goal.

From that moment on until the tunnel was complete, Rose himself was the digger, working solidly through Sunday 7th and achieving twice as much in one day as the full teams had managed on their own. He slept Sunday night, and then on the Monday morning started up again. At midnight he reached a post, which he guessed marked the far side of the vacant lot, so he began digging upwards. As he broke through the surface, he heard the watch call out 1.30 a.m. He was free.

After taking a few moments to breathe in the fresh air, he took a walk around the prison exterior, avoiding the guards both there, and at the Pemberton Buildings, another military prison close by. He then re-entered the tunnel, pulled a piece of wood over the top of the entrance to hide it from prying eyes, and made his way back to Rat Hell, arriving back there around three o'clock. He and Hamilton wanted to make their getaway immediately, but the others wanted to wait, so that they'd have a full night to make a clean break, rather than just the few hours before dawn. Reluctantly the officers agreed, and a schedule for exiting was arranged: each digger could bring another man with him, and there would be an hour's gap between parties. If the tunnel wasn't discovered, then the same thing could happen on a second and third night.

It was a great idea in theory. In practice, the following night, when the breakout began, chaos ensued, as word spread around the prison about the tunnel. Instead of a dozen or so men every hour, there was a constant stream of prisoners trying to get through, which quickly turned into a stampede. A false alarm suggesting guards were coming led to panic, with men trampled underfoot as they tried to return to their rooms, but still 109 men, starting with Rose and Hamilton, were able to get through the tunnel that night. The fireplace was put back in position to hide the tunnel down to Rat Hell, and the last man through had put the plank of wood back over the exit in the shed.

As far as the authorities were concerned, the disappearance of over a hundred soldiers was like a miracle. The roll call on Wednesday morning took four hours to complete, since the guards simply could not believe the disparity in numbers. The guards who had been on duty the previous night were immediately accused of complicity in the escape, since there seemed no other way that the Yankees could have achieved it, until two of the prison officers made a thorough inspection of the basement.

When they found the tunnel, they sent a young slave boy down through it, and joined him at the exit on the far side of the vacant lot. Rose's calculations had been so exact that the prison guards were convinced the diggers must have had outside help to reach the precise spot they needed. The guards who had been locked up suspected of conspiracy were immediately released, "the manner of the escape being too evident", as the *Daily Richmond Examiner* explained.

Four of the officers were recaptured, even before the escape had been discovered, some miles from Richmond. The fugitives had all taken separate routes as quickly as possible to minimize the chance of too many of them being caught. Four more were caught during Wednesday, fourteen further on Thursday. One soldier was caught by a freed slave, who asked where he was going. When told "nowhere", the man marched the soldier to the authorities "with courage and patriotism worthy of immortality", according to the *Enquirer*. Three fugitives gave themselves up after they went the wrong way on the river, and ended up nearly frozen. By Friday, thirty-four had been recaptured, although one, at least, had bluffed his way past a checkpoint.

By the end of the weekend, the total of recaptured Yankees had reached forty-eight, including Colonel Rose, who had had the misfortune to run into a group of Confederate soldiers who had disguised themselves in the enemy uniforms. When he realized his mistake, he tried to bluff his way out, but without success, and then, a few hours later, attempted to make a break for it, despite having a broken foot. He was apprehended by another patrol and returned to Libby. Quite a few of the prisoners were found still in Richmond, one of them caught by a newspaper boy as he tried to swap his Union Army jacket for a slave's greatcoat. Some of them were unable to stop themselves from trying to attack Confederate soldiers they saw, and paid the price with their liberty.

Although most official sources today claim that only forty-eight were recaptured, with two drowned, contemporary newspaper reports note that fifty-eight had been returned by 20 February, and twenty-one were known to have reached safety in Fort Monroe or Williamsburg, including Major Hamilton. One of the remaining thirty was found on 21 February, meaning fifty in total succeeded in reaching their goal.

Those who returned to Libby were thrown into what one writer described as "a narrow and loathsome cell" and found a regime that had been unavoidably affected by the prison break.

An alarm was raised when one guard thought he saw something – which turned out to be his own shadow. In the end, many of the key prisoners were exchanged: Colonel Rose was repatriated on 30 April 1864 and fought with conspicuous gallantry to the close of the Civil War.

Sources:

Daily Richmond Examiner, 11 February 1864: "Escape Of One Hundred And Nine Commissioned Yankee Officers From The Libby Prison"

Richmond Enquirer, 11 February 1864: "Extraordinary Escape From The Libby Prison"

Richmond Enquirer, 12 February 1864: "The Recent Escape from the Libby Prison – Recapture of Twenty Two Officers"

Richmond Enquirer, 13 February 1864: "Recapture Of More Yankee Officers"

Richmond Examiner, 15 February 1864: "The Re-Captured Yankee Officers"

Richmond Sentinel, 20 February 1864: "More Capture of Escaped Yankees"

Harper's New Monthly Magazine, April 1864: "My Escape from Richmond"

Moran, Frank E., *Famous Adventures and Prison Escapes of the Civil War* (The Century Co., 1898)

National Tribune, 14 May 1885: "Libby Tunnel"

Civil War Richmond: http://www.mdgorman.com/index.html (An invaluable resource, with all of the contemporary news reports, many of which were referenced for this piece; the ones listed above are those from which specific details and anecdotes were taken.)

This Room For Rent

One of the largest mass escapes of the twentieth century occurred in Uruguay over forty years ago when over a hundred members of revolutionary group the Tupamaros tunnelled out of the Punta Carretas federal prison in the capital, Montevideo, leaving behind them a set of cheeky signs to taunt their guards. It was in keeping with the Robin Hood-like roots of the organization – and perhaps there's a certain appropriateness to the fact that twenty years after the escape, the prison was turned into one of Uruguay's most prestigious shopping malls. A McDonalds restaurant now resides in the feared prison administration building.

The Tupamaros were founded in the early 1960s by Raul Sendic, a former law student who had qualified as an attorney, but not quite finished his legal studies during the 1950s. He had become prominent in the Socialist Party of Uruguay, and took a great interest in the plight of the sugar-cane workers, helping to organize them into unions, and arranging marches on Montevideo. Their motto was "Por la tierra y con Sendic" (For the land and with Sendic), a slogan that was ironically left at the prison end of the tunnel that Sendic would organize while within Punta Carreta.

When the marchers were suppressed by the government forces, Sendic decided that the only way that the workers would receive what they were due was if the government were forced to listen to them. The success of Fidel Castro's revolution in Cuba inspired Sendic, and a robbery at the Swiss Gun Club in Colonia in 1963 is usually seen as the start of the armed conflict and the birth of the Movimiento de Liberación Nacional Tupamaros. The group was named after Tupac Amaro, the last leader of the Incas in the sixteenth century, who had waged war against the invading Spaniards.

During the rest of the 1960s, the Tupamaros had a mixed reputation. They were renowned for redistributing food and money to the poor, but they were also responsible for bombings, kidnapping and murder. After a shootout between Tupamaros and the police in 1966, the revolutionaries were arrested or forced to go into hiding, either in Uruguay, or in Cuba, where some of them were trained in military techniques. A state of emergency and martial law was declared in Uruguay in June 1968, and the Tupamaros gained some sympathy from the public since they were fighting the repressive measures.

In July 1970, the Tupamaros kidnapped Dan Mitrione, an American FBI agent and specialist in torture who was in the country to train the Uruguayan police in interrogation techniques. They offered him in exchange for 150 prisoners, but when the authorities refused, the Tupamaros shot him. This didn't go down well, particularly as Mitrione was a father of nine.

Mitrione's death may have been a direct result of the arrest of Sendic and other Tupamaros leaders on 7 August. "Those captured lost all contact with the others," Sendic later told the *New York Times*, "and when the deadline came the group that was left with Mitrione did not know what to do. So they decided to carry out the threat."

Sendic and many of his fellow Tupamaros were sent to the Punta Carretas prison, which had been built in the early twentieth century. Conditions there, while not comfortable, certainly weren't as bad as in some South American prisons. The Tupamaros quickly took control, exerting pressure on the warden to keep things relatively easy (snap inspections of cells were stopped because it made the prisoners nervous, for example), and bribing guards to arrange for food and other items to be brought in. The inmates were allowed to gamble and buy lottery tickets.

According to Arturo Dubra, one of the key people involved in the tunnel, there never was any doubt that the Tupamaros would escape from Punta Carretas. They considered taking over the prison but that was dismissed because it would have been "very bloody" since they would have had to come in shooting, and deal with the sixty to eighty army soldiers who patrolled the outside walls. When they realized that there was no way to capture it without violence, an alternative was sought.

The cells were basic, made of eighteen-inch-thick brick blocks, with wood and metal doors, and it didn't take long before the prisoners discovered that they could remove the bricks between cells by using wires obtained from the woodwork classes to remove the mortar. A throughway between cells was created, and they even managed to create a vertical passage by digging through the floors and ceilings, and putting in a disguised hatch. They got rid of the dust from the mortar down the toilet, or out on the football field where they were allowed to exercise regularly, and replaced the mortar with plaster that had been brought into the prison in bags of "flour".

Now all they needed to do was dig a tunnel.

The Tupamaros in Punta Carretas were encouraged by the escape of women from their ranks who had been held at the Cabildo women's prison. A year earlier, thirteen of their comrades had walked out of Cabildo after mass; this time thirty-eight women would risk their lives. They planned it carefully: a cypher system of communication was devised based on copies of *Don Quixote*, using numbers rolled in cigarette papers and pills, and a novel about the Jewish resistance in Warsaw inspired them to check out the local sewer system. On 31 July, the women travelled through a tunnel to the sewers, and from there to a nearby house where they changed and disappeared into the Uruguayan underground, some of them for many years.

In the lead-up to the escape from Punta Carretas, which was codenamed "El Abuso" (the women's escape had been known as "Operación Estrella"), plans for the prison were smuggled in, torn up into small pieces and then put in small capsules: some of these were passed orally between wives and husbands when they embraced at visiting time; others had a rather longer passage through the prisoners' insides! One of the Tupamaros had lived for a time in the sewers, mapping them out, so knew roughly what was beneath the streets beside the prison. Arrangements were made to transfer prisoners whose sentences were coming close to their end into cells on the opposite side of the hallway from where the tunnel would begin. By the time that the escape took place, all of the Tupamaros who would be departing from the prison were therefore on the second and third floors of the prison, with access via the hatch to the ground floor. The cell from which they were going to dig was used by "common" (i.e. non-political) prisoners, and the Tupamaros struck a deal with them to allow use of the cell – the six men could join in the escape.

Intricate plans were drawn up to deal with the dirt from the tunnel. The men suddenly decided that they were going to become obsessed with hygiene. They got permission to put curtains around the toilets in the cells, and bed skirts on the beds. Linens brought in from outside were sewn up to create bags.

The tunnel took sixteen days to dig, using modified soap dishes and tools made from bed frames. The digger at the front would loosen the dirt and rocks and pass it back down to another man, who would drag it in a cart to the surface. From there it was put in the bags, and trodden down to remove excess air. These were then hidden behind the curtains in the toilets, or underneath the beds. Dirt was also stored inside an intersecting tunnel that had been built for an escape in 1931 that had never been filled in.

Air came from a makeshift plastic and cardboard bellows, which pumped air down a tube of taped-together cardboard tubes and rolled-up magazines. Unsurprisingly, it wasn't that effective, and when the tunnel reached the level of the sewer, a hole was cut through to allow some (albeit fetid) air in from there. (There was no point trying to head out through the sewers: after the women's escape, the police were patrolling them regularly.)

The two-foot-square tunnel passed beneath the prison walls, under Solano Garcia street, towards the living room of a house belonging to Billy Rial Castillo, a Mormon missionary, measuring nearly 130 feet in total. Around seven o'clock on the evening of Sunday 5 September, Rial opened the door to find a well-dressed young man standing there. When he asked what he wanted, the man pulled out a pistol and told him, "Stay calm. I am a Tupamaro and we are going to use your house." At first Rial thought it was a joke, but when he saw a second armed man approaching, he realized it was serious. The Tupamaros went into the living room and knelt down on the floor, listening carefully through a doctor's stethoscope. At the same time, a Volkswagen van drew up outside the house next door: the six Tupamaros inside took over that house too, brought in a dozen suitcases filled with arms, clothing, money and false papers, and knocked a hole through the adjoining wall into the Rials' home. Elsewhere in the city, at La Teja, other Tupamaros kicked up a fuss, overturning cars and burning tyres in the street, which drew the police away from the prison area.

The escape had to take place that night. The truce which the Tupamaros had agreed with the prison governor regarding cell inspections expired the next day, and all of their hard work would have been for nothing. At 10 p.m., as soon as the lights were switched off for the night, the call "Abuso" was passed between the cells. The inmates who were going to escape all started to gather in the end cells, by the mouth of the tunnel. However, around eleven o'clock, one of the common prisoners started to make a fuss, complaining of toothache. The Tupamaros suspected that he was doing it deliberately to draw the guards' attention, and one of the doctors quickly returned to his cell, since he knew that the guards would come to him for a pain-killer. He was able to pass the pill through his cell door hatch and stood carefully to ensure that the guard couldn't see past him to the disrupted cell walls.

Even once that had been sorted out, everything didn't go that smoothly. The tunnel didn't quite extend far enough: the houses were three feet higher than they had anticipated. Around midnight, the diggers frantically tapped to get their comrades' attention in the Rial living room, but the sound was so indistinct that the Tupamaros inside the house had to dig up most of the floor trying to find the source of the noise, which had become muffled by the earth between them. Eventually, after hours of increasingly desperate searching, they were able to break through in the right place, although it meant that the escaping prisoners, led by Raul Sendic, had to be hoisted out of the tunnel through a sixteen by twenty inch hole – which caused problems for one inmate who had a deformed arm, and thus had to be pulled up by the other arm.

By this time, the Tupamaros had a number of hostages to deal with, as well as processing the escapees. Rial's mother, his girlfriend and a couple of neighbours all came to the house during the evening, and were taken prisoner, although none of them complained about being badly handled by the Tupamaros – in fact, speaking to the press straight after the incident, Rial said they were treated "correctly".

As each of the 111 escapees exited the tunnel, they took off their prison jumpsuits, which they left in a pile, and were given a survival kit with the false IDs, a revolver and the equivalent of around ten US dollars. They were then sent through to the neighbouring house where they were divided into groups and taken by trucks and vans to cars waiting around the city. From there they fled into hiding. Because they were running late, one group missed their rendezvous, and the truck driver hid them in his home outside Montevideo overnight, then brought them back into town once fresh arrangements had been made – passing through roadblocks that were checking all outgoing vehicles!

Shortly after 4 a.m., the last inmate had come through the tunnel, and the Tupamaros released the Rial family. As soon as their captors had left, Billy Rial called the police to alert them that the Tupamaros had escaped from the prison through his house. The police didn't believe him, but said they'd call the prison to check. To Rial's disbelief, a few minutes later, the policeman said, "Everything is tranquil at the prison." Rial went outside his front door, and called up to the guards on the prison walls, "The Tupamaros escaped!" Still there was no reaction. Finally, around 5 a.m., a police truck came to check on Rial's story, and the guards inside the prison then checked the cells, finding the perforated walls, the bags of dirt under the beds and in the toilets. Notices had been left behind: "This room for rent. Good references required," ran one. "MLN-Transit Authority – keep left," was posted at the entrance to the tunnel. "Through the ground with Sendic" was a rewrite of the Tupamaros' original motto.

A manhunt was set up, but by that time the Tupamaros had dispersed. Heads rolled quickly. The prison governor resigned before he could be sacked. The government fired Colonel Pascual Cirilo, the director general of the prison service, the next day; he was tried before a military court of honour, although the results were never announced. Both the Interior Minister and the Defence Minister offered their resignations. Many guards and other officials were dismissed following charges of bribery, inefficiency and corruption. Three days later, the Tupamaros issued a press release explaining that as a result of the escapes from both Cabildo and Punta Carretas, they had decided to release one of their key political hostages, the British Ambassador to Uruguay, Geoffrey Jackson, after eight months.

This helped to rehabilitate the Tupamaros' reputation with the public, but not with the authorities. Uruguayan President Jorge Pacheco was running in the elections that November on a platform of law and order, and he turned the hunt for them over to the military. While some of the escapees were captured as a result of the arrest two weeks later of one of the five common prisoners who had been allowed to accompany the Tupamaros, many were caught up in the wide net thrown by their pursuers.

So they promptly decided to escape again. On 12 April 1972, fifteen Tupamaros, as well as ten common criminals, broke out of Punta Carretas through a tunnel that had been dug from the city sewers to a spot beneath the dentist's office. Around seven o'clock, Jose Mujica Cordano, one of the Tupamaro leaders, and the other twenty-four prisoners filed into the office, apparently needing treatment. Once they had all assembled, they overpowered the dentist and several guards using knives that they had made from spoons. They then lifted a steel grating in the floor, which gave them access to the tunnel dug from the outside by their colleagues.

To make sure the inmates weren't followed, the Tupamaros had thoughtfully provided their colleagues with some explosive booby traps which they could leave behind them. The guards following them spotted these in time, and called the Army in to defuse them, but by the time they could proceed down the tunnel, the Tupamaros had reached the sewer system beneath a large residential area, which gave them multiple exit routes. Despite an extensive search of the area by police and the Army, none of them was caught immediately.

The new president, Juan M. Bordaberry, was angered and embarrassed by this escape, and redoubled the efforts against the Tupamaros. By the end of 1972, the entire Tupamaros leadership was back behind bars, with nine of them held as hostages by the government: if the Tupamaros continued their fight, then the hostages would be killed. Sendic was shot in the face when he was recaptured in September 1972. Only after the fall of the dictatorship in 1985 were the Tupamaros released from prison, and allowed to form a political party. Sendic died of cancer in 1989; other Tupamaros involved in the escape went on to achieve political success, including Arturo Dubra, Fernandez Huidobro and Jose Mujica.

The escape itself was listed for many years as one of the Greatest Jail Breaks in the *Guinness Book of World Records*.

Sources:

Delta Democrat Times, 7 September 1971: "'Everything calm' with 111 inmates gone"

St Petersburg Times, 7 September 1971: "Tupamaros Pull Mass Escape"

Schenectady Gazette, 13 April 1972: "Tupamaros Free 25 at Uruguay Prison"

Oxford Companion to Military History

Latin America News Dispatch, 21 December 2009: "Burying the Past? Former Uruguyan Prison Becomes Shopping Mall"

RadioAmbulante blog, 31 July 2012: "Escape from Cabildo"

New York Times, 29 April 1989: "Obituary: Raul Sendic, 64, Founder of Uruguay Rebel Group"

Northwest Review, 1 January 2007: "The Great Escape"

Time magazine, 20 September 2007: "The Tupamaros Tunnel Out"

The Darkest Day

Described by Oklahoma Governor David Boren as he declared a week-long state-wide period of mourning as "the worst single tragedy in the forty-year history of this outstanding law enforcement agency", the deaths of three Oklahoma state troopers marked the end of a manhunt for two fugitives who crossed multiple state boundaries. Ten people – including escapees Claude Eugene Dennis and Michael Charles Lancaster – died as a result of the escape from the Oklahoma State Penitentiary (OSP) in April 1978; the town of Caddo has never been the same subsequently.

The riots at the OSP in 1973 had left millions of dollars' worth of damage, not all of which had been cleared up by the time of Dennis and Lancaster's escape five years later. Dennis had been arrested following the discovery of the bodies of John Witt and Mary Litrell in a farmhouse on 31 January 1975 in the small village of Doyle, not far from Marlow, Oklahoma. They were the new tenants of the farm, which had previously been owned by Dennis. Although he tried to claim self-defence, and went through various appeals to try to gain a verdict which would mean a lesser sentence, he was found guilty of first-degree manslaughter and sentenced to fifty years' imprisonment. He was also found guilty of a separate offence, the second-degree murder of Arthur Lake in Bryan County, Oklahoma; he had in fact originally been picked up by the sheriff's department investigating this crime, rather than the deaths of Witt and Litrell, and maintained that he had been framed for this crime by the sheriff.

While his various appeals against his sentences were going on, Dennis was housed at the OSP, along with armed robber Michael Charles Lancaster, who was serving a sentence of twenty-five years, with eligibility for parole after fifteen. Lancaster had escaped from Oklahoma State Reformatory in Granite in 1970, and later from Cleveland County Jail; during one of these escapes he had held up a liquor store and become involved in a gunfight with an Oklahoma state trooper. Dennis had briefly escaped from the Stephens County Jail in 1976, but had quickly been recaptured. Neither man had much likelihood of seeing the outside world before the start of the twenty-first century; both had appealed against what they perceived as unfair trials, but were stuck inside the OSP.

Tunnelling out of prison is nothing new, but usually prisoners have to go through the laborious process of actually digging the tunnel, getting rid of the earth and other refuse, and keeping it hidden from sight before they use it as an underground route to freedom. Dennis and Lancaster benefitted from OSP's location: various tunnels from the town's coal-mining days still remain beneath the streets of McAlester, and the pair were able to locate a way into them from the abandoned power plant in the industrial area of the prison. Although the authorities at first thought that the pair had scaled the walls when they departed from the prison on the afternoon of Sunday 23 April 1978 – with various guards at risk of negligence charges for not spotting them in time – certain evidence given to them by the first person the pair came in contact with led them to suspect the tunnels. Put bluntly, the pair smelled of shit. The tunnel that they had located, which ran beneath Tower 6 and then under the OSP walls, was a sewer outlet, and even though they disposed of their shirts soon after the escape, they still had a definite odour of the lavatory about them.

Around 3 p.m., Dennis and Lancaster took stolen tools they had obtained – including a sledgehammer, a crowbar and a shovel – and entered the tunnel. They were able to get through a thirty-inch-thick concrete plug before finding the tunnel to freedom. They headed first for the home of one of the prison correction officers, Sam Keys, a block or so north of the OSP, getting there around four o'clock. Keys had left for his 4 p.m. to midnight shift only a few minutes earlier when the two desperate men broke in to find Keys' wife and ten-year-old daughter on the premises. While one of them threatened Mrs

Keys with a knife, the other stole a 357 magnum pistol, a 12-gauge shotgun, a 30-30 rifle and ammunition for the weapons. The two debated taking the little girl as a hostage, but Mrs Keys made it clear that that would only happen over her dead body. The daughter was able to run to a neighbour's house, from where she called the police to tell them that "two men, dressed only in blue jeans" were holding her mother at knife point. After a brief scuffle Mrs Keys was able to flee to the neighbour's house, before the police arrived. The convicts sped off in the Keys' family car, a blue Datsun 210, similar to so many in the area.

Notified by the police of the incident, the OSP authorities began a headcount and realized that Dennis and Lancaster were missing from F Cell House, and they found evidence that indicated that the fugitives had been planning their escape for some time. Lancaster had written to Dianna Taylor, an inmate in the Wyoming State Prison, telling her about the plans, and letting her know that he was coming to get her out of prison. For whatever reason, this never happened.

A massive manhunt inevitably was begun, with dogs and helicopters all trying to track the fugitives. The car was eventually found near Holdenville, Oklahoma, near an area where a pickup truck was reported stolen on 24 April; its owner was never found. The trail seemed to go cold for six days, but then evidence of their activities was provided in the worst possible way: on Saturday 30 April, the body of twenty-six-year-old Kenneth Bobo from Garland, Texas, was found buried under some brush in Collin County, near Farmersville, Texas, not far from Highway 78. Bobo's car and fishing equipment were missing.

That green Ford was spotted on 2 May 1978 at 10.06 p.m. at the Sigmor Service Station some twenty-five miles further south on Highway 78. Lancaster went in and asked for a pack of Marlboro cigarettes, but instead of paying for them, produced a revolver and demanded the money from the cash register. If there was ever any doubt about the two fugitives' murderous intent, it was wiped away then: when attendant Mathal Thannikal Mathew stepped round from behind the counter, Lancaster shot him in the lower stomach, killing him.

Their next probable victim (although his body was never located) was minister James Dowdy of Hemphill, in Sabine County, Texas, who was reported missing on 5 May. He had taken his Chevrolet pickup to the local rubbish dumping ground, but had never returned. The truck was itself dumped after Lancaster and Dennis' next murder.

On 10 May, around 9.30 p.m., the two men went into the Rogers Sports Center, in Denison, Grayson County, Texas, Lancaster taking the lead. Waving the same revolver around that he used to shoot the gas station attendant, he told Mrs Loretta F. Spencer to open the cash register. Meanwhile Dennis ordered her husband, Bobby Lee, to go into the office. Lancaster took all the cash from the register, and a load of packets of cigarettes from the shelves, then tied a brass chain around Loretta Spencer's wrist and led her out to a gold-and-white pickup truck – the one they had obtained from James Dowdy.

Loretta was absolutely petrified. Everyone knew of the escaped convicts, and that they had already killed. She was forced into the back of the pickup truck, lying alongside two rubber life rafts, which had already been inflated, clothing, and other camping equipment. As Lancaster lay beside her, Loretta heard what she thought was the sound of a door slamming inside the store. Dennis then came out, started up the truck, and drove along to the Red River Bridge, where Lancaster forced Loretta out of the car and tied her to a tree. He and Dennis then emptied the truck, and Dennis went to abandon it a quarter of a mile away. While he was waiting for his partner in crime to return, Lancaster told Loretta that his name was Mike, and that they were both escapees from OSP.

Untying Loretta from the tree, Dennis pushed her into the raft and lay on top of her, fondling her during a three-mile trip eastwards on the river. Once back on dry land, they hid their equipment in some trees, and then Dennis raped Loretta twice. When the two men had fallen asleep, Loretta was able to open one of the links in the brass chain with her teeth, got free from the padlocks, and headed for the nearby highway. She was picked up by a passing driver and taken to Denison Police Department. There she learned that the "slamming door" sound had been the noise of the shotgun blast that blew her husband's face off. His body had been found fifty minutes after the pair of convicts had arrived at the store.

Based on Loretta's information, the manhunt focused its attention on the river area, with nearly six officers involved in the search including Oklahoma state crime bureau agents and Texas Rangers, as well as county officers and highway patrolmen from the two states and Corps of Engineers Rangers. Tracking dogs were brought to the scene, but in the end they weren't used.

Loretta's escape forced Dennis and Lancaster to change their plans. An hour after she raised the alarm, they came out from the woods, and approached fifteen-year-old Chris Bowling, who was mowing the lawn outside his home. They kicked the door of the house open, pushed him inside, and forced him to lie down on the floor. Lancaster asked him for the keys for the blue 1966 Chevrolet parked outside; Dennis got them from the cabinet, while Lancaster tied the boy with electrical cable. Warning Bowling that if they saw him come out of the house "I will blow your f***ing head off" Lancaster and Dennis stole the car. The car was believed to be spotted a few hours later, but by the time the officers who noticed it had turned around to begin pursuit, it had gone. The Oklahoma Highway Patrol set up a roadblock but the car didn't pass it.

Around 8 p.m. that evening, Mrs Judy Clemmons (or Clement) had a very lucky escape. She went to answer a knock on the door of her farmhouse near Mill Creek, Oklahoma, some sixty miles north of Denison to find two men there. She refused to let them in, even though they pulled a gun on her. When she screamed and slammed the door, they drove off in the stolen Chevrolet, which was found abandoned about twelve miles away the following morning.

After stealing a Ford Explorer pickup from a farmhouse nearby they continued on their spree, hitting a service station in Kewanee, Mississippi, on Monday 15 May around 10.50 p.m. and then changing cars for a red Camaro. Five hours after their raid on the service station, they were stopped by officer Larsen Dean Roberts in Butler, Alabama, for a routine traffic violation. As he came round the car to talk to Dennis, who was driving, Lancaster stepped out from the car, and fired a shotgun five times at him. Roberts was hit in the left shoulder and arm, but was able to run to the nearby Choctaw County General Hospital.

They were ordered to stop again two days later, this time by Alabama state trooper John Christenberry, in their latest stolen vehicle, a black-and-yellow Mercury they had obtained from Choctaw County. Trying to stop them a few miles north of the county line, Christenberry turned on his blue lights, but Lancaster opened fire, blowing out one of his tyres and shattering the windshield. Christenberry, whose wife was expecting a baby later that week, was miraculously unscathed. "The good Lord was riding with me," he commented later.

A number of false leads were followed up over the next couple of days. Two men were identified as Dennis and Lancaster by a store owner, but turned out to be local residents; another pair seen boarding a night train were simply vagrants looking for a place to sleep.

The next positive lead came on 19 May when a trailer was broken into near the Shalom Church, near Whitfield, Alabama, and firearms, goods and pillowcases were taken. Local law enforcement officers searched the area, and found what they believed was the stolen Mercury but they didn't approach it, waiting for fingerprint officers. The officers involved were later convinced that Dennis and Lancaster had been in the car at the time, and couldn't understand why the two escapees hadn't killed them. The next day the search was stepped up when it was confirmed that this was the fugitives' latest car. More than a hundred officers, helicopters and bloodhounds were involved. But despite the numbers, and the promises of more forces if needed, Dennis and Lancaster remained at loose.

Retired school teacher, sixty-eight-year-old Stacie Beavers, was not going to let the threat of two dangerous convicts in the area frighten her, and she carried on with life as normal. However, returning from a women's club meeting at her church in Cuba, Alabama, on the night of Monday 22 May, she was accosted as soon as she turned the key in her front door. According to one police report, Dennis and Lancaster then hit her on the head and shot her behind the ear, although most contemporary newspaper reports suggest that her throat had been slashed. They stole the keys to her home and car, and a plate of food that she had brought back from the meeting.

Her body was found the next day after relatives hadn't been able to get through on the phone – one of the escapees' regular tricks was to cut the phone lines at the houses that they burgled – giving Dennis and Lancaster a good ten hours' head start. Her station wagon was found around 9 p.m. on Wednesday 24 May, abandoned in a ravine not far from Little City, Oklahoma. Little City is part of Bryan County. Claude Eugene Dennis had come home.

Believing that he might try to make contact with them – either to gain help, or for less pleasant purposes – the sheriff's department kept an eye on Dennis' former wife (she had divorced him about eighteen months previously, keeping custody of their three children), his mother and other relatives. They also tightened their own security. Dennis had made it abundantly clear that he regarded the sheriff as responsible for framing him for the murder of Arthur Lake, and there was no doubt that the law enforcement officers who had been attacked so far were merely an appetiser compared with what he wanted to do to those who were responsible for taking away his freedom.

No sign was found of either man on Thursday 25 May, despite the FBI becoming involved, after federal warrants charging them with unlawful flight to avoid prosecution were filed. Off-duty policemen joined the many different agencies searching the entire area, going through farmhouses, barns, sheds, and the heavy brush and oak.

On Friday 26 May, the hunt came to an end. It began with an encounter at the home of rancher Russell Washington, who had spent the previous night staying at his parents' home. When he got back, his dachshund began acting up, as if she sensed that there was someone in the house. He and farmhand G.D. "Buzz" Busby were suspicious, and took a rifle with them into the house. Busby went into the living room where he saw Dennis and Lancaster. The convicts told Busby to call Washington in, and then made the two men lie spread eagle on the kitchen floor. Lancaster cut electrical cord to tie the two men with, then went back to eating the sandwich he had been preparing when Washington and Busby had arrived.

As the two men lay on the floor, wondering if they would survive the meeting, Dennis said to the rancher, "I'll bet you don't remember, but you let me come hunting on your place one time." Washington did remember him: Dennis and some friends had dove hunted on his land about three or four years earlier. Dennis assured him that he wasn't going to kill him: "I know you're a family man and a hard-working old boy." Anxious to keep Dennis in a stable frame of mind, Washington kept chatting with him about hunting, although from time to time the murderer would mention something about the killing spree he and Lancaster had been indulging in. "Dennis told me 'People make you kill them. They know you've got a gun on them and they still try to get away'," Washington recalled later. He also told Washington that had the rancher been on the jury that convicted him of the murder of Arthur Lake, he would have killed him on sight.

Once they'd finished their meal, Dennis and Lancaster took some food and money, and the keys to Washington's pickup truck. As soon as they were gone, Washington used his pocket knife, which the convicts had failed to find, and cut himself loose. He called the Oklahoma Highway Patrol, who, for the first time, had almost real-time information on the fugitives' whereabouts.

Within minutes Dennis and Lancaster ran into the police: mobile patrol unit 54, manned by patrolmen Houston Summers and Billy Young. Without any warning, Dennis and Lancaster opened fire on them from around seventy-five feet distance, blasting away with a rifle each. Both patrolmen were killed: Summers survived the initial onslaught and was able to let headquarters know they had been hit before being shot with a shotgun at point-blank range.

The Highway Patrol airplane, which had been assisting with the search for the men, was immediately dispatched to the scene. Pilot Trooper Lloyd Basinger dropped down and saw a blue Ford pickup matching the description of Washington's truck travelling at a high speed – as he commented later, no farmer was going to drive like that. He made sure that Dennis and

Lancaster were well aware of his presence, and bird-dogged the truck as it headed rapidly towards the west edge of the town of Caddo.

At the same time, a highway patrol car driven by Lt Hoyt Hughes was also heading towards Caddo, and by the time the fugitives reached the town, the two vehicles were only about four blocks apart. Although Dennis knew the area moderately, the pressure of the chase was telling on him: he kept turning into dead ends and had to turn the truck round. In the air, Basinger was telling Hughes and his partner Lt Pat Grimes where to go.

Both vehicles turned into Court Street from opposite ends. Dennis pulled the pickup into a yard, mowing down a honeysuckle bush and skidding to a stop beneath a tree. They jumped from the vehicle and took up position crouching in front of the truck. As Hughes drove past, they opened fire, killing Lt Pat Grimes instantly. Hughes was shot in the shoulder.

Hughes stopped and exited from the car, knowing he was in a fight for his life. He fired at Lancaster, the bullet hitting the back of his head and exiting through his mouth. Lancaster fell to the ground and was dead within minutes. Dennis hid behind a tree, armed with the sawn-off shotgun. By this time Oklahoma Highway Patrolman Lieutenant Mike Williams had arrived at the house, along with others. A gun battle ensued that lasted a mere thirty seconds, but whose outcome was never in doubt. Williams shot Dennis eight times, bringing the murderous spree to an end. Three state troopers and at least five civilians had died before Dennis and Lancaster was stopped.

Fact vs. Fiction

The *Real Prison Breaks* reconstruction of the final shoot-out is based on Lt Pat Grimes' brother's account as given in the show, which doesn't completely tally with the facts recorded at the time – in particular the way in which Lancaster was shot. It also confuses the chronology of the fugitives' trail across the states.

Sources:

Jerry D. Wiggins, Grayson's County Sheriff's Department, 1 June 1978: "Supplementary Investigation Report" (chronology mainly derived from here)

The Durant Daily Democrat, 24 April 1978: "Convicted murderer of Countian escapes from prison"

The Durant Daily Democrat, 11 May 1978: "Store operator murdered, woman believed kidnapped"

The Durant Daily Democrat, 12 May 1978: "Escapees are sought in death of Texas man"

The Durant Daily Democrat, 14 May 1978: "Trail cold in search for Dennis, Lancaster"

The Durant Daily Democrat, 15 May 1978: "Escapees continue to evade officers"

The Durant Daily Democrat, 18 May 1978: "Officers comb County in search for killers"

The Durant Daily Democrat, 19 May 1978: "Manhunt ended after mistaken ID revealed"

The Durant Daily Democrat, 22 May 1978: "Alabama officers seek 2 Oklahoma fugitives"

The Durant Daily Democrat, 23 May 1978: "Elderly woman killed in Alabama by fugitives"

The Durant Daily Democrat, 24 May 1978: "Alabama officers find Dennis, Lancaster crafty fugitives"

The Durant Daily Democrat, 25 May 1978: "Hunt for fugitives shifts back to Texoma area"

The Durant Daily Democrat, 26 May 1978: "3 Troopers, convicts die in gunbattle"

The Durant Daily Democrat, 28 May 1978: "Past meeting saved life of Washington, Busby"

The Durant Daily Democrat, 28 May 1978: "Teen credited for saving children"

The Durant Daily Democrat, 28 May 1978: "It cost them their lives"

The Durant Daily Democrat, 31 May 1978: "Trooper-Pilot sees fugitives' final minutes"

The Durant Daily Democrat, 8 June 1978: "Missing rancher is feared victim of Dennis, Lancaster"

The Meridian (Mississippi) Star, 29 May 1978: "An Odyssey of Frustration"

The Tulsa World, 27 May 1978: "33-Day reign of terror ends in Caddo gunfight"

The Victoria Advocate, 27 May 1978: "Five Killed in Shootout"

OHPTrooper.com: "OHP's Darkest Day: Remembering Caddo"

Real Prison Breaks, Cineflix Productions, 2011

Containing the Taliban

Some of the largest escapes in the first twelve years of the twenty-first century have come as a result of the conflicts that followed the bombing of the World Trade Center in 2001, and the wars in Afghanistan and Iran against the Taliban. On a number of occasions dozens of Taliban members have been freed – or come very close to freeing themselves – from the prisons and US Army camps around the area in which they are being held. During the latter half of 2012, as this book was being compiled, there were three incidents in which large enough numbers escaped that they were deemed worth reporting by the world's news agencies – but, as more than one pointed out, escapes are so common that they are not deemed newsworthy simply because they happened.

One of the first attempts came from the US Army Camp Bucca in Iraq in March 2005. Between the start of the US-led invasion of Iraq in March 2003 and the discovery of a huge tunnel shortly before at least 200 detainees made their escape on 24 March 2005, over 40,000 people were arrested by the US military. Over 10,000 were still being held at the three main prisons – Bucca, Abu Ghraib and Camp Cropper – at the end of that period. Many should never have been there in the first place: the commander of Bucca, Colonel Austin Schmidt, guessed that around a quarter of the prisoners had been swept up during raids, or had been victims of personal grudges.

Bucca, named after one of the fire marshals who died in the 9/11 attacks, operated between 2003 and 2009. Built near the border with Kuwait, it had a two-mile perimeter fence surrounding twelve compounds where the prisoners lived in canvas tents or air-conditioned plywood buildings, guarded by soldiers bearing automatic rifles, watching from three-storey wooden towers. There were teething problems: in January 2004, one detainee was able to escape through the wire, and the official report blamed inexperience, complacency, poor leadership and lack of communications. Five days after that, seven more escaped during the night, of whom five were recaptured; a fortnight later, several were able to crawl under the fence during a very heavy fog – visibility was down to ten to fifteen metres.

In January 2005, a riot broke out, which led to the deaths of four detainees. Around the same time, work on a tunnel started. It began underneath the wooden floorboards of one of the tents: the prisoners dug down three feet through the sand, put in a false bottom with plans, and then tunnelled down a further twelve feet where the sand was replaced by packed dirt. After the entrance was reinforced with pieces of plywood and sandbags, the tunnelling began in earnest, with over 200 inmates involved at some point.

The work could only be carried out at night, with teams of ten men operating between 1 a.m. and the dawn call to prayer, which preceded the daily headcount. With air provided by homemade bellows, the diggers, who used flattened tent poles wrapped with canvas grips, were only able to move forward three feet a day. Each would stay at the dirtface for five minutes at a time, filling up five-gallon water jugs and passing them back to be redistributed around the camp. Sacks from their bread rations were filled, and then spread across a soccer field.

It was that which alerted the Americans initially. Although it was invisible to the naked eye, satellite imagery showed that the field was changing colour because of the different dirt that was being tramped into it. Additionally, there were complaints of showers being clogged up, and two dozen portable toilets ceasing to function. Some guards even complained that the floor in some of the tents seemed to be rising.

By the end of March the tunnel was complete. It was 357 feet long, and the width of a man for the majority of its length, with around a hundred tons of soil moved in about eight weeks. It was illuminated with homemade torches built from radio diodes, and the walls were as smooth and strong as concrete, after being sculpted with water and milk. The plan was for groups of twenty-five men to go through at a time starting after midnight on 24 March.

Although the Americans were aware that something was wrong, they couldn't work out what. Informants within the camp weren't able to tell them anything other than yet another tunnel was being built – three others had been detected at very early stages during the first part of the year. However, when the tunnel was finished, one of the informants said that it began in Compound 5; his reason for betraying his friends was apparently that he feared there would be a bloodbath if the Americans caught the Iraqis escaping.

The Americans moved swiftly. The detainees were transferred into a holding area, and a bulldozer sent across the centre of the compound. That caused part of the tunnel to collapse, but they were unable to find the exit, despite bulldozing parallel with the compound fence. It was only by luck that it was found, considerably further away than the Americans had believed possible.

Oddly, it wasn't completely filled in: on 16 April, eleven detainees were able to access part of the tunnel and use it to escape. All of them were recaptured. As a result of the tunnel's discovery, and another riot that took place at the start of April, Camp Bucca was reorganized: the tents were replaced by buildings with proper concrete foundations. Although detainees tried to dig a further tunnel, unsuccessfully, there were few other reported escapes during Bucca's period of operation.

The first breakout which really attracted the attention of the world's press came when suicide bombers blew up trucks outside the main gates of Kandahar's Sarposa prison on the night of Friday 13 June 2008. This had followed unrest at the prison, with hundreds of the 1,100 prisoners going on hunger strike the previous month – forty-seven of them stitched their mouths together in protest – complaining about being held for over two years without trial. There were also allegations of torture.

The prison itself was meant to be a showcase for Western methods in Afghanistan: Canadian prison officials had been sent over to train the guards and teach them about human rights.

New uniforms were issued to the guards, and the towers of the sixty-year-old building were freshly painted.

This made it even more of a tempting target for the Taliban, who had been increasing their operations in the area around Kandahar, traditionally regarded as the home of the rulers of Afghanistan. At 9.20 p.m. a water tanker filled with explosives was driven to the front gates and detonated, destroying part of the mud walls of the prison. In the confusion following the explosion, a group of around thirty insurgents armed with rocket-propelled grenades and assault rifles rode in on motorcycles and began their attack, massacring fifteen guards, and heading for the political section of the prison, where the Taliban suspects were held. Another suicide bomber tried to destroy the rear gates, but the explosion didn't have the desired effect.

Initial estimates suggested that 1,200 inmates were freed over the next half hour, including around 450 hardline militants – non-political prisoners took advantage of the situation and ran for the pomegranate groves surrounding the prison. Coalition troops were based on the far side of the city: by the time they got there, the inmates had dispersed, with many of the Taliban boarding minibuses that were waiting for them outside the prison walls. Some early reports tried to claim that the guards had prevented 200 prisoners from leaving, but it soon became clear that no one had remained incarcerated, making it one of the largest ever prison breaks in history, dwarfing the 798 who escaped from Fort San Cristobal in 1938 (see chapter 7).

"We released all the prisoners, including 450 Taliban, we killed most of the guards, and we blocked the roads into the city so that our fighters could escape," Qari Yusuf Ahmadi, a Taliban spokesman for southern Afghanistan, announced to the press. "This was our first attack in the very heart of Kandahar, and this is a signal to the puppet government of Hamid Karzai and the infidel government of the West that they should not forget the Taliban."

Supporters of the Canadian involvement in Afghanistan were disheartened by the success of the Taliban operation. "The message this attack sends is that the insurgents can act with relative impunity even into downtown Kandahar," said Colin Kenny, the head of the Canadian senate's committee on security and national defence. "The other message it sends is to the insurgent rank and file: if you get captured, we'll get you out." The facility was rebuilt as a result of the raid, with several million dollars spent to ensure that there were no further breaches of security. Three years later, Sarposa prison was the cause of fresh embarrassment for the Coalition.

The Iraqi city of Tikrit was the scene of another mass breakout, with 109 prison officials and guards detained after sixteen prisoners were able to escape from a bathroom window in a palace that used to belong to Saddam Hussein. Just before midnight on 24 June 2009, they pried open the window and made their getaway down a twelve-foot-high concrete wall before the guards noticed. Although the police didn't believe that any of the guards were actively complicit in the escape, there "was great negligence" on their part.

House-to-house enquiries located two of the missing men and military working dogs were provided by the US Army to assist with the search. Five of the prisoners had links to al-Qaeda, and all of these were recaptured along with at least two others (one Iraqi news source suggested that all bar four were eventually caught). The location of the prison was moved to Tasfirat.

Such escapes weren't uncommon. In November 2009, thirteen inmates, including three key Taliban commanders, tunnelled out of the facility at Farah Prison; nine workers at the jail were arrested in connection with the breakout. Only one of the fugitives was recaptured, who revealed that the tunnel had taken ten days to dig, and they had hoped to empty the prison, which housed around 300 detainees, even though it was only designed to hold eighty.

Twenty-three suspects were able to get through a brick wall in Mosul, in northern Iraq on 2 April 2010 between being served breakfast at 6 a.m. and midday lunchtime. They had begun work the previous day, but used a blanket to cover the hole in the wall. The guards had noticed that it was unusual, but not taken any action, and as a result found themselves under suspicion.

Farah was the site of another jailbreak on 17 July 2010 which took a leaf out of the Kandahar Taliban's book. At 11 p.m., a suicide bomber attacked a police patrol but was killed before he could explode his device; police therefore rushed to the scene. An hour later, the Taliban attacked four security checkpoints, diverting police further. Then at 3 a.m., they blew up the prison gate; at the same time Taliban prisoners blew the locks off their cells using explosives that had been smuggled into the jail. One policeman was killed and four inmates were injured by the explosions. At least fourteen prisoners were able to get away.

Six months later, on 14 January 2011, twelve militants linked to the Sunni insurgent group, the Islamic State of Iraq, simply walked out of a prison in Basra in southern Iraq. They took the precaution of obtaining police uniforms first, but had no problems in passing the prison guards. They were the only prisoners held there, so one might have expected them to be spotted. In a statement of the obvious, Ali Ghanim al-Maliki, head of the security committee at Basra's provincial council, said, "Of course, there was collusion from within the compound, but we do not know who is involved at the moment." None of the guards was charged with any offence.

(According to a Reuters report of this incident, the militants were smuggled out by one of the guards who claimed there was an order to transfer them to another prison. This may, however, have been conflating accounts with an escape from Karkh prison in Baghdad in the summer of 2009, when the warden drove the insurgents out of the facility, which was referenced in local reports of this escape.)

April 2011 however, saw one of the biggest propaganda coups for the Taliban, when nearly 500 prisoners were released after the Mujahadeen were able to tunnel their way into Sarposa prison, the supposedly escape-proof jail in Kandahar. Despite the millions lavished on it, it wasn't as impregnable as the Coalition believed – Afghan president Hamid Karzai described the escape as a "disaster".

At around 4 a.m. on 25 April, the Governor of Kandahar, Tooryali Wisa, was notified that around 487 Taliban prisoners, including some of their senior commanders, had escaped. For five months a team of eighteen men had dug a tunnel that stretched over a thousand feet, seven feet underground, beneath the main Kandahar-Herat highway. It was five feet high, with battery-powered lights, and small fans providing air.

According to an account of the escape in the Arabic-language magazine *Al-Somood*, the Mujahedeen involved in the digging rented a house opposite the south corner of the prison, and refitted a room within the building, bringing in various concrete-making machines. At night they dug, and moved the dirt out in wheelbarrows attached to children's bicycles, and then sold the soil. They hit a snag when they realized that they hadn't been digging on a true course towards the prison – so they downloaded a map off the internet! They needed to bring people out from two separate locations, so they first dug to the arrest room, and confirmed that they were on target by raising a blade into the room through the dirt floor. They then continued the tunnel onto the main room, which held over 500 prisoners. When they had ascertained that they were in the right place (having first tried to come up a room early!), they passed the word to their contacts within the prison that the escape would be happening that night.

Four Taliban Mujahedeen went down the tunnel taking carjacks and solid iron poles to break through the floor. The arrest room was easy to access, but the floor of the political ward was heavy-duty concrete, and it took some time for them to break through it. However, once they had cut a huge hole, they passed guns and daggers up to the three inmates who had been aware of the tunnel's existence. They then went from cell to cell, inviting their comrades to join the escape. Some of these were freed from their cells with keys provided by "friends" within the prison, and around a third of the prison population made their way slowly along the tunnel over a four-and-a-half-hour period. Fresh clothes were waiting for them at the far end, as were vehicles to disperse them around the area. The Taliban claimed that they had a "martyrdom-seeking group" on standby in case there was any difficulties with the guard, but they weren't needed. According to them, 541 prisoners escaped; the operation cost around $20,000.

The first that the authorities knew of it was when a guard came on duty the next morning to find a completely empty building. Information on the escape had deliberately been kept to a minimum within the prison, to avoid any betrayal – the Taliban noted that known informers were knocked out during the escape.

Sixty-five of the prisoners were quickly caught, with a further two killed while resisting arrest. The majority, however, were quickly able to rejoin the fight. As one of the escapers told the press, "We had the full support of the people of Kandahar, who provided us with clothes and safe places to go. We have proved that whatever we want to do in Kandahar or anywhere else in the country, we can do it."

The Taliban didn't confine audacious plans to Iran and Afghanistan; in the early morning of 15 April 2012, hundreds of militants attacked the prison in Bannu, in north-west Pakistan. For more than two hours, they laid siege to the prison, entering the complex in at least fifty cars and pickup trucks, and throwing grenades. They were able to free 384 of the 944 inmates, including twenty-one who were on death row – although the authorities weren't exactly sure who, to begin with, since the Taliban destroyed the prison records during the attack. According to a BBC report, the guards called for help, but no one came for more than an hour and a half. Around a hundred of the escapees turned themselves in.

A couple of months later, on 7 June, the Taliban set off a bomb outside a prison in the northern Afghan province of Sar-e-Pol, which destroyed the walls. Prisoners promptly started to make their way out, although, for once, the guards were being attentive, and opened fire. Three inmates were killed in the subsequent gun battle, and many were quickly recaptured, although around fourteen evaded arrest. The Taliban claimed that 170 prisoners were freed. Sar-e-Pol police chief Abdul Yaqoob Zabuli and prison director Colonel Mohammad Aslam were both sacked the next day.

Fifteen Afghan field commanders who had been sentenced to death escaped from the Pul-e-Charkhi Prison, east of Kabul on 20 August. According to a report in the Russian press, "a large group of death-row prisoners 'vanished' from the third cell of the sixth block of the penitentiary". However, a couple of days later, the authorities said that there had been an attempted escape, but it was foiled by the guards. "To respect Eid, we wanted to provide a facility for the prisoners to congratulate each other during the Eid days and we opened the doors of the cells," the Central Prison Directorate Chief General Amir Mohammad Jamshid explained. "Taking advantage of this, eight prisoners managed to reach the prison yard but they were then identified and detained by the security guards."

Suicide bombers paved the way for another Taliban attack, this time at Tasfirat prison in Tikrit on 27 September, killing sixteen guards and freeing around 102 inmates. A plan to free prisoners the previous April had been foiled, but this time a group of gunmen was ready to storm the prison to liberate their comrades. They also destroyed personnel files, and stole papers which identified informers. Weapons had been brought into the prison during family visits, and the authorities were certain that some warders had deliberately left some locks open. Twenty-three prisoners were caught within twenty-four hours of the raid.

Sources:

Washington Post, 24 August 2005: "In Iraq Jail, Resistance Goes Underground"

New York Times, 14 June 2008: "Taliban Free 1,200 Inmates in Attack on Afghan Prison"

Daily Telegraph, 15 June 2008: "How Taliban sprang 450 terrorists from Kandahar's Sarposa prison in Afghanistan"

New York Times, 25 September 2009: "Qaeda Members Escape Prison in Iraq"

CNN, 26 September 2009: "Death row Iraqis among 8 escapees recaptured"

Washington Post, 28 November 2009: "Inmates escape prison in western Afghanistan"

New York Times, 18 July 2010: "Prison Break Precedes Afghan Conference"

BBC News, 14 January 2011: "Iraq seeks militants after Basra jail breakout"

Reuters, 14 January 2011: "Twelve insurgents escape from prison in Iraq's Basra"

IraqiNews.com, 7 July 2011: "Judiciary had not charged any officer with Basra prison escape last year, official says"

Christian Science Monitor, 25 April 2011: "Taliban tunnel: Five prison escapes in Iraq, Afghanistan"

Daily Telegraph, 25 April 2011: "Hundreds of Taliban escape from Kandahar jail"

The Guardian, 25 April 2011: "Taliban tunnel breakout outwits Afghan jailers"

The Guardian, 25 April 2011: "Afghanistan's great escape: how 480 Taliban prisoners broke out of jail"

Daily Mail, 25 April 2011: "500 Taliban prisoners freed through Great Escape-style tunnels in Afghanistan"

al-Šumid (Steadfastness), 5th year, volume 60, Jumada al-Thaniya 1432AH/May-June 2011} "Kandahar Prison Escape: the Taliban's Tale" (translated at http://www.alexstrick.com/2011/05/kandahar-prison-escape-the-talibans-tale/)

CNN, 15 April 2012: "384 prisoners escape after Taliban raid on Pakistan prison"

BBC News, 15 April 2012: "Militants free hundreds in attack on Pakistan jail"

AllVoices News, 15 April 2012: "Nearly 400 prisoners fled Bannu jail after Taliban's pre-dawn raid"

Associated Press, 8 June 2012: "Fourteen criminals, Taliban militants escape prison in N Afghanistan"

Tolonews, 22 August 2012: "Authorities Deny Pul-e-Charkhi Prison Break Saying Guards Foiled Attempt"

Afterword

A spot-check of Google News on 28 November 2012 reveals that in New Orleans the day before, a trio of prisoners were recaptured after injuring themselves on razor-wire during their flight. Dozens of prisoners escaped from Tete Provincial Prison in Mozambique on Sunday 25 November, after sabotaging the electricity supply and plunging the compound into darkness. Three inmates went on the run from Kamfinsa prison in Zambia the same day. A week earlier in India, four remand prisoners stabbed a warder, scaled the Kochi prison wall and escaped. Around the same time, in Jackson County, Oregon, a convicted bank robber was able to stand on another prisoner's shoulders, remove some metal mesh from a roof covering, and jump into a nearby tree. The trees have been cut down; despite a $6,000 reward there is no sign yet of Bradley William Monical . . .

Even if prisons are built like the ones that John Carpenter envisaged in his movies *Escape from New York* and *Escape from L.A.* (where Manhattan Island and Los Angeles respectively are turned into federal penitentiaries), the men and women incarcerated there will try to escape. As Emmanuel Goldstein said, "The primary obligation of any prisoner is to escape."

Appendix: The Philosophy of Escape

"If someone is determined to escape, it will be difficult to prevent him from doing so without making life virtually impossible for all concerned. There is room for a great deal of research and thought into the main factors which make people want to escape. In many cases a prisoner will make a cold and rational estimate of the position and will then decide whether or not it is worth taking the risk. Perhaps, in that sort of case, we must accept that one needs to watch him like a lynx. If a man is given such a long sentence and in such conditions that he has nothing to hope for, one cannot be surprised if he breaks out.

"The second category is comprised of those to whom the possibility of escape presents a challenge. Anyone who has read *The Prisoner of Zenda* or even *Huckleberry Finn* will know the feeling that exists in all of us, particularly when reading about these matters or when reading stories about escapes from prisoner-of-war camps. I believe that these feelings are sometimes projected into escapes from Her Majesty's Prisons. With the right kind of prisoner, one possible way of dealing with the problem would be to remove the challenge by offering him open conditions. Any challenge having been removed, there are certain types of prisoner who would no longer be impelled to escape.

"The third group comprises two categories of men. There is the man with a genuine or imaginary 'beef', because he is really innocent or because of something which has happened inside the prison. The other category is the man with a personal problem, possibly to whom some kind friend has indicated that his wife is carrying on with a neighbour. Unless he can be satisfied in some way, he will be impelled to break out.

"Then there is the man who is unable to resist temptation, and who, if he sees the hole to which my hon. Friend the

Member for Liverpool, Walton (Mr. Heller) referred, cannot resist walking through it. In that case, clearly the only satisfactory safeguard is to make sure that there are no holes of that kind left accidentally."

– Peter Archer, MP for Rowley Regis and Tipton, 16 February 1967, in the House of Commons debate following the escape of George Blake from Wandsworth Prison, and the Great Train Robbers. Extracted from Hansard

Acknowledgements

My grateful thanks to the many people who suggested stories for this book, and especially all those who checked out the histories of their part of the world for me to provide some of the more obscure tales contained in these pages: Brian J. Robb, Andy Frankham-Allen, Adina Mihaela Roman, and Patricia Hyatt.

My thanks also to:

Duncan Proudfoot for commissioning this in the first place, and for helping to ease the burden a little to allow real life to continue; and my copyeditor Gabriella Nemeth, who once again saved me from some idiocies of my own making.

Revd Clay Knowles for background information on St John of the Cross' escape.

Michael, our guide in Berlin at Easter 2012, who showed us round the route of the Wall, and shared stories about the escapes, many of which feature in this book.

Brian J. Robb again for wading through the material and providing some pithy comments which helped to focus the book.

The staff of The Laptop Workshop in Burgess Hill and Haywards Heath (http://www.laptopworkshop.com/) who were able to get me back up and running within 36 hours. (And to the maintainers of Dropbox for the secure facility that made sure nothing was lost!)

The librarians at the Hassocks branch of the West Sussex Public Library. I say this in every book, but it continues to be key: great as the internet is, it will never replace libraries, and I am grateful to the team for their help in tracking down some of the more obscure books needed for this volume.

Lee Harris, Amanda Rutter, Caitlin Fultz, Scott Pearson, and Clare Hey for providing other avenues while this was ongoing, and to the members of ASCAT church choir, All the Right Notes choir, and the Hurst Singers for the musical outlets.

Finally, and most importantly, my partner Barbara and daughter Sophie for their love and support, and for letting me disappear into the office to get this completed – and our terriers, Rani and Rodo, who have finally got the message about the correlation between desk, computer and staying quiet!